DISTANT JUSTICE

DISTANT JUSTICE
Policing the Alaskan Frontier

by William R. Hunt

Illustrated by Dale Bryner

University of Oklahoma Press : Norman and London

Also by William R. Hunt

North of 53 Degrees: The Wild Days of the Alaska-Yukon Mining Frontier, 1870–1914 (New York, 1974)

Arctic Passage (New York, 1975)

Alaska: A Bicentennial History (New York, 1976)

To Stand at the Pole: The Dr. Cook–Admiral Peary North Pole Controversy (New York, 1981)

Stef: A Biography of Vilhjalmur Stefansson (Vancouver, B.C., 1986)

Library of Congress Cataloging-in-Publication Data

Hunt, William R.
   Distant justice.

   Bibliography:
   Includes index.
   1. Criminal justice, Administration of—Alaska—History.   2. Law enforcement—Alaska—History.   I. Title.
HV9955.A4H86   1987   364′.9798   86-40528
ISBN 0-8061-2050-9 (alk. paper)

The paper in this book meets the guidelines for permanence and durability of the Committee on Production Guidelines for Book Longevity of the Council on Library Resources, Inc.

In memory of my dear friend
Jerry Collier,
who ever loved a good story

Contents

Illustrations

MAP

Preface

ALTHOUGH murders and other dastardly crimes may be examined in isolation with considerable pleasure, it is also beneficial to view them as illustrations of broader themes. Since Alaska has been my home ground, I wondered whether crimes and law enforcement there have expressed some unusual character. Certainly Alaska's history and geography are different from that of other western regions. Alaska, we know, is cold and far away; distances are great between various sections as well. These factors alone suggest that criminal history there, like other aspects of life, has been somewhat unique.

Political conditions were also different in Alaska. The territory did not become a state until 1959, and until that time all felonies were federal crimes and all the law enforcers, save for a few municipal police, were U.S. marshals and their deputies. All felonies were, of course, prosecuted in the federal district courts. All convicted persons languished in Alaska's federal jails or, if their sentence exceeded one year, at McNeil Island prison in Washington state or some other designated stateside prison.

All matters of law enforcement were directed by the U.S. attorney general and his assistants at the Department of Justice in Washington, where they sometimes had a hard time figuring out what their officers and Alaska residents were doing. The system was expensive and not particularly suitable to the huge, distant territory, but it did function with varying degrees of success from

1885 until statehood. To a large extent the honesty and efficiency of law enforcement were determined by the qualities of the judges, prosecuting attorneys, and marshals appointed by the presidents. Some were crooks; some were incompetents; and some were incompentent crooks. Others did their jobs properly and were a credit to their offices.

I am not sure that the machinery of the law administration system or the personalities of its officers surpass in significance the leading actors in this narrative, the criminals, actual or alleged. Most criminals are dull, unimaginative, stupid, or vicious, but there have been some Alaska men and women capable of rising above the mob in one way or another. We must not honor them, but if their wayward careers provide a lively story, we should not be ungrateful.

WILLIAM R. HUNT

Acknowledgments

ARCHIVISTS at the Federal Records Center in Seattle and the National Archives in Washington, D.C., have been very helpful, particularly David Piff and Joyce Justice in Seattle and R. Michael McReynolds and Cynthia Fox in Washington. My thanks too to Robert M. Yahn of the Justice Management Division of the Department of Justice. Readers and critics have included Robert DeArmond of Juneau and Terrence Cole of Anchorage. Cole's editorial eye and extensive knowledge of Alaskan history were especially valuable. As so often in the past I have had help from the staff of the Rasmuson Library, University of Alaska, Fairbanks, and from Phyllis DeMuth and Verda Carey of the Alaska State Library in Juneau. Robert Spude, Regional Historian, National Park Service—Anchorage, contributed substantially to the selection of illustrations. Thanks also to Bill Wilson, Mrs. Richard Dickens, Robert A. Henning, Gerald Williams, the late Herbert L. Heller, and my daughter, Maria, who did some typing for me.

DISTANT JUSTICE

1. Petroff's Alaska

You may have heard many horrible tales from Alaska and . . . they are no doubt true. —Countess Morajeski

BY AND LARGE, Americans appreciated the acquisition of Alaska in 1867. It was pleasant to have a new territory larger than Texas and California combined, a vast area of 586,212 square miles that might be a treasure box of resources.

Hayward M. Hutchinson and William Kohl, San Francisco merchants, took over the Russian-American Company's buildings and ships in 1868 and two years later, with Louis Sloss, formed the Alaska Commercial Company. The primary concern of the American entrepreneurs was with the fur seals of the Pribilof Islands, a readily marketable resource, but they also took over the Russian trading post at St. Michael, seventy miles upcoast from the Yukon River's mouth on Norton Sound, and in 1869 established a trading station at Nulato, an Indian village six hundred miles above St. Michael on the Yukon River.

When American soldiers landed at Sitka in late 1867, they swelled the territory's white population to about nine hundred, virtually all of them at Sitka, the former Russian-American Company headquarters.[1] No one knew for sure how many natives lived in Alaska, but most estimates fixed on thirty thousand as a likely figure.

While the Alaska Commercial Company's investments paid handsome profits annually, the early years of the American era were not marked by aggressive moves by the government in assuming administrative responsibilities. It seemed enough to encourage religious groups, particularly the mission-minded Presbyterians, to undertake education among southeastern Indians and leave law enforcement and other facets of governance to the army, the navy, and the treasury.

Eventually Congress responded to complaints and calls for a proper administration to consider the needs of Alaskans. A few white prospectors searching for gold started moving into the interior in the 1870s, encouraged by the 1870–72 gold discoveries along the coast at Sumdum Bay and Sitka and in the Cassiar district of British Columbia.

Among the experts who advised congressmen was Ivan Petroff, the sole agent of the Census Bureau charged with the 1880 census. The Russian-born adventurer was a good choice for census taker in Alaska. He had worked for the ACC at Kodiak and Kenai before 1871, then collected and translated Russian documents for historian-publisher Hubert Howe Bancroft in San Francisco. Bancroft employed Petroff for work on his *History of Alaska*, a book that remained the standard history of Alaska for decades.

In 1878, Petroff voyaged to Sitka, Kodiak, and Unalaska gathering historical data, then returned to California to edit the *Alaska Appeal*, a semimonthly periodical. Employment by the Bureau of the Census in 1880–81 gave Petroff an important place in Alaska's history. The results of his investigations, *Population, Industries, and Resources of Alaska, 1880,* published in 1884, influenced government policies and assured his employment for the 1890 census.

Petroff's 1880–81 itinerary was somewhat mysterious, although his stay of several weeks at Wrangell and his prodigious consumption of rum and whiskey, which earned him the nickname "Hollow Legs," established his first movements well enough.[2] Scholars who have tried since to follow his wavering track have concluded that when he did give a clear indication of his passage he was not always accurate, as, for example, the two seasons he claimed to have spent on the Yukon and Kuskokwim rivers, for which there did not seem enough time. It is not that Petroff was not conscientious about his duties, but he was severely restricted by lack of time and transportation for travel throughout the entire district that was known, and there were other large segments yet unexplored.

Alaska has six distinct geographic regions. The southeastern coastal strip, or panhandle, includes the narrow coastal strip west of the mountain walls along which lies Canada's boundary, many coastal islands, and the Alexander Archipelago. Sitka is in this region, and it was the most-populous and best-known community and, of course, the closest to the Pacific Coast cities of the United States. As Petroff voyaged through the spectacular Inland Passage, watching the calving glaciers and making wild estimates of the extent of marketable timber, the territory's first major gold discovery was making Juneau an important population center. Before long, Juneau was to surpass Sitka as the chief town of southeastern Alaska. The second region, as one moves along the coast, is the south central, which includes Cook Inlet and Kodiak Island and has as its northern border the huge Alaska Range. The third is the southwestern, which includes the Alaska Peninsula and its extension, the Aleutian Islands. The fourth is the interior, or central plateau, which lies between the Brooks Range to the north and the Alaska Range to the south. The fifth is western Alaska, stretching from the head of Bristol Bay to the Seward Peninsula and including some islands of the Bering Sea. Finally, there is the arctic, extending from Kotzebue, north of Seward Peninsula, to Canada's arctic border.

Of these regions Petroff visited only parts of the southeastern; parts of the south central, including Cook Inlet and Kodiak Island; and portions of the southwestern, the Alaska Peninsula, some islands south of it, some of the Aleutians and a portion of the Bering Sea coast, and lower portions of the Yukon and Kuskokwim rivers. The interior, arctic, and western regions were all but terra incognita to Petroff as a visitor, but he did secure valuable data from individuals who knew something of these regions. Whaling men, for example, filled him in on settlements they knew about along the Bering Sea and arctic coasts.

Alaska's population in 1880 was estimated at 33,426, with only 430 whites, excluding the military. The natives included coastal Indians (Tlingits, Haidas, and Tsimshians) of the southeastern region; Eskimos of the arctic region (the Innuits), the Bering Sea, and Pacific coast (the Yupiks); the Aleuts of the Aleutian Islands and other coastal regions; and the Athapaskan Indians of the interior. Breaking down his figures, Petroff showed 3,094 people in the

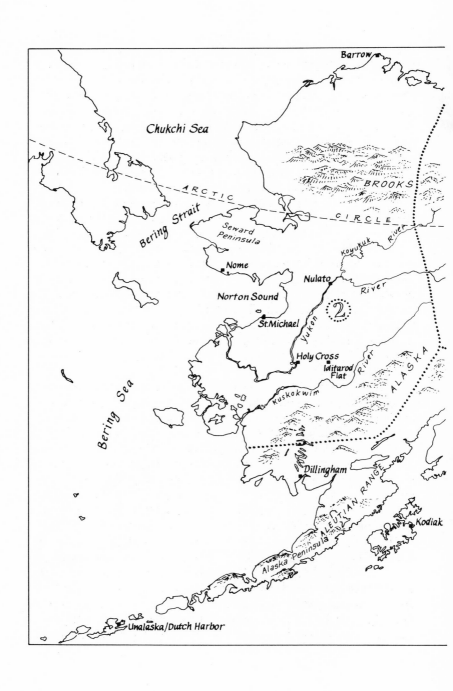

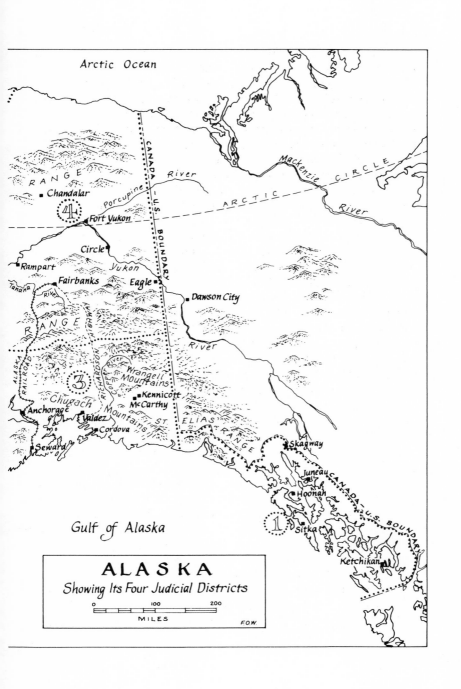

Arctic Ocean

RANGE

Chandalar

④ Fort Yukon

Circle

Rampart

Yukon

Fairbanks Eagle

Tanana

RANGE

ALASKA RAILROAD

③

Chugach Mountains

Anchorage

Valdez

Cordova

Seward

Wrangell Mountains

Kennicott

McCarthy

ST. ELIAS RANGE

RICHARDSON

COPPER River

River

Dawson City

CANADA - U.S. BOUNDARY

Porcupine River

Mackenzie

ARCTIC River

CIRCLE

Skagway

Juneau

Hoonah

① Sitka

CANADA-U.S. BOUNDARY

Ketchikan

Gulf of Alaska

ALASKA
Showing Its Four Judicial Districts

0   100   200

MILES

F.O.W.

arctic; 8,911 in the Kuskokwim; 6,870 in the Yukon; 8,911 in the Aleutians; 4,352 in the Kodiak division; and 7,748 in the southeastern. Aside from whites, there were 1,756 Creoles (mixed Russian and native); 17,617 Innuits; 2,145 Aleuts; and some 11,000 southeastern Indians, mostly Tlingits. Petroff's counts seem to have been reasonably accurate as he kept his strong Baron Munchausen tendencies in check for his census performance, except when a little lie was needed to cover his activities. Certainly folks in Sitka doubted the story that Copper Indians had seized his boat and held him prisoner for some months, but then they were angry with him for reporting a small white population for southeastern.

By the time Petroff's census was published in 1884, southeastern had experienced a boom with the gold discoveries at Juneau. Governor Alfred P. Swineford, Petroff's severe critic, estimated the white residents at 1,900 in 1885, with 800 at Juneau, 350 at Sitka, 250 at Wrangell, 100 at Killisnoo, and 100 at all other places. Of course, Alaskans were inclined to make high estimates in order to catch the attention of officials in Washington.[3]

Besides counting the residents, the first census taker reported on geography, education, health, climatology, fur and fish industries, timber, minerals, volcanoes, and ethnography. A lesser man of ordinary imagination might have been staggered by the task. But Petroff, despite a lack of scientific training, was undaunted.

At various times the articulate Russian had been sought by federal authorities for reasons other than his Alaskan expertise. In 1868, Private Petroff, who had served valiantly in the Union army during the Civil War before his engagement with the Russian-American Company, deserted. He had reenlisted the year before but left his unit when it was ordered from Fort Vancouver, Washington Territory, to Kenai, Alaska. He was caught, shipped north, and discharged in 1870. A year later he enlisted again and deserted again for journalistic opportunities with San Francisco newspapers. With the help of an influential officer of the Alaska Commercial Company, who explained that financial distress caused Petroff's problems, the deserter's record was cleared in 1883.

Petroff's place in the crime annals of Alaska is deserving in several respects. He was the author of a stirring account of the first murder on Cook Inlet, a story rich in erotic appeal and defamation of Russian traders and missionaries. His narrative, based on the journal of Father Juvenal, a Russian monk sent to Lake Iliamna in the late eighteenth century, first appeared in Bancroft's *History of Alaska* and was repeated faithfully by later historians.[4]

Poor Father Juvenal was making great strides Christianizing Indians when an amorous native girl slipped into his bed, seduced him, and caused his disgrace. The monk was honest enough to confess his sin to the village chief and continue to insist that the chief put away three of his four wives. "Who is he to talk?" the chief answered angrily. "When a woman touches him, he feels desire too. Tell him to get out of my house."[5] Later the chief and his brother clubbed the unfortunate missionary, and other Indians—disenchanted converts, presumably—stabbed him to death.

This fine and instructive story was a fabrication. Petroff committed a literary forgery worthy of Edmond Backhouse, the nineteenth-century scholar who fabricated *China Under the Empress Dowager* from imaginary sources.[6] Probably Petroff, a whimsical fellow at times, felt the need of a lively spicing of *History of Alaska,* and he was not friendly to the Russian church.

Some of Petroff's other forgeries were discovered long before the Juvenal tale, but not before they embarrassed the American government. In 1892 the State Department hired him to translate Russian documents relating to the British-American dispute over sealing in the Bering Sea. A scribe likes to show his usefulness, and Petroff inserted material in the translations that had not been in the original documents. His tampering was not capricious: the insertions bolstered the American government's case for jurisdiction over the seal fisheries. Someone noticed the fakery. Secretary of State John W. Foster had to apologize to the British. The State Department fired Petroff, and the superintendent of the census also fired him and expunged his name from the 1890 census report, then in press.

While Petroff counted Alaskans, others, such as treasury agent William G. Morris, described them: "There are in this country as God-abandoned, God-forsaken, desperate, and rascally a set of wretches as can be found on earth. Their whole life is made up of fraud, deceit, lying, and thieving, and selling liquor to the Indians which they manufacture themselves."[7] Morris' savage indictment

of the adventurers who flocked to the new territory and the hold-
overs from Russian rule did not stand alone. The American pioneers were opportunists. Tilling the soil was not part of their pro-
gram. Neither did fishing or lumbering attract them. They were
willing to buy furs from native trappers, sell provisions to residents, and, of course, compete in the lucrative liquor trade.

Liquor caused most of Alaska's crime and disorder during its first
eighteen years after 1867 as an American territory under the loose
supervision of military and U.S. Treasury personnel. Reporting in
1875, Henry W. Elliott, another treasury agent, described the
"one general evil . . . the curse of beer drinking and the disorders
which arise constantly from its effects." When government patrol
vessels disrupted the supply of imported whiskey, natives brewed
beer or distilled spirits. The beer, fermented from sugar, hops,
flour, dried apples, and other items willingly sold by white traders,
kept them "intoxicated and stupefied for weeks, and even months,
at a time; beating their wives and children, destroying their homes,
and . . . committing murder."[8]

Molasses rum, or hootzenoo, was a favorite concoction of both
natives and whites. U.S. soldiers stationed at Sitka—the old Russian headquarters and that for the U.S. military from 1867 to 1884
and the capital from 1884 until it was supplanted by Juneau—have
been credited with teaching the art to natives. Hootch makers constructed a crude still from a five-gallon coal-oil can, adding a nozzle
and a six-foot tin worm. Their mash of a gallon of molasses, five
pounds of flour, yeast, and water was soured, then boiled until the
distilled product resulted. "One gallon of the mixture," observed
Agent Morris in 1876, "will make three-fourths gallon of hootzenoo, and the three-fourths gallon will craze the brain of three Indians." Morris deplored the drink and its effects: "This is about
the most infernal decoction ever invented, producing intoxication,
debauchery, insanity, and death. The smell is abominable and the
taste atrocious. Previous to the arrival of the military its manufacture was unknown to the Indians."[9]

Hootch got its name from Kootznahoo Inlet on Admiralty Island,
a popular distilling place. Hootch (or hooch), it is sad to note, is the
only purely Alaskan term to have entered the American vernacular.

Morris, whose prose style far surpassed in force and elegance that usually found in government reports, described another common social evil: "Following in the steps of the troops, come the miners, who seem to have emulated the sons of Mars in the prosecution, performance, and mad riot of the quintessence of vicious enjoyment. A whole race of prostitutes have been created, and the *morbus incessens* of the Latins, which the Roman doctors declined to treat, is found in full feather and luxuriant blossom. Today there is not a single surgeon or physician in Southeastern Alaska, and when a victim becomes infected with the *lues venerea,* his fate can be predicted. Syphilitic diseases are the great bane of the country; but few of the women who indulge in promiscuous intercourse are free from the poisonous taint."[10]

The restless frontiersmen, sometimes called carpetbaggers and rogues, who moved to Alaska after 1867 did not debauch a Garden of Eden. Judging from Major John C. Tidball's rather unique characterization of Sitka's 391 people for the 1870 census, the Alaskans were not a classy bunch. Tidball damned the moral character of many of them: One man was a "worthless, drunken wretch" who drew rations last winter; another was a "worthless cuss," who worked formerly for the government, a "no account" fellow.

Tidball's annotations on some of the women listed included "slatternly looking"; "filthy," "small and dirty," "a destitute prostitute, Burmese poor"; "kept by . . . Franklin, or rather she keeps him. She says he don't pay her a cent for value received, gets drunk on her daughter's wages, not deserving."

Some men were "lazy, able-bodied, worthless, and needful of watching"; "worthless runaway, left his wife with lots of orphans"; "lazy, worthless, sells whiskey to the Indians and is in guard house for this"; "sharp, quick, steals, robs, rascal in every muscle"; "bilk of the worst kind, utterly worthless"; "worthless, lazy, ex-soldier"; "one who needs watching, has been implicated in smuggling."[11]

Of course, most of Sitka's residents worked or were willing to work, kept clean houses, and obeyed the law, although the withdrawal of the Russian-American Company had hurt the local economy and had created a general condition of destitution.

While the sharp-tongued major pulled no punches in unveiling the vices of worthless folks, he took pride in the cosmopolitan mix of the small population. It included Alaskan natives from southeastern,

Kodiak, Unalaska, and Atka and Caucasians and blacks from California, Washington, Connecticut, Massachusetts, Russia, Scotland, Germany, Ireland, Turkey, Maine, New Mexico, Canada, Mississippi, England, Martinique, Nevada, New York, and New Jersey.

Another observer, fur dealer Emil Teichmann, complained evenhandedly about the new and old Alaskans on his 1868 visit to Sitka. The Russians claim that "this sad state of affairs began with the arrival of American troops . . . but it seems quite evident that a very low state of morality reigned in the colony previously." People "live together without regard for age or sex" in sordid circumstances, threatening "even the strongest morality." Higher social circles revealed corruption as well: "There came to light almost every day some scandal not unlike those which have become familiar in the *demi-monde* of Paris." And, shockingly enough, men not only ignored their wives' whoring, "but in some cases even openly promoted it in order to gain a profit for themselves."[12]

As for the American soldiers, Teichmann watched the officers sit around drinking and gambling all day and having intriguing love affairs with the Russian women. While the officers amused themselves, they ignored their soldiers, who not only drank and gambled but indulged in robbery, arson, and violent assaults, to the terror of the citizens.

These comments on Alaska by visitors related only to Sitka; the Pribilof Islands, where the most viable remnant of the fur trade was centered; and to the few scattered southeastern coastal villages. No one knew much about conditions among people elsewhere in the vast territory.

The first real boom town attributable to gold was Juneau, northeast of Sitka on the mainland coast, founded in 1880–81, which soon became the most important town in the territory. Juneau's prosperity was a magnet luring other adventurers to the north, and from Juneau many expectant prospectors drifted into the interior. In 1886 the first interior gold strike was made at Forty Mile, not far from the border of Canada's Yukon Territory. Gold in modest quantities was also discovered on the Kenai Peninsula in 1888; then major strikes were made near Circle and Rampart on the Yukon River.

All these developments set the stage for one of history's outstanding dramatic events, the great bonanza findings on the Klondike River near the place where it emptied into the Yukon in Yukon Territory. The news of rich gold fields sparked the great stampedes of 1897–98, and soon prospectors ranged all over the north. Nome, on the Seward Peninsula, attracted thousands of stampeders in 1899 and 1900, and in 1902, Felix Pedro's patient searching of the Tanana Valley of the interior resulted in the founding of Fairbanks.

While the spectacular nature of these developments and the astonishing increase in Alaska's population could not have been foreseen, Congress had belatedly provided organization for Alaska with the Organic Act of 1884. The act provided for a governor and a judicial system, but not a legislature or representation in Congress. For legal guidance, officers were directed to consult the laws of the state of Oregon. Revisions followed in time, most notably with the criminal code in 1899 and the civil code in 1900, unique occurrences in that they were the first codes ever enacted by Congress for a specific territory.

Alaskans were not pleased by the slow pace of congressional response to their urgent needs; insofar as criminal law enforcement was concerned, the basic machinery established in 1884 was in place to meet the gold-rush booms in the panhandle towns in 1897–98, but only nominally was this true in the interior, where the prospectors flocked in before courts were established. In essence, the same basic structure for criminal administration established in 1884 remained in force until statehood in 1959. Presidents appointed the federal district judges, the marshals, and the U.S. attorneys through the Department of Justice under the U.S. attorney general. The Justice Department appointees served for four years if all went well and could be reappointed at the end of their terms. As with all other presidential appointees of the United States, the election of a president representing a party other than that of the current chief caused a general turnover among appointees. The Justice Department tried to supervise every aspect of Alaska's court and law enforcement system, from the purchase of a new lamp to the disposition of cases before the court or worthy of investigation. Obviously, geographic conditions and distances posed special problems, but the manner of conducting business from Washington was a familiar and long-established one for the bureaucrats charged with administration.

2. Uneasy Beginnings

Many able men drink far more than they should. —John McCafferty

THE laurels usually bestowed on founding fathers have been withheld from President Chester Arthur's first court appointees: Judge Ward McAllister, Jr., U.S. Attorney Edward W. Haskett, and U.S. Marshal Munson C. Hillyer. All were removed and disgraced after accusations of incompetence, wickedness, drunkenness, and unfairness were brought against them by the Reverend Dr. Sheldon Jackson. Jackson, the federal officers failed to note, had far more political clout in Washington than they did.

Judge McAllister, a young man still in his twenties with a mere two years' legal experience as an assistant U.S. attorney in San Francisco, owed his appointment to family connections. His grandfather, Matthew Hall McAllister, was California's first circuit judge and had a distinguished legal career. His father, Ward McAllister, Sr., established a prestigious law firm in San Francisco with his brother Hall and their father.[1] From 1850 to 1852, Ward, Sr. apparently did well enough in the litigation of mining claims to abandon practice for his true destiny as a social arbitrator. He moved to New York, married the daughter of a Georgia millionaire, and by his example and lavish entertaining established Newport, Rhode Island, as *the* summer resort for the wealthy. By the 1860s he ruled the social world of New York and chose the elitist four hundred. He has been well remembered for his social triumphs and would have gone unnoted in Alaska's history but for his lamentable ambition to see his clumsy son on the federal bench.

Still another influential McAllister was Ward, Sr.'s brother Hall, who achieved as much distinction in California legal circles as Ward did in New York society. He tried more cases, won more verdicts, and received larger fees than any other California lawyer of his time. A street in San Francisco bears his name, and his bronze image stands near city hall.[2]

Unfortunately, such distinguished lineage did not give the young judge either wisdom or strength of character, but it may have given him the feeling that his Alaska duties offered no serious challenge as he disembarked at Sitka, resplendent in dress and handsome with his fashionable handlebar moustache. A federal judgeship is an alluring prize beyond the ken of young attorneys in ordinary circumstances, but an assignment in rough, raw Sitka may have seemed a hardship to McAllister. It would not be odd if he longed for the pleasures of his hometown as he first viewed the motley folks he came to serve. Later the Presbyterians claimed that McAllister, Sr., had arranged the appointment to protect his son from the diversified debaucheries available in the Bay City, but it is unlikely that they could have known this to be true.

The untried judge did not have a strong supporting cast. Marshal Hillyer's confusion about his duties was scandalous, although much of the blame must rest with the failure of the Department of Justice to provide him with adequate instructions and enough money to perform his duties. Soon after his arrival in December 1884, Hillyer was directed by McAllister to send an insane person outside for confinement. While this was the sort of routine that could be anticipated, the order took Hillyer by surprise: "Where is the money coming from for all these expenses?" Hillyer asked Washington by mail while also complaining that he lacked funds and authority to pay reasonable salaries to deputies: "I can't get men for the fees and salaries involved." Later, in April 1885, he still did not know where the insane were supposed to be sent and queried Washington by slow mail.[3]

U.S. Attorney Haskett also had to explain some fundamental facts of Alaska's geography to the department. He had no clerk to carry on business while he was absent, and he was sometimes out

Russian buildings in Sitka used for the American courthouse and jail.
Alaska Historical Library

of Sitka for weeks, attending to business elsewhere, and entirely
dependent upon the limited steamer service for his movements.[4]

Lack of facilities for the court, jail, and offices was the most en-
during problem. The marshal did not find the buildings in Sitka
turned over to him by the collector of customs suitable for their
necessary purposes. He staggered the department by requesting
ten thousand dollars to alter the former clubhouse for the court
and another nineteen thousand dollars to build or alter facilities in
Juneau, Unalaska, and Wrangell.[5]

With all their other problems the court officers did not need a
confrontation with the Reverend Dr. Sheldon Jackson. In 1877,
Jackson made his first voyage to Alaska with the firm intention of
accomplishing great things. He was a well-respected Presbyterian
minister who had presided over the church's home missions among
Indians in eleven western states and territories and liked to be
called the "Rocky Mountain Superintendent." Jackson was ambitious, resourceful, relentless, and fiercely impatient with anyone

who resisted him; a mighty man—not physically, as he was slight and barely five feet tall—but because he commanded respectful attention in New York and Washington. Jackson was also a petty, vindictive man given to damning opponents by broadcasting unconfirmed slanders. As a crusader for the salvation of Alaska's natives, Jackson could spare no charity, or even basic justice, for his enemies; humility was not a conspicuous feature of his makeup. Alaska had attracted him inevitably; it was a new land to conquer.[6]

On his 1877 visit, Jackson left a teacher at Wrangell to begin the education work and returned to the States to promote his new cause through public lectures, writing, and lobbying. His winter base was Denver until he moved to Washington, D.C., in 1883, but he voyaged to Alaska each summer to supervise the progress of education and missionary work. Thanks to Jackson's fund raising, the Reverend John G. Brady was able to start the Sitka Industrial Training School in 1881, a boarding school that would remove youngsters from pernicious influences at home. Jackson gained considerable power in 1885 when Congress appointed him Alaska's first general agent of education.[7]

Judge McAllister apparently had not ingratiated himself with Sitka's Presbyterians before treating himself to a winter vacation in San Francisco after holding his first court session in 1885. This was his second dreadful mistake because, in his absence, U.S. Attorney Haskett opened war on the Sitka Industrial Training School. Whether Haskett was influenced by Sitka's Creoles, a sense of justice, religious bias, or a boozy disposition is not clear. The Creoles, upset as newer arrivals undermined their status and income, were much annoyed when the Presbyterians started construction of Indian cottages near the school. The land preempted was the only part of Sitka suitable for expansion and the church did not seem to have any better right to it than anyone else. It would be some years before Congress acted to clarify the rights of natives and others in regard to land.[8] In any event, Haskett, according to the Presbyterians, fueled racial hatred at public meetings and encouraged the angry Creoles to shout down Jackson when he tried to address the issue. Later Jackson had to flee to the woods as Creoles stormed his office. The Reverend Brady, who was also the U.S. commissioner, struck back by hearing assault charges against

Haskett, who was rumored to have been in a mob of men who invaded the girls' quarters at the school. Brady, whose court functioned like that of a justice of the peace over misdemeanors, was unable to secure conviction of Haskett but surely stirred his anger.[9]

While all this excitement was at its peak, Judge McAllister returned from his holiday and swiftly joined forces with Haskett against the missionaries. At issue was the question of whether the churchmen could hold children in school against their parents' wishes.

Haskett decided that Jackson's practice of removing Indian children from their homes to his boarding school for a five-year period amounted to indentured servitude. He found some parents willing to testify that they did not really understand the custody papers they had signed, so he filed petitions to free the children. McAllister was agreeable to the arguments of the prosecutor.

Wiser heads might have taken a more cautious course than one that appeared to be a challenge to the church by the officers of the court. It was the missionaries' view that children could be made decent Christians and be spared corruption only by boarding at the school. Probably Jackson did browbeat some parents into agreement to boarding, but the lawmen should have been wary of the appearance of fostering custody contests. Haskett seemed to be leading a direct attack on the school's very existence, and the judge did not look to be a neutral party.

Jackson, a redoubtable adversary, furious at being virtually run out of town and jailed for some hours to cause him to miss the steamer, wrote to another Presbyterian minister, who happened to be President Grover Cleveland's brother; to a zealous Christian admirer, who was the president's daughter; and to others. Other church members in Sitka added their outraged protests to those of Jackson, and without further inquiry the president sacked the judge, prosecutor, marshal, and, for good measure, Governor John H. Kinkead.

Kinkead was Sitka's first postmaster and a businessman from 1868 to 1871, then moved to Nevada, where he was governor from 1879 to 1883. Although the governor was a churchgoer whose wife helped initiate a temperance society at Sitka and although he had not opposed the Presbyterian housing colony that had excited the

Creoles, he must have incurred Jackson's wrath by remaining too neutral in the church-court dispute. Jackson told the president's brother that Kinkead was "a broken-down politician" who drank and gambled, a man without executive or intellectual force who "accomplishes nothing" and was hostile to the school.[10]

Jackson was fairly easy on the marshal, who, like Kinkead, was from Nevada. Hillyer did not drink, but he gambled. "He is a fair man as politicians go." As for the judge, he "is 25–27 years old. . . . He gets drunk and is a fast young man in every sense of the word." It was rumored, reported the rumor-mongering minister, that McAllister "slept with the woman" who sued the school over the custody of her ward and thus precipitated the drastic decline in enrollment when many Indian families decided to reclaim their children. Jackson believed that other unnamed government officials lived with Indian women. Worst of the bunch was Haskett, "uneducated, rowdy, vulgar, obscene in conversation, low in tastes," a gambler and a habitual drunkard who lacked legal knowledge and was one of those who attempted to break into the girls' building at the Sitka school.[11]

It is difficult to determine whether Jackson's outrage against the court officers and the governor was fully justified. Certainly law officers trying to stamp out the still lingering practice among Northwest Coast Indians of enslaving their neighbors had reason to inquire whether the Presbyterians had the legal right to hold children in boarding school against their parents' wishes. Perhaps the episode is a better example of certain attitudes current among whites and of political pressure than it is of justice on the frontier.

Some months after his dismissal, Kinkead, writing from Nevada, probably at the request of Ward McAllister, Sr., offered some explanations of the tawdry affair to the president. He "was glad to be relieved of his unsatisfactory and thankless position" but warned that no governor would fare better "under the inefficient Organic Act," which provided so little authority to the office. Kinkead did not want his job back but argued that most Alaskans had been grieved by the dismissals. The only happy people were Jackson and his party, whose "malicious misrepresentations" had been taken in Washington as the general opinion among "reliable citizens." The small Presbyterian coterie did not represent Alaska's citizens and was not trustworthy, he said. Jackson's denunciations flowed "from the diseased brain of a lunatic which in charity I believe Jackson to be." Jackson's "arbitrary course has paved the way for the Church of Rome" to win natives away from Protestants, Kinkead declared.[12]

Ward McAllister, Sr. did not take the removal of his son lightly. He secured a personal interview with the president, backed by letters of introduction acclaiming his "great distinction . . . very high social position" and reputation as "a good Democrat." The same letters observed that Ward, Jr. was "one of the strongest, most influential Democrats on the coast." Other friends of the McAllisters asked the president to appoint young Ward an assistant U.S. attorney in San Francisco if reinstatement to his judgeship was impractical. Instead, he was named federal special commissioner in Chinese habeas corpus cases. Later he resigned to become counsel for the Pacific Mail Steamship Company. Ward, Jr. also contended in federal court that the president could not remove a seated judge and demanded reinstatement and back pay, but the U.S. Supreme Court decided against him.[13]

Sitka's newspaper, the *Alaskan,* published by Kinkead's successor, Alfred Swineford, favored Jackson's side in the dispute although admitting that the clerics did make some mistakes. The news that Haskett fell to his death from a train near Needles, California, reminded residents of his "many bright and kindly qualities." When McAllister returned to Sitka to gather affidavits favorable to his reinstatement, the editor recalled that both sides had been partly wrong, but he did not favor the judge's return: "It is rather a humiliating spectacle to see the ermine sought in this way." After McAllister, Sr. reported on his meeting with the president in the *New York World,* claiming that this son's drunkenness had been the only charge discussed and that neither idleness nor incompetence was an issue, the *Alaskan* scoffed: Naturally the judge's idleness was not discussed because of his "zeal and energy in exploring the steamship route between his legitimate place of duty to the dude club room in San Francisco, and in turning an honest penny by charging to the government fares covered by an annual pass." As for his ability, he was "a dude of first class English pattern." His ignorance on the bench was tolerated by some "in return for the amusement his little hat and baby cane afforded," but the president should prevent "further humiliation to Alaskans in not returning McAllister." When the *San Francisco Argonaut* carried McAllister's side of the dispute, the *Alaskan* flailed both the judge and the magazine.[14]

After sacrificing McAllister to Presbyterian wrath, President Cleveland weighed the virtues of other meritorious Democrats. Edward J. Dawne, an attorney in Salem, Oregon, was one much-endorsed candidate. Dawne's application included a printed list of Oregon's notables among Democrats who assured the president that their man would make a very fine judge for Alaska. No less than 123 lawyers, judges, businessmen, and state and federal legislators joined Oregon's governor in petitioning in Dawne's support. Quite independently, Sheldon Jackson let the president's brother know that he had no objection: Dawne "is a Christian man with a Christian wife, and while I have not chosen him, he is well spoken of and will make an effective judge."[15]

The president rewarded the party faithful of Oregon by appointing their favorite to replace McAllister. Folks in Salem were stunned rather than gratified. Why, they asked themselves, would the president give a judgeship to a notorious charlatan, liar, braggart, and crook? Several Salem men suffered enough remorse to write the president, retracting their recommendations and apologizing for their thoughtless support of Dawne's petition; they had assumed that no one would take Dawne's bid seriously. He was actually a Salem joke, a man once described by one of his petition signers in a public speech as "a preacher without a pulpit; a doctor without a diploma; a broker without a dollar; and an attorney without a brief."[16] As details of Dawne's amazing career unfolded, action was taken to add the distinction of "a judge without a bench" to this remarkable list of credits.

Obviously, a man of gall could make his way in Oregon. Dawne moved there in 1872 as a Southern Methodist preacher but was dismissed from the ministry in 1874 for immoral conduct. Defrocked but undaunted, he took up lecturing at Willamette College's medical school until his lack of a medical degree was exposed. Turning to commerce he became an investment broker and later gained admission to Oregon's bar. His law credentials were legitimate, although earned through informal schooling, but he pre-

ferred brokerage work to law practice. Charges of misrepresentation and embezzlement, particularly in his brokerage transactions
between the time of his judicial appointment and his departure for
Alaska, now rose loudly from unhappy clients.[17]

By the time Judge Dawne had completed his cruise of the sparkling waters of the Inside Passage to disembark at Sitka in November 1885, the heat from Oregon and Washington, D.C., was altering his destiny. Alaskans had been for several months without a
court and were eager for the judge to attack his docket, but, hearing footsteps perhaps, Dawne showed no eagerness for work.
Rather suddenly, claiming urgent court business in Wrangell, the
judge hopped aboard a southbound steamer. In a series of furtive
movements, he went from Wrangell to British Columbia by canoe,
as no other transport was available, then entrained for Montreal
and sailed to Europe. His wife and family were left at Sitka to find
their own way back to Salem.[18]

Alaska's only newspaper used Dawne stories from Oregon newspapers without editorial comment. The stories showed that Oregonians were more embarrassed than Alaskans: "It would have been
a happy day for Oregon if Judge Dawne on his first setting foot on
Alaskan soil, had accidentally fallen into a deep crevasse and become as rigid as the ice encircling him." This accident would have
prevented the heralding of his previous record "from sea to sea."
Someone cautioned Oregonians to expect little hope of federal
offices whenever the president recalled the ridiculous affair: "Your
state has seen its Dawne; it has also seen its twilight, minus the
customary noonday."[19]

The other replacement officers did better. Mottrone D. Ball,
U.S. attorney, performed well until ill health forced his resignation in 1887. Barton Atkins, the new marshal, served until 1889.
Sheldon Jackson demanded his removal in March 1889, charging
that his "treatment of prisoners causes remark," that he used prisoners for his personal gain, and "it is reported that his accounts are
in great confusion."[20] An examination later established that Atkins'
accounts were in good order after he left office in 1889. It is not
clear whether his resignation was forced by Jackson, but neither he
nor any other officer ever again trifled with the Sitka Industrial
Training School, which survives today as Sheldon Jackson College.

It was not until 1888, after years of wailing from unpaid Sitka merchants, that Justice Department Examiner J. W. Nightingale reached Sitka to unravel the fiduciary snarls created by the much maligned Marshal Hillyer. The examiner looked over Hillyer's accomplishments in establishing an office, appointing deputies, keeping records, and acquainting himself with United States and Oregon statutes in discharge of his office with disdain: "I do not find that he gave particular attention to any of them." What irked the examiner in trying to establish what occurred during Hillyer's reign of ten months was the absence of all records except a few expense vouchers. The marshal, apparently fearing a scrutiny of his stormy administration, destroyed his files, leaving his successor in total confusion and the examiner in perplexity. "It was not my pleasure to meet him. I was told he resides somewhere in South America."[21] Nor were any of his deputies or former deputies on hand to shed light on the marshal's affairs. But for the clamor of creditors presenting bills, it was as if there had been no Hillyer administration.

Moralists, presumably including the Presbyterians, may have been satisfied by the post-dismissal woes of U.S. Attorney Haskell, who, while drinking heavily, accidentally killed himself in falling from a train near Needles, California.[22]

What transactions Nightingale pieced together smacked of skulduggery. Captain James Carroll, commander of the steamer *Ancon* and stockholder-officer of the Pacific Coast Steamship Company, wanted a five-dollar daily deputy marshal fee for twenty-eight days' service in conveying an insane man from Sitka to San Francisco and returning himself to Sitka. While the transport time was not unreasonable, it seemed "merely a money-making scheme," since it involved the government in paying the captain a salary for commanding his ship on its usual run. Carroll was prudent enough to eschew charging the government for his ship fare, but despite this restraint, Nightingale disallowed his claims.[23]

The examiner had other complaints too, particularly the excessive charges billed for the prisoners' meals: "One dollar a day for feeding Indians is exorbitant. The best food in the city can be had for that, and the Chinaman [the local restaurateur] didn't give them the best."[24]

Marshal Atkins showed some long-distance initiative in 1886

when timber thieving was reported to him. Downcoast of Sitka, ships' crews had cut timber from government land and steamed south, so the marshal boarded the mail steamer at Sitka for Wrangell to give chase. At Wrangell he learned that the fully loaded timber ships had left Alaskan waters and, as he could not return to Sitka before his steamer made its return voyage, Atkins remained aboard until reaching Port Townsend on the Washington coast. There he alerted the Revenue Cutter Service to intercept the ships. The effort failed at Port Townsend, but the ships were boarded at San Francisco and the company was prosecuted.[25] (The Revenue Cutter Service, forerunner of the U.S. Coast Guard, was called the Revenue Marine Division of the U.S. Treasury until 1894.)

Atkins did not always have an easy time with Judge Dawne's successor, Lafayette Dawson. When the Justice Department queried Atkins about courthouse expenses for janitorial services, he explained that the judge "became quite arbitrary and threatened the marshal with imprisonment" when he was slow to employ a janitor.[26]

In 1890, Examiner Nightingale sailed to Alaska to investigate charges made by Atkins' successor, Whit Grant, that Atkins had misappropriated government funds. The judge had defended Atkins, even though the funds on hand could not support anticipated court costs in 1889 and a scheduled court session had to be canceled. Nightingale found no evidence of wrongdoing and alerted Washington to its own shortcomings, observing that during his four-year term the marshal had never had his expenses reimbursed in a timely fashion. A year after he left office, the government still owed Atkins money.[27]

Cries of corruption of the court were never to die down for long in Alaska, but with the advent of Judge Lafayette Dawson as its third judge, the course was set in the general direction of justice and orderliness. The judge appreciated the importance of community respect for the court and even fined a courtroom spectator one dollar for putting his hat on while still in the room. In other ways, notably by playing his flute during leisure hours, Dawson elevated Sitka's culture level.

Judge Dawson stated his views of the priorities of law enforcement in his grand-jury charges. There were two murder cases in 1887, one involving an Indian charged with killing his wife "under circumstances of extreme cruelty." Jurors were not to consider "any question of tradition or custom that may have prevailed among the native peoples." Congress in 1885 "made all Indians answerable to the criminal laws of the United States."[28] Dawson's ruling on the natives' legal status convinced the grand jurors but did not escape challenge in subsequent trials.

The judge went on to other charges the jurors would consider: smuggling to evade customs; liquor sales; prohibition of the sale of breech-loading rifles to natives (an unfortunate restriction on native hunters as time passed and game became more scarce, and one protested often by officials and others concerned for their well-being); distilling or brewing liquor; and other matters. Customs in Juneau dance halls were noted: "Under some municipal arrangement founded, I suppose, in common consent, Indian men are required to retire at an early hour in the evening while Indian women are invited, enticed and persuaded into the dance halls, where they partake of the hilarity of the dance, and drink deep of the rude vulgarity of such places." There, the judge complained, "modesty has no resting place and . . . the licentious machinations of the libertine leads them to debauchery and ruin."

Dawson inveighed against cohabitation of unmarried men and women, a long-established custom noted by earlier visitors to Sitka. "Every precept of morality, every incentive to good society, every thought and desire for elevated morals, and every rational idea of the proprieties of life, cry out unmistakably for the suppression of this heathenish, immoral practice." Let them marry if they desire to live together, "and show a regard for the moral sentiment of the community."

These sharp judicial strictures were to be repeated in other forms to many grand juries over the years. Reasons for concern went beyond puritanical aversion to unsanctioned sex. Solid citizens of Alaska towns faced the task of building stable communities against the propensity of many unattached, uncommitted males to acquire native partners who could be discarded in time. The courts, urged by men who had brought their wives north or wished to, would not wink at the footloose man who used the community but made no commitment to it in return.

The judge concluded with an impressive appeal to enforce the

law: "Remember the history of the past. You, gentlemen, know
something of the confusion that prevailed here for long years before the establishment of a civil government." Shirk your responsibility and "you will find yourself as one adrift, cast upon the great
ocean of chance, confusion and uncertainty, driven by the waves of
individual passion and interests against each other." Dawson defined the law as "the ark of safety to all. Without it life itself is a
mere negative birthright and particularly here in our present condition emerging from a chaos of seventeen years growth, attempting
to establish and uphold a civilized society." Do your duty. Stand by
the law. "Let it crush whom it may crush, save whom it may save."
The law "is the only bulwark against the return of licentiousness,
brute violence, unspeakable cruelty and revolting barbarism."

With these ringing admonitions inspiring them, the grand jurors
usually worked with a will. Trial jurors, however, had to complete
the job, and sometimes—as will be seen—they lacked the virtues
that judges appealed to.

While all federal officials were on the same team, they did not invariably share a spirit of camaraderie. U.S. Collector of Customs
John McCafferty, "a friend of the people" and a spirited raconteur
with little regard for truth, secured his appointment against the
wishes of Alaska's second governor, Alfred P. Swineford (1885–89),
and U.S. Marshal Barton Atkins, who apparently had pushed a
friend for the job. [29] To forestall McCafferty and force his removal,
or so McCafferty believed, a warrant was issued for his arrest,
charging him with criminal libel. The collector had written the
Seattle Post-Intelligencer in July 1886 before receiving his appointment, complaining that none of the court officers had completed
formalities for qualification for their offices and condemning Judge
Dawson's actions against the captain of a small steamer, *Yukon,*
which had carried eight passengers from Seattle to Juneau. En
route he had borrowed a total of $50 from them. In Juneau the cap-
tain refused to pay up, so the passengers first sued in the U.S.
commissioner's court for $153, then raised the ante by asking the
district court for $2,200. Dawson awarded the claimants $300 after
refusing the captain a jury trial and the postponement necessary to
give him time to bring witnesses from Douglas, across the channel

from Juneau. "Go with the case. I want to get away from here," cried the judge, who whipped proceedings through from opening statement to judgment in twenty minutes.[30]

When the *Yukon*'s engineer gauged the judge's disposition, he hastily brought suit for $197 in back wages. Dawson quickened his pace. Five minutes was enough time to give the engineer his victory and the *Yukon* was attached by court order.

After settling the matter, Judge Dawson, "our corn-juice importation from the back woods of Missouri sailed for Sitka the next morning," related McCafferty. The Alaska appointees are nothing but "a gang of official desperados" who should not have been confirmed.[31]

When McCafferty arrived at Sitka to begin work, friends suggested that he apologize to Dawson, and McCafferty wrote the judge and admitted a harsh "outrage of your rights and privileges."[32] The collector did not mention the corn-juice remark in particular, although he told friends that he did regret the description, "for many able men drink far more than they should." But the judge was not satisfied with the apology and demanded an "unequivocal retraction" of the offensive remarks. Dawson's reply astonished McCafferty, although it is hard to see why, except that the collector was a most excitable fellow. McCafferty responded with bitter complaints to the Justice Department, calling for Dawson's removal. "His retention is a reflection against this administration and an outrage to democratic people . . . a man who sleeps with a jug of whiskey at the head of his bed should not be allowed to preside over the court."[33]

Later the criminal libel charges against McCafferty were dismissed, but only after the outcome of other criminal charges against him suggested that his disposition was not sound enough to warrant a trial. While the responsibilities for curtailing smuggling may have been a strain, McCafferty's methods of dealing with the problem were irrational. He initiated his trouble with an open letter to Sitka's newspaper in which he charged that a smuggling ring, headed by Captain James Carroll and protected by McCafferty's predecessor, Peter French, lay at the root of the persistent law violations. The editor of the *Alaskan* hinted in a comment following McCafferty's letter that McCafferty would perhaps join the ring himself. The collector and two friends called upon the editor and demanded a retraction. When the editor made flippant remarks and resisted, McCafferty attacked with fists and allegedly waved a pistol around in a menacing manner.[34]

The U.S. attorney charged McCafferty with assault and the Treasury fired him. McCafferty marveled that he was removed for merely defending the honor of the U.S. Treasury. The government appointed Arthur K. Delaney, a Sitka attorney and later Alaska's district judge, to replace McCafferty. Delaney had offered graciously to defend his predecessor against the assault charge, and he did a pretty good job. Alaska's jurors were not inclined to accept defenses based on temporary insanity, but this time they went along with the argument. Delaney pointed out the upsetting nature of the editor's remark, coupled with McCafferty's obsessive belief in a smuggling ring, as evidence of derangement at the newspaper office. McCafferty's close escape from punishment and his removal did not end his slander of court officials.

Speculation on "a ring of smugglers" where liquor was involved, or on "the courthouse ring" in most other involvements of the court, was a dominant activity in Alaska for decades. People enjoyed tracing unsavory conditions back to a conspiracy of powerful figures, and there did seem to be some substance to the conspiracy theory—at least at times—where smuggling was concerned.

From 1867 to 1899 the treasury worked first with the army and then, between 1879 and 1884, with the navy to stop the liquor trade. The collector at Sitka and deputy collectors at other ports had the support of their maritime arm, the Revenue Marine, predecessor of the U.S. Coast Guard. Inspectors were either assigned to voyage on particular ships or as assistants to deputy collectors. With the establishment of Alaska's court, treasury agents gained the advantages derived from federal jails and courts for prosecution but did not get any help policing Alaska's thirty-one thousand miles of shoreline. The marshals did not have a single boat at their disposal, nor did they have the manpower to police smugglers. Marshals did occasionally express longing for a sea or river vessel for the performance of their duties, but they did not express interest in assisting treasury agents in their traditional area of law enforcement.

Until 1904 the collector of customs was stationed at Sitka, usually with one deputy and a watchman at the port and single inspectors at other locations in southeastern, Kodiak, St. Michael, and the Aleutians. Weather, distance, and the lure of high profits to smugglers would have made enforcement difficult even for a huge force of police and a fleet of patrol vessels. As it was, the collector and his small band relied on a couple of ancient vessels, when they were not in repair yards, operated by the Revenue Marine.

Whalers, fishing vessels, foreign and American passenger ships and freighters, and Indian canoes conveyed liquor north from British Columbia or American ports with impunity. When salmon canneries started operations in the 1880s, cannery workers joined in the liquor trade with sustained enthusiasm. Traders of the ancient Hudson's Bay Company of Canada also were active in the illicit trade.

Since the federal government's concern for liquor prohibition did not extend to financing effective means of law enforcement in the form of personnel and vessels, the contraband trade may have corrupted the morals as well as the morale of customs men. Even small-time smugglers made officers look foolish. A deputy stationed at Wrangell complained that for six years he had nothing to do but "watch canoes pass and repass with smuggled goods." Governor Alfred Swineford protested in vain that "there is no water patrol, no revenue cutter, no transportation, not even a row-boat under [the customs district's] control, and as a consequence the smuggler pursues his nefarious calling with very little molestation from any quarter."[35]

Enticing profits encouraged dishonesty. Several officers were suspected of aiding smugglers. In 1891 the Department of Justice sent an examiner to follow up on the investigation of a special treasury agent, Tom E. Johnson, who was told that Assistant U.S. Attorney C. S. Blackett protected liquor sellers. The examiner found that Blackett did authorize sales but did not recommend prosecution because Blackett might have misunderstood customs regulations.

Treasury Department agents, whose responsibilities for fishery regulation and smuggling brought them into contact with Alaska's law officers, marveled at the shenanigans of U.S. Attorney Lytton Taylor. Joseph Murray spent a month in Juneau observing the town and the court, observing the territory's "two distinct classes": one law abiding and progressive, the other "the smuggling, law-defying, *shot-gun argument* element." It seemed odd that "twenty-seven saloons (many of them brothels) are in full blast in Juneau today and, although unlawful, there is no one here to say a word against them. The men who own and operate them are fully organized and by bribery, intimidation, and other questionable means, they manage to defy the law." People told Murray that Taylor "has become *peculiarly* indebted" to the lawbreakers. Men were arrested and brought to trial, but punishment was rare. "The District Attorney is in the habit of compromising the case and of allowing the criminal to go free for a very small fine or a very light sentence."[36]

Taylor prosecuted a deputy marshal for robbery, forgery, and embezzlement and accepted a guilty plea in exchange for a twenty-eight month jail term and a fifty dollar fine. Murray thought the deputy should have received a much longer sentence, but Taylor used the deputy's testimony to secure a grand-jury indictment against former Marshal Orville T. Porter while assuring Porter privately that there could not possibly be an indictment. Murray could not figure out what Taylor was trying to do or why a deputy who was convicted on evidence from the marshal could convince a grand jury that the marshal had something to do with his theft. Murray called for officers of nerve, ability, and honesty and recommended Taylor's dismissal. Taylor was honest but weak, and apparently under the influence of "stronger minded men, who are just now using him as a tool to further their own evil designs."[37]

Other strong complaints against Taylor were made by Collector Benjamin Moore and Sitka's U.S. Commissioner Robert C. Rogers.

Rogers cited several instances in which Taylor allowed criminals to escape punishment, describing his conduct as "eccentric . . . vicious" and so bizarre as to be crazed. Governor James Sheakley reported his opinion directly to the president: Taylor was insane.[38]

Taylor felt the heat and resigned. Then, having second thoughts, he wired Washington, withdrawing his resignation and asking for thirty days' leave. The leave was granted, but the Oregon lawyer was removed from office before he could return to his duties.

The lack of vigor in rooting out violators gave way in 1898 when a Juneau grand jury indicted seven former and serving customs officers. Four of them allegedly had helped smugglers bring liquor into the territory, while three others, stationed at Dyea, sold impounded liquor to thirsty folks in Skagway. Collector of Customs Joseph W. Ivey who held the post from 1897 to 1902, secured the release of Inspector Thomas Marquam and denounced the indictments as a plot against the customhouse directed by "the ring."[39]

Who led the ring? According to Ivey, its leaders were Alaska's district judge, Charles S. Johnson; District Attorney Burton Bennett; and W. A. Beddoe, a Juneau newspaper editor. Governor Brady investigated Ivey's charges and found no convincing evidence to support them. Brady, however, had been urging that Bennett be replaced since 1897.[40]

In a June 1898 report to the attorney general, Bennett warned that the seven accused men "are very much aroused" and asked for a Secret Service investigation. A month later he renewed his request, indicating that "some of the customs officers who were charged with its enforcement, but who violated their plain duty . . . were also indicted and the howl that they have sent forth must have reached you."[41]

Whether because of the howls or for other reasons, Bennett was replaced at the end of July 1898. The serving customs men who had been indicted resigned in early 1899, and Judge Johnson resigned in December of that year.

Prosecution of customs officers Thomas Marquam, W. E. Crews, C. S. Hannum, and Alonzo Cleaver proved impossible when key witnesses and defendants Hannum and Cleaver disappeared. The case that Bennett had been so proud of was dismissed by his successor in May 1901.[42]

Thomas Marquam's reputation did not hold him back too much. He practiced law at Skagway and Haines from 1898 to 1906; moved to Fairbanks, where he edited the *Fairbanks Times* in 1908; then practiced criminal law. He was denied his ambition of appointment as federal judge but was mayor of Fairbanks from 1920 to 1925, delegate to the Republican National Convention in 1924, and candidate for congressional delegate in 1926.

The gold rush ended large-scale smuggling in Alaska. With the flood of thousands of stampeders flowing into the territory, the few customs men were overwhelmed. "What is dutiable and what is not," Governor Brady noted, "nobody knows or pretends to care." [43] Now the advocates who long had urged that prohibition was unenforceable were heard. Congress lifted the ban and enacted a license system for liquor in 1899. With this change, the court's load of smuggling cases was reduced sharply, and the saloon license fees provided immediate funds for the support of two new district courts established in 1900.

3. Dreadful Murders

Alaska has been made the dumping ground for the political offal of the state of Oregon. —Juneau Mining Record

ALASKA'S first murder cases posed legal and logistical problems. The pioneer officers made some mistakes, although they functioned better under the pressure of serious crimes than in some of their petty, internecine local squabbles.

Charles Kie was already in the custody of the U.S. Navy when the first court officers arrived in Sitka. Kie, an Indian who lived near Juneau, had "cut with a knife Nancy, a human being, on the back, arms, and vital parts," causing her death.[1] Sally, another Indian woman, had witnessed the killing and told the white men that Kie had attacked Nancy when enraged by her infidelities with an Indian male.

The prosecutor presented evidence to Sitka's first grand jury with the help of a Russian versed in Indian languages who was hired for the occasion, and Kie was indicted for first-degree murder. Although the facts of the homicide were not in dispute, the court-appointed attorneys showed a commendable willingness to fight for their client's freedom on procedural grounds.

After his indictment Kie was returned to jail to await trial. He was a very sick man and his attorney asked for his release on bail. "He has suffered from a disease which has affected his mind to cause melancholia; further delay could make him insane or dead," argued John L. McLean.[2]

The prosecutor resisted the bail petition, partly out of purported concern for Kie's well-being. Since Kie was a Stickman Tribe member and his wife, Nancy, had been a Chilkat and "the long established custom of both tribes is that friends must slay the slayer," Kie should remain in jail for his own safety, the prosecutor asserted.[3]

The defense also tried to gain Kie's release on the ground that he had been denied his right to a speedy trial. McLean referred to the common knowledge in Sitka that the government forces were embarrassed by a lack of funds. Well, then, the defense counsel said, Kie should not have to languish in jail until the next court session in May because the marshal lacked money to pay for the transportation of trial witnesses from Juneau and elsewhere to Sitka. But the court resisted this argument and established a rather important precedent in Alaska that was used whenever the issue of speedy trial was raised: Alaska was different and delays were not unusual. "The defendant must wait for the regular May term when the Marshal will probably have the money," said the court. No undue hardship was involved. "Kie is simply undergoing a just, proper, and reasonable period of confinement."[4]

At the May term Kie was convicted of manslaughter, sentenced to ten years and fined one hundred dollars, although he was given credit for the time he had spent in jail. Defense attorney Alfred S. Frank appealed to the circuit court in San Francisco, raising arguments based on procedural errors and one that was to become familiar in early Alaska cases involving natives: Kie's killing of Nancy was justified by racial customs and traditions. We should not be shocked by such traditions, Frank told the court, because, "by the ancient Hebrew faith and customs, a woman caught in the act of adultery was stoned to death." Kie had no choice of action: "By the stern faith and customs of his ancient and virtuous people death at the hands of the husband in such a case is imperatively demanded."[5]

The circuit court refused to consider whether the customs of the ancient Hebrews or the Indians of southeastern deserved respect, since other issues were of overriding significance. The court had consulted Petroff's census report on the customs of southeastern Indians and took notice of the effect of recent white intrusions in Alaska: "But for the discovery of gold in the vicinity no civilized man would ever be tempted to seriously interfere with or contest the right" of Indians to their villages. Congress would do well, the court advised, to "provide that, for minor offenses peculiar to their social life and condition, the members of these tribes shall only be tried and punished by their own laws or customs, where they have any." But it was clear that the Organic Act of 1884 intended to "impart to this people the elements of our civilization" and they may "not be allowed to practice with impunity such acts of barbarity" as Kie's.[6]

Kie's conviction was reversed on other grounds and a new trial was ordered. The trial court had slightly exceeded the statutory term of punishment for manslaughter and it did not appear that Kie was actually present in court during all the proceedings. Although the records do not clarify the situation fully, it appears that Kie might have been too far gone with venereal disease to make an appearance in the courtroom, and since there is no record of a second trial, it is probable that he died before he could be tried again.

In an early civil case tried before Judge Dawson the court ruled against another Indian tradition, that of slavery, a common practice among Indians of the Northwest Coast. Sah Quah had been captured and sold into slavery as a boy. After years of servitude he petitioned the court for his release. His Indian owners answered "that they are uncivilized natives; that they and their ancestors have inhabited Alaskan shores from time whereof the memory of man runneth not to the contrary, in communities independent of any other law, authority, or jurisdiction except that established by their own rules and customs; that the buying, selling, and holding of slaves is one of the rules and customs of their race and tribe; that the civil authorities have no jurisdiction over them; and," as the judge observed, "impliedly asserting that Alaska is Indian country, and that they as inhabitants are subject to no law, save the usages and customs of Indians."[7]

Sah Quah's fate touched a commiserate and eloquent strain in Judge Dawson, who looked at the man's obvious degradation: an eye missing, mutilated ears, altogether "a sad spectacle of humiliated manhood." Here was a case where American justice could rise above the petty bickerings so often heard to save an individual from "the blighting curse of slavery." It was no defense, said the judge, "that slavery in its most shocking form has been thoroughly interwoven with the social policy of the Indians of Alaska." The practice was intolerable in a civilized, Christian community. "Does not every precept of religion, every principle that underlies our system of government, every axiom of our political fabric, cry out against such monstrous inhumanity?" Yes, answered the judge, and sent the slave away a free man.[8]

Frank Fuller was the first white man charged with murder in Alaska. His victim was Roman Catholic Bishop Charles John Seghers of Vancouver, British Columbia, who traveled into the interior in 1886 to start a Catholic mission for Yukon Indians at Nulato. The good bishop did not intend that the Presbyterians should continue their domination of northern peoples, not that, in his view, the Presbyterians had accomplished much. Several people told him that the Presbyterians had no influence on adults at all and whispered of scandals that made Seghers blush: "They themselves are not going to heaven . . . and they prevent others from getting there."[9]

If the Presbyterians could have read the bishop's thoughts or his diary, they might not have wished him well on his Yukon travels, but they had nothing to do with his disaster. Seghers' nemesis was a member of his own party, Frank Fuller, a good-looking, thirty-five-year old six-footer with blond, curly hair and moustache and rather strange blue eyes. Fuller was the bishop's helper, a good Catholic who had been serving in various capacities with Jesuit priests.

Seghers and his party reached the Yukon via Chilkoot Pass and traveled by dog sled downriver to Nulato, averaging twenty to twenty-five miles daily over the fresh snow. After several weeks on the trail, Seghers, Fuller, and two Indians got within forty miles of their destination on Saturday, November 27, 1886. The bishop was excited about the possibility of reaching Nulato on Sunday. Fuller, morose and ill-tempered, wanted a day to rest. The men quarreled over this as they had over other matters on the trail. Fuller's dark moods and irrational accusations had made the bishop uneasy throughout the journey. "Fuller asks me how it can be that I encourage Indians to make fun of him," Seghers noted in his diary. Fuller thought that Indians made fun of him in the Rocky Mountains, "and here they are doing the same thing."

Later Fuller wanted to know "why I sent one of our Indians

Frank Fuller, the slayer of Bishop Seghers, aboard ship and bound for trial in Sitka. University of Alaska Archives, Bunnell Collection

ahead to burn the sleigh and himself, Fuller." Obviously Fuller was a sick man, alarmingly paranoid, wildly suspicious of the man he had begged for the opportunity of helping on the Alaska mission, a man he had promised to give his life for. Seghers' last diary words on the twenty-fifth recorded another Fuller accusation: Fuller wished to know why a white man who accompanied the party earlier predicted that the bishop "would give him a black name."

On Saturday the party camped in an Indian smokehouse on an island in the Yukon. Seghers retired in good humor. Fuller rose repeatedly during the night to pace around the embers of the campfire. Between six and seven o'clock the next morning, the four men got up. Then, without warning, Fuller raised his .44-caliber Winchester and fired a single shot at the bishop as he bent to pick up his mittens. Seghers died instantly.

George Snitna tried to wrest Fuller's gun from him, but the stronger slayer resisted in a friendly way, shook hands with the Indian, and explained that he felt no urge to shoot anyone else. He had just wanted to kill the bishop and, having accomplished that, he was eager to push on to Nulato with the others. His awed Indian companions were grateful that Fuller remained peaceful during the rest of the trip. The Nulato trader seemed comfortable with Fuller even after hearing the Indians' story, and Fuller agreed to go back and help bring in the bishop's body. To the trader's question of why Fuller shot Seghers, the killer replied: "Oh, I did; that's all. I have taken the bishop's life, and mine will be short now."

Nothing could be done about Fuller that winter, once he had been taken downriver to the larger trading station at St. Michael. As there was no jail, Fuller was free to roam around and make everyone uneasy with his bizarre behavior. It was August before Lieutenant Charles Kennedy of the Revenue Marine Cutter Service's *Bear* arrested Fuller on a warrant issued by the U.S. commissioner at Unalaska. Fuller seemed to enjoy the attention he received from his escort, doffing his hat and waving his manacled hands to the silent spectators at St. Michael as he was rowed out to the *Bear.* From Unalaska, Fuller was transferred to the *Richard Rush* for the voyage to Sitka, where he stood trial in November.

Bishop Seghers' murder was the first Alaska crime to gain national prominence. Few people in the States knew anything about the Yukon River, but the slaying of a member of the Catholic hierarchy created a sensation, particularly because Fuller usually was identified, inaccurately, as a Jesuit lay brother.

The *Portland Oregonian* reflected on the death of a good man intent upon letting "the light shine in dark places that others may see," observing that Seghers expected dangers on his journey but "civilization supported his only enemy. . . . If those Indians possessed cultivated reasoning faculties they would feel like disputing the advance of civilization which could nurture one so heartless as the man Fuller."

The *Baltimore Catholic Mirror* concluded that the inhuman act could have been committed only by a deranged man, and another paper lamented that the honors of martyrdom were denied the bishop because he did not suffer at the hands of Indians but through the "irresponsible frenzy of a mad man."

In Sitka, Fuller appeared calm and cool most of the time, although he did keep altering his story of the shooting. A. K. Delaney, U.S. collector of customs in Alaska, was appointed to defend the accused and did not hesitate long before resolving on a defense of insanity.

At trial Fuller sat staring at the floor, showing interest only when George Snitna and other Alaskans testified. He seemed not to expect that jurors would accept an Indian's testimony against him and even guided his counsel in cross-examination of Snitna.

Fuller's testimony surprised the court. He claimed that the shooting had been an accident resulting from an attack on him by Snitna's Indian companion. When he took the rifle away from the attacker, he said, it discharged the fatal bullet. Delaney ignored Fuller's story and concentrated on medical witnesses, who explained that Fuller's statements after the killing showed his delusions and melancholia.

Prosecutor Whit M. Grant demanded a conviction for first degree murder, and Judge Lafayette Dawson instructed jurors on the distinction between murder and manslaughter and on the nature of temporary insanity. On retiring, the jurors were none too happy with the government's case. Of those individuals who had been in contact with Fuller before and after the killing, only James Walker and Snitna had been subpoenaed. And there had been no autopsy—in fact, the bishop's body remained at St. Michael awaiting shipment to the States. Evidence conflicted with the basic point of whether the bishop had been shot in the body or the head. The government's sloppiness was traceable to the high costs involved. It would take some time yet before Washington grew accustomed to the expenses of Alaska justice. The bill for conveying Walker and Snitna to Sitka and returning them to the Yukon via San Francisco reached fifteen hundred dollars. Bringing other witnesses would have raised costs and necessitated a postponement of the trial.

After forty hours and nineteen ballots, the jury asked the judge's advice. Could they find manslaughter? Yes, said Judge Dawson, if you find that Fuller did not intend to kill. After more debate the jury agreed on manslaughter, a verdict that provoked general dismay among those following the trial. Critics complained that Fuller was either insane and not guilty for that reason or sane and guilty of intentional murder. Yet the compromise arrived at by the jury was not an unusual one, even if flawed. Clearly the jurors doubted Fuller's sanity, but they did not care to free him. A conviction for manslaughter would result in a prison sentence.

Fuller did not help clarify things by insisting on his innocence at the time of his sentencing: "I believe I am innocent. I had anything but murder in my heart when I came to Alaska." Judge Dawson cautioned Fuller to count his blessings: "I am of the opinion that the jury showed a merciful consideration when they convicted you of manslaughter." And Fuller—always ready for the last, inconsistent word—argued that "it may turn out that the bishop was not shot after all. He may have died from natural causes."

Fuller's sentence was ten years and a one-thousand dollar fine. In press interviews he did not blame those who tried him but deplored that his friends among the clergy failed to come to his assistance. "They should not have left me in the lurch as they did," he declared.

In May 1896, Fuller completed his sentence at McNeil Island and created a flurry of publicity with press interviews. His new version of the killing described a quarrel with Seghers over an Indian woman. Some Catholics considered this story Fuller's ultimate infamy, while others charged that the anti-Catholic American Protective Association had incited Fuller's statement. Seghers' biographer points out that the quarrel Fuller mentioned had nothing to do with sexual rivalry. The white men had intervened to prevent an Indian man from beating his wife. Fuller wanted to shoot the man, but Seghers disapproved.

A few years after his release, Fuller's tortured life was ended when a Portland neighbor with whom he had quarreled shot him dead.

4. Justice Questioned

I'll freeze in hell before helping the courthouse gang get a conviction.
—Peter Trout

Panhandle residents liked to attend trials and follow courthouse gossip. Usually there was not a whole lot going on in town in the way of entertainment, so court sessions fulfilled a cultural need. Everyone knew the officers of the court and the lawyers, and it was interesting to compare notes on their effectiveness. Defendants in criminal trials were usually familiar characters as well, and if one were a particularly colorful individual, or if the crime had sensational elements, the courtroom would be packed.

Jack Dalton was rather well known in Juneau when he got into trouble. Local opinions of him were mixed. His friends bragged that he was a man of courage and commercial vision who would do anything for you. He might look kind of tough, but he was actually mild mannered and kind. Others looked at Dalton's short, thick, powerful figure, observed his curt, somewhat menacing manner and his quick, intense way of moving, as if he might run over anyone who dared get in his way, and did not like the man. The trouble with Dalton, some folks said, was that he took himself and his schemes too seriously. He thought he could bull his way over other folks to get what he wanted. The marshal made a mistake giving Dalton a deputy's badge; Dalton already thought he was a law unto himself.

In 1893, when the trouble occurred, we don't know whether Dalton had a clear vision of his future use of the Chilkat Pass trail that would later bear his name. He had been over the route with exploring parties from *Frank Leslie's Illustrated Weekly* in 1890 and 1891, and the suitability of the route to the interior had been discussed, but it was 1894 before Dalton took a pack train over it and 1896 when he started making improvements to the trail.

Dalton's plan in 1893 apparently was to use the trail to establish a trading post in the interior. He chose the route deliberately to avoid conflict with Indians. The Chilkats, a Tlingit people distinct from the Chilkoots, had long since established something of a monopoly of the Chilkoot Pass route. Frederick Schwatka, who led the U.S. Army reconnaissance of the Yukon River from source to mouth in 1883, employed Chilkat Indians as packers and guides. The Chilkats did not tolerate the use of the pass by other Indians because it gave them a trading advantage, and they even attempted to deny white prospectors entry until the U.S. Navy applied some force in 1880.[1]

A salmon cannery and store was established at Chilkat in the 1880s, and by 1893 the white population totaled thirteen. The Chilkats remained somewhat uneasy over the possible interference with their traditional interior trade, but they did no more than grumble as Dalton and his men cut through a route that avoided Chilkoot Pass's precipitous grade and could be used by pack animals and cattle.

On March 6, 1893, Dalton heard nasty rumors about young Daniel McGinnis, the village storekeeper. Dalton's hair-trigger temper exploded and he left the woods to confront the man, who may have been instigating the Indians to resist Dalton's plans. Storming into Murray's cannery store, Dalton challenged McGinnis: "What do you mean talking to Indians about me, about my going into the interior?"[2]

As the frightened storekeeper professed his ignorance, Dalton ordered an Indian interpreter to repeat what other Indians had heard from McGinnis. "Jack Dalton is going in there," said the Indian, "and make a trading post and then we get poor."

McGinnis remained sitting while Dalton shouted, "I don't want you talking this way about me."

"I don't want you to talk about me either," the little clerk replied lamely.

"I never talked about you. You have, McGinnis, and you are a liar."

At this insult McGinnis foolishly rose from his chair. Dalton pushed him back down, drew his revolver, and smashed McGinnis on the head three times, repeating, "You are a liar," with each blow. McGinnis threw up his hands and the gun went off—by accident or design. McGinnis fell with a mortal wound.

Patrick Woods and others tried to bind the dying man's wounds and prepared a boat to take him to Juneau for medical aid. Dalton left the store. He remained very cool and said nothing. If any of the white men or Indians felt like avenging McGinnis, the menacing spectacle of Dalton pacing the beach with rifle in hand dissuaded them.

After an inquest, a murder complaint was filed with U.S. Commissioner W. R. Hoyt on March 7. Dalton was arrested and taken to Juneau, where trial was set for June.

Newspapers reported the shooting, describing Dalton as a sober, industrious man of seven years' residence in Alaska, with headquarters at Sitka. "It was a sad and horrible affair and Dalton's acquaintances express great surprise."[3] Adding to the shock were Dalton's official office as a deputy U.S. marshal and the physical mismatch between Dalton and the 120-pound clerk. Did an armed officer who was also a notably strong man have any reason to use a gun on his puny victim? people asked.

Dalton's attorneys, A. K. Delaney and J. F. Maloney, presented Indian witnesses, including Schwatka, who as a young man assumed the army explorer's name after guiding the soldiers to the Yukon in 1883. Witnesses confirmed McGinnis' incitement of them to stop Dalton's construction. Such incitements "were a constant menace to the life of Dalton," his lawyer argued.[4]

In cross-examining Patrick Woods, the affray's only witness, the defense suggested that Woods had bolted to the store's privy and hid when the fight started, thus missing McGinnis' attack on Dalton with an ax. Dalton testified that Indians had threatened to kill the first white man who went into the interior, "whether Jack Dalton or not."[5] McGinnis' treachery had made Dalton angry, but Dalton shot him only in self-defense when the young man threatened him with an ax.

Jurors listened solemnly to witnesses and to the judge's instructions on self-defense and other aspects of the law. Then, in the privacy of the jury room, they may have reflected on McGinnis' disloyalty to their race and Dalton's sterling labor in opening up the country. In no time at all they returned with an acquittal.

Dalton won his freedom for distinctly unheroic conduct because the jury chose to ignore evidence that pointed to an unprovoked assault, and its finding angered Juneau's citizens. Talk of lynching Dalton raged, but at a civic-indignation meeting "better counsel prevailed and it was decided not to lynch Dalton, but to notify him that he had to leave the Territory within three days, and that if he failed to do so, he should forfeit his life."[6]

According to the *Alaskan,* published in Sitka, Juneau folks were also outraged at E. O. Sylvester, editor of the *Alaska Journal* at Juneau, for his defense of the jury and his blatant misrepresentation of the immediate response to the verdict. Sylvester reported that when the not-guilty verdict was rendered, "it was with great difficulty that Deputy Marshal Endelman prevented the people from noisily demonstrating their satisfaction." In fact, said the *Alaskan,* hooting and other demonstrations of disapproval disrupted the courtroom and the jurors who were employees of the dominant Alaska Treadwell Gold Mining Co. were "immediately discharged from the company's employ."[7]

Months later the *Alaskan,* perhaps motivated by the editor's personal vendetta against E. O. Sylvester, rejoiced that the *Alaska Journal* had folded, ascribing its unlamented demise to popular feeling about its misrepresentation of the Dalton trial. The trial had been a "travesty of justice," although the prosecutor and judge had done their duty properly, and everyone tainted by the outcome had left Juneau for "pastures new."[8]

Federal prosecutors in Juneau apparently believed that jury fixing had been instrumental in Dalton's acquittal and blamed John F. Maloney, Dalton's lawyer. Maloney, a six-footer given to drinking and brawling when not pursuing shrewd investments that would eventually make him one of Juneau's richest men, including his backing of the Dalton Trail construction and the Dalton Pony Express Company, was not a friend of court officers. "Maloney led the bad element resulting in the Dalton case result," Assistant U.S. Attorney John G. Heid complained to the attorney general. Heid did favor the law-and-order league formed after the Dalton trial because it was composed of right-minded citizens who offered to help lawmen "with money or force" against the likes of Maloney. [9]

Obviously the federal prosecutors lacked the evidence needed to bring charges against Maloney, who, undeterred by their angry mutterings, went on to great successes as the developer of the rich Porcupine mining district and the founder of the Alaska Light and Power Company. Maloney's reputation became better as his wealth increased. Folks came to forget allegations that he had fled from Montana to Alaska in 1885 to avoid a forgery indictment, nor did they remember some incidents of client hustling in his early Alaska years. The outstanding example of the latter activity occurred in 1887 when Walter Pierce was charged with the murder of an Indian. Maloney found other Indians who were interested in helping the prosecutor secure a conviction and accepted a fee to act as special prosecutor. Then he called on Pierce and accepted a fee to act as his defense attorney. Judge Lafayette Dawson had to explain to Maloney that the American legal system required that each side be represented by independent advocates: "The law is a jealous mistress," explained the judge. [10] Maloney was required to return his fee to the Indians, but he had shown his acumen in changing sides: Pierce was acquitted.

Whether Dalton actually left the territory until passions cooled is not clear. He may have returned to work, feeling confident that the Juneau men were not apt to menace him on his ground. It is likely, judging from his character, that he would have welcomed the arrival of fellows who seemed brave as mob members and shouted deadly threats while they were safe in Juneau. Dalton understood well enough that men who faced him as individuals usually spoke softly.

Within a few years the Klondike stampede proved Dalton's wisdom and foresight. In 1898 he charged a $2.50 toll for each steer, horse, and mule and various rates for wagons, freight, sheep, swine, dog teams, and foot passengers who used his trail. There were plenty of roughnecks who were tempted to bluff their way without paying, but Dalton possessed a certain presence that other hard fellows saw reason to respect. Everyone learned that he guarded his trail fiercely, and there were rumors that cheaters on the toll often vanished along the way. Dalton held his monopoly of the livestock traffic until the White Pass and Yukon Railway was completed. He did all right for himself and earned the gratitude of people in Dawson when two thousand beef cattle were driven over his trail to feed the hungry miners in 1898.

Thanks to his service during the gold rush and to the passage of time, Dalton's indiscretion of 1893 was forgotten. He became a firmly established legend for perseverance, integrity, success—and, yes, for some violence when a good cause demanded force. "Alaskans have absolute faith in him," reported the *Seattle Star* in 1915. "Dalton is easily the first citizen of Alaska." Dalton was then involved in organizing the transportation for the construction of the Alaska Railroad, "a herculean job, but he's been tackling herculean jobs all his life." He had "blazed the trail for the Copper River Railroad and the coal trail from Chickaloon on the Matanuska River to Knik for the government." A bit of violence on the latter job merely improved upon his standing. It seems that a government agent refused to pay the workers, with the idea of hindering the work, so the "active, extremely muscular," middle-aged pioneer flattened the agent with a blow to the jaw and then paid the workers out of his own pocket.[11]

Thus the Dalton legend grew, fueled by legitimate accomplishments in opening the country. Maybe it was just as well that the much defamed jurors of Juneau indulged in a "travesty of justice."

Alaska's newspaper editors feared the court enough to show a measure of restraint even when an unpopular decision upset them. But a shooting affray in Juneau shortly after the Dalton trial excited the kind of personal and vindictive journalism that inflamatory, community-rocking events were likely to arouse.

It all started with the April 15, 1895, issue of the *Alaska Mining Record*. Editor Frank E. Howard, succumbing to the temptation to mock the employee of a rival paper whom he despised, described the man's work as a volunteer firefighter as a comic, disruptive, drunken exhibition.

Unfortunate Jack Timmins, business manager of the *Alaska Searchlight,* grew outraged as he read that he had been "out having a good time with the boys when the vigorous ringing of the fire-bell and the clank of hurrying feet aroused him from a stupid state of inebriety." Timmins was not looking for praise when he climbed up on the roof of the burning building to direct other firefighters, but he did not expect to be called a "self-conceited ass," "an egotist," and "a drunken fool" whose bellowing at the fireboys "sounded like a steam calliope playing Yankee Doodle at a county fair." And the paper even claimed that other firefighters got mad at him and turned the hose on him, "suddenly shutting off the chattering parrot's wind, removing him from his elevated position and sobering him up," and probably would expel him at their next meeting. [12]

Timmins roared into the *Record* office, found editor Howard, and shouted:

"Am I indebted to you for that article . . . ?"

"I guess you are," was the cold reply.

"Well, what did you put it in for?"

"It is news and it's satisfactory."

"Then you shoulder the responsibility of the article, do you?"

"I do. I think we are about even now." [13]

But Timmins did not think the game even. What happened next was disputed. According to the *Record:* "With that Timmins partially turned toward the door and Howard thinking that was all to be said, arose from his chair, being completely thrown off his guard by Timmins' clever ruse. No sooner had he made a step from the position where he had been sitting when Timmins turned like a flash, grabbed Howard's right hand with his left, and with lightning-like rapidity drew a 38-calibre revolver from his breast pocket and began shooting." Frank grappled with his assailant and the revolver discharged, the ball taking effect in his left groin. "Weakened by the continued struggle and the loss of blood from the wound in his groin, Frank with one last Herculean effort knocked the pistol aside, but not in time to escape the ball. It entered his head just to the left of his left eye, ploughing its way through the skull to a point back of his ear where it still remains."

The *Record* of April 22, 1895, followed the shooting story with an account of Timmins' career. He had been in Juneau nine years and

was known to police of San Francisco, Portland, and Seattle "as a tough man who would not stoop in any crime human ingenuity could concoct." In Seattle they called him "Black Jack," in Portland "Roaring Jack," from "his habit of using his bull-like voice to such advantage when drunk." His periodic sprees inspired awe and terror, featuring the chewing and spitting of bar glasses, the smashing of furniture with Indian clubs, and the slugging of his best friends. One friend, a cripple who had nursed Jack through a long illness, suffered a broken nose for his pains.

Other violent acts by Timmins included butting Billy Lawson in the face, thereby knocking his teeth out, and threatening to shoot him until restrained; shooting William Hennig in the groin during a card-game dispute; smashing an Indian woman's head with a bowling ball; chewing John Curry's fingers in a drunken brawl; the armed robbery of Frank Leroy, who had won twenty dollars from him in a card game; drawing on a card player who accused him—rightfully—of cheating; and so on. Oh yes, Timmins used to run an illicit distillery at Chilkat. "The saloon that Timmins formerly ran in Juneau was known far and wide as the rendezvous of every murderous cutthroat in the territory." Many a poor drunk awakened in that den "to find himself in the street without a copper in the world."

What else? Well, the rumors of bribe taking and perjury time and again have never been refuted. And until his marriage Timmins associated openly and notoriously with fallen women. "He has lived off their shame and has descended to the lowest possible depths of degradation for a man." All Juneau knew of his disgraceful liaison with Mollie West, known as "Irish Mollie," and the time he gambled away all his money, demanded hers, knocked her down, choked her, robbed her, and spent the stolen gains on riotous drinking. "Lack of space prevents us giving this man's record on the Sound, at Portland, and in San Francisco," the *Record* explained, "but we assure our readers it is just as unsavory, just as rotten, vile and despicable as his life has been since coming to Juneau."

The *Record* kept its readers advised on Frank Howard's condition, which improved rapidly, thanks to his "wonderfully strong constitution together with naturally great vitality"; and on the cover-up journalism of the *Alaska Searchlight,* the newspaper Timmins reported for. In a half-dozen lines the *Searchlight* referred to the "little affray" as something of an accident. "Is this journalism?" editorialized the *Record.* "It might be considered so by the chattering idiots of an insane asylum, but among intelligent, well-read, and well-bred people, who know right from wrong, it must appear as the vapid musings of a demented creature whose pusillanimity and abject cowardice is only equalled by his egotistical mutterings and craven actions."[14]

No, clearly it was not journalism, but "as huge a piece of brazen effrontery and journalistic rot as one might expect to emanate from the pen of a thing whose very vitality and what few brains he ever possessed had long, long ago been sapped out. The entire population of Juneau and vicinity, every man, woman, and child, every siwash, and every yellow dog knows that Timmins had murder in his mind and the devil in his heart when he left his office for the Record office."

While the newspaper villification and outrage entertained readers, the more orderly process of law moved forward. District Attorney Lytton Taylor brought Timmins before the U.S. commissioner for a preliminary examination three weeks after the shooting. Jail had cooled Timmins' spirit. He was nervous and downcast as bail was set at $7,500. Taylor made his seriousness obvious by asking for a $10,000 bond, since the death of Howard within a year and a day would mean a murder prosecution. Defense attorney Maloney argued for a $5,000 bond, accusing the U.S. attorney of harassment because medical testimony indicated Howard was in no danger of perishing. Taylor probably spoke for the Juneau community in censoring the shooting of a citizen "like a dog." Even a $10,000 bond "scarcely covers such a crime as has been committed in your midst by the defendant."[15]

Mention in the Juneau newspapers of the Jack Dalton case suggests that the incident was viewed as part of the conflict between pro- and anti-Maloney forces championed by different newspapers. Of course, the circumstances of Dalton's shooting of Daniel McGinnis and the assault on Howard were similar enough to suggest comparisons even if competing factors were not involved. "Juneau's respectable and honest residents are not in the humor to stand another Dalton outrage," observed the *Alaska News*, "and far less the bloodthirsty acts of one who is trying to assume the former's mantle of crime without his reputed courage." The *News* noted that *Searchlight* publisher E. O. Sylvester, in 1893 the editor of the *Alaska Journal*, had approved of Dalton's killing of an unarmed man and the acquittal of him as a source of "general satisfaction." Timmins' cowardly act cannot be covered up by Sylvester, the *News* warned, "by the use of hypocritical language . . . to bully-rag the public and convey the idea that his local reporter and business manager was justified. . . . This double-faced pharisee has tried to pose before this community as a moral reformer, has piled on the sheep's clothing to hide the devilry of a hydra-headed wolf, but his base make-up always cops out when law, order, and respectability are marshalled against crime and base cowardice." In truth, Sylvester held a grudge against Howard. "It would be well for this masker behind cloaks to study well the fall of Oscar Wilde in England, whose disgusting life is something of a parallel example."[16]

To turn from such press fulminations to the court's disposition of the assault case is a relief. The parallels between the Dalton and Timmons cases do not extend beyond the facts of the assault. Juneau jurors took their duties seriously; and as Timmins lacked Dalton's popularity as a folk hero, he was convicted of assault with a dangerous weapon.

5. Vigilantes

We are not dealing with sane men, but a crowd of gold lunatics. —Captain
P. H. Ray

SKAGWAY'S natural endowments included a deep harbor, sylvan forests, and nearby mountains through which passes extended into
the interior to reach the headwaters of the Yukon River. White
Pass, named by William Ogilvie, dominion land surveyor, in 1887,
was forty-five miles long. Pioneer William Moore concluded that a
townsite at the head of Lynn Canal on Skagway Bay would be a
grand investment for the future, so he built himself a cabin near the
base of White Pass. Not far away, near Dyea Inlet, Chilkoot Pass
led to the interior along a thirty-five-mile route. Chilkoot, more
precipitous than White, was the chosen route of thousands of stampeders in 1897–98. Merchant John J. Healy had observed the Indians' use of the route and built a trading post at Dyea in 1886. Both
Dyea and Skagway flourished as gold-rush centers, particularly
Skagway because of its harbor.

Skagway was only about 100 miles from Juneau and not much
farther from Sitka, yet it could be reached only by sea, and the
court officers at Sitka were not remarkably alert in providing for
the town's orderly development. Of course there existed a number
of precedents for the orderly growth of towns in western mining
regions, and for periods of disorder as well. Sudden booms strained
the system until municipal authority could be organized, and the

emergency measures that could be effected during awkward stages were not always available or well handled when they were.

The miners' meeting did not work in Skagway as it had in Forty Mile, Circle, and Rampart. It worked in the interior towns because their populations were relatively stable, even though the towns themselves were short lived as large centers. Skagway was a place of passage for everyone except the merchants and a gang of rascals who found better pickings by staying on than by moving into the interior with the masses.

Soapy Smith, a gambler and con man from Colorado, noticed the opportunities in Skagway on a quick visit in 1897. He was an intelligent fellow who had managed to take control of Creede, Colorado, in 1892 by rigging the election of cronies as officials. His reign was brief and he did not accomplish much in Denver, where both the criminal and the law-enforcement classes were better established, but he had talents enough to tap the rich resources of incoming and outgoing stampeders through Skagway for several months in 1897–98.

Smith's headquarters in Skagway was a saloon, but his sharpers drifted around the town and the trails to the interior to trap the unwary into crooked card games or to unburden them of cash with tricks and plain thievery. In town, Smith posed as a public spirited citizen to fool most of the people most of the time.

There is no question that Dawson was a more colorful and exciting town than Skagway, yet throughout the great boom, order was maintained by the North-West Mounted Police in a commendable fashion. The Mounties seemed always to be on hand to clap any evildoer into jail before ugly things could happen. There were no murders in Dawson in 1897–98, an amazing fact given the migration of thousands of men and women. The Mounties did not allow guns in town and otherwise watched the potentially criminal class, mostly Americans, closely. Almost everyone appreciated the Canadian police and made unfavorable comparisons with the law-enforcement situation on the American side of the border throughout the gold-rush era.

Alaskans also praised the Mounties for solution of the most celebrated murder case in the early gold-rush era. In 1899, three men set out from Dawson for Skagway and other points, one with a bi-

cycle that did not function too well in the extreme cold. The travelers were last seen alive Christmas Day enjoying a feast at a roadhouse near Minto in Yukon Territory. Shortly thereafter they were
waylaid, killed, and hidden under snow and ice. Their bodies were
not discovered until spring, but by then the Mounties' chief suspect
had been languishing in jail for months as police investigators gathered evidence. The conviction and execution of George O'Brien followed in due course, and the legend of the Mounties grew apace.

Among those who reported on the lawlessness of Skagway was
Colonel Sam Steele of the North-West Mounted Police. He and another officer were awakened in their room by gunfire, shouts, and
curses but were not tempted to intervene. "Bullets came through
the thin boards [of our room], but the circumstance was such a

common event that we did not even rise from our beds."[1] No doubt Steele exaggerated because the disparity between Skagway and Dawson enhanced the Mounties' reputation, but he appears sincere in describing the Alaska town as being "about the toughest place in the world." Steele did overstate the case in claiming that Soapy Smith's gang had more than one hundred members and that they "ran the town and did what they pleased; almost the only persons safe from them were the members of our force. . . . Neither law nor order prevailed, honest persons had no protection from the gangs of rascals who plied their nefarious trade. Might was right."

Steele and a fellow officer, Major Zachary Taylor Wood, grandson of a former president of the United States, confronted the Smith gang in the spring of 1898. Wood had to ship custom fees totaling

$150,000 to Ottawa and feared thieves on the American side of the border. Rather than mount an impressive escort and attract attention, Wood and others carried the money in their saddlebags, pretending that Wood was going to the outside for a change of duty assignments. According to Steele, this ruse worked until Wood boarded a launch for Skagway and a waiting steamer when the gang tried to intervene. Wood held the gang off until he reached the ship, where armed Canadian sailors outfaced a menacing band of armed Smith men standing on the dock. Whether true or not, the story does reflect the Mounties' opinion of Skagway.

Besides Soapy there was another Smith in Dyea and Skagway who helped create disdain for American law enforcement. John U. Smith, an Oregonian recommended by Oregon's U.S. Senator George McBride, was appointed U.S. commissioner by the president on the recommendation of the secretary of interior in July 1897. Smith, the ex officio justice of the peace for Dyea and Skagway, was not of the criminal class, but he had, as Governor John Brady put it, "a hunger and thirst for fees." Alaska's governors complained for years about the fee system, which continued for commissioners even after 1900 legislation made the attorney general, rather than the secretary of the interior, responsible for appointments. "The fee system," Brady observed, "is an abominable method to secure the administration of justice in such a country as Alaska." Some commissioners and deputy marshals, who also earned fees, "will work together to make business by stirring up strife and contentions to get fees." There was no way to make the office pay except through such methods, "for his earnings will hardly pay for the salt that goes in his mush." [2]

Commissioner Smith's handling of his office helped mold Brady's opinions. Complaints against Smith began shortly after he took office. He gouged high recorder fees in the all important transactions of filing on mining claims, and he assessed exorbitant court costs at hearings. He also was accused of charging high fees for defending clients as their attorney in district court, although in such instances he acted in a private capacity, as he was entitled to do.

Juneau's U.S. Attorney Alfred Daly looked into complaints against Smith in September 1897 and seemed reasonably satisfied with the commissioner's explanations. Before Daly had the opportunity to report on Smith, the commissioner appealed to his patron, Senator McBride, just to be on the safe side: "Stand by me against old enemies and other envious parties." Smith went on to describe his heroic labors holding court in a crowded tent while parties waited outside in pouring rain.[3]

As complaints continued, the Justice Department sent an examiner to investigate. James S. Easley-Smith arrived in Juneau, talked to Governor Brady and others, and reported without bothering to wait two weeks for the next steamer bound for Dyea. He had learned enough; besides, Smith's office was Interior's responsibility, not Justice's. Brady had visited Dyea and Skagway in August to learn that the commissioner's work was "a public scandal."[4] One defendant in Smith's court had been fined twenty dollars for assault and assessed forty dollars in costs. Fines went to the government, costs and fees to the commissioner. Someone determined that the actual court costs were eighteen dollars.

Smith tried a man who had committed an assault in his presence. He agreed to reduce the charge from attempted murder—a felony which would have to be tried in district court—to assault and battery for which the fine and fees totaled $150. Contrary to Smith's expectations, the accused man did not think the reduced charge in exchange for $150 was a good deal and complained vigorously to the district court.

While Smith was trying to make a living, he did not entirely ignore the threat to order promised by the impending rush to the Klondike. In December 1897 he requested a squad of soldiers to police trails out of Skagway and Dyea to the Canadian border. The government agreed that two deputy marshals probably could not do the job and assigned an infantry troop to Dyea.

Governor Brady visited Skagway and Dyea again in February 1898 after calling at Haines, an Indian village sixteen miles southwest of Skagway. Brady, a former missionary, was enraged to learn that Smith had been in Haines a short time before to collect four hundred dollars in recording fees for town lots the Indians long had occupied. When he arrived in Skagway, Brady heard complaints against Smith from newspaper editor J. F. A. Strong and attorney J. G. Price, then told the commissioner "how universally he is detested."[5]

The governor sensed an ugly situation. Commissioner Smith's greed had encouraged contempt for the law. Skagway was a powder keg likely to explode, and Brady hoped that the brief appearance of the USS *Wheeling,* a navy ship that had conveyed him from Juneau, would remind the unruly element that the government did have some force at its command. At the time Skagway was quiet because people were "careful how they moved about at night." Dyea was calmer because people were moving toward the mountain pass in preparation for a spring crossing. Brady did hear of a vigilante incident at Sheep Camp along the trail. Three Californians had cached their provisions there in the fall of 1897 and returned to the outside for the winter. When they got back, they found their cache plundered. Two men were caught with some of the items in their possession. A miner's meeting was quickly held in a saloon tent at Sheep Camp, and the two men were convicted of theft. One broke away to make a dash for freedom but was swiftly pursued. As the miners reached him, he shot himself, fatally, in the head. The suicide victim must have anticipated a punishment worse than his self-inflicted exit, yet the miners let his companion off with fifty strokes with a knotted rope and a parade into Dyea wearing a large sign inscribed "Thief." Brady acknowledged that "this may not be legal, but it will be salutary for thieves for some time upon the trail and will be better than a whole lot of moral suasion."[6]

Charles A. Sehlbrede succeeded the dismissed Commissioner Smith in March 1898 and did a better job. One bad Smith had been taken care of, but the major character of that name was still in midterm of his glittering career as "King of Skagway."

Despite his apprehension over the problems attendant to sudden growth and an acceleration in crime, Governor Brady often saw the bright side of things, maintaining that the stampeders "reflect the goodness of our institutions" with their concern for school and church building. "If the coming multitudes compare with the people at Skagway and Dyea now," he wrote in December 1897, Alaska would become the "most noble state in the Union." Brady, back in Skagway for the 1898 Fourth of July celebration, watched "5,000 . . . celebrate in great style. A great display of Americanism in a one year old town." The pleased governor saw only two or three drunks and no rowdies at all. Brady said nothing about

Jefferson ("Soapy") Smith's riding a white horse as parade marshal, as reported by others, but he was able to give a name to the man who threatened trouble: "Everything is orderly now but there is a character there now by the sobriquet 'Soapy Smith' and he seems to have the gambling element completely under his control."[7]

Brady anticipated the season's major gold shipment out of Dawson and advised that troops from Dyea and Wrangell meet the NWMP escort at the border to guard the shipment to tidewater. More troops would be welcome, he told the secretary of the interior, because still another boom could be expected when two thousand workers arrived to start building the railroad through White Pass. Smith "might find it convenient to have the men strike just after a payday and rush them into the town to help his business."[8]

Perhaps beguiled by the patriotic display of the Glorious Fourth, Brady did not see how close Skagway was to eruption. A committee of citizens led by editor J. F. A. Strong and Frank Reid, a civil engineer who had laid out the town's site, had issued a public notice:

WARNING

A word to the wise should be sufficient. All confidence sharks, bunco men, sure-thing men, and all other objectional characters are notified to leave Skagway and the White Pass. Failure to comply with this warning will be followed by prompt action!

Signed—Committee of One Hundred and One.

Unimpressed, Soapy Smith countered with a challenge from the Committee of 303:

ANNOUNCEMENT

The business interests of Skagway propose to put a stop to the lawless acts of many newcomers. We hereby summon all good citizens to a meeting at which these matters will be discussed. COME ONE, COME ALL!.

Immediate action will be taken for relief.

Let this be a warning to those cheechawcos who are disgracing our city! This meeting will be held at Sylvester Hall at 8:00 p.m. sharp.

(Signed) Jefferson R. Smith, Chairman.[9]

At the public meeting Smith charged that outsiders were trying to take over the town from true pioneers. Rogues abounded in Skagway, he warned, and they were trying to harm the good folks.

A noisy audience cheered lustily as Smith avowed the determination of all respectable citizens to clamp a lid on Skagway.

Those in town who were not bamboozled by Smith's pose as a keeper of order either joined the vigilantes or, sensing that trouble loomed, arranged to stay out of the line of fire.

Smith issued still another public notice:

PUBLIC WARNING

The body of men calling themselves the Committee of One Hundred and One are hereby notified that any overt act committed by them will be met promptly by the law-abiding citizens of Skagway and each member and their property will be held responsible for any unlawful act on their part. The Law and Order Committee of Three Hundred and Three will see that justice is dealt out to its fullest extent and no Blackmailers or Vigilantes will be tolerated."

The vigilantes did nothing for a time beyond appealing to the U.S. Army garrison at Dyea for help. But to no avail; the commander, a prudent man, refused to move without orders from his superiors or a request from the governor.

It seems strange that the U.S. marshal or the U.S. attorney in Sitka did not look more intently at the Skagway problem. The key officer throughout the disturbing times was the Skagway deputy marshal, Sylvester S. Taylor, who was in cahoots with Soapy Smith and consequently was not inclined to alert his superiors. His treachery was obvious enough to informed people in Skagway by May 1898 or even before, and several complaints were made to federal officials in Washington and to the Seattle press by early June.

On June 3 a Seattle newspaper carried the charges of Mrs. Mattie Silks and her call upon the government "to straighten out the lawless condition of affairs at Skagway." Mrs. Silks, an arrival from Skagway on the steamer *Farallon,* laid it out: Deputy Marshal Taylor shares in Smith's plunder even when murder is involved: "On the afternoon of May 28th Ella Wilson, a mulatto prostitute, was strangled to death and robbed in her house on one of the principal streets of Skagway. A large trunk in her room, which was supposed to contain her money, was found broken open. It was the only thing in the room that was molested."

Taylor took charge of the "investigation" to discover the murderer, and Mrs. Silks, whose room in the Occidental Hotel adjoined that used by Taylor for his office, got an earful of incriminating scandal. She heard Soapy Smith, Bill Tanner, and John Bowers ("the latter two being well-known crooks") join Taylor to divide $3,800 taken from poor Ella. Apparently, Tanner and Bowers murdered her for the money at the instigation of Smith and Taylor. Then a shocked Mrs. Silks heard the men discuss their next victim: It was to be her! "After hearing this plot Mrs. Silks came to the conclusion that Skagway had become too hot to hold her and she accordingly took her departure on the next boat."[10]

Another passenger on the *Farallon* confirmed Mrs. Silks's views of the debased state of Skagway: "The condition of affairs in Skagway is a disgrace to civilized government. The United States officials make no pretense at enforcing the law. They are making money hand over fist, and any sort of crime can be committed as long as the officials of the United States get their share of the loot. The only law that is respected is the rifle or the revolver, and unless something is done pretty soon Skagway will be absolutely unsafe for any man to venture into who values his life."[11]

Tacoma Park Commissioner Lewis Levy, also arriving on the *Farallon*, wrote to a friend in government in Washington, D.C., and to the attorney general: "Some of the experiences I have had are beyond description. I have seen American citizens deliberately plundered before the marshal's eyes in dens kept for that purpose. . . . I had to pay the marshal $20 after he had recovered stolen property, before he would make a return to the court commissioner, as he threatened to turn it back to the thieves, unless I did so."[12]

Levy referred to Mrs. Silks's interview in the *Seattle Times* and advised "that it would be very dangerous for a government agent to go there, if his business was known." Smith's men had even dominated the coroner's jury in its consideration of Wilson's death; they found no foul play. Wrote Levy: "In justice to our beloved country I would implore your speedy investigation as there is an organized band of cutthroats in control."[13]

In contrast to these passionate warnings, the attorney general heard only good news from his representative in Sitka. U.S. Attorney Burton E. Bennett reported on June 17 and July 3 of the May term of court in Sitka in glowing terms without mention of Skagway's serious problems. Skagway, of course, was within Bennett's jurisdiction. "This term of court has been such as to make all respect the law and more fervently than ever believe in our free institutions." [14] One may suspect that the attorney general and his staff interpreted Bennett's patriotic sentiments as scarcely disguised braggery and wondered whether he had ever heard of Soapy Smith.

Meanwhile, the seething caldron of Skagway was about to boil over. A few days after the Fourth of July festivities that pleased Governor Brady, the Committee of 101 met to consider Smith's activities. The vigilantes, infuriated by the blatant robbery of a returning Klondiker, then met with Smith and demanded that he return the stolen gold. At this encounter on July 7, Smith agreed to return the loot if "no roar" was made in the papers. Then Smith did some drinking, consulted his cronies, and decided that no bunch of soft businessmen was going to threaten him. "There'll be trouble if you don't return the gold," cautioned a *Skagway News* reporter. "By God," shouted Smith, "trouble is what I am looking for." Thereupon he gathered his gang and marched them to the wharf, where the vigilantes were holding another meeting. There, Smith, armed with a Winchester, exchanged shots with Frank Reid, who had a .38-caliber revolver. Both fell with mortal wounds. [15]

"SOAPY SMITH IS DEAD!" proclaimed an edition of the *News* the morning after. "Shot through the heart, his cold body lies on a slab at People's undertaking parlors, and the confidence men and bunco steerers which have had their headquarters here for some time, have suddenly taken their departure, the tragic death of their leader having completely unnerved them." The vigilantes, led by Josiah M. Tanner, who was sworn in as a temporary U.S. deputy marshal by U.S. Commissioner Charles A. Sehlbrede after Deputy Taylor was restrained, began a roundup of the town's bad actors. "All last night the measured tread of the guards could be heard as they patrolled the streets. All the haunts where any of those supposed to be in any way connected with 'Soapy's gang' were liable to be found, were visited. But in most cases, the birds had taken warning and fled. However, quite a number were placed under arrest."

Escape routes from Skagway were blocked by vigilantes who

watched the wharf and small-boat moorages, combed the nearby town of Dyea, and sent a detachment to Lake Bennett, the jumping-off place to Canada's Yukon Territory. "The entire trail from Skagway to Bennett is closely watched. Business is practically suspended today. Hundreds of men, the majority of them armed with Winchesters," tracked Smith's men.

Turner Jackson was a fugitive who fled no farther than his hotel bed. At a rude hour he looked up at Marshal Tanner's six-shooter with affected astonishment. "What do you want? I was sleeping. Gimme back my blanket." Tanner ordered Jackson to dress, then marched him from the Astoria Hotel to Skagway's jail. Jackson did not recognize Tanner as the man he had threatened with a pistol in support of Smith's challenge of the vigilantes on the dock the day before. But Tanner recognized him, as he did George Wilder, another member of the dock party. The trial of these men in Sitka concluded the Soapy Smith saga.

Marshal James M. Shoup was the other federal official who shared responsibility for the law in Skagway. Whatever his state of ignorance or hesitancy before, he moved fast in learning of the great shootout four days after its occurrence. Shoup immediately wrote the attorney general: "About twenty lawless characters are in the hands of the committee, and it is supposed that a number will be lynched. U.S. Deputy Marshal S. S. Taylor is accused of being in collusion with the robbers and is also in custody. There being no other marshal there, I leave today for Skagway."[16]

Shoup got to the troubled town on the thirteenth. By that time the vigilantes had ordered thirty undesirables to clear out, and Josiah Tanner, appointed a temporary deputy marshal by Commissioner Charles A. Sehlbrede at Dyea, held fifteen others in jail; after closer investigation, four of these were released. Portraits were taken of those shipped south on the *Tartar,* according to the *Alaskan:* "They were taken twice and each time had to doff their hats and look pleasant."[17]

The vigilantes welcomed Shoup: "Everything was turned over to me as soon as I arrived and none of the citizens offered any resistance or obstruction." But Shoup smelled trouble as Frank Reid lingered near death: "An attempt would immediately follow his death to lynch some of the prisoners by overcoming the guards, [so] I chartered a boat and brought all the prisoners to Sitka."[18]

While Shoup had no convincing evidence that Taylor had been involved in the robbery of J. D. Stewart, the crime that led to the Smith-vigilante confrontation, or any other crime, his overall conduct raised suspicion: "I became convinced that he had not performed his duty as an officer." Shoup fired Taylor within hours after he arrived and held him for prosecution.

Governor Brady, who received the shootout news at the same time Marshal Shoup got it, wrote immediately to the secretary of the interior, describing the events and including the report that Taylor had offered to return six hundred dollars of Stewart's money if the vigilantes would let him go. Brady, like Shoup, predicted a lynching and hoped that the Skagway experience might foster a lasting improvement in law enforcement. Ask Congress to provide a small steamer for the marshal and empower him to appoint as many officers as necessary in an emergency, he urged. Brady's call for a steamer is one that echoed persistently throughout the territorial period—and was never heeded in Washington.

One of the bright spots of the Skagway mess concerns the role of the U.S. Army. When the shootout news reached Captain R. T. Yeatman, commander of the army detachment at Dyea, he offered help. Commissioner Sehlbrede refused firmly: "We have control of matters here. We do not need you. If we do, we will let you know."[19] Obviously Sehlbrede felt more comfortable about using the vigilantes than the army since the civilian force had indicated its willingness to act under the commissioner's and Tanner's direction. Americans did not mind seeing the army standing by, but they remained jealous of their civil institutions despite the faltering of the law enforcement system.

Several members of the Smith gang were subsequently prosecuted in Sitka. Turner Jackson and George Wilder were indicted for the murder of Reid but were not prosecuted. It made more sense to try them for an assault on Marshal Tanner during the dock affray than to try to convince a jury that they shared Smith's guilt. Defense lawyers tried unsuccessfully to suppress evidence of their clients' connection with Smith. Jackson got seven years and Wilder ten. Jackson appealed to the circuit court on various technical grounds, including the argument that his admission to Tanner that he pointed his gun "at someone" was made under "fear and duress."[20] The appeal court accepted the trial court's finding that the vigilantes behaved in a calm, orderly fashion and did not threaten Jackson with violence.

W. E. Foster, Van Triplet, and John Bowers were prosecuted for their robbery of Stewart and found guilty. Foster and Bowers also were convicted of assault on Stewart. The accused men insisted that Stewart lost his bag of gold to them on a daring wager that he regretted after losing—as poor sports will sometimes do—but the jury did not believe them.

The prosecutor longed to convict Deputy Marshal Taylor of something, since rumors raged of his complicity in all of Smith's larcenous activities. But rumors were not evidence, so he tried Taylor for neglect of duty in failing to arrest Foster, Triplet, and Bowers on warrants issued by the commissioner on July 8. Unfortunately, the robbers of Stewart had not yet been identified, so John Doe warrants were issued. While it is probable that Taylor knew the culprits, the John Doe warrants gave him an excuse for delaying. Taylor argued that he had been in hot pursuit of the robbers for only three and one-half hours before the vigilantes ordered him to stay home or risk lynching. Taylor took the warning seriously, remaining indoors until he was arrested by Shoup on July 14.[21]

Jurors listened to Taylor's excuse, his heartfelt references to his wife and four children, his sterling past service as constable, deputy sheriff, and U.S. deputy marshal in Idaho, and acquitted him. The prosecution's case was too weak. Everyone in the courtroom believed that Taylor's neglect of duty had made Smith's various scams possible, but for lack of evidence Taylor's role before July 8 was not even before the court.

A review of events shows that Soapy Smith was not responsible for all the crimes of 1898; the law enforcement system worked well enough at times. At Dyea on March 13, Sam Roberts, proprietor of the Wonder Hotel, a lively gambling place, was killed in a robbery attempt. After closing the joint at 2 A.M. he carried his money bag home under the protection of two employees, entered his log cabin, struck a match, and was shot by someone waiting for him. As the victim reeled outside, other shots were fired from inside the cabin.

Deputy Marshal John Cudihee arrived to find Roberts dead and witnesses who had identified the robbers in the moonlight. John Fitzpatrick, Henry Brooks, and William Corbett were arrested after Cudihee found bloody clothes in their cabin. Corbett was nursing a pistol wound in his shoulder.

At trial there was much argument about the light of the moon on the fatal night. Defense lawyer A. K. Delaney objected to the prosecutor's introduction of an almanac into evidence and his insistence that the moon rose in Dyea at the same time as in San Francisco. Fitzpatrick got life, the others ten years.[22] Thus the wheels of justice were grinding away just a few miles from Skagway during Soapy's reign. Dyea had a good deputy and no Smith gang.

Who was to blame for Skagway's woes? According to Governor Brady, "the marshal has not been sufficiently impressed that he and his deputies have police duties to perform as well as to be executive officers of the processes of the courts. I would suggest that the Attorney General be conferred with and that he lay down the law plainly to these officers." Brady was reporting to the secretary of the interior. "It is my opinion that if these bunco men had been taken in hand vigorously there never would have been any necessity for this outburst."[23] But Brady went beyond naming negligent officers, noting flaws in the system: "We are placed in the valley of humiliation when compared with the Canadians just over the border." What Americans lacked was a real police force, capable of making criminal investigations, organized like the Mounties, and having adequate means of land and water transport.

Ultimately the Skagway troubles must be traced to the American frontier system of law enforcement. Local government was expected to exercise its police power in organized towns. Gambling and saloons would receive the attention of town cops. The problem at Skagway was due to the lack of civil organization of the town and to the corruption and neglect of federal law enforcement officers, as noted by Governor Brady. We can hardly blame the federal government for not establishing a special territorial police force like the Mounties when there was no precedent for it. The system imposed upon Alaska was like that established in other western territories, where on several notorious occasions, citizens evoked mob rule with frightful consequences. Skagway's woes were a far cry from those experienced earlier in Virginia City and San Francisco.

After the passage of a couple of years during which the traffic to the Klondike via Skagway dwindled to manageable proportions and the town established its own government, residents viewed the 1898 events with detachment. Conditions had not been "as bad as others pictured them," argued the *Alaskan* in 1901. The newspaper's "Criminology of a Frontier Town" listed all the criminal cases filed in Skagway from December 1899 through December 1900. There were only 130 cases, mostly dealing with petty crimes. There were no murders. Without question, law and order had come to Skagway.

The *Alaskan*'s editor professed to be puzzled about all the excitement over Soapy Smith and the events of 1898. Skagway got a bad name that year "not from the fact that it was as disorderly as represented, but because the citizens of the town took it upon themselves to see law and order enforced." Soapy Smith attempted to prey on people, and when an actual case of swindling and robbery "was brought to the doors of this same Soapy Smith the citizens took immediate action." Smith offered to return the stolen gold dust if the affair were forgotten. Citizens rejected his proposal to compound a felony, and the shootout followed. "That is all there is to the old story. The yellow journals used it to show what a terribly disorderly place the frontier town was. Yet, with the exception of a couple of barroom shooting scrapes that ended fatally, this was the only shooting, to speak of, in this wild far northern border town." The yellow journals should have focused "on the desire of citizens to enforce law and order" instead of making "a dime novel hero of Soapy."

What really made the editor mad was a statement made by Governor Brady "as recently as last summer . . . that Skagway was a very tough town." Of course we know that "Brady knows nothing whatever of Skagway except its geographical position."[24]

6. Policing the Interior

Up and down the Yukon Valley the news spread like a great stage-whisper.
—Pierre Berton

IN 1896, on the eve of the gold rush, Alaska had one judge, one marshal, and ten deputy marshals. Additional law-enforcement help came from commissioners with justice-of-peace authority, who, like the twenty Indian police scattered in villages, were directed by the Department of the Interior.

The first center of mining activity in the interior in the early 1890s was the log cabin community of Forty Mile, which was actually in Canada. Several hundred miners worked claims along the Fortymile River, a tributary which flowed into the Yukon River on the Canadian side of the border with Alaska where the mining fields were located. Miners were not sure whether Forty Mile was in Canada or Alaska, but the North-West Mounted Police visited in 1895 because of complaints by storekeeper John J. Healy of the North American Transportation and Trading Company and by Anglican Bishop William Bompas. Healy, enraged by a decision against him at a miners' meeting, wanted the presence of established law officers. The miners' meeting, an informal tribunal organized to meet law-enforcement needs in the north as it had in earlier western mining camps, was much praised by pioneers, yet it was only a primitive means of keeping order.

Gold discoveries at Circle, 240 miles down the Yukon from Forty

Mile, in 1893 created the first community that took on the characteristics of a real town. By 1895 the population was five hundred and Circle was the largest community on the Yukon until Dawson City surpassed it in 1897. Clearly, Circle needed law officers, but Sitka's court officials did not respond until after the great Klondike strike in 1896. By 1897 it appeared that the Klondike held fabulous wealth and would draw thousands of stampeders to the interior of Yukon Territory and Alaska.

Miners' meetings kept order in Circle. Warning signs posted in saloons and at roadhouses along the trails promised whipping and banishment for all thieves convicted at meetings. Such crude methods helped keep the lid on restless men, but more civilized institutions were demanded for Circle and other parts of the interior likely to boom.

Congress reacted in 1897–98 to create the district of North Alaska under the secretary of war, and army troops were sent to St. Michael and Skagway, while a revenue ship was ordered to patrol the Yukon River. The army also sent Captain Patrick H. Ray and Lieutenant Wilds P. Richardson to investigate conditions on the Yukon in 1897 and to recommend sites for military posts. In 1899, Fort Egbert was established at Eagle, followed two years later by Fort Gibbon at Tanana.

U.S. Marshal James Shoup sent recently appointed Deputy J. J. Rutledge to Circle in 1897. Rutledge apparently took the Chilkoot Trail out of Dyea to the upper Yukon but did not reach Circle because the golden exuberance of Dawson unsettled his resolve. Months passed before Shoup became aware that his sole lawman in the interior was grubbing for gold in the Klondike rather than attending to miscreants from his duty station. Rutledge revealed an opportunist's gall when he finally communicated with Shoup. He wrote to his wife in Blaine, Washington, on September 28, 1897, enclosing a letter she was to send back to Sitka for the marshal. Shoup got the letter three months after it had been written to learn that Rutledge was having a hard time leaving Dawson. It seemed that he had heard there were no provisions at Circle and no steamboat transport heading that way. He had been advised not to risk a voyage by small boat because the freeze-up might catch him; besides, boat owners were charging three hundred to five hundred dollars per passenger. But the errant deputy modestly confessed that he had other options: "I have the promise of a share in the provisions of a mining camp here and which is run by friends if it is not possible to do better; but that is encouraging as compared with the luck of many others." All the marshal had to do to further his deputy's Canadian mining venture during the winter was "to see that my wife is in receipt of my small salary whilst I am endeavoring to arrive at my destination through such trying circumstances and I have not the slightest doubt but that the Department will take the same view of the situation on presentation of the facts by you." Still hopeful of getting someone to Circle, Shoup probably was too angry to be amused at Rutledge's presumption. He advised the attorney general that his deputy "has not made a true statement of his case . . . several thousand men have gone from Dawson to Circle City since his arrival at Dawson" and dismissed Rutledge.[1]

Marshal Shoup appointed Frank Canton deputy for Circle in February 1898 at a salary of $750 a year. Arrangements had been made for Canton's hiring in 1897, but the official appointment could not be made until Rutledge's whereabouts were learned and his removal made. Canton, a tall, lean, handsome, and menacing-looking man, differed from the usual run of deputy appointees in a number of ways. By 1897 he had achieved some eminence as a peace officer in Wyoming and Oklahoma Territory, plus a certain infamy as a Texas criminal under his real name, Joe Horner. In 1897 his name was not well known nationally, but years of service against criminals, particularly livestock rustlers, remained ahead of him, and his exploits were to give him a lofty ranking among western lawmen. His many detractors, however, have remembered him as a cold killer for hire.

Canton's appointment, which exposed some confusion and negligence among Justice Department officials in Washington, was achieved through the influence of Portus B. Weare. He and John J. Healy's North American Transportation and Trading Company had challenged the Alaska Commercial Company's monopoly of the Yukon River trade in 1892. In 1894, Weare felt that the trading company and the needs of law enforcement could be served admirably if the government appointed a vigorous U.S. marshal, one likely to care about interior conditions. Weare's candidate was Can-

Frank Canton, first United States deputy marshal on the Yukon. American Heritage Center, University of Wyoming

ton, formerly the sheriff of Johnson County, Wyoming, a longtime inspector for cattlemen's associations, who was working temporarily and unhappily at a Weare stockyard.

Writing to U.S. Senator George Shoup of Idaho, Weare called attention to whiskey and opium smuggling in Alaska and suggested that Canton replace Marshal Orville Porter at Sitka. Weare pointed out that Canton was known to the secretary of agriculture "and many others of our best western men." But the Sitka appointment went to Louis Williams in 1894 and to Senator Shoup's brother, James Shoup, in 1897. Since Alaska had only one judicial district until 1900, there was only one marshal, but Weare and others did succeed in calling attention to the interior situation by 1897. Canton, who also had been a candidate for U.S. customs inspector for Alaska in 1894, had since moved to Oklahoma Territory as a federal deputy marshal, and had come to some grief, thus was willing to lower his sights in 1897. Weare's interests were served by getting a law officer to the interior and, after a long delay, a place was made for Canton at Circle.[2]

The deputy marshal's job was not a plum—in terms of salary and fees—but Canton wanted to avoid a scandal in Oklahoma and had caught the Klondike gold fever then sweeping the country. Besides, Weare agreed to pay him an additional salary for looking after NAT&T interests.

Canton voyaged from Seattle to St. Michael on the steamer *Cleveland,* arriving on September 10, rather late in the season for reaching Circle. Reports of food shortages on the upper Yukon alarmed the *Cleveland* passengers, so sixty of them, including Canton, banded together to purchase the little riverboat *St. Michael* and forty-five tons of provisions, although Canton took passage on the steamboat *P. B. Weare* in company with Lieutenant Wilds Richardson, whom Canton knew from Wyoming, and Captain Patrick Ray. The army officers were starting their reconnaissance of Yukon conditions and were able to reach Fort Yukon before navigation closed on the river. Canton and his fellow stockholders in the *St. Michael* stopped at the mouth of Big Minook Creek.

Canton and two friends, Frank Kress and someone else he identified as Bill Painter, built a log cabin and joined a meeting with other stampeders to christen the little community Rampart. The new deputy marshal of Circle decided he could not reach his distant post until the spring breakup, although the expensive, hazardous option of going overland was another possible course of action. As he was not yet officially appointed, he was free to stay at Rampart.

Rampart was then the liveliest spot along the American Yukon because of gold discoveries on Minook Creek. Canton and others started for the diggings as soon as they were settled, trudging with packs in cold rain that soon turned into the season's first heavy snowfall. The party's inexperience and inadequate dress led to disaster. One young man named Tucker got lost and died of exposure. The others staggered back to Rampart wiser in the needs of interior Alaskan travel.

Novelist Rex Beach was one of those who wintered at Rampart: "We were some fifteen hundred souls and twelve saloon keepers, all dumped out on the bank of the Yukon to shift for ourselves in a region unmapped and unexplored," he wrote.[3] Beach spent two years at Rampart before moving on to Nome. Later he wrote novels and stories set in both towns and at the time approached Jack London in renown as literary chronicler of the gold-rush era. But in Rampart with Canton and other friends, he was only known as a big, college-educated fellow with tremendous strength and a lively sense of humor.

In November, Canton reviewed his expectations in a letter to his wife: "I came to this country to make some money and I intend to do it if there is any earthly show." After four months Canton had his doubts: "I frankly admit that if I had known the conditions here and the hardships that one has to endure, I would not have come, but I am here and I am going to stay until I do something or demonstrate thoroughly that there is nothing in it." Boosting Alaska's projects was not Canton's inclination: "If I had a friend who wanted to come, I would say decidedly, DO NOT COME, for mining purposes at any rate."[4]

While Canton settled down at Rampart, army officers Ray and Richardson had a busier time. Ray, reporting from Fort Yukon in September 1897, was aware that the army represented the government's only authority in the interior. He did not mention either Rutledge or Canton specifically in his report, but he assumed that the interior would not have a serving deputy for some time and doubted that any appointees would keep order effectively: "I do not believe it would be possible to obtain civil officers who will remain in one place long enough to be of any service, and the performance of their duties will be secondary to their interest in mines." The U.S. commissioner appointed to serve with Canton at Circle "has stopped at Dawson and in all probability will never qualify," and "Mr. Ross, the collector at the same place, has spent a large portion of his time in the Klondike."[5]

It is not strange that Ray distrusted civilian officials or that civilian officers questioned military authority. Army officers can feel the bite of ambition, and this drive might have influenced Ray's recommendation that northern Alaska "be given a provisional form of government of a semi-military character."[6]

Ray, in the deputy's absence, found lively work at Circle in early October. Miners had held up the steamer *Bella* the day he arrived and landed part of the Dawson-bound cargo. They did not intend to starve during the winter and told Ray "there is no law or any person in authority to whom we can appeal."[7] Ray urged the men to take only what they required because Dawson's needs were urgent too; they complied and paid for the stores landed.

Still another Circle incident involved the *Weare*, sent down from Dawson to Fort Yukon to carry supplies stored there back to Dawson. When the *Weare*'s captain, fearing the running ice, wanted to remain at Circle, some fifty Dawson men aboard demanded that he push on to Fort Yukon, threatening to seize the boat and its stores if he did not. Ray called Circle men to his assistance and prepared to defend the *Weare*. The captain, no soberer than the Dawson men, agreed to get moving, but overnight the ice froze solidly around the boat. Both incidents of near violence and interference with the NAT&T affairs were contingencies that P. B. Weare might have anticipated in hiring Canton and lobbying for his deputy's appointment, but his designated troubleshooter was still waiting for his appointment.

To forestall further trouble with the Dawson men, Ray induced the trading company to supply four small boats so that the men could drift through the broken ice to Fort Yukon to get stores for the winter. Sixty men started downriver; Ray, fearing violence at Fort Yukon, followed. Eventually all the destitute miners got

The Dawson waterfront in 1899. University of Alaska Archives, Bassoc Collection

to Fort Yukon with Ray's help. Lieutenant Richardson, who had remained at Fort Yukon on the *Weare's* upriver voyage, pressured the trader there to provide food to the refugees on their arrival, thereby preventing disorder.

Captain Ray did not tolerate cheating by the destitute miners he provided for at Fort Yukon. One of the charity cases, O. E. Weymouth, received enough provisions for the winter after swearing to his poverty, then contracted with a freighter to haul them to Circle at a charge of twelve cents per pound. At Ray's insistence, Commissioner J. E. Crane jailed Weymouth for obtaining goods under false pretenses. Circle's miners met, decided that Weymouth was getting a raw deal, and broke open the jail to free him. Weymouth brought the disputed provisions over to the saloon where the meeting had been held, auctioned them to his saviors, then left for Dawson, where he claimed to have another outfit. Crane wanted Ray to come up to Circle to restore order, but there was little that could be done. Ray reported to Washington on "the peculiar trend of the public mind in the matter of justice as administered by a miners' meeting in this country" and the rising tide of lawlessness. "If the commercial interests of the citizens of the United States are to be protected in the coming summer," he wrote, "they can not well be left to the tender mercy of such meetings, composed of men who are not citizens of the Territory, have no fixed place of abode, are here for what they can make, too often regardless of methods, and are in a large majority." But the good news was that people along the river were hearing about the small force of soldiers established at St. Michael, and the "better element who have interests at stake . . . express satisfaction that at last the Government is taking action." Ray gave Crane credit for doing his best at Circle. He met with "a few of the respectable citizens" to organize a force to preserve law and order, but the vigilante group did not materialize. One man insisted that Crane jail another who had threatened to shoot him on sight. Since the frightened man and his friends had helped free Weymouth, Crane demanded their help in guarding the jail, but the citizens could not reach any sort of agreement.[8]

Meanwhile, Canton, Rex Beach, and Bill Painter, restless as the winter advanced, responded to rumors of gold strikes on tributaries of the Tanana River. The men considered themselves seasoned travelers by this time and mushed some one hundred miles south of Rampart to stake on Troublesome River, then returned safely to the amenities of Rampart.

It was April before anyone reminded Canton that he was a deputy marshal, although he may not yet have received the February letter of appointment. His visitor was the captain of a steamboat, the *Walrus* (or *Seattle No. 1*), wintering some one hundred miles below Rampart near the mouth of the Koyukuk. Among the *Walrus*'s 150 passengers, some tough types dominated the camp and intended to appropriate the captain's small steam launch when navigation opened. Rumors of disorderly activity at the Koyukuk camp had reached Canton earlier from other sources, so, as he was bored at Rampart, he agreed to go. His adventures, if truly reported, were interesting.

After a two-day hike the deputy reached the camp, confronted the three villains who had usurped the captain's authority, disarmed them at revolver point, and called a general meeting of all the stranded travelers to explain his presence. The people were delighted to cooperate against the outlaws, who had been stealing left and right while menacing any protesters. Canton swore in twenty special deputies, organized a trial, and, as self-appointed judge, fined the three thieves a total of two thousand dollars.

As the camp settled down, Canton kept a wary eye on Tom Barkley, the outlaw ringleader. Canton believed him to be a fugitive from Idaho, wanted for a Coeur d'Alene mine dynamiting that had killed three workers. Since Idaho had posted a $2,500 reward for Barkley's return, Canton intended to arrest him as soon as navigation opened. Even Barkley's nearly successful assassination of him did not shake his resolve to earn the reward. Someone put a bullet within inches of Canton's head one night; Canton followed the shooter's tracks to Barkley's cabin and resisted his first impulse to kill Barkley on sight because he wanted the reward. After this, Canton had his deputies watch Barkley day and night and thus learned of the outlaw's amorous adventures. Barkley and the young wife of the steamboat's clerk were meeting secretly for lovers' games. Soon nature and Canton influenced the destiny of the loving pair.

The excitement started with the sudden movement of the Yukon ice, "miles of it, slowly at first, but in less than twenty minutes the noise of acres of thick ice, bursting and jamming, sounded like the explosion of thousands of tons of dynamite. Large pieces of ice the size of an acre of land and ten feet thick would shoot out of the water onto the land and uproot big trees."[9] Floodwaters tossing massive ice chunks surged into the log huts housing the *Walrus* passengers, and terrified people climbed trees or clambered to rooftops. One couple, the clerk and his erring spouse, were isolated atop their cabin by swirling waters. Stampeding ice threatened to demolish their cabin and dash them into the raging river.

Barkley and another man launched a lifeboat, desperately fighting the current and raging ice blocks and effecting the couple's rescue at enormous risk to their own lives. It was "the most splendid exhibition of nerve that I ever witnessed," said Canton, who alone knew Barkley's inspiration.[10]

Canton, a legend for his daring capture of the notorious outlaw Teton Jackson, as well as other exploits, was influenced by Barkley's courage. He acknowledged it when he apprehended Barkley and his lover as they were preparing a furtive lifeboat voyage downriver to St. Michael. The deputy disarmed Barkley and made an offer: Barkley could either paddle off alone, "be shot like a wolf," or go to Circle in chains. Canton was willing to forgo the reward because of the heroic rescue "and give him one more chance to make good."[11]

Naturally the outlaw chose freedom and life and left the camp. The next day the *Walrus* moved upriver, carrying Canton back to Rampart. His generosity to Barkley, an uncharacteristic gesture of sentimentality, was also pragmatic. He was still a long way from Circle, where there was no jail capable of holding a desperate man, and much further from Idaho, where the reward might have been withdrawn. Getting rid of Barkley made sense.

At Rampart, Canton sold his cabin to Rex Beach. The cabin later housed another well-known character when Tex Rickard, he of boxing fame, introduced Wyatt Earp to Beach. Earp and his wife, new arrivals at Rampart in summer 1898, rented the cabin and wintered there before moving on to Nome. Canton moved upriver to Circle but before settling there voyaged up to Dawson to guard a shipment of gold for the NAT&T all the way down the Yukon to St. Michael. Back at Circle again, he signed his official commission and assumed office.

Circle's community of miners had been reduced by the Klondike stampede, so there were not many demands on the deputy's skills.

He had help too in the presence of U.S. troops. Soldiers commanded by the new Captain Wilds Richardson had arrived to barrack in some of Circle's abandoned houses.

Canton's letters to Marshal Shoup at Sitka during 1898–99 document Yukon lawkeeping and administrative concerns. In reporting on the last two quarters of 1898, the deputy earned only $22.50 in fees for himself. Expenses charged against the government were far higher than the limits set by the attorney general. No one in Circle would contract to feed prisoners for $3 daily, and jail guards would not work at the government rate. Canton requested funds for building a suitable jail and reimbursement for his own outlays on jailkeeping: "It has been a hardship on me to discharge the duties of the office as I have had no funds at my command and have been compelled to borrow money to meet expenses."[12]

Serving subpoenas and other U.S. commissioner court business kept the deputy reasonably busy, and there were some serious crimes, particularly a store robbery and shooting. Canton arrested one of the holdup men and turned him over to the army for safekeeping. He did not relish the thought trying to hold a desperate criminal in an inadequate jail until June, when transport to Sitka for trial could be arranged.

Another serious crime involved the robbery of the U.S. custom house at Fort Yukon. Canton got twenty arrest warrants from the commissioner and prepared for the eighty-mile trip in January 1899: "This will be a hard trip for me and an expensive one as I shall have to employ an Indian guide with dog teams, and also guards."[13]

The military's role in Alaska law enforcement confused Canton. Richardson told him that the army had authority to arrest lawbreakers, as it did by virtue of Congress' creation of a military district for northern Alaska. "In my past experience for sixteen years as Deputy U.S. Marshal I have never known the military to be vested with that power when there was no reservation or where martial law had not been declared. I hold that the civil law is supreme in time of peace until the marshal calls upon the military for assistance," Canton said. Richardson and Canton had debated this delicate matter in friendly fashion, but the deputy wanted clarification from his superior. He also wanted Shoup to understand that "the civil authority is fully capable to cope with the criminal element in this country and to enforce the civil law."[14]

Canton's confidence was commendable and understandable. He was a Texan steeped in the tradition of the efficient, deadly Texas Rangers, men whose tradition held that one officer was equal to any disturbance (although this was the legend rather than the practice). Canton had never been a Ranger, although he claimed service in later years, but he respected the Rangers' reputation, perhaps because they had arrested him a few times.[15]

By March 1899, Canton's report to Shoup revealed his disgust with conditions on the Yukon. The first regular mail received that winter reached Circle on March 22 but did not include money for running the marshal's office. "Now I want to say this to you," wrote the angry deputy. "I wrote and mailed my accounts to you from here about January 2nd and never had any returns. I need some money very bad and wish you would send in some funds at once."[16] Canton had eight prisoners to take or send to Sitka when navigation opened and had been paying for their food and guarding all winter.

It did Canton's mood no good to report the failure to capture a Captain Danahan (or Deneham) wanted in Juneau on grand-larceny charges. The warrant arrived by private messenger while he was ill. He sent two men upriver thirty-five miles where the fugitive was wintering, but to no avail. A Dawson prostitute known by the alluring name of Bene Joy warned Danahan before the officers arrived. They chased him four days by dog team, but he crossed the Canadian line.

Not only did Canton receive no funds from Shoup, he was dismissed from office. The reason was the trouble he and other deputies in the Oklahoma Territory marshal's office had encountered in 1897 when their fraudulent expense claims were exposed. Canton had resigned his Oklahoma position before the Justice Department could conclude its investigation and fire him, as it did him and his colleagues eventually. The department was sufficiently annoyed to have all the deputies indicted in March 1898, but only later did it become aware of Canton's appointment in Alaska. Marshal Shoup's stern message of dismissal, written in February 1899, reached Canton in May.

"It surprises me that after so long a time the Attorney General should take action in a case of this kind especially after I had been assigned to this isolated country and after having been thoroughly advised that there would be no trouble," Canton wrote. He never did say who advised him, nor did he ever admit that his padded expenses were a serious matter, but even though the indictments were dropped the department refused to exonerate him. Six years later he was appointed deputy in Oklahoma Territory and again dismissed when the 1897 troubles caught Washington's attention. [17]

While Canton's service in Alaska did not enhance his reputation as a gunfighter, he holds a place in history as the first officially appointed law officer in the interior who actually served, and he performed his duties effectively while he lasted. The dismissal left him in bad shape. He was broke and the government was reluctant to reimburse him for his considerable out-of-pocket expenses until a leisurely review of his accounts could be concluded. He had to borrow money to get to Seattle, where he hired on as a packer, probably in desperation, with the U.S. Army's expeditionary force to China.

In writing about Alaska in his memoir *Frontier Trails,* a life story professing to be "the plain, uncolored truth," Canton was most discreet. What happened, he recalled, was an unfortunate occurrence of snow blindness on a journey from Circle to Fort Yukon to arrest three men. He got his men but had to spend two weeks in darkness once safely back in Circle. "The United States Surgeon of the Medical Department advised me to leave Alaska as soon as possible, and go out to the States where I could get treatment for my eyes." [18]

Canton thought he was in line for any new marshal's position that would be created but for the emergence of the Oklahoma scandal. The new marshals were assigned to Nome and the interior in 1900. Had he become the marshal of Nome, events there might have taken a different course by his opposing the audacious plot to take over rich gold mines under color of judicial office. Despite his fiddling with expense accounts, Canton's career was not tainted with any major corruption of office. As a young man he killed another in a brawl, robbed a bank, held up a stage, and served time in the Texas prison before escaping, but he did serve honestly as a law enforcement officer before and after winning a pardon from the governor of Texas in 1894, although some believed he ambushed suspected rustlers in Wyoming.

In later years he read Rex Beach's Alaska novels *The Spoilers* (1906) and *The Barrier* (1908) and identified himself as the hero of *The Spoilers,* a strong young man who was honest and tough enough to upset the machinations of Alexander McKenzie and his crew of rascals. Canton also believed that Owen Wister modeled the hero of *The Virginian* after him, but neither Wister nor Beach supported Canton's quietly held opinion.

7. No Place Like Nome

Alaskans were of the kind who had left Washington and other western states and changed their names and gone to Alaska to hide their past— President William Howard Taft.

OF all the lands to be associated with the glitter of gold and the colorful squandering of it in the heat of excitement, the Seward Peninsula was one of the most unlikely. Yet it was there on the barren shores of the Bering Sea, some fifty miles across from Siberia, that "Alaska's Klondike" was born. The discovery of gold on the treeless tundra of the Seward Peninsula occurred in 1898 and resulted in two stampedes, one in 1899 by those who were already in the north and the other in 1900 by expectant outsiders who dreamed of riches. Comparing the Nome gold fields with the Klondike made sense in terms of the quantity of gold mined and the masses of stampeders. No other earlier discovery in Alaska had been so spectacular, and the only other comparable field found later was that in the Tanana Valley, which led to the founding of Fairbanks.

Transportation during the winter posed a problem for miners in the Klondike and Alaska's Yukon interior, but Nome was even more difficult to reach. The Bering Sea was open to navigation only from June to October, and during that season Nome could be reached directly by steamer from Seattle or another Pacific Coast port with ease, but during the other eight months the way was long. Travelers during the winter had to reach the Yukon from Skagway via the White Pass rail route, then follow the Yukon Trail almost all the way down to the river's mouth before cutting across to the Seward Peninsula. But of course such hardships as winter travel entailed made little difference to the seekers of gold. Men will go anywhere under any conditions when lured by precious metal.

The winter of 1898–99 had stopped the flow of rivers and its snowy mantle lay over the land when rumors of discoveries by a couple of different parties of prospectors reached the Yukon. The stampede drew men from Rampart, Forty Mile, Circle, Dawson, and elsewhere. They came by dog sled, by bicycle, and on foot. By late summer the new town held three thousand people. It was expected that as many as twenty thousand more would come in the summer of 1900.

The stampeders of 1899 sowed deeply the seeds of future discord even as they followed the familiar frontier process of throwing up dwellings and business places, mostly tents, because wood was scarce. A military garrison from St. Michael was dispatched in time to prevent serious disorders, but, as always, the army was limited in what it could do to solve civilian problems.

Charles Johnson, Alaska's only judge in 1899, managed to visit the boom town in August and advised people to organize a local government, but otherwise the Sitka law officers left Nome to its own resources. Folks would just have to get along until summer 1900. By that time the federal government undoubtably would establish a court.

On September 12 the Nome voters, some fourteen hundred in all, elected a mayor, a city council, a chief of police, and other officials. Key Pittman, a twenty-seven-year-old lawyer who had stampeded from Dawson, was appointed city attorney. Pittman, one of many members of the Nome bar to gain fame, later became a powerful U.S. senator from Nevada. Tex Rickard, later to be a boxing promoter, was a city councilman.

Many men who came to Nome were destitute, suffered from scurvy and were bitterly disappointed about their failure to find gold at the other locations they had worked. Some were riffraff, disgusted with the strictness of Canadian law. Their bitterness was magnified when they arrived at Nome and found that the entire region had been staked. By December 1899 approximately forty-five hundred mining claims had been recorded. Enterprising prospectors there before them had spent their first season staking claims in preference to working them. Optimists believed that gold was to be found in every stream, and they staked from beach to skyline in their own names, for their friends and relatives, as agents, or with powers of attorneys for others. The law required that a mineral discovery be made before a claim was staked and filed, but nobody had time to verify the presence of wealth. Claim jumping and relocating resulted from this wild scrambling, and there would have been enough disputes to keep the court docket filled endlessly if there had been a court.

As bleak as the town and its environs appeared, it was obvious that prospects of moneymaking were very high indeed, and public-spirited citizens with a respect for private property demanded that law and order be maintained. The chamber of commerce was the first organized body in the town, and its president issued a decree against violence: "We will hang the first man who unnecessarily spills human blood if we have to go to Council City to get the tree to hang him on."[1] Since Council City was a far distance to go for a hanging tree, the merchants wished to show potential killers their determination.

Actually, disease posed a bigger threat than crime, since there was no sanitation system and the area was full of refuse and offal. Eventually this was carried out onto the Bering Sea ice before the thaw, but not before typhoid and other diseases took lives and raised alarm.

The throngs of miners who reached Nome in the summer of 1899 came in time for the second stage of the drama: the discovery of gold on the sandy beaches of Nome. Never had mining been easier. No slow burning of a shaft through permafrost many feet to bedrock was necessary on the beach. A crude rocker set up on the beach was enough equipment for the job. The rich sand was shoved in and shaken down until the gold particles were trapped in the rocker. In the first season after the discovery of beach gold, more than $2 million worth of gold was recovered by this simple process. During the same time span, the creeks of the Nome district produced $1 million worth, although it was hard to keep miners working the creek placers as long as beach possibilities remained available. Overall production exceeded $4 million a year later, and that figure was maintained for each of the next six years.

There were no claims on the beaches of Nome. Prospectors simply worked at a hole between high and low water marks as long as they could. The tide smoothed off all the diggings every time it came in. Then, once it had receded, the thick swarms of men would return to set up their rockers once more at one spot or another.

The noted geologist Alfred H. Brooks journeyed to the town in the fall of 1899 and noticed that all the larger buildings in Nome were saloons or dance halls. Law and order was difficult to maintain because of the number of gamblers and con men who flocked to the camp. One means of keeping order was extremely effective if illegal. Spotting in the camp a dozen men who were well-known criminals, the city fathers asked the U.S. Revenue Cutter Service to take them outside on the last sailing before winter closed the navigation season. Captain David H. Jarvis of the *Bear* accommodated, and the hoods were rounded up and taken aboard the *Bear* to Seattle, where they were set free. None of the unwilling passengers sued the government for what could only be considered false arrest and false imprisonment.

The eviction of known rogues and the exodus of many who were prosperous enough to buy a boat ticket eased both the health and law enforcement situations in the winter of 1899–1900. Many of those who preferred to winter outside planned to return when Bering Sea navigation opened. But the claim jumping went on, and some of it was done under color of legal authority. Rich ground on Anvil Creek was a particular source of contention because the original claimants were the three "lucky Swedes." Erik Lindblom and John Byrneson were Swedes, but Jafet Lindeberg was a Norwegian Laplander. The Americans who had not been as lucky considered it a hard thing that foreigners should profit from their nation's natural wealth. One of these patriotic grumblers had a great idea: Why not dispossess the Swedes through the orderly proceeding of a miners' meeting? At a proper meeting the assembled body could declare that aliens could not hold claims and that would fix the vexing matter. If the schemers knew that the Oregon Code, which had been promulgated for Alaska, explicitly stated that aliens had

Nome courthouse. University of Alaska Archives

full rights to mining claims, they did not care. Once their resolution carried, a signal fire would be lighted and a waiting mob would forcibly eject the Swedes from their claims. Unfortunately for the enterprising Yanks, their meeting was disrupted by Lieutenant Oliver Spaulding and a few soldiers from recently established Fort Davis near Nome. Spaulding ordered the miners to withdraw their resolution. When they refused, the soldiers cleared the saloon where the meeting was held at bayonet point. Spaulding's decisive action may have prevented bloodshed, but it did not end the controversy over alien ownership.

In November, Chief of Police W. M. Eddy received a little help from the Mounties at Dawson, who had compiled a list of undesirable characters, including "the worst criminals ever known on this continent." The Mounties intended the list as a warning to U.S. Army personnel stationed on the Yukon who might have cared to intercept the rogues, who were supposed to be on the way to Nome. Included were:

H. M. Carr—Curly Carr, Prize fighter, has just done a term of six months in Dawson for vagrancy.

Sammy Deering—has several short sentences for theft in the U.S.

Fred Walsh—alias Big Fred; clever confidence man and general crook, and ex-member of "Soapy Smith's" gang.

Doc West—all round crook and clever pickpocket.

Sam Berry—gambler and all round crook.

Steve McNichols—general crook, has a bad record in Butte, Montana.

Paul and W. H. Stackhouse—or Reardon Brothers, ex-members of O'Leary gang of Skagway.

Barstow Page—all round crook, was sent out of Dawson.

Nick Burkhardt—New York thief and confidence man; has been ordered out of a great many cities of the U.S.

Front Street in Nome in 1900. University of Alaska Archives, Bunnell
Collection

C. B. Heath—alias Hobo Kid; general crook, clever poker player, will most likely be found living with a dance hall girl.

Sam Bell—was connected with Jim Marshall's gang of train robbers in California.

Ed Ramsey—all round crook.

James Pounce—sneak thief, has just completed a term in Dawson for theft.

Tom Fisk—all round crook, ex-member of "Soapy Smith's" gang.

Bill Doherty—general tough, killed a man in Boise, Idaho, and two men in Butte, Montana.

Paddy MacDonald—all round crook.

Tom Triggs—general tough, has been in several shooting scrapes in the U.S.; used to travel with Doherty.

Hank Freize—gambler; runs a sure thing game.

Ed McDonald and Ed Ross—sneak thieves.

Frank Bulive—gambler and all round crook.

Ed Reid—clever pickpocket.[2]

Whether the list helped is not known, but the first name on it appeared in the papers when a twenty-round fight between Curly Carr and Ed Kelly, middleweights, was scheduled at the Dexter Saloon. Wyatt Earp owned the Dexter, but the man from Tombstone and other scenes of violent exploits was a quiet businessman in Nome. Aside from a fifty-dollar fine for interfering with a police officer and a minor assault involving a patron, he did not figure on the police blotter. Other luminaries-to-be involved themselves in prize fighting, including Wilson Mizner, sharper, bon vivant, and Hollywood screen writer; Jack Kearns, later Jack Dempsey's manager; and Nome saloonkeeper Tex Rickard.

The close of navigation encouraged a lot of pilfering, particularly of food, coal, and driftwood, but most of Chief Eddy's arrests were for drunkenness. Other disturbances included fighting—lots of it— and robberies. There was some fraud, as when mail carrier Joe Carroll collected money to deliver letters on the first stage to the outside but mushed out of town without them. The mayor and police chief caused a little scandal when it was reported that they had been seen "breaking a window and tumbling a female in the snow on the street."[3] Three tolerant members of the city council outvoted two others on the issue of whether the officers should resign.

Considering the possibilities, Nome's first year passed serenely, but the scene became frenzied when the first ships of the 1900 season landed their eager passengers. Ships continued to come in all summer as every vessel on the coast capable of making the long voyage was pressed into service. At one point, seventy ships stood off the town; landing was a slow process for lack of deep water near shore and docks.

Honest men and women jostled with gamblers, con men, whores, pimps, thieves, and trigger-happy gunmen on the crooked streets of Nome. Shootouts, muggings, and saloon brawls were endemic in what was in 1900–1901 as turbulent a community as ever existed in the Old West. Geologist Alfred H. Brooks, a veteran of all the other northern mining camps, making his second visit, armed himself for the first time in Nome. Town government broke down as one scandal followed another among the officials. Nome was not a pretty place, or a safe place, but it was surely one of the most exciting places in the world, and men swarmed all over the region, looking for ground to claim or good sites to buy from the original stakers. The beach front was especially lively because the first ships had hauled in all kinds of mechanical monsters, machines of diverse design, engineered to dredge gold from the richly saturated underwater sands supposed to lie off Nome.

C. S. Frost, special agent of the Department of Justice, reported to Attorney General John W. Griggs in August 1900:

> To this place has flocked thousands of people attracted by the riches of the gold diggings, and thousands more have followed them to engage in every sort of business and scheme that would be liable to run into their pockets some of the proceeds of the miners' labor. With them have come some of the sharpest criminals, the most dangerous cutthroats and bad men that civilization has produced, and it is a conservative thing to say that Nome has within its limits the worst aggregation of criminals and unprincipled men and women that were ever drawn together in this country. The saloons and gambling houses and the narrow streets and dark alley ways along the beach offer every opportunity to this class of criminals successfully [to] engage in their practices.
>
> Compared with Nome, today Butte, Montana, which is famous as the wickedest city in the United States, is a righteous and law-abiding community.[4]

Frost himself was one of the crooks, but his involvement takes nothing away from the truth of his assessment, which was corroborated by many others in Nome.

Yet the reality of Nome's conditions belied its potential for violence. Records show only six murders between September 1899 and October 1900, and street gunfighting was an even rarer occurrence. Robberies, burglaries, assaults, and petty thefts were numerous, and newspaper editors called for more policing. The *Nome Chronicle* insisted that the town had more felonies than a city of half a million population and urged that the military take over. "While all the officials talk the burglar and footpad ply their vocations and honest pedestrians mush home with their hands on large sized guns they carry in outside pockets. . . . Nothing is done to discourage crime."[5] The military did not take over, but it did calm things somewhat in 1900, as it did in 1899, by putting a six-man patrol on the streets after dark.

The *Nome News* cried out against the prevalance of crime even after the exodus on the last ships of the season had reduced the population of some twenty thousand to the level of four to six thousand. Days were darker, so thieves dared to work around the clock. "We are at the mercy of a gang of thieves. A reign of terror exists. None dare testify against the crooks for fear of vengeance. If correction does not come lynching will, and that will hurt our reputation."[6] But *News* editor J. F. A. Strong did not recommend vigilante action, arguing that vigilance committees had not been successful in Alaska. He did not clarify his assertion, but he had been active with the vigilantes of Skagway, who took on Soapy Smith, so he did have personal knowledge.

There was good reason for disorder in Nome during its first year as people struggled to form an effective local government and had to do without a district court and federal marshal. But despite the masses of new arrivals, things should have been better with the arrival of the federal court party in the summer of 1900. One reason for the continued turbulence is easy to see: The court was corrupt and little concerned with the orderly administration of justice. Officers had their own interests to consider, and these included the most audacious swindles ever to disgrace the honor of the American judiciary.

8. The New Court

As long as I am President of the United States, Wickersham shall be judge in Alaska. —Teddy Roosevelt

WITH his usual quick thinking, James Wickersham used a parliamentary maneuver at a Republican party caucus in Tacoma, Washington, to win a United States Senate seat for his friend Addison G. Foster. Foster owed Wickersham and recommended him for presidential appointment as consul general to Japan or as district judge in Alaska. To his disappointment, Wickersham got the Alaska job—and not the better of the two judgeships created in 1900, either. He got the third division at Eagle; Arthur H. Noyes, who had more powerful backers, got the second division at Nome. Yet, as it turned out, Wickersham and Alaska seemed made for each other. He served for years as judge and congressional delegate and further identified himself with the territory as historian, bibliographer, and dauntless enthusiast. Wickersham was not the object of universal love in Alaska or in Washington, but those who opposed him always knew what to expect: an all-out eye-gouging struggle waged above, and sometimes a bit below, the board.

Wickersham chose Albert R. Heilig, a Tacoma lawyer who had served in the Washington state legislature with him, as court clerk, and another friend as court stenographer. The Justice Department ordered him to meet the second-division court party in Seattle so that the new judges could fix the boundaries between their two districts. Wickersham described Judge Arthur H. Noyes as "an agreeable man, though he seemed to be immoderately fond of the bottle." Wickersham was not aware of McKenzie's schemes when he met him in Seattle, but he was impressed with the Nome party's sense of purpose. "It seemed to me that my companions were rather unimportant and probably blessed with only moderate ability. Members of the Nome group were alert, aggressive, and busily engaged in planning huge mining ventures." Wickersham's humility did not spring from an innate character trait; it was just that the Nome excitement was sweeping the world at the time. The spectacular discoveries on the Seward Peninsula promised to give Alaska its first mining region of comparable wealth to that of the fabled Klondike. "The members of my modest party felt that they were being shunted to an obscure place in the Yukon wilderness. The great Nome camp was everywhere the main topic of conversation, whereas no one knew whether our Eagle City division had mining possibilities. We were not interesting to the Seattle crowds which stood open-mouthed about those bound for Nome."[1]

Others in Wickersham's party included U.S. Attorney Alfred M. Post, U.S. Marshal George Perry, and Plato Mountjoy, a special accounting officer from the Department of Justice. Mountjoy, who was making his first of several trips to Alaska, would help install a bookkeeping system for the clerk and marshal. Mountjoy was one of several Justice officials who would leave an imprint on Alaska's law enforcement system, just as he had in other western territories. The customary role of such officers as were dispatched from Washington was that of troubleshooter or special examiner when nasty things were going on in the field. A description from the *Oklahoma State Capital* cleverly catches the spirit of an examiner and the glee his visits excited among critics of the court:

> Mr. Plato Mountjoy is someone that federal pie eaters do not know exactly what to make of. Nothing can be found out about his business. He tells neither to warm-hearted federal officials nor the newspapers, but comes here looking into the condition of different departments. It can, however, be seen which way the shoe pinches by the extra politeness and bowings and scrapings, when certain ones who feel that their tenure of office is short, greet him. He is a little man. He is gray and gentle and sweet voiced, but he is as dangerous as Menelik, king of Ethiopia . . . a

satrap and autocrat, who can cut off a head by a word and make it fall into the basket.[2]

But such fears as these did not hang over either the Eagle or the Nome court officials—at least not yet.

Wickersham sailed north on the SS *City of Seattle* on July 2, 1900, calling at Ketchikan, Wrangell, Treadwell (the great mine on Douglas Island opposite Juneau), Juneau, and Skagway. At Skagway, Wickersham met with Melville C. Brown, first-division judge, to decide on a boundary between the Eagle court division and that of Juneau. Juneau had been designated the seat of government in the Civil Code of 1900, although the official move was postponed until appropriate facilities could be constructed.

Wickersham heard all about Soapy Smith and Frank Reid at Skagway and gathered other information as he traveled, in comfort not available two years earlier to the stampeders over the White Pass and Yukon Railway, to Bennett for transfer to steamboats for lake and Yukon River passages to his destination. Fellow travelers told him about law enforcement in the interior when the first prospectors went into the country. The earliest serious crimes occurred in 1878, when the wife of trader James Bean was shot by Indians on the Tanana River, and in 1885, when George Holt, an Alaska Commercial Company trader, was killed by Copper Indians. In neither case were attempts made to punish the Indian murderers because there were too few white men in the country to do anything about it. But it was different in 1888 when prospector John Bremner was killed by two Koyukuk Indians. A party of prospectors on the lower Yukon voyaged upriver on a small steamer, surrounded the Indian camp, arrested the men who supposedly committed the murder, and hanged one of them. There were no repercussions. Indians of Alaska's interior had little in common with the fierce warriors of the western plains; instances of violence to whites or any resistance to their intrusions were isolated.

The judge reached Eagle, the seat of his division near the Canadian border on the Yukon, on July 15, 1900. Fort Egbert, the army post located there at the recommendation of officers Patrick Ray and Wilds Richardson, had been established in 1899. The town also had stores of the two major Alaskan trading companies, two restaurants, five saloons, and log cabins housing a couple of hundred resi-

*Judge James Wick-
ersham.* Alaska His-
torical Library,
Alaska Centennial
Collection

dents reasonably well pleased to have the town distinguished as the interior's judicial center.

The third division's boundaries extended to encompass some three hundred thousand square miles between the Arctic Ocean and the North Pacific, including the vast Yukon Valley. Only fifteen hundred whites had been counted in the 1900 census. There were several thousand Indians and Eskimos widely scattered over the region.

Wickersham's first chores were to build a log house for himself, his wife, and his son and supervise the construction of a courthouse and jail. And he did not waste time before convening court at Eagle. There were not too many pending cases, but he was able to collect license fees from all the saloonkeepers in his district. Alaska's officials had finally convinced Congress that high license fees for saloon operators could support government services, and this made more sense than a blanket prohibition of liquor that had proved unenforceable. The judge needed these fees to keep things going. Pay warrants and expense reimbursements were remarkably delayed. The court party's first payday came eight months after arrival.

The three Alaska judges lacked some of the amenities familiar to their colleagues outside, but they certainly had more power. By the Civil Code of 1900 the court held administrative as well as judicial functions. It heard petitions for liquor licenses and divided the fees collected; it called elections and supervised the incorporation of towns; it approved bonds for schools; it organized commissioner precincts and appointed the commissioners, whose duties included those of justice of the peace for lesser civil and criminal matters, coroner, road commissioner, probate judge, notary public, land office supervisor, and others. In effect, the Civil Code had strengthened the judiciary without adding any other public officials. The governor's powers were very limited; there was no legislature and no congressional representation. Although the governor, appointed by the secretary of the interior, might speak for Alaska, actual governance rested in the Department of Justice through its appointees.

Later Judge Wickersham was to complain that the judges held too much power, but in first viewing his domain he was more concerned with what was lacking: "It contained no court-house, jail, school or other public building. There were only four log churches within its wide spread boundaries. There was not a mile of public wagon road or trail. No money had been appropriated or promised by Congress for any of these purposes, except that the district court judge had been authorized to reserve two town lots and build a courthouse and jail out of license funds." Thus the situation did not differ much from what it had been in 1897–99 when U.S. Commissioner Crane and Deputy Marshal Canton inaugurated the court's presence at Circle. Canton had depended on the NAT&T for credit; Wickersham relied on the Alaska Commercial Company. "That company financed us and thereby loyally aided in establishing American government in the Alaska-Yukon basin," he wrote.[3]

The Yukon also had a mail service, and the court officers were grateful for its existence. The Post Office handled mail routes through contractors, who bid on the various routes. Ben S. Downing, a tall Missourian, packed mail on the Yukon River between Dawson and Fort Gibbon. Earlier on the western plains he had

Judge Wickersham's first courthouse in the Alaska interior at Eagle.
University of Alaska Archives

been a wagoner; in the north he learned to drive dogs for winter travel. His mail contract did not prevent his carrying other freight and passengers. Since traffic was particularly heavy between Dawson and Eagle, he ran a four-horse bobsled, switching to the conventional dog sled for the route below Eagle.

Downing used eight to ten dogs, hitched tandem, for his mail sleds. He could carry a passenger if the mail and freight load was light; otherwise the passenger had to run at the handlebars. Teams were expected to cover a distance of twenty-five to thirty miles a day, depending on the spacing of stations, and loads were calculated at about one hundred pounds per dog. Such travel was dangerous along the Yukon before the ice reached winter thickness in the fall and in the spring when breakup time approached.

The judge's first murder case involved Downing. The mail carrier had not only witnessed a killing but came close to being killed himself. Yet for some reason he refused a subpoena commanding his appearance at the September 1900 murder trial of Charles Hubbard in Circle, the first jury term of court held in the interior. Downing was either too busy to go to Circle or reluctant to perform as a key government witness. But Judge Wickersham expected folks to do their duty, regardless of inconvenience or pecuniary loss. How else could law and order be established in the interior?

Charles Hubbard's murder trial began on September 4. When the judge heard that Downing was missing, he found him in contempt and the trial went on. Wickersham and the U.S. attorney realized that the case against Hubbard would be much stronger with Downing's testimony, but they did not dare postpone the trial. Getting an indictment from the grand jury had been difficult enough. It was not that the boys figured Hubbard was innocent, but the shooting was just one of those things. Wickersham got rough with them as their reluctance surfaced: "I called them in and gave pointed instructions." If they refused to indict, "I told them I would hold Hubbard over to the next grand jury."[4]

According to the facts, Charles Hubbard woke up one morning in Dawson to discover that his friend Tom McNamee had absconded. Hubbard had lent McNamee $5,000, "all he had in the world." McNamee's mining ventures had not paid off. He had $2,500, not nearly enough to pay Hubbard, and there were other creditors too. So he took off as soon as the ice went out of the Yukon River in May after allegedly telling another man, "If that damn Hubbard bothers me any more, I will kill him like I would a Siwash."[5]

Hubbard set out in pursuit. He was mad and drunk. And he stayed mad and drunk as he pushed on past Forty Mile, Eagle, and Circle, getting news of McNamee's progress along the way.

Meanwhile, McNamee, sensing the hot breath of Hubbard behind him, got a break. At Circle he ran into Downing, an old friend, who, since the river was open, was carrying the Dawson mail out by canoe. McNamee begged to go along.

"What's the hurry?" asked Downing. "You can't get a ship from St. Michael until July."

"Well," McNamee said, "I've got to get moving anyway. I made my stake by hard work. Now I want to visit my folks in Ireland."

Downing needed help with the canoe, so he was willing. The men left Circle on May 19 and reached Fort Yukon that night. Along the way, Downing insisted on pulling into shore to fix some hot grub, although "McNamee was very anxious to keep moving."

Departure time from Fort Yukon was set for 4:00 A.M. At 3:00

A.M. as the men slept in the mail carrier's cabin, Hubbard knocked on the door, asking for McNamee. Hubbard, red eyed and shaky, demanded at least one thousand dollars from the Irishman. If he got one thousand dollars, he would forget the rest of the money. If he didn't, he would kill him. McNamee, who always called bluffs, flatly refused, left Hubbard standing there, and rushed back into the cabin.

Hubbard was not bluffing. He fired his revolver as the door closed, then kicked it open and marched in. Downing thought Hubbard was after the registered mail and reached for his shotgun. McNamee jumped behind Downing, figuring the big man made a useful shield. Hubbard fired. The bullet pierced the left flap of Downing's shirt without hitting flesh and smashed into McNamee's heart.

"I would have blown Hubbard's brains out," said Downing, "but he threw his gun down and I picked it up. I laid Tom's body on the bed, went to the N.C. store and told the men to hold a coroner's inquest, deputize me as marshal, and I'd take Hubbard to Rampart."

A miners' meeting convened to handle the formalities. McNamee's effects were recorded. He had $1.50 in silver, a dollar bill, a pocket knife, a catechism, a pipe, letters, and bank drafts for $1,500 and $1,000. The $2.50 cash was held for the cost of a coffin and grave digging. The committee appointed William Rhoades to go along with Downing and make charges against Hubbard.[6]

At trial, Hubbard claimed self-defense. McNamee had threatened him in Dawson and at Fort Yukon. He shot McNamee out of fear for his own life. In the absence of Downing's testimony—the basis for the summary of events given here—the prosecution's case rested on the complaint made by Rhoades and hearsay reports of what Downing had told the Fort Yukon men. This was not the best evidence. Jurors deliberated for a while, then asked the judge to tell them the various penalties for murder one, murder two, and manslaughter. Since manslaughter involved only a ten-year sentence, the jurors chose it as their verdict.

Judge Wickersham, who had convened court in a church for want of a more suitable building, was satisfied with the verdict. He did not believe Hubbard killed in self-defense, but Alaskans did not appreciate debt absconders. When Hubbard was considered for release from McNeil Island in 1906, the judge gave his approval.[7]

It took the court a long time to get Downing's version of the bloody event. Wickersham's clerk recorded a statement made in June 1904 and filed it with the rest of the record.

The Hubbard case was not particularly sensational or significant from any legal aspect, but it had telling points. It encapsulated some major gold-rush themes: quick wealth, greed, treachery, personal vengeance, and the tardy pace of formalized justice. It tells much of the tyranny of Alaska's geography in fixing the movements and sometimes the behavior of its people, and even more convincingly it shows the danger of self-help.

At the judge's instructions, Eagle's U.S. attorney hauled all of the town's bawdy-house keepers, prostitutes, and gamblers into court. Wickersham wanted to fine them "a reasonable amount each quarter in vindication of the laws and as an aid to the fund to maintain the police." An effort by the commissioner to fine the sporting class the year before failed because jurors refused to convict, and they showed the same reluctance in the first two cases Wickersham heard. Privately, Wickersham villified the "weakness and cowardice of the men of Eagle. . . . Men who should stand by the courts abuse them and acquit flagrant law violators."[8] There is no record of what the judge said to jurors in court, but he commanded the kind of tongue that could lash through even the thickest skulls, and suddenly all parties came to understand their civic responsibilities.

Defendants learned to plead guilty and jurors hastened to assess proper fines. The old, easy days had passed on the Yukon.

With the Yukon River open to navigation, the court party voyaged downriver for sessions at Circle and Rampart and returned in stately ease on Yukon steamers. Court business did not take long in either place, and the officials were soon able to return to Eagle. On October 19 the judge had the honor of sending the first telegram out of the interior on the completed army telegraph line. Soon the river iced up and the land fell to the grip of winter. After some months of relative inactivity, the judge wrote the attorney general, offering to assist either of his two more heavily burdened colleagues. Some relief to monotony was provided with news of claim jumping at Rampart. It seemed a good excuse for undertaking his first dog-sled journey, five hundred miles down the Yukon Trail: "Our long, Indian-made, spruce-basket sled was filled with dunnage bags, and dog feed, generally rice and bacon, sometimes dried fish; with blankets, dry sacks and warm clothing." The travelers also packed a big grub box, extra dog harness, and soft caribou-skin moccasins for trail-sore dog feet.

Over the load a tarpaulin was thrown and securely lashed down with ropes. "On the right side of the front end of the sled the gee-pole extended forward; the driver ran astride the low hanging rope which attached the dogs to the sled." A driver guided the team with whip and voice and the sled with the gee pole. "At the rear of the sled a pair of handle bars, similar to those of a common plow, enabled the rear guide to manage the sled and to keep it in an upright position on sloping ice ways. [9]

Temperatures dropped to fifty below between February 9 and March 2, when the dog-sled party bustled into Rampart. For a middle-aged man, the judge was in excellent condition, and he loved the excitement and novelty of the journey.

Late in March 1901, Wickersham was ordered by Washington to take an even more extensive trip to Unalaska in the Aleutian Islands. Unalaska was within the territory of the Nome court, but it seemed obvious that Judge Noyes was already over his head trying to clear his local docket. He could not go before holding the July term of court at Eagle, so his departure was delayed until August 1. He voyaged down the Yukon to St. Michael, then went by steamer via Nome to Unalaska. In a few hours at Nome, he realized that he would probably be assigned there after holding court in the Aleutians. Judge Noyes had left town in disgraceful circumstances, and all Nome roared for some attention to a logjam of pending litigation.

9. Alexander the Great

Give me a barnyard of Swedes and I'll drive them like sheep. —Alexander
McKenzie in Rex Beach's "The Looting of Alaska"

ALEXANDER MCKENZIE's scheme of grabbing the richest gold
mines of Nome involved the corruption of U.S. senators and officers of the Department of Justice. It was basically a simple plot to
take advantage of litigation over mining claims with swift, decisive
action under legal authority. McKenzie was able to move behind
puppets whose appointments to office he had arranged: District
Judge Arthur H. Noyes, District Attorney Joseph Wood, and U.S.
Commissioner R. N. Stevens. U.S. Marshal C. L. Vawter was also
a McKenzie appointee, although he showed some resistance to the
boss at times.

Mastermind McKenzie, the Republican national committeeman
from North Dakota for twenty-one years, advised friends never to
write a letter. "Walk across the state if necessary, but never write
a letter. Sure, what you say goes up in smoke, but what you *write*
is before you always."[1] He was born in Ontario in 1850 and labored
as a youth on the Northern Pacific Railroad construction in the
1870s. During the Black Hills gold rush, he became the sheriff of
Bismarck and was on his way to being the most powerful politician
in the territory. Railroads and other corporations supported his
rise to power with a Republican party machine that dominated politics in North Dakota for decades. His was a day of general graft and

corruption, yet no one surpassed him in political venality. He directed the "theft" of the territorial capital from Yankton to Bismarck in 1883 and lobbied in territorial and state legislatures for the railroads, insurance companies, banks, and other corporations he looked after. His hold on the major elective offices in North Dakota, and most of the federal appointments as well, lasted from 1889 until state progressives revolted against the ring in 1906. Seven of the first eight Republican governors had ties with his machine. He selected nearly every U.S. senator from North Dakota during the first twenty-four years of statehood, including Henry C. Hansbrough in 1891, who played a key role in his Alaska scam.

The Nome law firm of Hubbard, Beeman and Hume had a vital interest in the claims of the lucky Swedes. In return for their services for the claim jumpers who contested the aliens' right to mine gold, the lawyers shared ownership of about one hundred property titles, including some of the richest ground on the Seward Peninsula. Between 1899 and 1900, Oliver P. Hubbard, who had been with the attorney general's office during the Cleveland administration, looked around Chicago, New York, London, and Washington, D.C., for investors in the claim shares owned by the Nome law firm. Apparently he did not have too much luck exciting anyone over the claim jumpers' chances of winning their suits until he met Alexander McKenzie. McKenzie, a man of purpose and vision, saw right away how the risky proposition Hubbard offered could be transformed into a sure thing.

McKenzie agreed to use his influence in the U.S. Senate to nullify alien claims. The timing was perfect. Congress had Alaska's civil code under consideration. If one of McKenzie's cronies could slip a restriction on alien rights into the bill, the Nome lawyers and their new partner, McKenzie, would win their lawsuits with ease.

McKenzie organized the Alaska Gold Mining Company, capitalized on paper at $15 million. With corporate stock, McKenzie bought hundreds of jumpers' claims and gave Hubbard, Beeman, and Hume $750,000 in stock in trade for part of their interest in their one hundred claims. Hubbard was made secretary of the corporation.

It is reasonable to assume that McKenzie gave stock or something else of value to the two senators who would aid his plans.

Hansbrough of North Dakota was one friend; Thomas H. Carter of Montana was another. Carter had been chairman of the Republican National Committee from 1892 to 1896 and was a legitimate expert on mining law. As chairman of the Senate Committee on the Territories in 1900, he was the key man in the passage of Alaska's civil code.

Carter, who sponsored the bill, pushed hard for passage in 1898, insisting that "I have no more interest in the passage of this bill than any other Senator, but my interest and the interest of the Senate are profound."[2] Circumstantial evidence and Carter's devious work on the floor suggest that Carter and Hansbrough were in collusion with McKenzie. There is no evidence that the senators expected to share the Nome millions, but if they helped their friend get millions, perhaps they would benefit in kind. There is evidence that Carter and Hansbrough met McKenzie at his hotels in New York and Washington to discuss affairs.

It was difficult for the senators to avoid tipping their hand because the code, as sent out of committee, used the language of the Oregon Code, explicitly giving aliens the right to acquire mining property, a right that "shall not be questioned nor in any manner affected by reasons of the alienage of any person from or through whom such title may have been derived." Much of the disputed Nome property was held by Americans who had purchased from the lucky Swedes, so the purchasers' rights were specifically protected. But once the code was on the floor, Carter commanded the gall to argue that the alien provision had "crept into this compilation" and must be stricken to prevent its confirming "shady or doubtful titles" and giving "rights where none existed under the law." Like the claim jumpers of Nome, Senator Carter's interest was patriotic: numerous aliens had illegally and immorally taken the richest claims of Nome, he told colleagues, and now the code had to be amended to protect the rights of American citizens. Carter also offered his version of Nome's history, distorting the priorities of discovery and the actions of the military in breaking up the miners' meetings of claim jumpers. In spread-eagle form, Carter warned "it will be a dark and evil day for this country when the badge of American citizenship will not be at least as good a cloak for protection as the ancient citizenship of Rome was in the days of that great Republic."[3]

This was fine rhetoric, even if it ignored the rights of Americans who had acquired property from the aliens, and Carter provided a solution to the injustice for his colleagues. It just happened that Senator Hansbrough had drawn up an amendment to the original version of the code, "moved by a high sense of duty to a distant body of his fellow-countrymen, men on an ice-bound coast 8,000 miles away."[4] The amendment would invalidate the title of any claim purchased from an alien locator and give courts a right to inquire into a locator's citizenship. Since the U.S. Supreme Court had ruled that only the government—as distinguished as a litigant in a law suit—could raise the question of alienage, the amendment was doubly bold.

Carter warned of the yellow peril. Swedes and Laps were one thing, but should "we should give notice to the . . . people of Japan that they . . . may proceed to Cape Nome . . . and there participate like our own citizens? . . . It would be equivalent to turning Alaska over to the aliens who might desire to come there from all over the world."[5]

Some senators were aware that they were being asked to pass special legislation. Comments were made on the interest of attorney Hubbard, who was seen with Hansbrough. Charles D. Lane, a notable California mining man with many properties in Nome, some purchased from aliens, was the important impediment to the spoilers' schemes. Lane had Senator William M. Stewart of Nevada explain to other senators what the amendment meant: it was "grossly unjust . . . an unheard of proposition." As the debate dragged on, Carter became desperate enough to withdraw the Hansbrough amendment in favor of one of his own that was identical except for a preamble declaration that it did not change existing mining law. An eloquent senator from Tennessee exposed Carter's cunning language: "There is, Mr. President, a serpent coiled beneath that rose; a dagger behind that smile."[6]

Finally Carter had to compromise. He withdrew the amendments in return for alterations in the bill to delete the Oregon Code language explicitly stating alien rights. This would leave the alien matter to be settled in court, although a court examining precedent would be likely to hold for aliens.

McKenzie did not get his amendment, but he did get the judge who was likely to decide on the question in Nome. Arthur H.

Noyes, an old friend of the North Dakota boss got the appointment, and one may assume that a certain mutuality of accord was
arrived at between the two pals. Thus it was that Nome got the
judge and other court officers that were so desperately awaited by
beleaguered residents crying for law and order.

The Nome court party arrived on July 19, 1900. Within four
days, Alexander McKenzie, abandoning his customary behind-the-
scenes role as power broker, controlled the richest placer mining
claims of Nome. He had been appointed as receiver by Judge Noyes
to administer the very mining claims he was challenging in court—
while they were in litigation. A receiver is supposed to be a disin-
terested party charged with holding disputed property in trust so
that its value is not dissipated before judicial determinations can be
made. Obviously the safest way to preserve the gold was to leave
it in the ground; instead, the receiver hired every miner he could
find to work the claims before seasonal changes halted operations.
McKenzie did not disguise his peculiar position. He called on Hubbard's law partners, W. T. Hume and Edwin Beeman, demanding
cooperation in return for a "large and ample fortune." If they failed
to cooperate, he would ruin them and "see to it that they won no
suits in the district court . . . as he controlled the judge." The deal
ensured that the "weak and vacillating" judge had a part of the law
firm's profits. District Attorney Joseph Wood was to get a quarter-
share of the business, and another quarter went to McKenzie "in
trust" for Noyes. A contract was signed on July 22.[7]

Hume supervised the work of a flock of secretaries while McKenzie paced the floor of the office. There were reasons for urgency; the
sooner the lawyers applied for the appointment of receiver Mc-
Kenzie to supervise the claims, the sooner the present owners of
the mines could be forced off. They were bringing up gold that
McKenzie coveted. On July 23, Judge Noyes signed the necessary
papers without even bothering to read them. McKenzie, standing
by with horse-drawn wagons and a deputy marshal, dashed for the
mines with court orders forcing owners to give him "immediate
possession, control, and management."[8]

These bizarre events caught the miners off guard or they might
have resisted by force. Most people in Nome assumed that everything was proper because the judge had sanctioned it and because

they did not understand that the claim jumpers, whose suits depended on the alien ownership argument, did not have very strong cases. When the U.S. Circuit Court of Appeals reviewed the matter later, it stated that "a fair examination of the law" would have found that the claim jumpers' allegations were insufficient grounds to support a court action, much less the appointment of a receiver.[9]

Attorneys for Charles Lane and Jafet Lindeberg, chief opponents of the claim jumpers, protested the receivership to Noyes without getting any response. McKenzie got more action when he told the judge that Lindeberg's mining men were interfering with him. Noyes empowered the receiver to confiscate all property, equipment, and gold on the claims, an order, as the circuit court observed, "so arbitrary and unwarranted in law as to baffle the mind in its effort to comprehend how it could have issued from a court of justice."[10] But the Nome court was a tool, not a court of justice. McKenzie could not be stopped. As the owners and their lawyers cried of outrage, he said: "To hell with them all! Nobody can hurt me! I am too strong at headquarters." It was patently true that McKenzie's Washington friends held high positions and that he could drive "a barnyard of Swedes" like sheep.[11]

The stirring events in Nome were, of course, brought to the Justice Department's attention by its officers. Marshal Vawter reported to the attorney general early in August 1900, describing the town's chaotic state, with "twenty to thirty thousand people along the beach," including "more murderers, cut-throats, thieves, confidence men, gamblers, prostitutes and bad characters than any camp I ever saw or heard of, and I have been on the frontier continuously for over thirty years." District Attorney Wood confirmed the presence of much riffraff: "It appears that ex-convicts and criminals from all parts of the country have congregated here, and are as active as it is possible to imagine." Vawter wanted permission to hire six more deputies, and Wood asked approval after the fact for hiring W. T. Hume, "a splendid lawyer," as assistant district attorney and W. N. Landers as clerk. Hume, of course, proved less complaisant than the spoilers expected.[12]

A report of C. S. Frost, special examiner and watchdog for the Justice Department, alerted the attorney general in August to trouble over the judge's appointment of unnamed receivers in mining disputes. Unhappy mine owners had appealed receivership orders to Noyes, but he, "with justice and fairness to all parties and without bias or prejudices," rejected their appeals. Now these litigants planned "to force an appeal on the appellate court" and were trying to intimidate the judge. These men also planned to send someone to Washington to discredit the court. They did not want honest officials who could not be bought. "If any statements made by persons who seek to discredit Judge Noyes reach your ears, they will, I am sure, if sifted well, be found utterly without foundation." An upright judge and other officials "take their lives in their hands" in Nome, but for all the peril to life and reputation, they would prevail.[13]

Judge Noyes sent his first report on August 20, complaining that all of Nome's twenty-five thousand people "seem to be engaged in contests over lots or mining properties." He assured Attorney General John W. Griggs that he was performing vigorously and appointing a receiver (not named) for valuable mines in dispute. The judge explained that the mining would go on under the receiver as "it would be greatly against the community to in any manner shut down the work." He expected "harsh criticism," but "I have been guided by what in my conscience I believe to be the best thing to do." For one whose court was so burdened with criminal and civil matters, Noyes made the unusual request that Wood be authorized to winter in Washington, where he could explain Nome's "crying needs." This clever ploy would have protected the spoilers as their victims' screams reached Washington, but the department thought Wood should stay on the job in Nome.[14]

Marshal C. L. Vawter, a North Dakotan, had been selected for the appointment by McKenzie, yet he seems not to have been a willing, informed partner to the spoilers' schemes. He had not been involved in any criminal activity and did not care to go down with a sinking ship, so he documented some of the court party's skulduggery for the circuit court. Since some of the unlawful acts occurred as early as July 1900, soon after the court opened its first Alaska session at St. Michael, he might have spoken sooner had he been braver and willing to sacrifice his job. He was allowed to resign as marshal in 1901 and take a deputy's job at distant Unga, one of several he held for many years until his retirement. Vawter reported that A. K. Wheeler, Noyes's private secretary, used the judge's chambers as his private law office. This cozy arrangement helped folks wishing to do business with the judge understand the significance of Noyes's advice to "go see Wheeler." Noyes was not above picking up a few dollars before he even reached what became his headquarters at Nome from the managers of the Alaska Commercial Company and the North American Transportation and Trading Company in transactions that the managers swore to in support of Vawter. The traders were concerned that the court wanted the companies to pay higher liquor license fees—wholesale rather than retail rates for their St. Michael stores. Upon explaining that their operations were only retail, they learned of Wheeler's availability as counsel and each trader paid him five hundred dollars to settle the matter favorably. This deal, Vawter swore, was made "with the knowledge and consent of Noyes."[15]

Other Wheeler-Noyes cons cost owners of the Black Chief Mining Company heavily. After Noyes advised them to retain Wheeler, they refused the secretary's demand for a half-interest in their mine. Wheeler reduced his demand to three-tenths, then one-eighth, and when the owners continued to resist, claim jumpers asked for an injunction and the appointment of a receiver. The receiver, William B. Cameron, worked the mine with machinery leased "at an extravagant price" from McKenzie's company and otherwise wasted money.

Vawter pinpointed several instances of Frost's role in keeping the spoilers in control of Nome's wealth, including his acceptance of attorney fees directly from McKenzie. Frost had also hired "three detectives at government expense to spy upon and watch the attorneys" of disputed mine owners. During the desperate days after the circuit court served a writ on McKenzie, Frost tried to get Vawter to resist the return of gold held in a bank to the mine owners. Get a posse to guard the bank, demanded Frost, but Vawter thought he could call upon the army for help if any trouble occurred. "To hell with the military," said Frost, "you can't trust them." Frost was probably right. Major John J. Van Orsdale had been more than cooperative with Noyes and McKenzie but could hardly be expected to resist a court order. Nor did Vawter fancy himself in the role of a posse leader standing off a court order and perhaps the army in a valiant effort to save McKenzie's ill-gotten gains. When Vawter refused to do his bidding, Frost approached Deputy U.S. Marshal George A. Leekley and asked him "to get something" on the marshal. In return, Leekley would be rewarded, perhaps with Vawter's job when the judge removed him. But Leekley refused to help.[16]

Ironically enough, McKenzie's very speed defeated him. Had he delayed his plan for a couple of weeks, opposing attorneys might not have had time before the winter freeze-up to bypass Noyes's court for the circuit court in San Francisco. Noyes had denied motion for appeal on August 15, so lawyers hurried to California to appeal their denial. By late August, Judge William Morrow ruled that Noyes "had grossly abused the judgment and discretion vested in him by law" and ordered the receiver to return all the property he held. Just as significantly, since Morrow appreciated the degree of corruption, he ordered Noyes to stay all proceedings relating to the contested claims.[17]

The circuit court's orders reached Nome on September 14. McKenzie, anticipating the decision, had already sent an SOS to Carter through James L. Galen, Carter's brother-in-law, who had accompanied the court party to Nome. But no one in Washington could think of a way to thwart the circuit court.

Much jubilation followed the news of Morrow's decision. "The ring is broken," reported the *Chronicle* on September 14, "its leader has been deposed and deprived of his power."[18] McKenzie fought back, denying the validity of the circuit court order. Noyes stayed out of sight, passing the word that he was sick and powerless to make the receiver give property back because the circuit court had usurped his jurisdiction over the case. Once more lawyers steamed off for San Francisco, three thousand miles distant, to complain. Meanwhile, bloodshed seemed likely as Lindeberg's men drove the receiver's men from the mines. Both sides asked the army for help, but Major Van Orsdale, officer in command, was friendly to McKenzie and fearful of acting against the district court. Noyes came out of seclusion long enough to order the army officers to ignore the writs from California.

The circuit court writ of supersedeas was a matter that called for some comment by the judge to his superiors. The judge assured

Washington on October 12 that his conduct and McKenzie's "will bear the most severe and strictest scrutiny." He professed to believe that the circuit court would soon reverse itself so that his defiance would be condoned. He apologized for being too busy to report on "trouble among the officials," a reference to Marshal Vawter's damaging affidavits to the circuit court, and was saddened that his marshal had disrupted the harmony of the court. Tracing the source of the circuit court's mistakes was easy. C. D. Lane, the mine owner, "loud mouthed and blatant," and a heavy contributor to Democrat William J. Bryan's presidential campaign, was the culprit of a nasty attempt to bring the court into disrepute.[19]

Many people in Nome feared that McKenzie would grab the quarter of a million dollars in gold he had deposited in the bank and head outside. Armed men watched every move of McKenzie to the bank, and after a near confrontation the deposed receiver agreed that soldiers should see that the gold remained in the bank.[20]

Folks watched as eagerly for a mid-October ship likely to bear news from the circuit court as they did in the summer for the first ship through the receding ice. The *Oregon* arrived on October 15 with two deputy marshals from California bearing writs backing Morrow's orders and an arrest warrant for McKenzie. McKenzie was taken back for trial.

While everyone awaited the course of events in San Francisco, Frost wrote the Department of Justice on October 27, suggesting that the unhappy mine owners crying out against the judge were being aided by a treacherous member of the court. He charged that Court Clerk George Borchsenius, a foe of the judge and friend of "the Swede element," was helping to discredit the court. The clerk put out the story that the court hired private detectives to shadow attorneys of the mine owners in the hope of countering their moves, whereas, in fact, the detectives had been hired to catch jury bribers. And, of course, the same attorneys were suspected of bribing jurors. Neither Noyes nor Wood would employ detectives except in the government's interest, and Frost, of course, would never lend himself to dishonest dealing.[21] Later Noyes did fire Borchsenius, who was reinstated.

The timing of decisive events did not allow the attorney general the leisure to investigate Noyes, much less replace him before navigation closed in October 1900. Nothing much could be done during the winter, either. The department's leadership changed during the winter when Philander C. Knox replaced John W. Griggs as attorney general. It must have seemed easier, and safer politically, to await the outcome of circuit-court proceedings.

The department heard complaints about Nome over the winter. Senator Stewart discussed the circuit court's actions in the Senate, and his scolding of the Nome district-court officers was picked up by the press. Nome mine operator W. L. Leland was one of several to call for Noyes's removal: "While I am a good Republican I am ashamed of the present administration," he said. Another complaint made to the president referred to Nome's "Reign of the Receiver."[22]

Of course the big winter news came from San Francisco. At his trial before the circuit court, the judges found that McKenzie had deliberately and intentionally disobeyed the writs "in furtherance of the high-handed and grossly illegal proceedings initiated almost as soon as Judge Noyes and McKenzie had set foot on Alaskan territory at Nome." McKenzie's actions "may be safely and fortunately said to have no parallel in the jurisprudence of this country."[23]

This was, in a way, high praise for "Alexander the Great," who really lost nothing in stature by the nasty affair. In February he was sentenced to a year in the Alameda County Jail, but after a bit more than three months a compassionate President McKinley, learning that the North Dakota boss's health was failing, pardoned him. McKenzie's debility did not keep him from sprinting from the jail door to the train station or from continuing to exercise his political power for twenty more years before he died.

Judge Noyes stayed on through the winter without getting much done except drinking. His work in clearing the crowded civil and criminal dockets was farcical and infuriating to attorneys and their clients.

U.S. Attorney Wood was embarrassed in December when he tried to prosecute R. J. Parks for gambling. Tex Rickard and other saloon men testified in Parks's defense that Wood had demanded $3,000 monthly or he would close them down. The gamblers got together and offered Wood $750, but Wood demanded more. Finally the gamblers consulted attorney W. T. Hume, who outlined the story in municipal court: "We want to see if a jury will convict saloon men because they refused to give $3,000 a month to District Attorney Wood." The *Nome Chronicle* editor was most critical of Wood but conceded that "at least he's no pugilist. He didn't fight Hume."[24]

Noyes took time in March to respond to statements of Governor Brady carried by the wire services. It pained him that Brady, who had visited Nome for only two or three days in October and had expressed confidence in him, should now say that Noyes's life was in danger because of widespread disgust in Nome. No one opposes me except the Pioneer and Wild Goose mining companies, Noyes informed the attorney general, so "it is only just and right that I should remain here until the investigation is made and that I shall expect as my just due." Later Noyes passed along to Washington a report by his deputy clerk summarizing all the cases heard at court and praising the judge's marvelous work.[25]

The Justice Department had not nerved itself to a decision about Noyes by the time navigation opened. While argument could be made for the department's restraint with the judge, the same could not be said for the same dilatory conduct where the district attorney was concerned. Wood remained on the job until required to answer contempt charges in October 1901 at San Francisco. This gave him the opportunity to try to fix blame on his opponents, particularly W. H. Metson and Samuel Knight, attorneys for the Pioneer, Wild Goose, and other mining companies, for bringing the court into disrepute. These attorneys had offered five hundred to three thousand dollars for false affidavits accusing Wood of misconduct and protecting a gang of robbers from legal sanctions by packing juries. "Probably in no other place of earth, in proportion to its population, are there so many affidavit men, and persons who will commit perjury for a consideration." These people and those hiring them hate Wood "because I am the chief obstacle in their way." Yet, through many travails and relentless efforts to rob him of his good name, Wood had established law and order.[26]

On July 19, Noyes responded to formal charges made by the attorney general. He had not received the letter from Washington until July 4 because he had voyaged to St. Michael on June 17 to open court and his ship had been held in the ice for fifteen days. On July 5 he received his summons from the circuit court. The judge offered a splendid suggestion for a "searching investigation": let Congress appoint a committee. This notion may have raised a smile from the attorney general. Executive departments had to endure oversight from Congress often enough but were not accustomed to requesting help in housecleaning. Noyes, of course, understood that any hope that existed for his protection lay with powerful senators willing to help a coverup. The department was willing to help out on one Noyes request: asking the army to allow Major John J. Van Orsdale to appear as the judge's witness in San Francisco.[27]

W. T. Hume's testimony to the circuit court, implicating his partner Hubbard with McKenzie, Noyes, and friendly senators in a conspiracy, contributed significantly to the conviction of the spoilers. District Attorney Joseph Wood gave Nome some juicy gossip with his livid response to Hume's affidavit in July 1901. The federal prosecutor interrupted a city council meeting to demand the firing of Hume, who served part time as city attorney. If you do not get rid of him, Wood threatened, "I'll close down every gambling game in town and drive out every woman of ill repute." According to the *Nome Nugget*, "the council told Hume they wanted no clashes with federal authorities and intimated to him that oil will be poured over the troubled waters if his resignation was forthcoming." Hume resisted, but the council insisted. Hume must resign because he called Wood "a grafter." But, Hume protested, "that's my privilege as a private citizen." Odd things happened all the time in Nome, and it was well that several newspapers helped folks keep up on stirring events, even if their editors sometimes lied for and defended their favorites and savaged their enemies. The *Nugget*'s only comment on this little diversion was in describing Hume as "placid," and Wood as "impulsive and inclined to be choleric and sarcastic." The men were rated equally as "probably good haters."[28]

Nome's lawyers, aside from those representing the Pioneer and Wild Goose owners, did not gain courage to complain openly about the judge until August 1901. They were stimulated only when attorney T. M. Reed gathered seventeen signatures of lawyers attesting to Noyes's "strict integrity." Reed, later to become the first-division judge (1921–28), argued that "if the judge erred it was of the head not of the heart." Since some of the petitioners, who included Frost and other friends of the court, were honest men, it must be that they sincerely believed that a new judge "not acquainted with our conditions would hamper rather than advance the cause of justice."[29]

Two days later the majority of the bar, fifty-four members, wired President McKinley requesting Noyes's removal "to prevent riot and bloodshed," charging that he "is vacillating and dilatory, weak, petty, negligent, careless and absolutely incompetent."[30] For all their professional belligerency, lawyers are fearful of opposing judges, yet by mid-August northern Alaskans become acutely aware of seasonal change. If the Justice Department did not act by October, it would be too late for another year. Of course the attorney general did move in September by sending Judge Wickersham to Nome as a temporary replacement for Noyes.

Noyes left Nome in August for home visits and an appointment in Washington before the circuit-court hearing. He obviously wanted an attorney with him when he saw the attorney general and so informed the department indirectly by wire from Seattle. He referred to his companion as "my private secretary and stenographer . . . it is absolutely necessary to have my secretary with me." This necessary helper was none other than C. S. Frost, who had been special examiner, then assistant U.S. attorney to Wood.

On September 6, 1901, Teddy Roosevelt succeeded the assassinated President McKinley, and before long he learned a lot about Nome. If Roosevelt had been unaware of the involvement of U.S. senators with the spoilers, it was spelled out by a Montana man in October. "Careful investigation," wrote C. W. Wiley, "will show that Senator Carter was about as deeply involved in the mire of Cape Nome scandals as was Alex McKenzie" and he is "boss and dictator" of the corrupt Republican party in Montana.[31] Roosevelt knew better than to make careful investigations of senators and did not need to do so. The former Dakota cowboy knew all about Alexander McKenzie and Carter.

U.S. Attorney Wood was sentenced to four months in jail for

contempt and was fired by the Justice Department, as was C. S. Frost, the Justice Department man who found Nome more wicked than Butte. Judges told Wood that he had "grossly betrayed the interests of the United States which were entrusted to his care," and gave him a year in jail.[32]

The Washington friends of the spoilers fought for their vindication even after the conviction of McKenzie in February 1901 and those of Noyes, Wood, Frost, and Dudley Du Bose in January 1902. They probably felt that they owed their friends some help, or perhaps feared being linked with the scandal. After kind words for Noyes were made on the Senate floor, Attorney General Philander Knox was inspired to schedule a departmental hearing on Noyes's affairs in February 1902 to consider whether the contempt prosecution arose from an insidious plot to force his removal rather than from "the vindication of the processes of the [circuit] court."

Among those invited was E. S. Pillsbury, who had written an amicus curiae brief at the request of the circuit court. Pillsbury knew that Knox's investigation had something to do with support for Noyes in the Senate, but he was not sympathetic. He had worked for three months without pay "solely in vindication of the process of the court." The circuit court, acting on his belief and other evidence, had convicted Noyes and others. Pillsbury not only refused to appear at Knox's hearing but seized the occasion any attorney might relish of lecturing the U.S. attorney general on constitutional processes: "I do not consider that the Court has need of vindication from any source. If it is desired to review the action of that tribunal, the law provides the method for so doing."[33]

At the hearing, Francis J. Heney appeared as one of the Noyes's lawyers. Professing illness, Noyes remained in California. Heney was then a rising star in the American bar, noted for being a barroom brawler in Arizona and for his more mature court pugnaciousness in San Francisco. Later he prosecuted the notorious gang of grafters led by Abe Ruef in San Francisco and became a favorite of Teddy Roosevelt after prosecuting successfully the rings of looters of Oregon and California public lands.

Attorney General Knox led the interrogation of Noyes's attorneys. He asked Heney how Noyes justified appointing mine receivers when the alleged owners were in possession and accessible. Heney conceded that the appointments were a mistake, but one "that inexperienced judges very frequently make."[34] Knox observed that Noyes had persisted in the mistake and accused Heney of making light of obvious repetitions of partiality on Noyes's part. For all his skill, Heney was hard pressed to make any sense of Noyes's receiver appointments except in reference to McKenzie's scheme, and no one was impolitic enough at the hearing to discuss McKenzie candidly.

Heney was even less effective in fending off Knox's persistent demands for an explanation of Noyes's behavior after the circuit court's writs reached Nome. The only time Heney felt comfortable with Knox's questions was in reference to the public hostility to the judge in Nome. "The other side bought a newspaper for villifying Noyes and bought the support of another" and even tried to bribe the good judge on four separate occasions, Heney said. Noyes's opponents were "conspirators against justice" who had used the circuit court as a tool to destroy him. This was not the first time Knox had heard that Noyes had been victimized by "conspirators against justice," but he was no fool and recognized the last-ditch defense for the nonsense it was.[35]

Sam Dunham, a Nome miner who suffered huge losses to the spoilers and who, as an occasional poet, had registered his dismay in published verse, wrote Knox about the same time. He wanted Knox to authorize fifteen cents a mile for witness fees (the rate for travel within Alaska) rather than the standard five cents he received for the 7,358-mile Nome–San Francisco round trip. His boat fare had been covered by the five-cent fee, but since he had been forced to winter outside, he was losing a good deal of money for testimony before the circuit court on "matters of common notoriety." He was irked by the contrast with those who had caused his mining losses in Nome, whose prosecution required his presence outside: "the criminals who are responsible for my financial embarrassment are spending the winter in the states on leave of absence granted by your Department and drawing their salaries and enjoying a liberal allowance for subsistence."[36]

President Roosevelt received several letters from Noyes's victims, including one from E. S. Coy, who lost both thirty thousand dollars on a mine and his son, who was drowned on a prospecting trip soon after being "driven from work on his father's mine" by receiver McKenzie. Coy thought other Masons were keeping Noyes out of jail and as a Mason he resented it. [37]

Certain Alaskans commanded Roosevelt's attention, particularly David H. Jarvis, collector of customs at Nome. The president admired heroes, and Jarvis was a legitimate one. As a Revenue Cutter Service officer in 1897, Jarvis had led an expedition, including a reindeer herd, in relief of whalers stranded without provisions at Point Barrow. For this well-publicized feat he was rewarded with a gold medal from Congress. He added to his fame by taking charge of preventive measures when a smallpox epidemic threatened Nome in 1900. In 1906, Roosevelt chose him to be governor of Alaska, but Jarvis declined the job. Jarvis' message to the president in early 1902 was an unequivocal denunciation of "one of the most outrageous conspiracies and attempts to rob the country . . . through this court and its connections . . . the attempt was bold, direct and perfectly patent to everybody." The circuit court convicted district-court officers "and declared that a conspiracy existed." There was only one way for the government to preserve respect for the Nome court: "Only the immediate removal of everybody connected with this conspiracy will give the people confidence in the good intentions of the administration." Jarvis tacitly rejected Noyes's supporters: Congress "should have no weight against the people who suffer under this court." Below this unsigned memo Roosevelt scrawled his own message to the attorney general: "This is from Jarvis who certainly knows Alaska." [38]

From the manner in which Knox handled the hearing, it appears that he caught the president's meaning. Noyes was finally removed from office on February 24, 1902. [39]

In February 1902 the *Nugget* carried a story from San Francisco on the Noyes trial under the heading "ALASKANS ALL LIARS—According to Judge Noyes An Eminent Authority." Noyes had denied the truth of attorney Hume's affidavit, of statements by Marshal Vawter, and of former District Judge Charles S. Johnson. Johnson told the court how, in defending a private client whose mine had been placed in receivership, he told Noyes in chambers and in open court that he could prove a conspiracy with McKenzie to control the mines. Noyes's explanation of the disparity between his stories and those of others was ingenious: "If you live one winter in Alaska you'll hate everybody and everybody will hate you."[40]

When the convictions were reported, *Nugget* editor J. F. A. Strong editorialized "on one of the most amazing conspiracies . . . known in the history of jurisprudence" and "the brazen effrontery displayed by McKenzie, his tools, hirelings, and henchmen." He expressed no sympathy for the "freebooters who foolishly imagined themselves the people"; they mocked the law "and the men who were supposed to administer it in justice and equity were the subservient tools—that is, those of the number who were not actually a part and parcel of the conspiracy."[41]

Many individuals were annoyed that the spoilers got off so easily and that charges of conspiracy were never brought against the chief actors. The attorney general or president could have ordered a prosecution, but perhaps they believed that the gain would not be worth the embarrassment to government, the courts, and certain leading politicians. This failure to prosecute was not necessarily a coverup. Even Judge Wickersham, who had nothing to fear from association with the tainted officials, adamantly resisted efforts in Nome to get a grand-jury indictment. He persuaded the grand jury to ignore the court officials and "certain U.S. Senators" accused of conspiracy: "The quicker the people of Nome and the court forgot those black days the better it would be for the administration of justice in that district."[42]

Strangely enough, the Nome scandal did not get full national exposure until 1906, when a series of articles by old Nome hand Rex Beach was published in *Appleton's Booklovers Magazine.* "The Looting of Alaska" charged that the scandal "was smothered and the public kept in ignorance. Criminals were pardoned, records expunged, thieves exalted to new honors."[43] The exposure led to defeat for McKenzie's ring in North Dakota's 1906 elections. That same year, Beach published *The Spoilers,* a novel based on Nome events that sold eight hundred thousand copies within ten years after publication and more in other reprintings over the years.

Five movies between 1914 and 1955, with such stars as Marlene Dietrich, John Wayne, Gary Cooper, Rory Calhoun, William Boyd, and Randolph Scott, retold Beach's romantic story.

Any lasting damage to Alaskans' veneration for the law is harder to assess, but it is possible that those who knew about the spoilers were reluctant to assume the credibility of their law-enforcement officers.

10. Teddy Wants Answers

Like so many others appointed to Alaska, Wright was hopelessly incompetent.—Albert Fink

AMAZEMENT followed amazement in the court circles of Nome, where scandals never seemed to end. Maybe there was too much gold for the community's well-being. Miners would deny there was such a thing as too much gold, but the Justice Department officials in Washington had reason to wish that their field men had fewer temptations.

The bright side of the second wave of devious scandals involving Nome court officers is that the judges were not sullied and the freebooters lacked the lofty, larcenous ambitions and organizational power of the McKenzie gang. Yet there remained signs of undue influences in Washington and a curious reluctance in the Department of Justice to move hastily in throwing offensive appointees out of office.

Judge Wickersham was winding up court business at Dutch Harbor when the attorney general ordered him to take over for Judge Noyes at Nome. Wickersham landed at Nome on September 16, 1901, "thrown suddenly, just as the season closed, into a maelstrom of scandal, intrigue and bitterness which then involved the court."[1] He feared riots and anarchy over the long-disputed mine-ownership cases. Soldiers were guarding the most valuable mines, but frustrated victims of the McKenzie plot might be expected to take over their properties by force. The court docket was clogged. Some claimants clamored for immediate trial, while others hoped to gain compromises and settlements through postponement.

Wickersham met with the military commander, asking him to withdraw his troops from the mines. The civil authorities would assume responsibility for policing once more. The judge then reviewed the pending cases, noting that Noyes had issued no written decisions on mining cases during his year on the bench. Two hundred cases were ready for trial, but during the four weeks that Wickersham's review consumed, the pressures for immediate trial dropped dramatically because many litigants and attorneys preferred wintering outside. The navigation season would close sometime in October.

On October 16, Wickersham opened the first jury trial after announcing "that no member of the bar shall in my private office, or any other place, except in the courtroom or in the presence of opposing counsel, speak to me at any time upon any matter connected with litigation."[2] With this warning that he intended to clean Nome's "Augean stables" with strict impartiality, the judge went to work. During the winter he tried fifty-six jury cases, twenty criminal and thirty-six civil, and 140 equity cases without a jury.[3] He also dismissed 226 cases for want of prompt prosecution, most of which were filed capriciously by claim jumpers who used the threat of litigation as a means of extortion.

Judge Wickersham felt pleased with his work in clearing the docket and removing one member of the McKenzie ring who still held office. R. N. Stevens, a brother-in-law of Senator Thomas Carter of North Dakota, had been McKenzie's appointee as U.S. commissioner. He was "a shrewd and clever lawyer, and McKenzie made a mistake," Wickersham believed, "in not procuring his appointment as district judge instead of Noyes, for Stevens would have kept the boss out of much of his trouble."[4]

Stevens had arranged things very handsomely for himself in Nome. He occupied a house opposite the courthouse, kept his court and recorder's office in the front room and lived with his family in back rooms. Stevens had ignored the requirement of submitting quarterly accounts of expenses to the court during his year's service, and when Wickersham demanded them, Stevens came up with some surprising figures. Over the year, receipts totaled $22,895.65 while his expenses were $22,700.45—a scanty yield to the government because Stevens charged $100 rent to the government for his front-room office and heating and general expenses for the whole house. With these expenses and the salaries of himself and family members deducted from revenues, it was little wonder the government had so little coming. Wickersham recommended to Washington that Stevens be removed and his dismissal followed.

Stevens had another source of income through his appointment as municipal judge by Nome's city council. Adding this position "made him the sole depository of all judicial powers in Nome except that held by his chief, Judge Noyes." Stevens earned nine thousand dollars in fees and fines, "a good fat salary and heavy expenses," from this office.[5] When a citizen contested Nome's authority to create a municipal court, Wickersham was given the chance to end Stevens' graft. The nine thousand dollars in fees and fines should have gone to the U.S. commissioner's court rather than directly to Steven's pocket, already brimming with salary and expenses received for doing as municipal judge what he should have done as U.S. commissioner.

Another instance of expense padding involved U.S. Marshal Frank Richards, who replaced Cornelius L. Vawter in 1901 and appeared to be "another of the McKenzie crowd."[6] The expense-account padding was a trifling affair compared with Stevens' lucrative setup, but the repercussions proved to be very heavy for Wickersham. The difficulties arose when Richards submitted his expenses for the Hardy trial in Unalaska, over which Wickersham had presided. Since all the court officials felt good about bringing the murderer of Con Sullivan and others to justice, Richards may have assumed that the judge would overlook some padding of his hotel bill. But Wickersham did not have warm regard for the marshal (see note 9 below) and upon interrogating the hotel keeper he learned that padding was a customary favor to court officials. The judge returned Richards's account and asked him to set them right. Richards was angry. He complied, but his character was not transformed.

Marshal Richards' chief problem, aside from his crookedness, lay in his belief that practical politics solved more problems—and probably rendered more perfect justice—than unthinking adherence to abstract concepts. At bottom he believed in loyalty to one's party, friends, and associates. Good men acting in concert could prevent miscarriages of justice and protect one another by using their heads. The judicial system was man made and prone to human imperfection in its results. What, in the name of God, he wondered, was wrong with manipulating the system when necessary to achieve good ends?

The embezzlement case against Nome's postmaster, Joseph Wright, offered a perfect example of the need for occasional fudging. Good old Joe was guilty as hell in a sense, but the poor guy held a job that was way over his head. He was too dumb to balance his accounts accurately or to know whether his clerks were ripping off postal funds. Sure, technically, Joe was responsible for shortages, but he was a well-meaning and popular fellow who liked his drinks and card games and meant no harm to anyone. His friends owed him some loyalty. Why should they treat Joe like some hardened felon and expose him to the law's rigor when he had already been punished by losing his job?

Joe's friends, who were also Richards' friends, talked to the marshal, and he assured them he would help. They all agreed that U.S. Attorney John McGinn, a roaring drunk himself, and the too scrupulous Judge Wickersham, whose past, according to rumor, encompassed some sordid adventures, were pressing too hard against Wright. By helping Joe out, Richards, still smarting over the padded-expense embarrassment, would also deliver a lesson in practical politics to McGinn and Wickersham.

Alerted to the tainted jury panel, Wickersham gave direct orders to Richards that he choose a new panel of jurors, one that did not include Wright's friends. Richards defied the judge by directing his deputies to round up some fellows who could be counted on. Wright's acquittal followed. McGinn was outraged, as he had a right to be. The judge, who had been sent to Nome because of the stench of court corruption, now saw his own work tarnished by a nasty business carried on right under his nose. Both men resolved to convict Richards of contempt and were pleased mightily when they succeeded.[7]

While Richards rallied his forces to appeal his conviction and gained the immediate support of the Justice Department, his attorneys directed a cunning campaign against Wickersham and McGinn. Since attorneys Albert Fink and P. C. Sullivan saw the Richards' adroitness in packing juries as a major element in their conspiracy to fleece Nome's gamblers, they zealously opposed the contempt conviction. Aside from gathering false affidavits and encouraging letters of protest to Washington, Fink addressed his personal interpretation of events to Attorney General Philander Knox. A shrewd fellow, Fink spoke less as Richards's attorney than as a conscientious member of Nome's bar, an officer of the court, keen to give Knox the benefit of his inside knowledge. Fink praised Wickersham's efficiency and integrity. Poor Wickersham, Fink explained, lost his head because of an ancient bias against Richards. Fink, a friend of both men, had tried to patch up their quarrel, which dated from animosity over political differences in Washington state before they came to Alaska.

The Wright acquittal should not have been attributed to jury fixing, Fink confided. While Post Office funds were missing, Wright did not benefit. "Like many others appointed to Alaska, Wright was hopelessly incompetent."[8] He was not dishonest but could not handle the job. It was McGinn's carelessness that determined the acquittal. McGinn submitted evidence of cash shortages that showed mathematical errors on their face. Who could convict on such evidence? McGinn, desperate to cover his own poor preparation, persuaded Wickersham that the jury had been fixed and also encouraged him to use federal funds allotted for crime suppression to hire detectives for the investigation of the jury.

Similar letters were orchestrated by Fink from the mayor, clergymen, and other lawyers, who added fresh details, such as McGinn's intoxication in court. The strategy should not have worked, but it did. From the record we cannot know whether Knox was moved by his distrust of Wickersham, by his fear of Richards' supporters, or for other reasons, but he did intervene to question the decision of a judge of proven honesty and ability on the word of biased parties.

Fink's cleverest explanation may have been that concerning the Washington-state feud between Richards and Wickersham. Everyone in politics understood how this sort of thing could happen, and, often enough new Alaskans encountered old friends or foes from the outside. Like the fabricated affidavits, this charge was made a part of the appeal record and was not contested by the government attorneys. But the Justice Department should have noticed that there was something phony about the allegation. Why would Richards pass up a jury trial and ask that Wickersham decide all the issues if he feared his bias? Wickersham insisted that he first met Richards in Nome in August 1901. "That whole matter," as Wickersham explained in 1904, "is a figment of his attorney's brain and wholly for the purpose of a defense against a just verdict." While Wickersham's indignation at charges of bias are understandable, Richards was not actually a stranger to him.[9]

Even if Wickersham had not met Richards earlier, he had experienced some anxiety through Richards while waiting for his judicial appointment. Richards, who then wanted the collector-of-customs office in Alaska, threatened to air Wickersham's prosecution for seduction in Tacoma (see Chapter 19) unless he received his appointment before Wickersham received his. Richards used the same threats against E. C. Bellows, a friend of Wickersham's, who was also in the running for the collector's position. Bellows offered to withdraw himself from consideration, but Wickersham said, "No. Let them file anything they please but none of my friends should suffer for it (Wickersham diary, February 27, 1900). Eventually Bellows was appointed consul general in Japan. With this background it is not surprising that Wickersham was alert to any missteps Richards might make. The judge was not a forgiving man.

Richards' easy manner and persuasiveness helped him fool several Justice Department examiners, particularly as they sensed that he had friends in high places. In 1903 agents Stanley W. Finch and Alvin M. McNish found Judge Alfred Moore, who had replaced Wickersham at Nome, incompetent, and they concluded that the belief which Judge Moore shared in Richards' unfitness derived from an unreasonable reliance on McGinn. They did find U.S. Attorney Melvin Grigsby "incompetent and unqualified," but Richards won their hearts. Oh, the marshal was not perfect; he could do a better job handling the jail accounts, but certainly he had not rigged juries or done anything else unlawful. "Richards is well qualified but a politician and has enemies. He stands well with the businessmen and better class."[10] Such reports in the face of persistent accusations against Richards finally irritated President Roosevelt to the point of intervening and demanding of the attorney general that he take a closer look at the charges.

Frank Richards' survival in office after his 1902 conviction of contempt was inexplicable. His friends in D.C. must have had powerful influence in the Department of Justice. Of course, his cause was aided when the circuit court reversed his conviction, yet, as Judge Wickersham made clear, the reversal was less a vindication than another example of Richards' corruption and the Justice Department's willingness to go along with it.

Governor Brady was one of the Alaskans who marveled that Richards was still Nome's marshal in May 1903. Writing to the secretary of the interior, he wondered how "people were supposed to feel their lives and property were safeguarded" with a jury tamperer as marshal and an absentee district attorney. "It seems to me that since Nome was started that there has been some evil and sinister influence in the background working against its best interests."[11] Brady, although an ordained minister, was not thinking of the devil's influence but of certain U.S. senators and those for whom they acted.

Judge Wickersham still saw Richards as a disgrace to law enforcers and his tenacity in office as an infamous example of corruption in Washington—as well as a personal affront. Wickersham had made his views clear earlier but got another chance in February 1904 when he submitted a review of events to the attorney general. Whether it was requested or he volunteered is not clear. Wickersham was having a very hard time holding on to his job since friends of the spoilers and Richards in the U.S. Senate managed each year to refuse approval of his appointment; he remained in office only because the president granted him a temporary appointment each year.

Wickersham's review of the Richards case did not spare the Department of Justice. He pointed out that Justice had virtually overruled Richards' conviction within seventeen days of the court's decision by ordering Judge Alfred Moore to review the case, and then it permitted Grigsby to fire McGinn for defending Richards' con-

viction before Judge Moore. "For all practical purposes," the Department of Justice had "reversed the judgment of the trial court,
condemned its action, and held the prosecuting officer for dismissal
if requested by his superior."[12]

Wickersham saw nothing mysterious about Grigsby's absence
from Nome in 1902–1903. Two special examiners were in Nome to
investigate Richards, and there were rumors that they would recommend his dismissal, so Richards and his friends hired Grigsby to
defend him in Washington.

The Justice Department was also responsible for the circuit
court's reversal of Richards' conviction. Special examiners Mountjoy
and Taylor learned during their 1902 investigation of Richards that
three affidavits included in Richards' appeal record were perjured
statements purchased for $150 each. Since the district attorney
made no effort to contest Richards' appeal once Washington made
its sympathies obvious, the circuit court assumed the false affidavits to be true. If a government attorney had objected to the affidavits, the circuit court would not have reversed the district court.
It was not until May 11, 1903, that Justice ordered the U.S. attorney in San Francisco to defend against Richards' appeal. It was
too late then to offset the condemnation of Wickersham by Justice
and the charges against him in false affidavits.

It was the investigation of William A. Day in 1904 that finally led
to Richards' removal in November. Day observed "that the prevalence of jury bribery and subordination of perjury has produced a
feeling of insecurity as to property titles and general dishonesty in
the administration of justice which constitutes one of the chief
causes of the disturbed conditions that have so long prevailed in the
2nd district." It was time to turn "a new and more promising leaf in
the affairs of Nome . . . to restore that community to a normal and
sane condition."[13]

Day knew that his report would be attacked savagely by Richards'
friends, but there was ample evidence of Richards' unfitness for
office: "If only one half of what attorneys and parties say about
Richards' office is true it will be impossible to rely on the fairness of
any jury verdict regardless of the evidence." Because of the situation, claim jumping occurred all the time: "Possession is nine points
of the law in Nome mining . . . most property was tied up in litiga-

tion."[14] Day recognized that the animosity between Richards and Moore also affected the orderly course of justice. He found Moore incompetent and recommended his removal.

Upon his removal, Richards complained that "it was unjust and un-american to remove me without a chance to answer charges," but the attorney general figured he had heard enough about Richards and Nome, a town where court and law-enforcement scandals set a standard beyond parallel in American frontier history.[15]

The attorney general sent Melvin Grigsby to replace corrupt U.S. Attorney Joseph Wood, who was convicted with the other spoilers. Colonel Grigsby owed his title and his 1902 appointment to Spanish-American War service with Teddy Roosevelt's Rough Riders, although his unit did not actually see action. For Alaskans longing for an honest, efficient law-enforcement system, the change from Wood to Grigsby amounted to the substitution of a free-lance buccaneer for a corporate one. The colonel must have resolved before he hit the beach at Nome that his appointment would pay off in supplementary benefits because he wasted no time shaking the money tree when he arrived.

Among the curiosities of Justice Department rules in those days was one allowing district attorneys to accept private clients. A federal prosecutor was supposed to work full time for the government and avoid any cases that involved a conflict with official duties, yet within these limitations he could moonlight at the bar. Grigsby was aggressive, greedy, and well connected for wrestling Seward Peninsula gold from those who mined it. But his self-confidence and stupidity threw up imposing obstacles to what should have been an easy fortune. The colonel's blatant initial moves and his reluctance to winter over in Nome caused him to disobey a direct order from his chief in Washington. His days were numbered with such a start, yet it is wonderful how many days he survived in office despite his awkwardness.

Only a few insiders knew about the deal the colonel made with the Pioneer Mining Company soon after he took over his office in the courthouse. Pioneer's gold production was exceeded only by that of the Wild Goose Company among the region's operators. Jafet Lindeberg, L. H. French, and the Chilberg brothers faced serious personal and business legal problems, including the threatened federal prosecution of Lindeberg for ejecting McKenzie's minions from a number of claims with armed force. This or other federal prosecutions might force a closing by court order or otherwise cost the partners plenty in lost production or fines. They had an ample legal staff, but there was only one U.S. Attorney. They recognized the glint in the colonel's eye as the prosecutor confessed to being a poor man who needed to practice on the side. Swiftly the men reached an agreement: Pioneer would retain Grigsby at ten thousand dollars per annum. Specific tasks were not discussed. It was understood that Grigsby could look after his leading client in ways that need never be recorded.[16]

Once he had closed this lucrative deal and perhaps other similar ones, the colonel felt restless. If he could winter in Washington, D.C., he could lobby for his clients, and perhaps he could protect his job from critics more effectively there than he could in Nome. All the talk he had heard about the approaching close of navigation on the Bering Sea, plus the obvious preparations for winter he saw going on about town, excited his desires for livelier places. "Let George do it!" he cried, quietly buying a ticket on the last steamer for the outside. George would do it because he was the colonel's son and an assistant U.S. attorney. One Grigsby is enough to handle Nome during the slack season, Melvin probably rationalized as he appointed George acting U.S. attorney.

The press reported unkindly on the colonel's desertion, or at least that element of the press that had customarily viewed the machinations of Noyes, Wood, and Marshal Richards with dread and loathing. Justice Department officials were angry when Grigsby appeared in D.C. to explain that he had to take leave even though his request for it had been rejected. Facing the options of removing Grigsby, forcing him to return on the winter overland route, or tolerating his nine-month absence to give him another chance to make good, the attorney general chose the last-named course. Tolerance probably spared the attorney general the reproaches of those who had gained Grigsby his appointment.

Once back in Nome to resume his duties, Melvin Grigsby crowned his reputation for nepotism, absenteeism, and favoritism with Nome residents by asking the court to review the conviction of Marshal Richards. Most court watchers enjoyed the spectacle of two federal prosecutors, John McGinn and his chief, Grigsby, taking opposing sides in court. McGinn was asked by Judge Moore, who was appointed to the Nome district court in 1902, to defend Judge Wickersham's conviction of Richards and, as McGinn had been the prosecutor, he did so effectively. Judge Moore dismissed Grigsby's petition for a rehearing, saying the matter was one for review by the circuit court. But Grigsby was not acting frivolously in opposing Richards' contempt conviction; he was acting with the express orders of the attorney general, and when he complained to the attorney general that McGinn had opposed him, he was told that he could fire McGinn if he desired. And he did.

Among those who were urging Grigsby's removal in 1902–1903 was John Clum, a special agent for the Post Office. Clum's adventures on the frontier had included founding the *Tombstone Epitaph* in 1880 and the negotiation of the surrender of Geronimo and his Apaches to the army. It was Clum's responsibility to check on mail service in Alaska, and he spent enough time in Nome to become an expert on law-enforcement scandals. His interest in Grigsby and Richards ran deep because the jury-fixing charges against the marshal were incidental to the prosecution of Postmaster Joseph Wright.

President Teddy Roosevelt had asked Clum to report to him directly on the Nome scandals. The president had heard charges and countercharges from federal officials and their friends and longed to settle the town's murky, disgraceful wrangling.

In February 1902, Clum accurately described "one of the great outrages at Nome last season. . . . One of Col. Grigsby's first official acts was to oppose Richards' contempt conviction proceedings by a vigorous speech in open court whereas it was his duty to defend them or at least to remain silent."[17] Of course, Clum did not realize that the scandal ran higher than he imagined because Grigsby's orders had come from someone at or near the top level of the Justice Department who wanted to save Richards by overturning Wickersham's conviction of him.

Clum's letter made clear to the president that the Wright trial, the jury fixing, and attempts by Grigsby and Richards to reverse Richards' conviction were related issues that kept the pot of discord bubbling in Nome and showed the essential unfitness of both officials. As postal inspector, Clum knew that Wright had been guilty "on evidence of records in his office and his own confessions." It was obvious that Wright would have been convicted if Richards had not fixed the jury; that Richards had been rightly convicted; and that Grigsby's and Richards' challenge to Judge Wickersham's decision should be answered by firing them both.

To support further his opinion of Richards, Clum told Roosevelt about the marshal's persecution of Deputy Marshal Adam Johnson, who had dared to testify honestly at Richards' trial. Richards fired Johnson after advising his many creditors to attach his final salary payment. Then Richards sent Mike Sullivan, a local tough who performed unsavory unofficial chores for the marshal, to offer Johnson his job back in return for Johnson's reneging on his court testimony. Since Johnson refused to be intimidated or purchased, Richards revealed his capacity for imaginative, venomous retribution. Johnson's wife, a handsome, frivolous woman to whom he was devoted, had responded to her husband's troubles by drinking and playing around with a Revenue Marine officer at the Golden Gate Hotel gambling saloon. Johnson ordered his mother-in-law to bring his wife home and gave her a little push. Richards, a fellow who played hard ball, had Johnson arrested for assault. Later he told the revelers at the Golden Gate that Johnson "has just beaten two women and thrown them out in the mud. He broke his wife's arm and ought to be hung."

In jail Johnson was lodged in the secure cell usually reserved for murderers and was denied a blanket, food, and water. Next morning, Mike Sullivan arrived, perhaps to present his deal again with the aid of some muscle, but Johnson's friends followed Sullivan, offered bail, and refused to leave the jail until Johnson was released.

At trial the defense showed that Johnson did not touch his wife and barely touched his mother-in-law. George Grigsby "prosecuted bitterly" but failed to get a conviction except on the minor charge of disorderly conduct because Johnson's wife and mother-in-law refused to go along with the contrived assault story.

Clum considered the episode a significant one in highlighting the conduct of the marshal and U.S. attorney's office. He reported it to special agents of the Justice Department who investigated Nome conditions in 1902, but they did not seem too impressed. "Thirty years on the frontier showed me the need for protection against this kind of persecution," Clum told the president, and he had only seen one or two other examples as atrocious as the Johnson incident.

President Roosevelt referred Clum's report to the attorney general, but no action was taken against either Grigsby or Richards at the time. Meanwhile, several special investigators for the Justice Department had submitted conflicting reports on the Nome officers. In February 1903, Roosevelt asked Cabell Whitehead, a friend who had Nome business interests, to give his opinion. Whitehead's letter was as lucid as Clum's and clearly identified the culprits.

Don't blame the unusual character of Nome's people for the fresh scandals there each season, cautioned Whitehead, because all the troubles are "actually due to the character of men in responsible positions." Richards still held office despite his cheating on expenses and "notorious tampering with juries," and Colonel Grigsby, his "warm defender," had aroused suspicion since the day he arrived. "One miner told me that nine friends of Grigsby advised him to hire Grigsby when he had filed a law suit—or he would lose the case because Grigsby is a friend of the president and of the court." [18]

Roosevelt's secretary sent Whitehead's letter to the attorney general, complaining that none of the examiners' reports had raised any questions about Grigsby's conduct except for his unauthorized absence in 1902–1903. Roosevelt did not believe that the charges against Richards had been "satisfactorily explained," either. "The president is not satisfied with the matter and would like a full report from your department in view of Whitehead's letter." [19]

Attorney General Knox got Roosevelt's message. The president was angry, and the whitewash of Richards and Grigsby had better end. Once more an examiner was dispatched to Nome, and this time he was either better directed or better chosen for his ability to discern the cause of turbulence.

In fall 1903, Grigsby was instructed to travel to D.C. to defend himself. He appeared at a hearing before the president. In March 1904 the attorney general removed him from office, charging that he had been derelict in his duties by his 1902–1903 absence from Nome.

Grigsby protested his removal to the president, arguing foolishly

that his lawyers had been prepared to defend the bribery charges
alleged by the Pioneer Mining Company but had not been prepared, for lack of notice, to answer the old complaint about his unauthorized leave. Grigsby thought the treatment unfair because his
pay had been docked earlier as punishment for his absence.[20] This
protest was probably just a matter of form. Grigsby was not too
astute, yet he could figure out that the stated grounds for his dismissal were intended to save his face and perhaps that of Justice
Department officials who had defended him beyond the call of
reason.

11. Nome Settles Down?

Be it ever so bumfull, there's no place like Nome. —Egg Island Yellow Journal

EDITOR J. F. A. Strong of the *Nome Nugget* blamed U.S. Attorney John L. McGinn for several of the ugly things that harmed his friends. Besides that, McGinn was a Republican and Strong liked Democrats. Strong had not cared for Judge Wickersham but showed a little caution in attacking the judge while he was in Nome. After Wickersham left the editor had less to fear from his successor and, as McGinn remained in office, Strong treated *Nugget* readers to vituperative attacks on McGinn.

Editor Strong believed in himself and figured he knew more about the north and its people than most others did. He had edited a paper at Skagway in 1897 and was a leader among the citizens who tried to overturn the wicked rule of Soapy Smith. He started a paper at Dawson in 1898, then moved his press to Nome in 1899 to publish its first paper. Everywhere he boosted the community's prospects and kept his subscribers alert with forceful prose and lively feuds. Later he followed other gold rushes or related opportunities to Katalla, Iditarod, and Juneau. In 1913, President Woodrow Wilson wanted a good Democrat as governor of Alaska and rewarded Strong. Strong proved to be a capable governor, although he was fired when his Canadian birth was discovered. He had claimed Kentucky birth falsely and had not been naturalized.

He was also a bigamist, having not divorced his Canadian wife before remarrying.

John L. McGinn came to Nome in 1900 looking for gold, and did in fact mine for a few months before receiving an appointment as assistant U.S. attorney in October 1900. In July 1901 he became Nome's U.S. attorney until Melvin Grigsby got the top job. Then he stayed on as an assistant. He resigned in January 1903, was appointed acting U.S. attorney by Judge Moore when Moore removed George Grigsby, and was fired shortly after Melvin Grigsby returned. McGinn was from Portland, Oregon, and saw service in the Philippines during the Spanish-American War. In 1905 he moved to Fairbanks, where he had a good practice and made enough money to invest in oil and enjoy winters in the balmier climes of San Mateo, California.

It was McGinn's prosecution of Marshal Frank Richards for jury fixing that enraged Strong against him. Strong and Richards were cronies, and the editor had been accustomed to defending Richards and, before their disgrace, even Judge Noyes and Alexander McKenzie. Will Steel, editor of the *Nome News,* opposed Strong on most issues and accused Strong of switching from support of Wickersham and McGinn to becoming their implacable enemy after his good friend Richards was convicted: "It was a spectacle to strike men blind to see this great, lumbering buffoon toady to and beslobber a man who has shown himself to be an upright judge." The *New's* praise of McGinn, Steel said, "rambles in the feeble brain of the antiquated editor of our semi-weekly competitor."[1]

Strong responded in kind to Steel and opened up on McGinn in prose and poetry, including the savage verses of "A Gambler's Soliloquy":

> *Of all speculations the market holds forth,*
> *The best I know for a lover of self, is to buy*
> *Mc . . . n up at the price he is worth,*
> *And then sell him at which he sets on himself.*[2]

Subsequently, Strong charged that "Mr. McGinn seems to be of that stripe of prosecuting attorney that would, without scruple, send an innocent man to the gallows merely for the sake of making a record."[3]

Strong did not leave McGinn alone when the lawyer left the U.S. attorney's office. The *Nugget* put its own interpretation on McGinn's resignation: "He disgraced the office which he unworthily filled, and at the twelfth hour he resigned well knowing that it was the most prudent course for him to pursue."[4] It was true that McGinn resigned under pressure, but his only disgrace was excessive drinking.

By this time McGinn, a sharp lawyer and as pugnacious a man as Strong, had had enough. He sued Strong for libel, asking fifty thousand dollars on seven counts for statements published in the newspaper between August 1902 and February 1903. The *Nugget* reported on the suit but had "space for the publication of but one of McGinn's 'causes' for action, and it may be taken as a fair sample of all others." Strong reprinted "A Gambler's Soliloquy," being rather proud of his poetry, and remarked, "For publishing the following he only wants $5,000."[5]

Spectators jammed the courtroom in anticipation of sparkling forensic displays when the libel suit was heard. McGinn performed to everyone's expectations in a trial described by the *News* as "one of the most notable ever heard in Nome." The *News* hoped for McGinn's victory as it would destroy a rival paper and a personal enemy. Of McGinn's summation before the jury the *News* declared: "Not within the history of the bar at Nome has there been a more eloquent or forceful speech." It was certainly lengthy. McGinn went on from court opening to late afternoon with only a lunch break. "During the long argument not once did the jurors manifest any signs of weariness or impatience and the audience were on the verge of breaking into loud applause a number of times."[6]

McGinn stressed the relationship between his successful prosecution of Richards for jury fixing and Strong's furious attacks on him. Strong, Richards, and their friends had conspired to ruin him. "Then it was that the cry went forth that McGinn must be ruined—visit his haunts, search Nome, search Council City, go over the whole district with a fine toothed comb . . . we must annihilate him so that he won't annihilate us."

Marshal Richards and his hirelings watched McGinn diligently. Every drink he took in a saloon was noted; each occasion on which he laid a dollar on the roulette wheel was recorded. "All this was done simply because I had brought suit against them." Richards had a perfectly destructive hatchet man in editor Strong: "The defendant has circulated many slanders and malicious falsehoods concerning me and has ever used the weapon of a fool since the foundation of the world." McGinn knew that libel was hard to establish and depended upon an emotional appeal to bridge the gap that was always hard to span: showing that the defendant intended to do harm. "The heart of the libeler is more base and low than the heart of the assassin or the heart of the man who commits midnight arson." How could a lawyer survive if he were robbed of his most precious possession, his reputation? "Take away the reputation of a lawyer and what is there left?" One who would circulate "these filthy libels and slanders is not worthy the attention given to a mangy malemute dog . . . the editor of the character of the defendant is ever ready to throw the stink pots of the scavenger at the objects of his hatred."[7]

In his defense Strong testified with coolness, strength, and conviction and did not back away from any of his statements against McGinn. He believed firmly that McGinn was capable of judicial murder: "I believe these things are true . . . you got drunk . . . you asked members of the jury if they were A B's [Arctic Brotherhood members] . . . you formed combinations to hold up the gamblers of the community . . . therefore I drew the conclusion that you are the kind of man who would send innocent men to the gallows."[8]

Jurors initially voted ten to two in favor of giving McGinn five thousand dollars in damages, but the debate went on until the amount of damages went down to one hundred dollars and one or two jurors still favored Strong. Finally the jury said it could not agree and was discharged. Strong had won.

When the chief of police kills his deputy on the street, it is a reflection on the community's cultural level. Of course the town was Nome, where exaggerations in law enforcement compared with the high level of infamy reached by crooks. But in 1903 respectable folks yearned to put the wicked, lawless days behind them and boast of schools, churches, public works, prosperity, and security. So they were a little annoyed at Chief John J. Jolley's shooting of Officer Sam James and most reluctant to view the sordid affair as a romance.

John L. McGinn, much to the displeasure of acting U.S. Attorney George Grigsby, presented evidence against Jolley to the grand jury. McGinn was sure that Grigsby wanted to protect Jolley, a friend of U.S. Marshal Frank Richards. Another witness was S. H. Stevens, editor of the *Nome Gold Digger* and deadly foe of the Richards faction, who explained that the shooting was a case of thieves falling out. "Certain classes" in Nome paid protection money to Jolley and James to avoid prosecution.[9] James had either wanted a larger share of the graft or had threatened to expose his chief, hence his execution.

Not so, not so, cried Chief Jolley. The shooting was the culmination of an unfortunate chain of events. It had all started when Miss Lottie, a young woman of the demimonde, summoned Jolley to visit her at her lodgings. Miss Lottie demanded seventy-five dollars for services performed for Officer James.

"I says to her, 'why, my dear lady, I cannot help that.'"[10]
"'Well,' she says, 'I can send him to McNeil Island, and I will if he don't pay me this $75.'
"I says, 'why do you want to send this man to McNeil Island? What has he done?'"
Lottie told of many crimes. James had stolen coal from the Northern Commercial Company, coal oil from the city, and pistols from someone.
"I says, 'That's kind of funny you should keep tabs on him like that.' She flew at me then. I ought to pay $75. I told her to go and do her best. I goes to James' room immediately. I says, 'James, this woman Lottie sent for me this morning and accuses you of stealing coal'. . . . I says, 'God knows what you haven't stolen.' I says, 'James, I am going to lay you off and investigate these charges. . . . Jim, you have been drinking a good deal lately, you have been gambling a good deal lately and I am afraid you have been neglecting your duty as a policeman.'"

The following day, Jolley heard that Lottie had spent the night in James's room, and the chief upbraided him again for drinking and staying with a woman who put a charge on him: "You are going to the dogs as fast as you can."

A day or two later, James met Jolley on the street and told him there was nothing to worry about as Lottie had not reported James to Deputy Marshal Joe Warren as she had threatened to do. "You better sober up," Jolley advised James. "I believe that woman." Later that week, James came to Jolley's house and threatened to kill him unless he got his job back. "He called me a horse thief and a SOB. He was drunk," Jolley said. Subsequently, James confronted Jolley on Front Street and in the saloons, invariably mouthing drunken threats despite the chief's kindly words on each occasion.

The reckoning came on a snowy, windy afternoon as James stopped Jolley in front of the Hunter Saloon, poking a derringer in his ribs and shouting, "I'm going to blow your belly out now." The forbearing chief edged away to talk to someone else across the street, keeping a wary eye on James. Then, from ten feet away, James took purposeful aim with his derringer. Jolley drew his pistol and shot him, then stood over the fallen man, pumping in a few more shots to make sure he stayed down. Spectators flocked to the scene from saloons and offices along Front Street. Jolley asked them to observe that James's derringer lay on the street, partly covered by his hat. Jolley turned himself in to the marshal and a week later had the grace to resign.

In June the former chief stood trial. Lottie Wilson, the dead man's girl friend, confirmed Jolley's story in all particulars. Jurors acquitted Jolley, but he did not get his job back. Nome's reputation was shaky enough without having police shootouts on Front Street.

Let Tombstone, Arizona, advertise the O.K. Corral affair if that is what it wanted to be known by, but the people of Nome craved respectability.

The grand jury was not happy with Jolley's acquittal, so it reviewed the trial. The majority of jurors censured George Grigsby's handling of the case as acting U.S. attorney. Grigsby's work was a "repetition of similar efforts that have been made in the past to shield criminal offenders who were able to render pecuniary or political services to a ring of as infamous plotters and plunderers as ever reigned in the darkest days of iniquity upon these bleak and barren shores."[11] This fine rhetoric and Judge Moore's antagonism led to George Grigsby's removal by the judge, but he lived on to become territorial attorney general (1916–1919), congressional delegate (1919–1920) and the grand old man of Alaska's bar in Ketchikan, Juneau, and Anchorage before retiring in 1959.

By the third year of its existence, Nome was a very well-established community glittering with some of the attractions that encouraged boosters to call the place "the Paris of the North." But community stability did not mean that its residents had become complacent, whether they had made any money or not. Years yet would pass before Alaskans heard rumors of a new gold discovery with equanimity. Most Alaskans had located there in response to news of gold discoveries and were not inclined to miss out on bonanzas. If information concerning a new prospect appeared sound, many individuals were willing to take the trail for an investigation or to back others adventurous enough to do so.

So it was that the arrival of George W. Duncan and Charles R. Griggs caused excitement at Nome in January 1903. Both men were experienced prospectors known to others in town. They looked as if they had been traveling for a long time with considerable hardship yet were obviously bursting with good news that they did not wish to indulge in any detail. Soon everyone in town heard that the prospectors had tried to record claims at the court clerk's office. Clerk George V. Borchsenius refused to record their claims because the men refused to divulge the location of their ground. Duncan grew indignant and insolent: "What a hell of a note that after a year or more of hardships in prospecting a new country, and after having traveled 600–800 miles to the clerk's office, we're told we can't record."

A day or two later the prospectors appeared at the clerk's office again, this time in company with an attorney. Once more the clerk explained the situation, but the men seemed determined to guard their secret at all costs. Soon Duncan and Griggs went to the clerk again with another attorney. Borchsenius and the attorney persuaded the miners to identify their location within a radius of one hundred miles. Still this was not good enough because the location might have been in either one or another of two or three different designated recording districts. Again an impasse resulted. Unless we know the district of your "sacred creek," Borchsenius told them, you may not record claims. Later the prospectors came back with District Judge Alfred S. Moore. Duncan's anxiety impressed the clerk: "It would not be easy to forget," he recalled later, "the appeals Duncan made for something to be done to save them the property which cost them so dearly." Judge Moore was impressed too and broke the deadlock by creating a new district that embraced the prospectors' sixty-four locations on Midas Creek, a tributary of the Koyukuk River. "There was no suppression of anything in forming the new district," and swiftly all Nome knew that wonderful riches could be found on Midas Creek. No one knew where Midas Creek was, but there were those who meant to find it and locate claims near those of Duncan and Griggs.[12] The lucky prospectors may have been reluctant to tell the location of their finds until legal requirements made it necessary, but they had been willing to show impressively large nuggets around town.

A few Nome men grew hot enough to try a winter trip into the distant Koyukuk country in hope of finding Midas Creek and beating others who would wait for the spring breakup. Duncan and Griggs felt too secure to concern themselves with such folly. They announced that they were going outside for the winter, presumably over the long trail up the Yukon River to Whitehorse and down to Skagway since Bering Sea navigation long had since closed for the season. Before they returned in June on one of the first ships of the season, the unfortunate prospectors who had tried to find Midas during the winter without guidance had long since given up.

On their return Duncan and Griggs announced the formation of the Treasure and Midas Creeks Gold Mining Association of Alaska, organized and incorporated in Oregon. Company assets included four claims of twenty acres each. Investors could buy 174 to 240 shares to become stockholders. Each share represented twenty square feet of ground, the same ground that had yielded $449.50 in gold per cubic yard to the original discoverers.

Some people in Nome remained skeptical. The *Nugget* even published a lampoon purporting to be an interview with a company man, Mr. Othmer, who "could never think of Midas without associating it with the figure of $300,000,000." Mr. Othmer assured readers that such an amount of money was enough "to free Ireland or to convert the United States to socialism," but it was not clear that he would divert his profits to either cause.[13]

The company prepared to send a party of investors into the field, but others who did not buy stock left earlier, seeking Midas about two hundred miles above the mouth of the Koyukuk. According to persistent rumor, the golden creek could be found at that point. Other prospectors waited until Duncan and Griggs left Nome on a small motorboat, the *Louise,* then tried to follow the *Louise* or the *Research,* which carried company stockholders, in boats of their own. The stampede was on, and soon there were no boats worthy of taking to sea to be found in Nome or its vicinity.

When company stockholders, a group of fifty men including the commissioner for the new district, F. T. Merritt, reached St. Michael, they were disappointed when Duncan and Griggs did not rendezvous with them as planned. They cursed their lost leaders for delaying them, or worse, but pushed on up the Yukon to the mouth of the Koyukuk, then turned up the Koyukuk. Their map showed the Midas as a tributary of the Hogikakat River, so they intended to search for Midas, although with deepening suspicion of treachery.

Back in Nome, folks heard some news of Duncan and Griggs, the "Midas Prophets." Reportedly they had landed forty miles up the Koyukuk River. It disturbed those who still believed in them to hear that the prospectors carried only eighty dollars' worth of food, enough to get them to a ship for the outside but hardly enough for men planning to settle in for a season of mining. Soon opinion in

Nome crystallized: Duncan and Griggs were great rogues who by this time were outside with their fraudulently acquired gains from shareholders. Men who did not invest because they had lacked means assured others who passed up the opportunity that they had known all the time that the promoters were fakes.

It turned out that Duncan and Griggs had voyaged to the Koyukuk to confuse their pursuers. Once there they found the riverboat they had concealed on their original journey and drifted back down to the Yukon. From concealment on the bank they watched the *Research* enter the Koyukuk, then they turned down the Yukon for St. Michael and transport to the outside.

Other rumors kept Nome gossips happy for weeks. Someone said the Midas fakers had turned up in Fort Yukon, boasting of their fifty thousand dollar swindle. Estimates of their take varied, but fifty thousand dollars was the amount heard most frequently. Of this, thirty thousand dollars was said to have been raised outside; the rest came from Nome investors.

Midas argonauts on the *Research* and others following in their wake had a hard time after leaving the boat to tramp the rough, swampy ground. Game was scarce; mosquitoes and gnats wanted to eat them alive; they had to kill some of their horses for food. In September they abandoned the search begun in July and returned to Nome, plotting revenge.

The district attorney ordered a grand-jury investigation that produced some information. Apparently the Midas Prophets bought the fifteen hundred dollars' worth of gold nuggets and dust they showed in Nome from a miner in Bettles. They had done a little digging at the mouth of Koyukuk River without finding anything. From the outset the whole scheme had been a deliberate swindle. Nome's newspapers encouraged the grand jury to reach a sensible decision: "If ever men deserved punishment for crime committed, these two are they."[14] Editor J. F. A. Strong had not been an investor, but he shared the feeling of the community that vengeance must be swift in cases like the Midas swindle.

Feeling ran high in Nome against prominent men who had seemed to favor the Midas scam. Accusations against Judge Moore and Court Clerk George Borchsenius were sent to the attorney general. Both court officials denied any role beyond that of carrying out their recording duties. Borchsenius assured Washington that all dealings had been aboveboard. The court had not kept its dealings with the Prophets secret, although the appointment of a district commissioner was withheld until the Prophets made it clear that they were returning to their claims on their return to Nome in June. "The parties complaining of suppressions of facts," Borchsenius told the attorney general, "had published to the world much more than I ever knew about the matters." Charges that court officers had an interest in Midas were indignantly denied.[15]

Finally, in October, Nome's newspapers carried the headline everyone was hoping for: "DUNCAN AND GRIGGS PICKED UP IN PORTLAND."[16] The grand jury issued indictments immediately, and Deputy Marshal Al Cody left for Portland with arrest warrants. Navigation closed before Cody could return, but Griggs was lodged safely in the Portland jail. Meanwhile Duncan disappeared.

Cody returned Griggs for trial in July 1905 after wasting the winter looking for Duncan. Griggs's defense lawyers asked for a change of venue. It did not seem possible to get a fair trial in Nome for such a notorious case. The court was not inclined to grant venue changes in Alaska even when the defense's contention had merit, as in this case. It was obvious to the Justice Department that a venue change would be granted automatically in other jurisdictions and the cause of strict justice would gain by a transfer, but Alaska was different. Washington was painfully aware of how much the case had cost already in keeping Cody outside, transporting Griggs and witnesses, and in other incidentals, and it did not encourage a transfer certain to make expenses even higher. Editor Strong was pleased when the court refused the defense request: "So Mr. Griggs will have justice meted out to him in Nome—as it should be met."[17]

The prosecution allowed jurors to hear from fifteen witnesses. Griggs remained tight lipped on the matter of where the money had gone. People hoped that Duncan had cheated Griggs and that either someone else would rob Duncan or that he might be found. Griggs got five years. Duncan was never found.

The conviction of George Allen for robbery in February 1901 startled people in Nome and outside. Young Allen, charged with

Tom Dolan and George Hawkins, was the son of eminent Seattle attorney and former United States Senator John P. Allen. Young Allen had an alibi. He could not have held up R. J. Embleton at 2 A.M. because at that very hour he had sat down for dinner at the Butler Restaurant. With him were three friends. Wilson Mizner was one. But perhaps Wilson Mizner's reputation for veracity did not convince jurors. He was a bon vivant, a gambler, entertainer, con artist, famed raconteur, and perhaps the wittiest man of the thousands of stampeders to Dawson and Nome. Books were written about him, and he wrote many film scripts in Hollywood. But his 1901 fame in Nome rested more on his princely standing among the town's demimonde for cunning fleecings of innocents who had more money than sense.[18] One other witness was even better known. This worthy was Albert Fink, a trial lawyer of commanding skill, daring, and deviousness, a lawyer whose success in criminal practice would one day excite the interest of a beleaguered Al Capone in Chicago.

If jurors could not credit Wilson Mizner, would they believe the testimony of Albert Fink, a distinguished officer of the court? No, they would not. According to rumors in Nome, Fink busied himself in shakedowns of gamblers, jury fixing, and other nefarious activities. And there is ample evidence that these rumors were true. It must be said to Fink's credit, however, that he contributed more to Nome's daytime culture than the late-carousing Mizner. Fink was an active dog racer and a founder of the All Alaska Sweepstakes, the town's most celebrated sporting event.

Long before the Allen case was resolved, Fink showed enough sportiness to assault editor S. H. Stevens of the *Nome Gold Digger*. Stevens offended Fink by publishing the affidavit of Claudius McBride, an assistant clerk in the district court.[19] Plenty of money would be given McBride, promised Fink, if the clerk would agree to influence Court Clerk George Borchsenius and Judge Alfred Moore in behalf of Fink's client, the Wild Goose Mining Company. McBride told Stevens about the bribe offer. Stevens printed the story. Fink and Stevens fought briefly and were fined twenty dollars for their unseemly behavior. Fink disdained to appear in court.[20]

Even if the Allen trial jurors could not trust the witnesses, they listened to a compelling story. It was an intensely cold night in late December when Embleton, who had been carousing and showing a wad of money in Front Street saloons from 8 P.M. to 2 A.M., encountered three men on a dark street. He was attacked, relieved of his purse, and left unconscious. Fortunately, he was found thirty minutes later and carried to the hospital.

The assailants were identified by L. C. Cherry, a young man who left his bed at 2 A.M. to urinate in the street. This key identification was remarkable. Why would a man dressed only in an undershirt and trousers walk two hundred feet from his building before urinating, a cold process unnecessary to his physical needs but responsible for his getting within sight of the scuffle? And how could he identify men he did not know on a dark, snow-blown street at a distance of thirty to forty feet?

The defense hinted that young Cherry, unemployed, broke, and living in an unheated room, testified falsely when a reward was offered. It was also argued that Embleton had not been attacked at all. He was terribly drunk and fell down, injuring himself. The defense was not permitted to show that Embleton sometimes got so drunk he would stagger out over the Bering Sea ice and pass out. But for timely rescues, he might have died.

The prosecutor presented another bombshell in the testimony of A. S. Palmer, who overheard a conversation in the Grotto Saloon the night of the robbery. Wilson Mizner, Allen, and Hawkins discussed Embleton, who was pouring down drinks at the bar. "He has a roll, and I will take him down the street, and you stick me up," said Mizner.[21] According to the *Nome Chronicle,* this "sensational story fell flat."[22] Perhaps Palmer's credibility was not high among jurors or with the *Chronicle,* but it did not hurt the prosecutor's case, although Mizner was not indicted as a co-conspirator. Allen, Dolan, and Hawkins got fifteen years at McNeil Island.

U.S. Attorney Joseph K. Wood had opposed defense attorney Fink's request for a trial continuance. Fink wanted the court to wait a week for Tom Noyes to return to Nome from the Fairhaven mining area. Noyes would testify that he had given Allen one hundred dollars the morning of December 21 for faro playing. Wood argued that the trial should go on. Mrs. Noyes had told someone that Fink wanted Noyes to tell the story about giving Allen one hundred dollars, but Noyes had not done so and did not want to testify. The judge agreed with Wood and refused to delay the trial in spite of Fink's affidavit from Mrs. Noyes denying that she had said what Wood reported.

The U.S. Circuit Court of Appeals noted that the jurors had heard Wood's remarks, which "were well calculated, if not intended, to cast an imputation, not only upon the defendant, but also upon his counsel. The inference to be drawn therefrom was that both of them had attempted to procure a witness to testify to a falsehood, and that they had each subscribed to an affidavit they knew was untrue."[23] While it was never clear that Noyes's testimony had much relevance to Allen's guilt, the refusal and Wood's remarks placed Allen under suspicion.

Other grounds for reversal were found in the trial judge's allowing Wood to cross-examine Allen on his work, or rather the lack of work, in Alaska from 1897 and on certain unspecified "trouble" he had in Skagway in 1897. Apparently Allen's mother voyaged to Skagway to help him out of some difficulty in 1897. Allen was only seventeen years old at the time. Wood's questions were set up to expose Allen as a saloon loafer and gambler who had never held a job in Alaska. This was true, but it was not pertinent to the robbery and, of course, was highly prejudicial to the defendant. "The questions indicate the purpose for which they were asked as closely as the needle points to the pole," observed the circuit court, "that it was for the purpose of showing that his habits were bad, and that he was a vagrant and a bad man, hanging around gambling resorts, and to secure his conviction upon general principles, independent of the testimony offered as to his guilt or innocence."[24]

With two grounds for reversal the circuit court ignored the many other grounds Fink had appealed upon. The court also made clear its reservations about the substance of the prosecution's case: "The fact of the robbery and identity of the defendant depended alone upon the testimony of one witness, which was, to say the least, highly improbable, and in many respects unreasonable, and of such a peculiar character as to cast suspicion and raise a doubt as to its truth."[25]

A historian must be grateful that the circuit court's judges uttered this dictum on witness Cherry's testimony. It shows that even

comfortably situated San Francisco jurists could imagine themselves in Nome in the dead of winter with the need to urinate.
Would they crawl out of bed in the dark, grope out of an unheated
building undressed, then wander off at some distance to relieve
themselves? Indeed not! Then how could jurors in Nome believe
such a tale? they wondered. But the U.S. attorney's office in Nome
did not take the hint from San Francisco and dismiss its case
against Allen. George was released from McNeil Island in February
1902, but his family had to post bail to avoid a jail cell at Nome. The
prosecutor intended to try Allen again.

Senator Allen asked Attorney General P. C. Knox to dismiss the
case. Such an appeal was a desperate measure. People suspected
political influence in such a case, and Knox would want to avoid
scandalous accusations. But Allen feared for the health of his son,
"a mere school boy," who had already served several months in
jail.[26] And he had a good argument in the Nome court's delay of the
new trial. He had asked for a trial during the 1902 navigation season but had been denied.

Senator Allen reminded Knox of Nome's judicial scandal involving
Judge Arthur Noyes. When Allen had defended his son at trial, his
involvement in Noyes's conviction by the circuit court identified him
as an opponent of the Nome court. It may be, Allen hinted, that the
court's reluctance to schedule the new trial was a measure of vengeance. Senator Allen's appeal was emotional: "I do not want to
hazard even the possibility of death overtaking him before another
year, with this undisposed of charge hanging over him. So far as I
can trace there is no blot on my family name, and I do not want the
cloud of this charge to longer shadow it than I can prevent."[27] But
Knox was not moved to grant relief. The grieving father, distracted
by George's disgrace and further depressed by the suicide of his
daughter, stood in a deeper shadow than his son. A few months
later, long before the case was resolved, the distinguished and
much respected attorney died.

Allen's widow carried on the struggle for a dismissal or early
trial. Despite the petitions of influential friends in Washington,
D.C., to the attorney general and the solicitor general, the case
against George was not dismissed. Allen's attorney could not even
get the trial scheduled before September 7, 1903, despite his plea

that Mrs. Allen, the Seattle attorneys, and some witnesses might be compelled to winter over in Nome if the trial continued into October.

As it turned out, there was plenty of time for everyone to get out of Nome. Jurors acquitted George Allen on September 10, 1903. The costs had been heavy to the Allen family and to the federal government. The case against Dolan, which had been reversed, was dismissed, and Hawkins' attorney petitioned for a new trial on the basis of the Allen and Dolan cases. The Department of Justice had achieved nothing for its tenacious prosecution of the three men.

U.S. Attorney Melvin Grigsby's desperation for evidence caused him embarrassment in one instance, plus a significant outlay in witness fees. While preparing for the retrial in 1903, he heard that W. S. Evans, formerly a Nome jail guard, could testify that Allen admitted the robbery in 1901. Since Evans had moved to Bozeman, Montana, Grigsby asked Evans' friends to contact him. Evans agreed to come to Nome without specifying his evidence beyond saying that the accused man had told him something "in confidence."[28] The expensive witness from Montana shocked Grigsby at trial by saying his use of "in confidence" had been inadvertent. Allen had not said anything to implicate himself in the robbery. Possibly Evans had been anxious to visit friends in Alaska at government expense and therefore took advantage of Grigsby's carelessness.

The Allen case seems curious because of the relative relentlessness of the prosecution, but there may have been more reasons for this than the court record alone reveals. Allen's original prosecutor, U.S. Attorney Joseph Wood, later fired and jailed for his own misconduct in the McKenzie conspiracy, cited his successful prosecution to the attorney general as a grand triumph in 1901. Wood had been frustrated by lying witnesses and jury packing, "through the assistance of one or two dishonest deputy marshals who were then in office and in sympathy with the criminal classes." The district attorney determined to break up this gang of criminals "or else have the town turned over to martial law." Allen's prosecution was an important first test of Wood's resolve, and "the usual number of alibis and character witnesses were on hand to testify, but after a desperate fight we succeeded in exposing the whole gang.

A verdict of guilty in that case broke the ice, and other convictions followed in rapid succession."

After Wood's brilliant work, Nome, in spite of an influx of population and widespread poverty, "became as peaceful as a country town."[29] We can discount the district attorney's little boast, but mark him down as a poor prophet. Trial fixing and jury packing was just in its infancy in Wood's time because Marshal Frank Richards had not yet arrived to refine the art. But Wood's concern in the Allen case can be accepted. Although he lied and cheated prodigiously to help the spoilers loot Nome's gold and to save his own neck, there is no reason to doubt the vigorous, even indignant, prosecution of crooks outside the protection of his own ring or his disdain for others' lying witnesses and dishonest jurors. Thus the Allen case reminds us that there were other crooks in Nome besides those who held federal office or had the protection of federal officers.

One example, a very confusing one, of less-serious crimes that occupied lawmen should be cited for what it tells of the mental states of some gold seekers and their willingness to burden the president with tawdry affairs. Alice Rollins Crane, a woman of talent and temperament, voyaged to Alaska in 1897 to pursue her studies of North American Indians, focusing on folklore and mythology. She had been a serious student of Indians and a member of the Southern California Academy of Sciences. Alice talked a lot, but did not always tell the truth. It appears that gold interested her more than science. She was also keen to make her reputation as a writer.

When she arrived in Dawson in July 1898, she disdained any interest in gold, yet before long she was part owner and manager of a mining company. Dawson newsmen found Alice good copy throughout her stay, praising her on arrival as "a delightful conversationalist" and an able journalist.[30] What particularly pleased the *Klondike Nugget* was her attack on the newspaper's bête noire in 1899, U.S. Consul J. J. McCook.

After Alice had a run-in with McCook, she announced her authorship of a drama, *Official Life in Dawson,* that would feature McCook in unflattering ways. McCook protested in a letter, which she ignored, and in a street encounter McCook accused her of trying to blackmail him. While the charge may have been true, Alice did not admit it and told a reporter that McCook was not only not a gentleman, he was a brute.

Alice went outside during the summer of 1899, showing her usual good rapport with journalists by getting favorable mention in the *Seattle Post-Intelligencer* as an "interesting, bright woman . . . who does not mince any words" in describing U.S. Consul McCook. She also bragged about her "professional pleasure in witnessing Dawson's first hanging"; she was "the only woman in attendance." By October, Alice was back in Dawson, having raised money in California for a mining venture and alleging a commission from the *San Francisco Examiner* to write Klondike stories.[31]

In 1901 she published a book entitled *Smiles and Tears from the Klondyke*. Earlier, before going to the north, she claimed to have published several novels, but *Smiles and Tears* was a compilation that included contributions by William Galpin, Ella Cunningham, and William Ogilvie, and apparently the contributors had not authorized the use of their stories.

William Ogilvie was one of Dawson's most respected men. He was a Canadian government surveyor who eliminated much of the chaos and claim jumping incident to gold stampedes with accurate, timely surveys of the town and mining district. William Galpin was acknowledged by Alice as one of "Dawson's leading businessmen and promoters . . . genial, straight-forward and daring." Later she would call him a foul conspirator, blackmailer, persecutor, and would-be killer.[32]

The story of Alice's change of mind about Galpin and her view of the circumstances was expressed in a 1904 letter to President Teddy Roosevelt, a letter that ranks as a literary classic in the annals of vituperation, complaints against officials, and self-serving cries of outraged innocence. "You may have heard many horrible tales from Alaska," Alice's letter began, "and if you have they are no doubt true, as such a place and such a people as this country consists of was never known before."[33] With this gripping, scandalous lead, the author hoped to catch the president's immediate attention—and probably did.

Alice's story concerned the atrocities of Alaska's lawmen, who abused and robbed her and her husband at Russian Mission and Nome. The outrages occurred after Alice married Count Victor

Morajeski, who told the unlikely story in spring 1903 that his father had died in Poland, leaving him a title and large estates. To gather this wealth, the Morajeskis left Dawson for a voyage down the Yukon, the first leg of a long journey to Europe. They asked Galpin to come along as a tutor and secretary to the count, and that is what caused all their subsequent woes. Thanks to Galpin's treachery, Alice lost her oil paintings, writings, clothes, Indian artifacts, and everything else she owned. Of all these losses the most serious involved her manuscripts, some two hundred pounds of writing. "You being a writer," she told Teddy, "would appreciate that loss to me. It tears my heart out."[34]

Ruffians who claimed to be deputy marshals almost killed her husband, and when she tried to save him, they knocked her down. Since she was pregnant, this and other rude handling, including a sled journey to Nome, permanently ruined her health. The marshal stripped her naked in the presence of Indian women, took her money, and abused her. The U.S. commissioner browbeat the Morajeskis for weeks, then decided he could not try them, so he sent them to Nome. "They could not try us so they tried to kill us." She arrived in Nome "more dead than alive," was jailed, then later removed to the hospital.[35]

Since Nome was a better-established community than Russian Mission, the Morajeskis expected to prevail at law. Galpin brought larceny charges against them in district court, but the grand jury refused to indict. Now the Morajeskis were free, but they demanded that the government arrange to get their possessions back from Russian Mission. The U.S. attorney refused to pay the costs. Eventually, perhaps as a result of Alice's letter to the president, the Morajeskis got the prosecutor to indict Galpin and U.S. Commissioner Duncan McDonnell for larceny and misconduct of office. A Nome jury returned a verdict of not guilty to both charges. In great disgust and dead broke, the Morajeskis took the last 1904 ship for Seattle. Using her old skills, Alice told her story to Seattle newsmen, a bitter denunciation of Alaskan injustice.

The *Nugget's* J. F. A. Strong observed that Seattle newspapers are easily taken in: "Just because someone has a tail to their name they are permitted an undue amount of latitude." The Morajeskis had threatened to sue federal officials, but "to those who know them all such vain vaporings and alleged charges of misconduct appear as the most absurd and veriest rot."[36]

What really happened on the Yukon as the three friends set off to gather Victor Morajeski's supposed fortune? William Galpin, who had been a mining partner with Alice until general dissatisfaction with her operation broke up the company, asked William Ogilvie's advice when the Morajeskis asked him to join them. "Don't go to Eagle or Circle to meet ze Prance and Prancess," Ogilvie said. "This is a trap for you." Ogilvie was at Stewart River when Galpin wrote him, and the Morajeskis had moved from Dawson to Eagle. Ogilvie harbored very strong suspicions of disaster, "maybe a murder by one or the other."[37] He had been present when the couple were courting in Dawson and believed that Alice's only interest was in Morajeski's title and what might be gained from it. There would be a day of reckoning when he began to understand her.

Ogilvie had not denounced Alice for using his stories in *Smiles and Tears,* but he had asked her to stop using his name in promoting the book. She had ignored his request. Ogilvie considered her illiterate; her literary pretensions were wholly fraudulent. Now she would use Morajeski's name "to sell her writings that she has stolen from others, as you and I know."[38] Poor Galpin did not heed his friend's advice. Possibly bedazzled by promises made him by the count or hopeful of getting money Alice owed him, he joined the couple in Eagle and was given the job of buying a river scow and provisions for a fine cruise down to St. Michael.

By the time the travelers got to Rampart, Alice and Galpin were at war. "I will murder you tonight and go behind the bars at Rampart for it, and I call you, Count, to witness what I say," she allegedly told Galpin. But instead of murdering Galpin, she left the boat, slept overnight ashore, then tried to incite the bemused Rampart folks against both men, screaming: "These men want to rob me. One is an Englishman and one is a dirty Polish Jew."[39] The men calmed her down for a time, but the next morning she fired a pistol at Galpin. However, because the count had removed the powder from the cartridge, no harm was done.

Apparently the two men had reached some accord concerning Alice's bizarre behavior, although the count told Galpin that earlier

he had believed all that Alice had accused him of and had been ready to kill him. Once Alice figured out that she had lost the count's sympathy, she had tried to rouse Rampart against him. When that failed, she jumped overboard and the men had to haul her back.

We don't know how long this and other distractions took or when the voyage began, but they found themselves at Russian Mission on October 7, when the freeze-up caught them. There they settled into a cabin and began quarreling in earnest. "At Russian Mission," Galpin told the court, "she assaulted me with a large pair of scissors, grasped me by the throat, sinking her nails into the flesh, obtained money by false pretenses, robbed me with violence of my diary and conspired with Victor to further rob me of valuable papers." [40] After Galpin turned over his papers, which included a promissory note for $7,500 Alice owed him, to a Russian Mission man for safekeeping, Victor got them away from the guardian by deceit.

Count Morajeski was forty years old and probably not too bright. He admitted after falling out with Galpin that earlier on the voyage he had been under Galpin's influence and had agreed gladly to help get Alice jailed at Russian Mission while the two men left to gather his inheritance and whatever they could get from the publication of Alice's manuscripts. Somehow, Alice turned Victor around at Russian Mission. Now Victor renounced the Huck Finn existence the men had planned, which would have involved them in the "ruining of women for the rest of their lives," and decided to protect his wife.[41]

Perhaps the count's conversion occurred after Galpin embarrassed him with a scheme to show Alice's unfaithfulness. If the story Victor told was true, he had agreed to hide under the cabin table while Galpin seduced Alice. Alice saw through this clumsy plan and berated both men.

The people in Russian Mission had never before heard anything as exciting as the charges and countercharges the Morajeskis and Galpin exchanged in the U.S. commissioner's court. It was a spectacular diversion and worth every effort expended by the jurors, who had to be called from miles around to hear charges against Victor for obtaining Galpin's papers by false pretenses. Of course, this was only one of the eight criminal complaints filed by the parties against each other, which also included a most unusual one based on Alice's charges of blackmail and conspiracy against Galpin and her husband.

The jury found Victor not guilty, and since the assault charges Galpin made against the Morajeskis were felonies, the commissioner sent them on to Nome for the grand jury's indictment. The Morajeskis' charges against Galpin and those who helped him recover his property were withdrawn by them because of Alice's bad health and the commissioner's prejudice. The commissioner dismissed these charges as malicious prosecution without probable cause and assessed costs to the Morajeskis.

The only other jury hearing at Russian Mission concerned Alice's charges of assault against a man who tried to restrain her efforts to protect Victor during the property squabble. He was found not guilty. The judge fined Alice five dollars for contempt in interrupting trial with violent outbursts and charges of bias.

While the circus did not gain much in meaning as it was transferred from the lower Yukon to Nome, it should be noted that all the juries that considered the tangled affairs of the Yukon voyagers refused to render any verdict except not guilty. Somebody must have been guilty of something, but jurors intelligently refused to sort out the confusion. The court and its officers wept with relief when the Morajeskis finally sailed off. And, oddly enough, the precious manuscripts Alice wrote, and around which much of the fighting may have revolved, were never published.

12. Tough Characters

No gentleman would beat his wife—with an ax.—L. T. Erwin

IN the summer of 1902, Judge Wickersham, relieved in Nome by Judge Noyes's successor, Alfred S. Moore, returned to his assigned third division. At St. Michael he met trader E. T. Barnette, who told him about rich gold strikes on the Tanana River. Wickersham suggested that Barnette's new town be named for Indiana's Senator Charles W. Fairbanks, one of Wickersham's political patrons and later vice-president of the United States. Political appointees, like explorers of new lands, saw no harm in seizing the opportunity of showing appreciation when the occasion offered itself. When the judge later visited Fairbanks and decided to move the court there, he named streets after two congressmen: Francis Cushman of Washington and John F. Lacey of Iowa.

The third division had been neglected in the judge's absence, and he had a backlog of civil and criminal cases, including murder charges. In later court sessions he had other serious felonies that excited the community, especially those involving gold robberies.

In towns sizable enough to warrant the expense, the Justice Department authorized the district judge's appointment of U.S. commissioners. When he appointed A. J. Balliet at Rampart, Judge Wickersham observed that "you are given almost supreme power in a region larger than many of the states. I sincerely hope for your good reputation that you will exercise that power judiciously and in accordance with the law."[1] To ensure devotion to the law, the Department of Justice had agreed to provide Balliet with the *Revised Statutes of the United States*. In the States, commissioners had to borrow or buy copies, but Wickersham had pointed out to the government that there was no copy of the book within four hundred miles of Rampart.

Balliet was a good candidate for the job. He was a lawyer with mining interests who had stampeded from his Seattle home to Dawson in 1897. At Yale University he had been a sports hero: stroke on the fastest crew Yale ever had, and in football, a lineman "as immovable as a mountain."[2] It was understood that the commissioner's duties would not be too taxing. Commissioners received no salary but kept fees levied for recording transactions and case filings. That suited Balliet, as did Wickersham's advice that he fine offenders wherever possible rather than jail them. The U.S. Treasury could use the fine money, the judge cautioned, so "why support men in idleness at great expense?"[3] A month later, Balliet had more excitement than he wanted. Rampart's first murder was committed on December 17, 1900.

T. M. Crawford was passing the time looking at goods in Rampart's NAT&T store and chatting with storekeeper Joe Muldowney when the commotion started. He heard Muldowney say, "Look out there!" but paid no attention.[4] When the storekeeper hollered the warning again, Crawford looked up, saw a man moving toward Muldowney, holding a revolver in both hands, and heard the weapon's roar. Muldowney bounced off the counter while his assailant continued toward him. Crawford stepped toward the gunman, whose cap, eyes, and beard were frosted with ice, then hesitated when the man turned to look at him. The man had a wild look. "After I saw that look in his eyes I stopped and did not go any closer." In some haste Crawford bolted out the door as the gunman fired at Muldowney again. Before his shouting raised others, he heard four shots. By the time Crawford and two other men had returned to the store, the killer had fled.

Muldowney lay in a pool of blood. "For God's sake," he said, "make someone lay me out, for I am done for."

"Who shot you?" asked Crawford.

"I don't know," answered Muldowney.

"Why did he shoot you?"

"I don't know."

It was not so strange that Muldowney did not recognize his killer, Dan Carolan, because Crawford, who had known Carolan for years, had not recognized him either, although Carolan had not been disguised.

Carolan did not go far, and his actions showed some presence of mind. He hurried over to the military barracks, confronted the soldier on duty, and asked for protection. "What for?" asked the soldier. "From a mob," answered Carolan. The soldier took Carolan's gun, placed him in a cell, grabbed his own rifle, and went outside. Five or six men ran up and wanted to know if the killer was there. "Yes he is and he's going to stay here," said the soldier with commendable determination. And that was enough to appease the Rampart men.

Soon everyone in town knew the circumstances of the shooting. Dan Carolan, a thirty-six-year old miner of "settled, industrious habits," spent much of his time working a claim on Little Minook Creek eight miles from town. His wife, Lucy, an Indian girl he had married in 1898, remained in town while he worked. On November 17, Muldowney allegedly had raped her.

What actually happened was not clear. Obviously she had been upset enough on November 17 to send her ten-year old sister for Dr. J. H. Hudgin. She did not tell the doctor about a rape, yet she was plainly very excited and nervous. The doctor assumed that it had something to do with the death of her little brother a short time earlier. The next day, Lucy sent for her husband, but she did not tell him about the rape either. It was not until mid-December, two or three days before the shooting, that Lucy told him that Muldowney had locked her in a storeroom of the NAT&T Co. store and raped her. He grew very red in the face and "acted like a crazy man," and several days later went to track down Muldowney.

A grand jury indicted Carolan for first-degree murder. Trial was set for the July 1901 term, when Judge James Wickersham would hold court in Rampart. Attorney J. Lindley Green prepared the defense. He would have been much happier if Carolan had shot Muldowney the day he got Lucy's news, and happier yet if the rape and shooting had been the same day. Of course, killing in a fit of passion was not technically a homicide defense, yet juries were usually quick to find temporary insanity when a husband responded to a forcible defilement of his marriage.

Green did his best. Both Dr. Hudgin and Dr. H. V. Tweedie, the army surgeon, agreed to testify to Carolan's insanity. Tweedie had examined the accused in jail, observing "a peculiar whiteness of skin, nervous movements, and twitching of the eyes." Green also had witnesses who would praise Carolan's character and habits; the family's happy home life; Lucy's disdain for the town's rowdy "squaw dances" and whiskey; and some disputed information on Muldowney's sexual aggression toward others on several occasions. And it did not hurt the defendant's cause when Lucy gave birth to a child in the spring. The tougher question Green faced was U.S. Attorney Nathan V. Harlan's evidence that Lucy hung around the store. Someone knew that Muldowney had once ordered her to leave. She always came back, as if to tease the storekeeper. The evidence of rape rested on her word alone. But even if she had been raped the evidence of her provocation hurt the cause.

At trial Green painted a picture of Lucy's injured innocence, waved Exhibit A with a flourish, the panties Lucy wore, which Muldowney may have torn in his lust, and told jurors that the outrage unhinged Carolan's mind. But the defense's hopes for the medical testimony crashed resoundingly when the prosecutor ridiculed Dr. Hudgin's expertise on insanity. Hudgin, who was also a storekeeper, was forced to admit that his experience with mental disease had been extremely limited. He was even reticent when Green asked whether Carolan's mind might "be more easily dethroned than that of a person with a stronger temperament." Dr. Tweedie changed his mind about testifying, leaving Green without competent evidence of the only substantial defense available to him.

Carolan tried to help by denying that he remembered what occurred in the store, and Green stressed the wild disfigurement of Carolan's features, which had made him unrecognizable to acquaintances, but this was not enough. Jurors could not even settle for second-degree murder because of the time lapse between Lucy's revelation and her husband's actions. And who could deny the intent of a killer who started shooting while still outside the store without saying one word to the victim? Thus Carolan was the first defendant convicted of murder one in a third-division court. Jurors stipulated "without capital punishment," and Carolan got life at McNeil Island.

In November 1901, two miners on Hutchinson Creek forty miles southwest of Eagle reached the boiling point and fought it out with knives. Carl Christenson fell, and Harry Owens left his cabin, stumbling over the trail eighteen miles to get help from his closest neighbors. The neighbors patched Owens up, then went to look at Owens' cabin. They had to break the door open because for some reason Owens had nailed it shut. Christenson lay dead on the floor in a pool of blood. The miners declared themselves a coroner's jury and interrogated Owens.

"What happened?"

"The little Dane knifed me."

"Did you have a fight?"

"No."

"Did you leave Christenson dead?"

"I don't know. I wished he was." [5]

Owens went on to explain that the victim came to his cabin and tried to take some grub from him. Owens refused the demand and Christenson drew his knife. Owens grabbed his own knife to defend himself.

A man had been killed; there were no witnesses. When a deputy from Eagle eventually reached the scene, bringing a doctor, who performed a rudimentary autopsy, he talked to Owens and the other residents of the remote mining area. The deputy's impressions were important. Since the other miners seemed suspicious of Owens, he recommended prosecution. The assistant U.S. attorney in Eagle decided to ask the grand jury for a murder indictment, although the evidence was slight.

Judge Wickersham convened court in Eagle in August 1902. In the backlog of cases awaiting his return was that of Harry Owens. Wickersham thought Owens' self-defense story was a lie. Jurors agreed. Owens was convicted of second-degree murder and sentenced to twenty-five years at McNeil Island.

In May 1904 the U.S. Circuit Court of Appeals reversed Wickersham's conviction because the judge's instructions to the jury were faulty. "By the frequent use of the words 'absolutely necessary' . . . the jurors may have drawn the inference that, before they would be justified in acquitting the defendant, it must appear to them that the killing of deceased was absolutely necessary." This view of the case would virtually deprive a defendant of a reasonable exercise of his own judgement "in determining from all the circumstances what was necessary to be done for the protection of his person or his life."[6]

Nathan V. Harlan, the government prosecutor, followed the usual procedure on reversals by arranging for a new trial. But the process caused delays, as Owens complained in a letter to Attorney General Philander Knox in November 1904. Owens was transferred from McNeil Island to San Quentin while the appeal was in process, then was taken back to Eagle. By this time, Wickersham's main court had been relocated in the new town of Fairbanks. After three months in the Eagle jail Owens was taken to Rampart, which did not bring his trial any closer. Why didn't they take him to Fairbanks in June and schedule the trial for the July term? asked Owens reasonably enough. "Or why don't they take me to Valdez this month [November] as there have been two terms of court in this district and they could have tried me."[7]

Owens knew a raw deal when he saw one. Before his first trial he had been in jail nine months. Then he had been at McNeil and San Quentin for twenty-one months. Here he was back in Alaska, and after six months, he still had not been retried. "Maybe I have to lay here until next June"—another seven months. He also complained that the court had been unfair at his first trial: "They subpoenaed only the witnesses they wanted. Maybe it will be the same this time." And Owens, a concerned citizen, proposed that Knox order his case dismissed: "I could be discharged without putting the government to any more expense."

Prosecutor Harlan did indeed postpone Owens' trial until the July term, not out of spite, but because an important witness had left Alaska for Canada's Northwest Territory. He could not compel Stephen Mosher, "one of the most important witnesses," to come.[8] Mosher demanded ten dollars per day and mileage expenses. Travel and the trial would take thirty-one days; travel expense for eleven hundred miles would bring the total costs to three hundred dollars. Harlan negotiated from February to June with Knox and Mosher before the expenses were approved. After all this trouble a Fairbanks jury acquitted Owens. Wickersham was miffed: "Another bad verdict," he confided to his diary, "Owens not guilty!"[9]

That was not the end of this expensive-trial story. Two other witnesses, Tom Neely and Charles Clausen, had been subpoenaed in March for the July 1905 trial. Unlike Mosher, they could not negotiate their expenses with the threat of noncompliance, although they faced a long journey as well.

The witnesses started June 5 from their diggings on Lucky Gulch, Roosevelt Creek, at the headwaters of the Susitna. They traveled southeast out of the Mount McKinley region to Copper Center "until finally finding an opening in the mountain range, passed to the headwaters of the Delta, down to its mouth, then down the Tanana to Fairbanks, making the last 100 miles by boat in 12 hours!" They reached Fairbanks on July 3, having "traveled 150 miles above the timber line . . . and by reason of swollen streams and lack of food suffered many hardships and deprivations, as well as dangers, traveling 500–600 miles. Over the last days they had only flour to eat and all of their dogs had died."[10]

When the trial ended on August 12, the witnesses realized that the season was too advanced for a return along the same route because of high water and snow. They had no pack animals or blankets, but even if they had had them the trip would be too dangerous. Since Clausen was a part-owner of a mine and left men working there and since Neely was his employee, they had to return at once. The only practical route was by steamboat downriver to the Yukon and its mouth at St. Michael, thence by ship to Skagway, where they could get passage to Cook Inlet. From the head of Cook Inlet, they would walk 160 miles.

When Judge Wickersham received the witnesses' petition for additional travel expenses, he was not sympathetic. There is no reason to believe that Wickersham denied the request because Owens had been acquitted; the court always had to exercise frugality. Wickersham was a keen student of Alaska geography and had traveled to Mount McKinley in 1903 for a climbing expedition. Perhaps he thought hardy Alaskans could get back to their mine without the necessity for such a roundabout trip. And he may have wondered why the miners traveled so far to the southeast instead of pushing north directly for Fairbanks. At any rate, he would not help, and the witnesses, who suffered hardship and expense to do their duty, were not further compensated for their pains.

Many men watched the seasonal output of interior gold mines being loaded at Fairbanks and other shipment points, imagining the fun they would have spending the loot. But how to get it? Boats are not easy to hold up, so most gold shipments moved serenely down the Tanana and Yukon rivers to St. Michael, or up the Yukon to Dawson, for eventual transfer to ocean ships and the Seattle mint.

Insiders might have a chance, however, and on a couple of occasions ambitious thieves took a crack at the big bonanza. Young Robert E. ("Bobby") Miller took a job as a watchman on the steamer *Tanana* in 1906 with larcenous intent. He and his confederates knew that the *Tanana* carried the Fairbanks gold shipments to Fort Gibbon on the first leg of the long voyage to Seattle. At Fort Gibbon the gold would be transferred to the steamer *Ida May* for the Yukon voyage downriver to St. Michael.

Before the *Tanana* left Fairbanks, Miller stashed heavy lead bird shot in his cabin. Once the boat got under way, he carried one gold box to his cabin, removed thirty-eight bricks of gold and hid them in his bunk. He filled the gold box with bird shot and replaced it with the cargo. At Nenana, Miller got the gold ashore, caching a quantity worth $50,000 in one place and a portion worth $29,000 elsewhere. Odd events followed. Some heisters stole the lead-weighted box that contained only two gold bricks from the *Ida May* after the usual transfer of cargo was made. They were apprehended before the *Ida May* left Fort Gibbon, and so was Miller. Miller, a pleasant, cooperative chap, led deputies to the $50,000 cache, then was taken to Fairbanks for indictment and trial.

People in the Tanana Valley boom town were excited about the bold theft, as they were about any news concerning gold and swiftly won fortunes. They were reminded of widely known train robberies by legendary outlaws on other western frontiers and were pleased to have some romance touch their lives. Fellows hanging around town with time on their hands—and grievances—

embellished events by spreading rumors that prominent citizens had been involved in the gold heist. "Good names can't be repaired," cautioned the *Fairbanks Times* in warning readers to discount such unsupported gossip.[11]

The discovery of Miller's theft came about in confused circumstances. "Hard Rock Charley" Tague had approached several men at Fort Gibbon, offering to sell gold at a discount. Tague and others had taken the box Miller already had plundered from the *Ida May* when it docked at Fort Gibbon. Six men were involved in the robbery. Arrests followed when a marshal's deputy spotted a well-known rogue named Kelso laboring under a heavy suitcase and avoiding the board sidewalks in Fairbanks for open, muddy ground. Anyone choosing to walk through muck with a heavy load must have a reason for avoiding people, reasoned the deputy, and he was right.

Miller, formerly a bartender at the Delta Saloon, "a well-educated, well-reared" young man, was the mastermind of the heist, or at least the original heist. But Fairbanks newspapers derided this "Napoleon of finance" when it was learned that two gang members, annoyed because Miller gave them only one thousand dollars for the essential job of carrying the gold to Seattle, helped authorities by preaching on Miller.[12]

Miller's conviction followed in due course, but folks wondered why he was given a light two-year sentence. Seattle newspapers professed to know all about it when Miller won his release from McNeil Island in 1908. Apparently crime did pay because Miller made a deal with the U.S. attorney before he consented to lead officers to the $50,000 cache. As a reward for finding the treasure, the prosecutor would ask for a minimum sentence and would not excite the judge over the mystery of the still-missing $29,000. This somewhat implausible deal was made even harder to believe by an imaginative reporter's insistence that Miller had never expected to get away with the gold: "There is no chance for a 'getaway' in Alaska." Miller knew that the insurance company and the bank shipping the gold would agree to a $50,000 return and allow him to keep the balance of the loot. "He says himself," the newspaper reported, "he would have taken the limit sentencing before he would have so far thrown down the magnificent financial structure he had erected."[13]

After serving eighteen months Miller went back to Fairbanks in August 1908, recovered his cached gold, "and now, despite detectives and other hindrances, he is back with a nicely certified paper for the mint value of the balance he held out and announces that, when opportunity comes, he will shed his name and his past, and, with the stake in hand, go somewhere where his ability for finance may have full swing."

While this colorful newspaper reporting based on a supposed interview with Miller is not too convincing, it is likely that Miller held on to some of the gold. It could not have been too much because James Beggs, Miller's confederate, lost $10,000 to police when he arrived in Seattle on an Alaska ship in September 1908. Police believed that this money came from the $29,000 cache. But if Miller did manage to keep any of the gold, he deserves a special place in Alaska's criminal files, particularly because of his involvement in the great escape of Hendrickson and Thornton from the steamer taking them to McNeil Island, a story related elsewhere.

Just a year after the Miller gold heist, Frederick Wright and R. P. Quinn evolved a scheme to divert a modest shipment of eighty-three ounces of gold dust valued at fifteen thousand dollars. They were studious fellows who reflected upon the Miller episode and believed that they were cunning enough to loot a steamer without detection. Unfortunately for their subsequent self-esteem, they demonstrated not only a lack of perception but the absence of certain essential manual skills as well.

This heist was to be an inside job too. Both men got jobs on the steamer, *Seattle No. 3.* To avoid the premature discovery of their theft, the hue and cry, and the suspicion likely to fall on any crew members, they hatched a sure-fire plan. Instead of trying to get the gold ashore along the route and risking observation by lynx-eyed custodians, they would simply heave the gold overboard, mark its location discreetly, and return at their leisure to gather their reward.

Wright and Quinn made their move just before the steamer arrived at Victor's wood camp on the Yukon River above Fort Gibbon. Somehow the wood stop came sooner than they anticipated or they had planned their plundering for another point, then altered their arrangements for some reason. Whatever the reason for their confusion, which may have been basic incompetence, they had no time to sew up the top of the sack they filled with gold. Worse yet, they did a clumsy job of securing their location float to the sack before they threw it overboard. When it hit the water, the golden sack made a satisfactory splash and parted from the rope securing the location marker.

Now all their best laid plans went awry. They had resolved to stay aboard and go about their duties with an air of innocence after hiding the gold, but Wright panicked and left the steamer at Victor's. Because of his desertion and other suspicious circumstances, officers searched the mail, found the gold missing, and raised the alarm. Quinn tried to tough out questions about the mysterious disappearance of his friend, but he found it hard to be casual throughout the excitement. He made the terrible error of telling another crewman "that a man who gave anything away [about Wright or the robbery] ought to have his head blown off."[14] On hearing this scarcely veiled threat, the crewman scurried to the officers and reported Quinn.

Meanwhile, Quinn left the steamer at Dawson and started downriver for a rendezvous with Wright and/or the gold. At Fort Gibbon he was arrested. By this time police had Wright in custody and the thief confessed his role after certain assurances were made to him. If he would testify against Quinn, the prosecutor would go easy on him. Since Quinn had not been his shipmate and comrade long enough to cement loyalties, Wright was willing to identify him as the mastermind.

At trial, Judge Silas Reid sentenced Quinn to five years and let Wright off lightly with a year in the Fairbanks jail. Wright even got several jail reprieves as he helped deputies search for the gold that had been cached on the bottom of the Yukon, but its location could not be determined. The moral of this might be that gold is hard enough to get the first time it is wrenched from nature; if you give it back, you must not expect a second chance.

George M. Pilcher was an 1898 gold-rush stampeder who never made it to Dawson. He was thirty-four years old and left a wife and two young daughters in Ohio to join the great adventure. In Seattle he invested his savings in a river launch, constructed there to his specifications, and other necessary equipment. A steamer carried Pilcher and his launch to St. Michael, where he started up the Yukon.

Pilcher's diary is evidence of his first-sight love of the north. On his passage from the sea to the river mouth, he observed with awe the broad meadows of grass, moss, and flowers, the heaps of drift-wood, the mirror-like sea in the distance: "This evening presents a picture of posy dreamland. As the sea is a perfect mirror while stretching from N.E. to S.W. is a sky festooned and draped in the most soothing mellow hues that show alike both sky and water completely obliterating the horizon. This can only be surpassed by the floweriest pictures of the gateway to paradise or soft low strains of music from heaven. Nothing in my sweetest dreams ever compared to this scene." [15]

His first love became his last. Pilcher forgot about Dawson and settled down on the lower Yukon as a trader, woodchopper, and occasional prospector. Years later he did achieve his original ambition of discovering gold, no huge bonanza, but enough to make his work worth while. But the event of interest here occurred in 1908. Pilcher's diary, a fascinating account of his life, is the best source. "I am alive tonight," he wrote January 25, "only through the kind providence of God. A murderer and a robber came to my cabin at noon, was made welcome, and ate a hearty dinner. After dinner he got ready to go on, and when my back was turned he placed a 38 caliber Iver Johnson revolver at the back of my head and fired." Pilcher heard the gun snap, whirled to face his assailant, and looked into the revolver's barrel as the would-be killer pulled the trigger once more. Amazingly enough, neither bullet hit Pilcher. As Pilcher dashed for his shotgun, Harry Loper ran out of the cabin. Pilcher pursued him downriver for two miles before giving up and returning home. The next morning, a Sunday, Pilcher's anxiety did not encourage him to perform his usual washing, shaving, and baking. "I took my gun and tramped the hills in search of my would be murderer but I saw no signs and after 6 hours of tramping I came home."

On Monday, Pilcher sent a native to Russian Mission, the nearest village, to report the shooting. On Tuesday he learned that Loper had not been seen there. He sent another native downriver to alert people, then set off into the hills himself to search. Obviously Loper had to be somewhere in the vicinity. There was no way to get out of the Yukon country in winter except on foot. The second messenger brought news of Loper on the twenty-eighth, and Pilcher hurried downriver in pursuit. Two days later he caught up with Loper at a native village, but the fugitive eluded him for two more days.

Finally Pilcher took Loper unaware and called for his surrender. "He started moving towards a depression in the ice and showed signs of a concealed weapon under his left arm. I opened fire, and emptied my gun, four shots [a .30-30 Winchester], and made no misses." Pilcher loaded the wounded man on his sled and started for St. Michael, two hundred miles distant. After a few miles Loper claimed he was dying. Pilcher hired a man to nurse him and pushed on to St. Michael, arriving there after a week on the trail.

Pilcher languished in jail after making his statement to U.S. Commissioner Edward H. Flynn. A month later Loper, a deserter from the U.S. Army post at St. Michael, was brought down the Yukon. Both men were taken to Nome for trial.

U.S. Commissioner Flynn had not been required to charge Pilcher, but it seemed safer to do so. Probably he knew nothing about the woodchopper except that he was an excellent rifle shot and a relentless pursuer. Yet, since Loper confirmed Pilcher's story in the substantial particulars and since most lower-Yukon residents knew Pilcher's peaceful reputation, a Nome trial might have been avoided.

In his statement Pilcher expressed his feelings very effectively, explaining that his act was intentional but not criminal. "I believed in doing my duty as an American citizen in defense of justice and protection of innocent, unprotected citizens who were an easy prey to a reckless murder." He asked the judge to look at the warning note he had sent to Russian Mission. "See if this note breathes fire or revenge. Also please inquire into a ten years residence on the Yukon and see if a vindictive spirit has ever been in evidence." [16]

He did not shoot Loper "in anger, nor for revenge, nor through a sordid thirst for blood. I shot him to arrest him, out of duty to deliver him to justice." Pilcher was now amazed to find that an "honest, law-abiding citizen was required to wear padded gloves in taking captive a foul murderer who had shown by his acts that he placed no value on human life."

Pilcher explained that he had every reason to believe Loper was armed, yet he observed the formalities of calling for a surrender and holding his fire until Loper resisted. What Pilcher wished the judge to recognize was the heavy responsibility the situation had imposed upon him. "No other white man knew a murderer was at large. No one else could forestall him. I must either capture a villain single-handed or let him go unchallenged. It would be a ridiculous folly to run about the country 200 miles for an officer and holler 'thief'." And the Alaska Code, Pilcher noted, gave citizens the right of arrest.

Despite his eloquence, Pilcher was taken to Nome in March but was freed early in April when the grand jury refused to indict him. Loper got three years at McNeil Island for shooting with intent to kill. But Pilcher's travails were not over. He was broke and longed for home. Home was 550 miles away, so he borrowed a few dollars to buy a bicycle and set off on April 7. The trails were slushy and the sun's glare caused snow blindness. Yet he pushed on. When his bike tires broke, he stuffed them with rope. After a month's tough going, he reached home with great joy.

Yankee whalers initially invaded northern waters in pursuit of the bowhead in 1845. Three years later the *Superior* of Sag Harbor, New York, sailed into the western Arctic Ocean via the Bering Strait to open another rich hunting ground. For decades ships from New England and other Atlantic ports made seasonal hunts. By the 1880s such long voyages were no longer profitable, and the center of whaling shifted to San Francisco.

Most whaling men ignored restrictions imposed by Russian and American governments against liquor importation. Trade with Eskimos was too appealing to resist, and neither the feeble Russian efforts nor the later patrols of the Revenue Marine Service (or Revenue Cutter Service, as it was later called) were difficult to evade. Missionaries among the Eskimos and other concerned individuals cried out for years against the whalers' debauchery of the natives, but the disgrace did not end until whale and walrus depletion ended the annual hunting voyages early in the twentieth century.

Captain Harston H. Bodfish made his first voyage from New Bedford to the Arctic in 1880 as a seaman. By the time he became a captain, the industry's base was San Francisco for short seasonal voyages into the Arctic. By his own admission, Bodfish was a tough character. Once when he was second mate aboard the *Mary D. Hume,* after his foot was smashed in a shipboard accident, he neatly amputated his own toe, disdaining to wait for the captain to do the job. On occasion he beat up Eskimos who stole articles from the ship and crew members who challenged his authority.

In the best of times a whaling mate or captain kept control of his men with force. Sailors often rebelled on the long, hazardous voyages that, according to maritime historian Samuel Eliot Morison, "brought out the worst traits of human nature." Brutality by officers was the rule. "Many whaling skippers who on shore passed as pious friends or church members, were coldblooded, heartless fiends on the quarterdeck." Such men, Morison believed, were "blackguards who disgraced the flag and the name of America."[7] Keeping order and preventing desertions taxed ship officers severely during the gold-rush era. Seamen, stricken by gold fever, jumped ship to the desolate shores of the Bering Sea, the Arctic, and elsewhere with the same zeal that propelled thousands of others to leave their homes for the north.

Bodfish described a mass desertion from the whaling fleet in the western Arctic that culminated in a pitched battle between officers and deserters. Before six men were returned to their ships, losses amounted to one sailor dead and another badly wounded. On another occasion Bodfish ended a mutiny by attacking the ringleader and laying him out, although he took a bad knife wound in the scuffle.

With this background it was no wonder that Alaskans viewed whaling men with suspicion. Accusations of brutality from any source—even deserting seamen with axes to grind—were accepted uncritically and were featured prominently in territorial newspapers.

In March 1906, Bodfish took the *William Baylies* north and ran into bad luck. A gale destroyed several boats and slowed passage to Dutch Harbor to thirty-two days. In early May, as Bodfish worked the edge of the Bering Sea ice pack, looking unsuccessfully for bowheads, steerer Ed LeGear acted up. "Put in irons," Bodfish's log noted. "Evidently crazy, and acts like softening of the brain." Three days later the seaman threatened the third officer with an ax and club when his chains were removed for exercise and fresh air. Soon after that the seaman set fire to his bedding. Bodfish moved him from the hold to a platform over the boiler, where he was chained to the pump pipe, "a clean, warm, and well ventilated place." It was not easy aboard a crowded whaler to find safe quarters for a madman. A week after LeGear's first signs of madness, he died "after singing all night."[18] Bodfish figured the sailor was a dope addict who became crazed when his supply of drugs was exhausted.

Before this misfortune the captain had experienced some difficulty with LeGear over stolen cigars the sailor shared with the crew. "During the investigation I had cuffed LeGear around somewhat, but the matter was not at all serious and I got a chuckle out of it after it was over."[19] But other seamen thought LeGear's theft of cigars from the captain led to his death.

In August the revenue cutter *Thetis* boarded the *William Baylies* to ask questions. A *William Baylies* sailor, interviewed by the *Nome Gold Digger,* had accused Bodfish of brutalizing LeGear. The captain tried to laugh off the charges. LeGear, a black, had another black friend aboard, plus five white friends. Bodfish believed that these men were Wobblies, members of the radical Industrial Workers of the World, who shipped with him only to reach the gold fields. They were making trouble now because they wanted to leave the ship.

Thetis officers took the testimony of captain and seamen, seemed satisfied, and left. A few days later they boarded the *Baylies* again off Icy Cape, accompanied by an assistant U.S. attorney and a deputy marshal from Nome. After more questioning the officers took eight seamen aboard the *Thetis* with Bodfish, held a U.S. commissioner's hearing, and bound Bodfish over for the Nome grand jury on a charge of manslaughter.

Bodfish was taken to Nome and released on bond. "I had invita-

U.S. revenue cutter Bear *north of Point Barrow, 1897. Revenue-cutter officers were sometimes deputized as U.S. commissioners to assist in law enforcement at remote points.* University of Alaska Archives

tions galore from the best people."[20] Later he took his ship to San Francisco, then appeared in federal court at Seattle, where his case had been transferred, with twelve of his seamen. At trial the jurors compared the testimony of Bodfish's twelve seamen with that of the eight crew members who had accused him and acquitted the captain.

The affair was costly to Bodfish. He had to pay the expenses of his seamen to have them available for testimony, and his ship's owners did not give him any assistance. He believed that everyone knew the charges against him were false. "I still believe that if I'd offered that district attorney up North twenty-five dollars he would have forgotten the whole thing."[21]

Arctic maritime traders were another small group of individuals who had opportunities for mischief in the isolated, scarcely policed world of their endeavors. A handful of skippers brought small schooners into the Arctic to compete with the whalers for the Eskimo trade. By skirting the ice pack's edge in early summer, they were able to cover most of the western arctic shoreline. The sparsely populated coast was not a particularly lucrative field of commerce, but there was enough profit to attract a few adventurers. One of the regular traders was Christian Klengenberg, a Dane, who, like Bodfish, was accused of mistreating his sailors. Charges against Klengenberg were much more serious and better founded, and their prosecution involved the Justice Dpartment in a good deal of effort and red tape.

Canadian Mounties first investigated Klengenberg at Herschel Island in 1906 after he completed a western arctic cruise with his schooner, the *Olga*. Several crewmen had disappeared under mysterious circumstances, and police were curious about the skipper, particularly because he had stolen the *Olga* from another trader at Herschel Island the previous year, then plundered a warehouse for provisions and trading goods before departing for Victoria Island.

Klengenberg told the Mounties and the polar explorer Vilhjalmur Stefansson, who acted as stenographer for the police, a sad tale about his men's raising hell on remote Victoria Island after looting the *Olga*'s stores to distill hootch from sugar and flour. The captain struggled to gain control of his besotted men; when he spoke severely to his chief engineer, the man reached for a gun. In self-defense, Captain Klengenberg shot the engineer dead.

As for the other three missing men, Klengenberg told another tragic story. One of them had died aboard the schooner of natural causes, while the other two fell through the thin sea ice while out on a hunting excursion. While the Mounties pondered these unusual happenings, Klengenberg tired of their interrogation, stole a whaleboat, and left Herschel Island furtively. Now the surviving seamen changed their stories, accusing Klengenberg of murder. The sailor who allegedly died of natural causes was in chains in the schooner's hold when he died and his demise had been actively stimulated by the captain. And the two men who accidentally fell through the ice had been out with the captain at the time. Crewmen did not believe their loss had been an accident; it seemed significant that the lost men had been the only witnesses to the captain's shooting of the engineer.

The sailors explained why they were reticent during the initial interviews with the Mounties. Klengenberg had called them on deck as the *Olga* approached Herschel Island: "Boys," he said, "you know the penalty for killing five men is the same as for killing four. You know what happened to the four of you who are not here today. The same thing will happen to the first man who tells on me, and maybe to the second and third."[22]

Discussions of the *Olga*'s bizarre mysteries occupied the highest levels of government in Britain, Canada, and the United States. James Bruce, ambassador to the United States, advised Secretary of State Elihu Root that the alleged crimes occurred in Canadian waters and Canadian authorities "were anxious to bring the perpetrators to justice"; however, the *Olga* was an American ship and its crew were American citizens, so Canada would relinquish jurisdiction if U.S. authorities would agree to prosecute.[23] Root took the hint and passed the word along to the attorney general, who ordered officers at Nome and Barrow to watch out for Klengenberg. Eventually the veteran arctic trader was arrested at Barrow, taken to San Francisco, indicted, and tried for murder.

Before the captain was arrested, several members of the *Olga*'s crew had appeared in San Francisco to make charges against him. Federal authorities took the sailors' affidavits and held them in jail from November 1906 until October 1907. Charles Gibson, a crewman who was released in February 1907, complained to the Justice Department, but the others, according to San Francisco officers, agreed to remain in jail because "they had no permanent place of abode and their incarceration was needed to prevent their disappearance."[24] Gibson did not believe his mates willingly stayed in jail to earn a dollar-a-day witness fee, and he wrote directly to President Theodore Roosevelt when the attorney general did not respond.

San Francisco newspapers featured the horrible stories told by the *Olga* survivors. Alfred Carlson, the cabin boy, probably survived only because the captain did not realize he had seen the quarrel that started all the trouble. The chief engineer did level a gun at Klengenberg, then agreed not to shoot in exchange for the captain's promise that he would forget the incident and not beat him up. Four days later Carlson heard five shots. Klengenberg ran up to him with his rifle in his hand, saying "come and look, I killed him." Carlson hurried to the wounded engineer, who had been lying in his bunk reading when Klengenberg opened fire. The dying man told Carlson he had refused Klengenberg's order to fetch wood. "Hell," said the skipper, "if you won't pick up wood you're a dead man," then shot him. [25]

As the engineer lingered near death, Klengenberg grew extremely impatient for his demise and ordered the cook to poison the wounded man. The cook substituted sugar for the poison Klengenberg gave him. "Klengenberg paced the deck at night and could stand it no longer so he put a pistol to the dying man's head and shot him." [26]

On the lesser side of atrocities, sailor Alfred Haley described his constant hunger pains. He could not sleep much at night during ten months of subsistence on wormy "trade flour" and walrus hides.

Nome's assistant U.S. attorney, W. N. Landers, voyaged to San Francisco to prosecute Klengenberg. Not only did Landers lose his case, because Klengenberg was an accomplished liar and because jurors were not sure that the revised stories of the crewmen, countering those made under oath at Herschel Island, were true, but also Landers got into trouble for not returning to Nome. In December, Landers wired the attorney general in response to a query on his absence from Nome. "Should I go over the ice or remain here?" he asked. The attorney general demanded to know why he had not returned immediately after the trial in October. "The trial ended October 30," Landers said. "The last boat sailed October 9. I can go overland [via Dawson or Fairbanks] and reach Nome in 60 days, if desired." [27] Presumably, officials in D.C. reviewed their information on the seasonal change at Nome and forgave Landers his absence from duty.

Considering the time involvement of lawmen in Alaska, California, and Washington; the costs of transportation in arresting and transporting Klengenberg; the jail boarding expenses for material witnesses; the cost of trial; and the loss of a Nome prosecutor for most of a year, the Department of Justice could not have been too happy with the trial result. In retrospect, some officials wondered why they had not left the whole affair to the Canadians.

David H. Jarvis is the fallen angel of Alaskan folklore. To President Teddy Roosevelt, Jarvis was the embodiment of manly virtues— courage, decisiveness, intelligence, integrity. Jarvis caught Roosevelt's attention in 1898 when, as an officer in the U.S. Revenue Marine, he directed an overland reindeer expedition in relief of whalers caught in the arctic ice. Later, as Alaska's collector of customs, Jarvis enhanced his reputation. Roosevelt offered his favorite Alaskan the position of territorial governor in 1906 and, when Jarvis declined, accepted his recommendation of Wilford B. Hoggatt. Jarvis chose a more lucrative job as a director for the Alaska Syndicate.

The Alaska Syndicate was formed in 1905 through the efforts of Stephen Birch, a bright, aggressive young man who from 1900 to 1902 purchased the fabulously rich Bonanza copper claims with backing from capitalist H. O. Havemeyer. The syndicate included the banking houses of the Guggenheim brothers and of J. P. Morgan, but the Guggenheims, because of their mining experience, directed development of several mines located on tributaries of the Copper River. In 1908 the enterprise was first reorganized as the Kennecott Mines Company, and then in 1915 as the Kennecott Copper Corporation with Birch as president.

In Alaska the syndicate, often called "the Guggs," was either lauded for its development of resources or condemned for monopolistic practices and political corruption. James Wickersham, a friend to Birch and Jarvis until becoming congressional delegate in 1908, described how the syndicate's "attempt to control the great national resources of Alaska in 1910 destroyed the last Republican administration, split the Republican party into two factions, which destroyed each other in 1912, and gave the country eight years of President Wilson and his policies."[28] Wickersham was referring to the celebrated Ballinger-Pinchot controversy, which had involved charges of fraud in the syndicate's acquisition of coal claims in Alaska and the subsequent withdrawal of coal lands to entry—an affair that established the company's significance in territorial history.[29] More directly pertinent to law enforcement in Alaska was the violent aggression attributed to agents of a syndicate subsidiary, the Copper River and Northwestern Railway (CR & NW).

In September 1907 the CR & NW, after abandoning routes from Valdez and Katalla, was pushing construction of a line along a 196-mile route up the Copper River, from Cordova on the coast to the Kennecott mines, when a rival railroad's construction diverted them. The Alaska Home Railroad, a short-lived scheme of Henry Reynolds, had graded several miles out of Valdez with the enthusiastic support of Valdez folks, who were unwilling to face the death of their hopes for a railroad. At Keystone Canyon, a narrow defile leading to Thompson Pass along the old Valdez-Eagle road, the Home Railroad crew was confronted by a rock barricade placed by CR & NW workers. Home Railroad backers, then on the verge of bankruptcy, resented the interference of the well-funded syndicate road. Since the syndicate had abandoned its Keystone Canyon grade, its defense of it seemed surly—and provocative. Of course, the CR & NW had the legal right to defend its grade against trespass, but this did not extend to the right to shoot trespassers. George Hazelet, a feisty mining man in charge of syndicate operations in the region, had arranged to awe the trespassers by getting U.S. Marshal George Perry to issue temporary deputy commissions to two syndicate employees, Edward C. Hasey and Duncan Dickson. Hazelet had armed the two men and had advised them, "Be patient, take it cool, but I look to you boys to protect my rights."[30]

Law officers anticipated but could not hold off violence. Perry wired Valdez Deputy Marshal James Lathrop on September 16, 1907, "See that Dixon [sic] and Hasey don't exceed authority and get us into trouble." Lathrop responded on September 19: "I am satisfied Hasey has overstepped his authority. Hazelet is not trying to hold canyon but only his grade. I advise you wire Hasey and Dickson to be careful and don't involve this office. Also wire Hazelet to same effect. I look for no trouble over there of any nature. It is a simple bluff."

On 25 September the Home Railroad men, armed with tools and clubs, marched in a menacing manner onto or near the syndicate's grade, and Hasey, sheltered behind the rock barricade with a rifle, shot three of them, including a Fred Rhinehart who later died of his wounds. As most Alaskans denounced Hasey's violent behavior, court officers swiftly convened a grand jury. Governor Hoggatt hurried to Valdez to investigate the affair. His sympathy for the syndicate was obvious, but U.S. Attorney Nathan V. Harlan refused the governor's demands for indictments against the Home Railroad men. The grand jury indicted Hasey for murder and assault, but, on the advice of Harlan and his deputy prosecutors W. T. Scott and L. V. Ray, they did not indict Hazelet. At the time they did not have evidence of Hazelet's instruction to Hasey to "protect my rights."

Hasey's case was transferred to Juneau to avoid the partisanship in Valdez, and to forestall chicanery, the Justice Department sent Secret Service Agent E. P. McAdams to assist the prosecutors. Preparing for trial in February 1908, McAdams found the atmosphere "terrible" and warned that the jury "will be subject to influences." Alaskans, who traditionally identified New York City and Washington, D.C., as the centers of corruption, would have been amazed at McAdams' opinion of their integrity: "It would take a Constitutional amendment to purify Alaska," he reported to his chief.[31] Part of the unrest in Juneau grew out of the dismissal of Harlan at the governor's instigation. Within a month of the shooting Hoggatt had opened his attack on Harlan, blaming him and Scott for failing to prevent the violence and for refusing to indict the Home Railroad workers for inciting riot. Hoggatt charged that both men were private counsels to the Home Railroad contractor and that Harlan was a conspicuous drunk. Harlan considered himself a victim of the syndicate for his vigorous prosecution and rallied friends to protest Hoggatt's charges. It does not appear that Harlan was entirely a martyr of the Keystone Canyon shootout because some of Hoggatt's charges, notably those concerning drinking, were confirmed by others.[32]

President Roosevelt, who always kept a close watch on Alaskan events, responded decisively to Hoggatt's charges: "It seems to me Harlan and his sort should be removed at once and steps taken to provide men who will prosecute leaders on both sides in the recent troubles in Alaska, as Hoggatt recommends." Soon after, the president heard from the attorney general of Hoggatt's interference in the case and reacted with anger: "It seems well-nigh impossible to be sure that we have got a decent man in Alaska."[33]

As the government's attorneys, John Boyce, William Barnhill, and W. T. Scott prepared to try Hasey for murder in Juneau, they were well aware that the attorney general and the president were watching closely. "With an honest jury we can't keep from winning," McAdams assured John Wilkie, chief of the secret service.[34] Hasey's defenders, Thomas Lyons of Juneau, John Carson of Tacoma, Fred Brown of Valdez, and John Ostrander of Valdez, conferred often with Jarvis, Birch, Hazelet, and the syndicate's law firm of Bogle and Spooner in Seattle. Ostrander, the defense-team leader, dismissed Scott and Boyce as "a pair of old grannies" and complained of Judge Royal Gunnison's slow pace. The presence of McAdams, "a bad actor" and "so-called detective," did not awe him: "I think we will be able to show him up." Ostrander planned to use M. B. Morrisey, a Home Railroad worker, as a defense witness, although he had been subpoenaed earlier by the government. Since Morrisey seemed eager to testify that some of the Home Railroad men had been armed, the prosecutor had no use for his testimony. "Morrisey is acting on the square," Ostrander believed.[35] The role of Morrisey later taxed investigators of the trial. It was not his testimony, which had corroboration by other defense witnesses, that aroused suspicion, but his open-handed entertainment of and loans to other witnesses. Morrisey spent money provided by the syndicate, and he drew a salary from it during the trial and afterwards until he departed for parts unknown.

In April 1908 the trial opened. Ostrander's confidence was not diminished by the sudden illness and death of Assistant U.S. Attorney Scott, or even the hostility of Judge Gunnison, "the most ignorant fool that ever sat on this or any bench."[36] After several weeks of trial jurors found that Hasey's apprehension of bodily harm from the Home Railroad gang justified his shooting and acquitted him of second-degree murder charges. The government persisted, trying Hasey for assault with intent to kill in February 1909. This time jurors decided that Hasey's gunplay had been unnecessary and unreasonable and found him guilty. Judge Gunnison sentenced him to eighteen months at McNeil Island. Initially Hasey's attorneys prepared to appeal, then dropped it when syndicate officers encouraged Hasey to serve his time in return for receiving his full pay and other benefits. According to rumor, the syndicate followed this course because of Morrisey's persistent demands for money.

With Hasey in jail, and the Alaska Home Railroad bankrupt and disgraced because of questionable activities by its promoter, the syndicate's reputation improved. Construction of the Copper River and Northwestern Railway and other developments captured public attention. Michael J. Heney, "the Irish Prince," was the railroad contractor and a universally admired figure. Heney had built the narrow-gage White Pass & Yukon Railway from Skagway to White-horse during the Klondike gold rush. The new railroad was a greater challenge because of its far greater length, wider gage, and the formidable obstacles posed by huge glaciers. It also answered a long expressed longing of Alaskans for an "All-American" route to the interior. Syndicate officers often declared their intent to carry construction of the railroad all the way to the Yukon River to achieve a combined rail-river route that would aid territorial devel-opment. Whether the syndicate was ever genuinely interested in building beyond Kennecott is not clear, but when the line reached the copper mines in 1911, construction was terminated.

The syndicate might have fared better in public regard but for its obvious determination to dominate Alaskan politics. CR & NW rail workers, many of whom were not eligible to vote, were en-couraged to vote against Wickersham at Cordova in the 1908 congressional-delegate election. This upset Wickersham, who had already been annoyed by the syndicate's publication of earlier cor-respondence showing Wickersham's interest in being retained as counsel by the "Guggs." Another exposure of letters revealed that earlier Wickersham had not favored home rule for Alaska, although he had made demands for a territorial legislature and other home-rule measures the thrust of his campaign. Once Wickersham gained office, he had to suffer the competition of the syndicate for the right to control political patronage. All these things made Wick-ersham determined to destroy the influence of the syndicate by any means at his disposal. By the time Stephen Birch got around to asking Wickersham to name his price for dropping his unrelenting attacks on the syndicate, it was far too late.[37] Wickersham had be-come the champion of the people against the powers of evil—and the evil was represented by the syndicate and its supporters. But for their blunders and corruption, the syndicate might have fared much better during the storm of the Ballinger-Pinchot controversy, and the syndicate's support of President Taft's plan for a military government for Alaska, rather than more democratic institutions, would have been less suspicious.

Wickersham gained the ammunition he needed when H. J. Douglas, recently fired as syndicate auditor, gave him evidence of Morrisey's role during the first Hasey trial. Douglas identified John Carson as the bag man who saw to it that Morrisey got money from the company's "corruption fund." It was suggestive of serious tampering that Carson had written to Jarvis extolling the services of Morrisey, whose "acquaintance with many of the government's witnesses and control over them placed him in a position to be of the greatest service."[38] The actual disbursements to Morrisey were not great enough to be convincing as bribery, but as Wickersham pointed out, Douglas did not have all the evidence that might exist.

Wickersham knew how to engage the attention of the press, and the syndicate men blundered further by providing him a congressional forum for inquiry when they brought charges against U.S. Attorney John Boyce and U.S. Marshal Dan Sutherland. Boyce and Sutherland were dismissed because of alleged excessiveness in prosecuting Juneau banker C. M. Summers for assault. Summers and his good friend, Governor Walter Clark, a syndicate sympathizer, convinced the attorney general that Boyce and Sutherland had gone after Summers because he was a foe of Wickersham. Whether that was true or not, the dispute over the firings and the replacement of the officers with John Rustgard and Herbert Faulkner might be aired when a Senate subcommittee met to consider the fitness of the new appointees. Wickersham and Sutherland argued that the dismissals followed the efforts of the officers to investigate Hasey jury-bribery charges. It is not clear that this was actually the case, but Wickersham did not make light of opportunities granted him to strike at his old enemies.[39]

The new officers were confirmed, but the attorney general could not resist Wickersham's demands for a thorough investigation of the Keystone Canyon trials, the election frauds at Cordova, and other questionable actions by the syndicate. Agents of the Justice Department went over the court records, interviewed a number of individuals, investigated the activities of suspects, and examined all the 1907–1908 telegraph communications of syndicate officers. When the examiner, S. McNamara, reported the results of the investigation in February 1911, he concluded that "Morrisey is preeminently a scoundrel" and that "irregular methods" had been used by the Hasey defense. U.S. Attorney Elmer E. Todd of Seattle reviewed McNamara's report and agreed with his conclusions: "Improper methods" had been used by the defense, but the government did not have enough evidence to support a successful prosecution. Both men called for further investigations of possible bribery in the Cordova election and possible Sherman Act violations in collusive bidding for government contracts between the syndicate and a rival company.[40]

Eventually a coal contract resulted in the prosecution of some syndicate officers, when H. J. Douglas reported that the syndicate's David Jarvis had agreed with officers of another company on the price for coal to be offered for shipment to Forts Davis and Liscum in Alaska. Further investigation and much urging from Wickersham led to a federal prosecution of company officers at Tacoma, Washington. Jarvis, who has been treated with great sympathy by historians of the event, was not among those who were convicted in October 1912 because he took his own life in June 1911, shortly after indictments were issued. He left a cryptic note: "Tired and worn out." The *New York Times* story on his suicide observed his boldness "beyond the realization of people who did not know Alaska—whether lobbying for legislation, seizing railroad right-of-ways by power of Winchester, fixing jurors, or playing corrupt politics."[41]

13. Long Trails

All ye icebergs make salaam
You belong to Uncle Sam.
　　　　　　—Bret Harte

ALONG the main trails in Alaska, the Yukon, the Valdez-Eagle, the Valdez-Fairbanks, and that between Nome and the Yukon, travel was eased somewhat by regularly spaced roadhouses. Travelers in winter might experience some hardship and even danger, but at least they could count on a warm stopping place for the night and hot food, assuming they could afford it. But there were parts of the territory, such as the arctic north of Fairbanks, where a small resident population and a paucity of travelers meant that roadhouse amenities were lacking. Traveling there in the cause of justice was a distinct burden for officers. But any travel in Alaska, even in settled areas, and under comparatively pleasant conditions, was an expensive business. Its authorization by a court officer caused concern in Washington unless the matter had been thrashed out beforehand.

During the time that winter travel could be accomplished only by dog sled, each court district designated one deputy marshal as trailsman. These hearty individuals had the duty of traveling to outlying areas to serve warrants, investigate crimes, bring back men charged with crimes, and even to bring back bodies. Deputy Bert Hansen, the third division's trailsman, made a number of hard journeys, and that undertaken to freight Oscar Gustafson's frozen corpse from Iditarod to Fairbanks in the winter of 1909 was particularly memorable. Gustafson was blasted by Felix Boucher's rifle in November 1909 because of a Willow Creek mining dispute.

Boucher explained the matter to the U.S. commissioner. Friends had warned him that Gustafson had been threatening his life, yet he let the Swede get the drop on him. Gustafson walked into Boucher's cabin holding a rifle Boucher had left on the porch. "Where is the man who is going to fix me?" shouted Gustafson as he aimed the rifle at Boucher's chest. "How are you going to fix me?"[1] This time there was no shooting, but the Swede warned Boucher that any further attempt to stake fractions on his ground would result in legal action. Later Gustafson approached Boucher while he was working and cursed him. Boucher retreated, stumbled, fell, and grabbed his rifle. Gustafson picked up an ax and advanced in a menacing manner. "Go away or I'll shoot," said Boucher. "Quit fooling with my ground and I will go away," retorted Gustafson, who then raised his ax and rushed into Boucher's rifle fire.[2]

The commissioner accepted Boucher's self-defense story, but Gustafson's brother complained to the U.S. attorney in Fairbanks. Why was my brother shot in the back? he asked. Since no one in Fairbanks had a clear notion of the wound's location, Hansen was sent out to exhume the dead miner and haul him in for a more competent autopsy than the remote Otter recording district offered on the spot.

Easier said than done, as Hansen knew when he set off from Fairbanks in March. After a couple of weeks on the trail he reached Otter Creek, found the place where the body had been buried, then persuaded a little Norwegian fellow to help him thaw the ground. Reaching Gustafson by thawing, digging, thawing, and digging was hard work. Eventually the diggers struck their goal: "He was a huge man, six foot two and weighing all of two hundred and twenty pounds . . . frozen stiff as a poker, and had turned black, with traces of mould on his face."[3] But Hansen had to finish the job without pausing for somber reflections or squeamish reactions. He wrestled with the corpse, got ropes under its shoulders and legs, and heaved. The Norwegian helper, only five feet tall, tried to help, but his legs, unlike Hansen's could not straddle the grave. Their joint struggle raised the body a foot or two but no further. Repeatedly they raised the burden a bit, then had to lower it back.

A U.S. commissioner's tent at Iditarod in 1910. Alaska Historical Library; Basil Clemons, photographer

Hansen rejoiced when three Irishmen came along, but they refused to handle a dead man, although the deputy showed his badge and showered them with curses. Finally one of them agreed to give a hand. Since he would not approach the body closely, it was some time before Hansen got the corpse on a tarp and loaded it on his sled. Now he was able to lash it down and think about the five hundred miles back to Fairbanks. Speed was necessary because the court term was in session and Boucher's trial had been scheduled for it. Another reason for hurrying was the cost of dog food. Prices were sky high, and the penny-pinching government did not care that one meal for nine dogs cost Hansen $15.50. Hard-working dogs liked to eat twice a day, but the standard food allowance given Hansen for his team was $15 a day.

In April the glare of the sun on the snow could blind a man. Hansen made sixty miles the first day to Dishkakat, stayed at a roadhouse, and pushed on the next morning. Before he reached Nulato, his eyes felt like someone had shaken hot pepper in them. When he arrived, he was virtually blind; further travel that day was out of the question. From Nulato, Hansen could only travel at night—lonely work with only the dogs and a dead man for company.

Everything looked better when Hansen reached Tanana. A roadhouse man helped him kennel his dogs and raise the sled to a six-

foot-high platform so that his or other hungry dogs could not eat his provisions, or, perish the thought, the body, which was needed for court evidence. Hansen made the terrible blunder of naming the sled's contents as the two men strained to lift it onto the platform. The helper dropped his end with a crash and bolted. After Hansen got someone else to help him secure the sled, he was embarrassed to discover that Gustafson's head had snapped off in the fall. Wise to the ways of the law, Hansen protected himself with an affidavit from his clumsy helper to offset any defense arguments that the body had been tampered with.

For all the grotesque features of the journey, the deputy was pleased at his speed record: eight hundred miles in ten and one-half days while snowblind, including the last seventy-five-mile stretch in ten and one-half hours. All the time, money, and Hansen's superlative dash were wasted as far as the prosecutor was concerned. The bullet hole was not in Gustafson's back. Jurors accepted Boucher's self-defense story and acquitted him of murder.

Hansen made a memorable journey in 1910 to investigate the possible murder of two Chandalar miners, Joseph Geraghty and J. D. Clarke. Information about the missing men originated with Jack Cornell, a census taker, who told the Reverend Hudson Stuck that the two men had been prospecting at the headwaters of the East Fork of the Chandalar River in late 1908. Thereafter they disappeared. By late 1909 it appeared that unless they had crossed the mountains to the arctic coast to replenish their supplies at the Flax-

man Island trading station, they must have starved or otherwise perished in the vast, scarcely populated arctic region. Cornell claimed that he devoted six months starting in spring 1910 to a search for the men. He found a pass in the Endicott Range 250 miles above the mouth of the East Fork, and there was evidence that white men had camped in the area on journeys to and from the northern coast. Cornell's feats of detection climaxed with the discovery of Clarke's body beside a broken sled and the tattered remains of a tent. No other body was found. Cornell reported his discovery to the U.S. marshal in Fairbanks, who had to make a decision.

On November 6, 1910, Hansen called at U.S. Marshal Harry Love's office and read Cornell's telegram: "Found body of Clarke prospector believe murdered on head waters upper Wind River tributary East Fork Chandalar. I covered body to protect it from animals."[4] Love hesitated to send Hansen into a country where there were no trails, trading posts, or any other amenities associated with habitation by whites. But Hansen was eager enough: "I'd just as soon go after the body . . . as to spend the winter plodding along the old trails. A dead man isn't such bad company, after all. He can't talk back and he stays put. I've had worse!"

Hansen's zeal pleased Love because there existed a deep suspicion of the Chandalar Indians. Several prospectors had vanished into the country during the past fifteen years, and persistent rumors of foul play were reinforced by Indian Chief Christian's action on one occasion in escorting a miner out of the region at gun-point. Such rumors had been discounted in the past. The U.S. marshal was not required to search for men who got lost, and, often enough, men believed to have perished in the wilderness had simply left the country without giving notice. Clarke and Geraghty could have died of starvation or exposure easily enough, yet Cornell must have seen some evidence of murder. Thus Love, Judge Thomas Lyons, and U.S. Attorney James Crossley wired the attorney general requesting authorization for Hansen's trip.

While awaiting authorization, the lawmen wired Cornell for the specific location of the body. Cornell was the designated census taken for the arctic region and was presumed to know the area better than anyone else. Unfortunately, the estimated coordinates placed the body somewhere near the North Pole on the marshal's map. The maps were all wrong, replied Cornell when this was explained.

Knowledge of the Chandalar Indians also was reviewed. Originally they had lived around Fort Yukon but moved north into the Chandalar country when the gold rush brought an influx of whites. Later a mining development in the Chandalar caused them to move farther north. Plainly, they wished to remain away from white men's towns, although they did visit Fort Yukon and Circle briefly for trading purposes each season. It was believed that some two hundred to three hundred people lived in a village somewhere on the south slope of the Endicott Mountains.

Hansen's provisioning included a ten-by-twelve-foot canvas tent, a sheet-iron Yukon stove, six hundred pounds of tallow for dog food, and food for himself. He spent several days making moccasins from wool blankets for the dogs' feet. "Each dog had to be fitted as carefully as a prima donna." And Hansen did not begrudge the effort. "My life depended upon my dogs." He took great care in selecting the twelve who would make up his team, dogs he felt had an instinctive sense of direction.

Hansen's clothes weighed only five pounds and included a Siberian-squirrel parka, the hood faced with fox and wolverine and lined with silk; lynx-foot mittens; and mukluks with feet of moose hide and tops of caribou hide. He would be warm at seventy below, and the linen underclothes he wore would allow evaporation and reduce frost.

In spite of his heavy sled, Hansen got to Circle after several days. He expected to find Cornell there and persuade him to travel with him. Cornell, a wiry fifty-year-old veteran miner, was drinking. He had no taste for a winter trip to the Chandalar but finally agreed. Fort Yukon was the next stop, and the way was not all hardship: "The mush down the Yukon was one of the most beautiful trails I have ever covered. The air was cold, full of frost, and the ice, rough in spots, making it hard going. But, winding our way in and out of the many small islands in the river, it was an ever-changing picture of beautiful scenery. The trees and brush were covered with a heavy frost, almost like fresh snow, but finer and lacier. We were mushing through a fairy-land, and the breath of the dogs, rising in little clouds, to hang a few feet suspended over their heads, gave an added beauty to it all."

Cornell, suffering from post-drinking-spree depression, saw no beauty and crabbed about the brisk pace Hansen maintained. At Fort Yukon the travelers enjoyed the last roadhouse they would see for a time, and Hansen replaced his heavy sled with light toboggans. Cornell boozed with friends while Hansen worked. During one session Hansen watched uneasily while Cornell's friend derided his attempts to place Clarke's location on the map. Take a boat with you, the friend advised Hansen; the body must lie in the Arctic Ocean according to Cornell's calculations.

It was time to search for truth. Hansen pressured Cornell until he admitted he had not seen Clarke's body at all. He had only heard about it from a trader while visiting Flaxman Island the previous summer. Now Hansen faced the prospect of crossing the Endicotts to Flaxman Island, where he might learn where the body was located. He was anxious to replace Cornell with a less reluctant companion and managed to hire a tough young white man and an Indian, both of whom claimed to know something of the Chandalar.

From Fort Yukon the mushers had to break trail ahead of their dogs. The temperature ranged to thirty-six degrees below zero. Fifteen miles daily was good progress achieved through strenuous effort. On December 11 they reached the Chandalar Indians' village on the Christian River, an aggregation of fifty log cabins fifty-five miles north of Fort Yukon. Resting near there, the travelers celebrated Christmas with caribou steaks, beans, dehydrated potatoes, plum pudding, bannocks, and tea. After the feast Hansen started off, disdaining the trail in favor of the unmarked tundra in hope of reducing the distance. Eventually they reached the most northern Chandalar village at Big Lake, the stronghold of the reputedly unfriendly Chief Christian. Hospitality was bountiful and in a meeting with the chief Hansen explained his purpose. The chief asked: "Is it so strange that a man should die in the Arctic? Does his death mean that my people are murderers?" As for Christian's expulsion of a white man from the area, he had a ready explanation: the man had been a booze seller. "Your people debauched my people. In one hand they brought their Bible, in the other they held your whiskey!" The Indians' effort to keep some distance from white men was a protective measure, and all the more remarkable for the Indians' acceptance of Christianity.

Hansen's companions quit the expedition at this point, but he was able to hire an Eskimo who knew the route but refused to travel without his wife and two babies. Hansen and the Eskimos mushed off for the Endicott Mountains and the arctic coast. A good, steady pace did not prevent Hansen's enjoyment of "the most beautiful mountains in the world." Nothing could be more beautiful. Peaks in the Alaska Range were higher but appeared less grand to Hansen. "Snow-clad, their tops a long battlement of needle-like spires and pinnacles, some of them looking so thin and fragile that I wondered the wind didn't blow them down. I simply stared and stared, getting my eyes full of their beauty."

Once over the mountains, the party raced across the flat, frozen tundra of the North Slope until a raging storm forced them to camp for three days. Gloom settled on them when, after digging themselves out of a five-foot snowfall, they suffered a tragic loss: one baby had frozen to death, "right at her mother's breast."

Finally they reached Flaxman Island. They rested and learned about the visit of Clarke and Geraghty from Henderson the trader. The miners had arrived on foot in August 1909, paying in gold dust for their provisions. Although they claimed the gold had come from earlier work at Caro, Henderson suspected they had found new wealth in the East Fork country and sent two Eskimos to watch their direction after crossing the summit. In the spring Henderson followed the miners' route and found their camp and Clarke's body. Clarke had not been dead more than three days. There were no rifles or food among his gear. Henderson thought Clarke had been shot in the neck. Once back at Flaxman Island, he dispatched a letter to Nome by way of a whaling ship. Later that summer, Cornell arrived on his census-taking tour and heard Henderson's story.

Before Hansen started back over the mountains for the body, he was warned that Chief Christian opposed its removal, fearing repercussions against his people if authorities in Fairbanks had an excuse for meddling. Hansen determined to accomplish his task despite the risk and had Henderson's Eskimos guide him to Clarke's resting place.

Finding the miners' camp was easier than removing the body. Henderson had covered it with the tent and a pile of logs, a mass now frozen solid. It took Hansen three days of chopping in bitterly cold weather before he uncovered the corpse. Finally he got a three-hundred-pound mass of partly decomposed flesh attached to gravel, sand, and ice on his sled and set off for Fairbanks. Many days later—Hansen had lost track of time—the musher reached the neighborhood of Fort Yukon. He was fortuitously found lying unconscious over the handlebars of his sled. His dogs were as gaunt as he was. The lead dog died at the moment of rescue. "I don't know what happened," Hansen said later. "I can remember driving ahead like in a nightmare . . . just sense enough to keep the dogs going . . . going . . . driving them like a fiend. . . . It must have been about at the Porcupine River when I passed completely out."

At Fort Yukon, Hansen lay in a delirium for days. In time he was able to go on to Fairbanks, relying more on will than physical strength, and arriving in an exhausted, emaciated condition. Once more he was hospitalized but recovered without ill effects. He reflected ruefully on his days of agony, "tugging around some cold dead thing . . . bringing it back from the white, clean place where it had laid itself down for final rest, just so my fellow-men could pat themselves on the back for doing the proper thing, and shoveling six feet of fresh earth on top of the coffin." "Leave me be if I die on the trail," he told friends. Had Clarke his own way, he probably would have wished to remain where he fell.

Deputy Hansen's grueling journey was not the only excursion into the remote Chandalar district connected with Clarke and Geraghty. In August 1910, Chandalar's U.S. Commissioner S. J. Marsh appointed Otis J. Nicholson special deputy to arrest Robert John. According to rumor, John had killed Clarke and Geraghty. At this time Clarke's body had not been found and no serious investigation of the pair's disappearance had been made, so the arrest of John seemed a little premature. Nevertheless, District Attorney James J. Crossley of Fairbanks wanted John brought in, and Nicholson was hired to do the job. Nicholson was a miner who took such assignments to make a little money, but he refused to go among the unfriendly Chandalar Indians without help. Marsh permitted him to hire Arthur Newton to go with him.

Nicholson hired six pack dogs at fifteen dollars per day, the going rate, and set out for Chandalar Village. The deputies arrived to find that John and other Indians were off hunting in the distant Wood River country, so they followed the Indian trail until their food supplies were exhausted, then turned back. They had been out twenty-nine days, "the same being twenty-nine days' extreme hardship," but had not been successful.[5]

Henry K. Love, U.S. marshal at Fairbanks, refused to pay all of Nicholson's charges. The special deputy spent $143 on provisions; $15 on pack saddles for the dogs; $218 for dog hire; and wanted $6 per day in wages for Newton and himself, a total of $942. Love cited Justice Department limits on deputies' fees and paid $45 for the service at a $5 daily rate. Before pursuing further payments, however, Nicholson accepted another appointment in December. He was to serve a subpoena on John Cornell at Fort Yukon, ordering Cornell to appear before Commissioner Marsh for a coroner's inquest concerning J. D. Clarke's body. This action was a little premature too because Clarke's body had not been found. While mushing to Fort Yukon with a hired six-dog team, Nicholson ran into Deputy Hansen who was heading north in search of the missing men. "Hansen informed me . . . it would be useless for me to serve the subpoena. . . . I, therefore, returned." Nicholson's expenses for two days' work, subsistence, and dog team hire were $56.50, "for which the U.S. marshal refused to allow me anything."

In August 1911, Nicholson was commissioned to take Robert John, still the Clarke-Geraghty murder suspect, to Fairbanks for trial. Summer travel in the interior could be as arduous and time consuming as winter travel. The deputy left McNett Basin on September 1 with a pole boat, proceeded down the Chandalar River and the Yukon to the Tanana River, and arrived on September 8. Two days later he caught a steamboat going up the Tanana to Fairbanks, arriving on the thirteenth. Had Nicholson not been required to appear as a court witness, he would have returned by steamboat down the Tanana and up the Yukon to Fort Yukon, taking three or four days at best, then using fifteen days to pole up the Chandalar to his home. Because of his court appearance and other activities, it was February before he left Fairbanks, so he took the winter trail for twenty-eight days to return home. His charges of $461 were reduced to $163 for payment, despite his economies in bringing John in alone. Traveling alone with a prisoner had required him to sleep while handcuffed to him and do his own cooking. He had also furnished his own equipment and had saved the government money by returning over the winter trail because he would have had to hire a helper for upriver poling on a summer return.[6]

Despite his second disappointment in the matter of fees, Nicholson made a trip in February 1911 to arrest Dave Coughrought, charged with insanity and attempted suicide. Once more he insisted that Marsh permit him to hire a companion because Coughrought was thought to be dangerous. The arresting officers were out thirteen days. Coughrought was dead when they reached his camp, 45 miles off the trail and 110 miles from Marsh's office. Of his $449 expense claim, the marshal allowed him $65.

Now Nicholson petitioned the attorney general of the United States, hoping he would see justice done and reimburse him for "disagreeable and dangerous work." If the government refused to do the right thing, no one will "undertake the hazard" of making arrests. "There is no regular deputy marshal maintained in all that vast territory [Chandalar]" occupied by forty whites and the Indians. Chandalar people must resort to summary handling of accused and insane people if the government will not show its responsibility, he said.[7]

By this time, Washington officials had learned a little about Chandalar geography and a Justice Department examiner then in Fairbanks looked over Nicholson's accounts at the marshal's request. As Marshal Love recommended payment, the department eventually paid most of what had been requested by late 1913.

All this travel by Hansen and Nicholson and the long, sustained correspondence between Alaska's officials, including the governor, and their chiefs in Washington made the prosecution of Robert John very costly. Everyone might have felt better about the costs if a conviction had followed, but jurors acquitted John; it appeared that he paid a higher price—as a presumably innocent victim—than the government.

According to missionary Hudson Stuck, who wrote a couple of popular books about his northern experiences and was ever a biting critic of the government, the entire affair showed shocking incompetence. Some of Stuck's concern was ill founded. He believed that Cornell had discovered the missing miners' bodies after unselfishly searching the arctic region for five months because the government had refused its responsibilities. Judging from Hansen's difficulties on the trail with Cornell, it is hard to accept Stuck's estimate of him. The government's delay in seeking the missing men, given the uncertainty of their plans and movements, does not seem as outrageous as Stuck believed it to be.

A more serious question lies with the treatment of John. Stuck believed that the marshal could not get Washington's approval of a search for the missing men unless murder charges were brought against someone.[8] Once there was "murder in the air, and an accused person bound over to the grand jury at Fairbanks, the marshal's office was unlocked, no expenses were spared and two special deputies were in the field." Clarke's remains were brought in and his virtually fleshless body showed no signs of a bullet wound or of any other foul play. For lack of evidence that a murder had occurred, the grand jury refused to indict. John, after six months in jail, was freed.

What further angered Stuck was the terrible inconvenience to John. He was free, broke, and three hundred miles from home. The government did not assume any obligation for helping him return, and the record does not show how he achieved it. In this respect the Alaska court did not differ from that of any other in its treatment of an accused person, but the distance and time involved certainly could become matters of great hardship.

Nicholson's hint to the attorney general that Chandalar miners would resort to summary action against criminals if the government defaulted was intended to intimidate, but incidents of Alaskans' taking the law into their own hands in extreme necessity showed its danger. The woes of George Pilcher illustrate that the exercise of self-sufficiency, however praised in theory, must meet the burdensome test of the court system.

Constant pressure from Washington must have done much to reduce the costs of justice in Alaska, yet there were curious slippages that strained the Justice Department's budget. Of these, the Fort Yukon scandal stands out.

For several years most of the Fort Yukon folks took winter vacations in Fairbanks at government expense. The court junkets pleased those with little income and plenty of time, especially the ones who were intrigued by the bright lights and sophisticated ways of Alaska's largest town. Strife was daily fare among the white residents in the little Yukon town noted as an important fur collection center and as home base for the Reverend Hudson Stuck, the hard traveling Episcopal archdeacon of the Yukon. Stuck, an Englishman, was, like other missionaries, bitter against whiskey-trading Americans and government officers whose indignation at the natives' corruption fell short of his own. But even an honest, hard-working marshal like Lewis Erwin echoed the distaste of American miners and fur traders for Stuck, "the most thoroughly hated and despised man throughout the whole territory of Alaska but a very smart and talented man indeed." [9]

Stuck could not hold office in Fort Yukon but his candidate, Dr. Grafton Burke, was the community's only official as U.S. commissioner. Burke and the other missionaries disdained the Americans as "low down whites" and debauchers of natives. Americans contended that the missionaries "were out to get Indian furs for nothing" and run Yankee traders out of the region. Thus the Fort Yukon atmosphere suffered from burning animosities, and Burke heated matters up, at great government expense, "by stirring up strife and bringing frivolous prosecutions for revenge." Erwin also believed that Burke deliberately contrived to benefit mission retainers with witness fees.

Trapper John A. Carroll wrote with amusement of three criminal trials set for hearing at Fairbanks in December 1912. For weeks beforehand the deputy marshal from Circle scoured the country to serve subpoenas to most of the area's forty whites and many Indians. Carroll was served, and when court time drew near, he dog-sledded seventy miles from his camp to Fort Yukon. There a party of witnesses formed a travel group. It took them three days to reach Circle and six more to Fairbanks. A court witness had to be hardy; there was no easy way to travel.

Carroll's good humor deserted him after a month's wait for the Fort Yukon trials in Fairbanks. While he was gaining his daily witness fees, he was losing the winter's trapping season; on his return he found that half of his traps were lost. But for the poorer individuals bored with their village, the Fairbanks excursion amounted to a bonanza.

Trespass and cohabitation were the most important cases tried. The man charged with cohabitation resolved his legal dilemma by marrying his housekeeper, something Carroll figured he could have thought of doing earlier to save them all a lot of trouble. The cost to the government for the winter diversion of Fort Yukon, according to Carroll's calculation, was twenty-five thousand dollars.

Fairbanks merchants were the big gainers, which may explain why there was no general outcry from the interior against the extravagance. When the court session ended the Fairbanks newspaper headlined its story:

> FORT YUKON LEAVING FAIRBANKS, BOUND FOR HOME.
> WE ALL REGRET TO SEE THEM LEAVE SO SOON.[10]

The same game was replayed in 1913 and 1914. Marshal Erwin, reporting to the attorney general in 1914, calculated a cost of thirty thousand dollars for Fort Yukon trials in the previous eight months. He blamed prosecutor James Crossley (with whom he was feuding), Commissioner Burke, and the Episcopal Church for encouraging a variety of minor charges that had netted a single conviction and a five hundred dollar fine. Erwin observed that most of the witnesses had nothing to say about the cases: "All mission whites are always brought and many Indians. The fees are an important income to the Indians."[11]

Erwin had tried to cool Fort Yukon tempers by assigning a deputy there. The missionaries complained to Washington about the deputy's conduct, forcing Erwin to explain matters to the attorney general. It seemed that the deputy had intervened when the Indian council threw a woman and her furniture out of her cabin "without due process." Missionaries had assured the council that their authority was the equivalent of that held by the U.S. marshal.

In time, Washington reacted to the Fort Yukon court-junket scandal. The delay can be explained only by the officials' fear of stirring the ever present hornet's nest of missionary interests in high places. A Justice Department examiner investigating Erwin's office recommended Burke's removal and the appointment of one "who will administer the law, instead of listening to and taking hand in petty complaints arising between members of the mission and white settlers." While observing that Fort Yukon has, "for the past four or five years, been the most expensive point on the Yukon River," the examiner indirectly exonerated prosecutor Crossley; he was required to present all cases bound over by a commissioner to the grand jury.[12] After 1915 little was heard from Fort Yukon. The little settlement did not die, yet its prosperity languished because of the government's stern austerity.

14. Hard to Convict

Generally speaking, those professing aversion to crooks, grafters, etc. bear watching.—Governor J. F. A. Strong

No ONE of the four judicial districts of Alaska can be distinguished from the others over the long territorial period for either the efficiency or the malfeasance of its Justice Department officials. Nor can any one be singled out—except at times of particular stress— for a greater degree of lawlessness than others. What distinctions the record reveals have more to do with geography than anything else. In the first division the climate was much more mild than in the other regions, and access to its ports from the States was convenient the year round. But geography and local economic activities provided a setting of some uniqueness for certain celebrated crimes in the southeastern district, and a few of them are worth describing.

A bench warrant for Joseph MacDonald's arrest on a murder charge was issued December 17, 1912, by the district court in Juneau. MacDonald's whereabouts was no mystery: he was superintendent of the Guanajuato Consolidated Mining and Milling Company in Mexico, a position similar to that he had held earlier at Douglas's Treadwell mine. Getting him back to Juneau, however, might have posed much difficulty if MacDonald had wanted to resist extradition. A revolution raged in Mexico, travel was difficult, and the beleaguered government considered MacDonald to be a responsible and valuable resident.

MacDonald believed the indictment to be a mistake, one that he wished to clear up by traveling willingly to Juneau. Instead of escaping when Mexican newspapers published the indictment news, he invited officials to place him under nominal arrest until conditions permitted travel. The Mexicans did not mention bail but asked him to spend one night in a military hospital until the extradition papers were signed. Even this brief incarceration angered Guanajuato miners and MacDonald's friends; he had to restrain their threat to attack the hospital—or so he claimed. With the papers signed, MacDonald was prepared to go, but officials confessed their inability to pay guards for taking the "prisoner" to the border. "Don't worry," said the former Alaskan, "I'll pay them myself."[1] Thus the party moved off to the border, where special agent Joe Warren waited for MacDonald.

If these proceedings seem bizarre, consider the dating of events: the alleged crime had been committed ten years before the extradition and authorities, who had considered prosecution earlier, had decided that the accused man was innocent. While it is true that the statute of limitations does not run out in murder cases, it is extremely unusual to indict years after a crime's occurrence. This was not a case brought to a climax by significant, belated detective work or by the discovery of an evasive fugitive. In essence, the U.S. attorney had the same case in 1912 that his predecessor had in 1902. But in 1902 the coroner's inquest found no basis for charges and the grand jury did not indict. Did the memories of witnesses grow more acute in the passage of time?

"No crime has been committed," reported the coroner's jury on May 14, 1902, after hearing the testimony of witnesses led by MacDonald and Robert Kinzie. The facts seemed straightforward. Obviously the dead man, N. C. Jones, suffered from insane delusions, a wildly distorted vision of religious obligations that caused him to threaten the Treadwell mine superintendent. The Treadwell mine was the area's largest employer by far, and its superintendent was not accustomed to threats. So when Jones entered MacDonald's office and announced, "I am sent to you by the Lord for to have you stop working on Sunday entirely, because there are a

thousand men here that are damning their souls every Sunday,"
MacDonald had every reason to get angry—or to laugh. But Mac-
Donald, if he can be believed, neither laughed nor got angry. He
merely explained in the manner of a cultured gentleman who may
have realized that Jones had problems with reality that "we could
not think of doing that. If Sunday work stopped men would not stay.
They would lose $15 per month."

Don't worry about the money, advised Jones, "the Lord will give
you plenty of men." The Lord will be here "in six weeks and he is
going to take this thing in hand." He will reward you and you can
"make yourself a good man" by shutting down on Sunday.

"Why didn't the Lord tell me?" asked MacDonald.

"You are not a Christian," replied Jones.

After Jones ended this fascinating confrontation by telling the superintendent he would be back later, MacDonald talked to the
marshal and the U.S. attorney about the incident. District Attorney Robert Friedrich, a pal of MacDonald, agreed that Jones
sounded crazy and promised his arrest, but nothing was done.

A couple of days later, MacDonald was eating breakfast at his
residence within the mine compound when employees warned him
that Jones was hanging around waiting to see him. MacDonald,
sensing that his men were worried about Jones's intentions, picked
up his morning cigar and his revolver, then headed for his office.
Jones stopped the mine boss, brandishing a small stick. According
to MacDonald, Jones packed a gun as well, although even the mine
employees who witnessed the shooting did not see any sign of
Jones's gun. "You did not do as I told you," shouted Jones, who,
according to MacDonald, then pulled a gun. MacDonald shot him in
the arm, and when Jones grappled with him, MacDonald shot him
in the other arm. Then, said the husky boss, "because I am lame,
and I knew I could not stand much more pulling around, I shot him
again," got his gun, and "he ran away." But Jones did not run very
far before he dropped dead with three bullet wounds.

Robert Kinzie, the Treadwell assistant superintendent confirmed the boss's story in all particulars, as a loyal subordinate
should. The U.S. attorney saw no reason to proceed once the coroner's jury was satisfied with the story told by the Treadwell men.

As the years passed, official satisfaction with the conclusion of
the Jones case vanished. Rumors persisted in Juneau that a terrible

miscarriage of justice had occurred. John Boyce succeeded Friedrich in 1903 and was succeeded in turn by John Rustgard in 1910. Eventually the complaints reached the Department of Justice, causing the attorney general to order an investigation in 1911.

Investigators learned that MacDonald was "a man of an unusually arrogant, overbearing and vicious temperament" and was reputed to have killed seven men in Montana and neighboring states. Often enough MacDonald bragged of his exploits as a gunman and gave demonstrations of marksmanship to back up his pretensions. "He evinced a general desire to be looked upon by the community as a professional gunman and to impress the community with his disregard for human life; he frequently drank and habitually used shockingly vile and violent language . . . and terrorized the community and practically had the great majority both on Douglas Island and at Juneau intimidated, cowed, and subdued." Eyewitnesses at the coroner's inquest were thoroughly frightened of MacDonald and his friends. It was only when the boss left the country that witnesses dared to speak openly of what they had seen.

Rustgard discovered another instance of MacDonald's domineering: in 1904 he assaulted Captain E. G. Baughman of the *Humboldt* with a revolver. Despite the evidence of his guilt, the grand jury did not indict.

The *Humboldt* affair shed some light on MacDonald's character and overwhelming arrogance. On her passage from Seattle the ship eased up to the Treadwell wharf just after midnight on June 13, 1904. The Treadwell watchman, acting under instructions, refused to allow any passengers to land except those he recognized. The captain protested that the dock was a public one and accompanied a passenger to the foot of the gangplank. By this time the watchman had summoned MacDonald, who brandished a gun, called the captain an S.O.B., and ordered both men up the gangplank, shouting and cursing.

Female passengers who watched the lively spectacle from the ship with mingled amusement and indignation commented loudly on MacDonald's truculence. The superintendent retorted that the captain seemed to have a cargo of whores aboard, a comment that caused even more excitement and comment upon the man's uncouth manner.

Another dramatic scene ensued when an unidentified Indian

tried to land. "God damn you, go back up there," roared Mac-
Donald, who then hit the passenger with something he held in his
hand, and, as the passenger retreated, chased him to deliver the
third blow.[2]

Outrage at such brutality and highhandedness swept through the
ship. A German consul introduced the theme of Americanism, lecturing MacDonald that "America was a free country and this was a
free dock." MacDonald pointed his gun at the speaker, denounced
him as an s.o.b., and threatened "to blow him full of holes."

Complaints were carried to the U.S. commissioner, and U.S. Attorney John Boyce tried to get an indictment for assault with a
deadly weapon; but, as Rustgard observed when he conducted his
historical research, the grand jury refused to indict. Judging from
the record, the grand jury may not have been as cowardly as Rustgard suspected. Its refusal to indict seems reasonable in view of
the fact that none of the complainants appeared. The *Humboldt* had
sailed on, and all the prosecutor had as evidence was an affidavit
from passenger G. W. Barlow. Neither the captain nor "John Doe,
Indian," who was the victim of the alleged assault, nor any other
prosecution witnesses was available.

Rustgard did have witnesses for the 1912 murder prosecution,
four or five eyewitnesses who told federal investigators what actually happened in front of the Treadwell butcher shop on May 14,
1902. One of the witnesses was T. A. Tubbs, who changed the
story he had told to the coroner's jury. Jones was walking along
whittling a stick as MacDonald and Kinzie approached. Kinzie hurried into his house to avoid seeing what his boss planned for Jones.
There was no conversation between Jones and the boss. Mac-
Donald started shooting as Jones held up his stick as if to ward off
the bullets.

Anna Olsen, Kinzie's domestic servant, heard butcher James
Thompson say to MacDonald after the shooting: "What have you
been doing—shooting dogs?" MacDonald laughed uproariously at
this clever sally. Anna ran upstairs and told other men that the superintendent had shot Jones. "Don't say anything," they advised,
"you may have to prove it."[3]

Clothilda Marcky also had seen Jones standing defenselessly before the boss's attack. Neither she nor any of the other witnesses
believed that Jones was armed with anything but his whittling stick.

Tubbs claimed that he would have told the truth in 1902 if Friedrich had shown any inclination to hear it. Friedrich had asked only a few questions "and made no effort whatever to really bring out any testimony which would be damaging to MacDonald." As a reward for his lies to the prosecutor and the coroner's jury, Tubbs got a one hundred dollar monthly raise, yet he believed "it was a cold-blooded murder if there ever was one in the world." Tubbs also claimed that MacDonald and Kinzie beat Jones up earlier in 1902 for serving a warrant on Treadwell property, threatening to send him back in a box if he ever came near the mine again.

In a better world, or one more favorable to prosecutor Rustgard, the Juneau jurors would have removed the ten-year-old blemish on the town's reputation for justice with a conviction of Joseph MacDonald. But, alas, the prosecutor lost his case; jurors could not find MacDonald guilty beyond a reasonable doubt.

The outcome is not surprising. Some, but not all, of the witnesses who gave information to the Bureau of Investigation testified, yet the prosecutor's evidence was not overwhelming. The defense argued that the conclusion reached earlier, when the matter was fresh, must be overcome by convincing, substantial evidence, and the prosecution did not offer enough strong evidence. Jurors probably felt that their responsibility was to be careful in 1912, out of concern for justice, rather than worry about the supposed domination of a 1902 jury by the mine boss.

The aging MacDonald looked pathetic enough at trial. Federal officials tried hard to prevent his pretrial release on bail despite his claims of poor health and meritorious conduct in accepting extradition from Mexico. He spent a couple of months in jail before bail was granted.

Where did justice lie in the case? the folks in Juneau wondered. If the federal authorities botched the job once, who could say that the later trial did not illustrate another chapter in a comedy of errors? And who could now help poor Jones?

In this and in other cases Rustgard showed his taste for battle. His career was a rather unusual one. He had been born in Norway and was educated in Minnesota after serving adventurously as a cabin boy on a clipper ship. He passed the bar in Minneapolis and joined the Nome gold rush in 1900, serving as mayor in 1903 and two terms as city attorney before gaining his first-division appointment. Subsequently he was territorial attorney general, and after leaving Alaska in the 1930s he wrote a number of books and popular articles on economic topics.

While the Department of Justice saw nothing suspicious about the district attorney's zeal in prosecuting MacDonald, there were gossips in Juneau who whispered that Rustgard hoped to silence critics who complained that he served Treadwell interests rather than the public's. Rustgard's reputation as a Treadwell man grew out of a 1910–11 dispute over a quartz-mining development by the Ebner Gold Mining Company. Ebner's property was adjacent to that of the Alaska-Juneau Gold Mining Company in Silver Bow Basin, and Ebner's plans for a two-hundred-stamp mill upset its rivals. Alaska-Juneau posted location notices on the land Ebner claimed; Ebner filed ejection suits in August 1910 and asked for restraining orders. Before the case could be heard, Alaska-Juneau started to build a dam that would divert water needed by Ebner and seriously affect its mining prospects. Two months later, Ebner's workers blasted rock on their claims in a manner that forced the dam builders to run for their lives. R. A. Kinzie, superintendent of both Alaska-Juneau and the huge Treadwell mine on Douglas Island, which employed two thousand men, charged Ebner's supervisors with assault with intent to kill.

According to Justice Department examiner M. C. Masterson, District Attorney Rustgard and Marshal Herbert Faulkner went after Ebner with inquisitional zeal. "Rustgard improperly used his office to intimidate the U.S. Commissioner. He brought charges before the grand jury in Ketchikan instead of Juneau contrary to tradition and agreement with the defendants' attorneys." He also made a false statement in his venue-change request, "giving the impression that the U.S. Marshal had telegraphed him that the Ebner people were again riotous." To Masterson it seemed a blatant interference with civil litigation through criminal proceedings. "The zeal of Rustgard in prosecution is so noticeable that the impression has gone out that he has been unduly influenced by and is working in the interest of Treadwell, for whom he was formerly employed." Public opinion in Juneau, where most resented Treadwell's domination, condemned Rustgard as a company tool. Yet Rustgard, when frustrated by the refusal of the grand jury to indict

Ebner's supervisors, refused to dismiss charges and brought new ones against Ebner's attorney.[4]

Back in Washington the attorney general reviewed Masterson's report and its recommendations that Rustgard and Faulkner be dismissed. He was appalled. Writing Rustgard in March 1911, he censured "a conspicuous lack of discretion and of that impartiality which could characterize a prosecuting officer of the United States . . . and impaired the confidence of this department in your judgment. I am authorized by the president to request your resignation."[5] Since Faulkner's involvement was peripheral, he was not asked to resign.

Rustgard refused to resign. Instead he wrote a long explanation of his conduct, supported by a thirty-two-page letter from Governor Walter E. Clark defending Rustgard and Faulkner. Other letters of support also reached Washington. Rustgard's explanations made sense, and Clark's knowledge of Juneau's customary volatile temper over mining disputes convinced the attorney general that Masterson had not fully understood the situation. Five weeks after he had demanded Rustgard's resignation, he withdrew his demand.[6]

Rustgard had survived, but perhaps he saw some wisdom in dissociating from Treadwell. The charges against MacDonald provided an opportunity to appear before Juneau's citizens as a righteous prosecutor of the powerful in defense of the little worker's right to live. He seized the chance to display himself in a more appealing role. Although he lost the case, his obvious determination helped restore his image.

With the admission of New Mexico and Arizona as the forty-seventh and forty-eighth states in 1912 the Justice Department's responsibilities for territorial courts and lawmen were sharply reduced. This did not mean that Alaska and the few U.S. overseas possessions received more attention. Alaska's population was declining, and the decline continued until World War II, so that there was no great demand for change. Marshals and district attorneys were still expected to investigate and apprehend criminals with the personnel on hand, although in certain hard cases their requests for outside help or special agents might be favored.

In October 1913, U.S. Attorney George R. Walker appealed urgently for help. People in the Valdez division were in a panic about several murders and disappearances. Even though gold mining had declined, prospectors still roamed the sparsely settled country, hoping to find new fields that would equal Nome or Fairbanks, and they dreaded violence. The bodies of two men with bashed-in heads had been found on the Fairbanks-Valdez Trail one hundred miles north of Valdez on Willow Creek early that month, and while there was no way of policing trails on departmental budgets, swift apprehension of the murderers would make all Alaskans happier and perhaps deter potential miscreants.

Judge Frederick M. Brown joined Walker's petition for the employment of a special detective, and so did Delegate James Wickersham. The requests allured the Justice Department because they named a legendary detective who was available for the duty. Philip R. McGuire was the sleuth wanted by Alaska officials. For the benefit of Washington bureaucrats, they recalled McGuire's exploits in investigating the multiple murders of Christmas Day 1900 on the Dawson-Skagway Trail. McGuire, a former Pinkerton detective, had helped the Mounties nail George O'Brien, the first man executed for murder in Canada's north. Washington responded with authorization for a three hundred dollar reward for the apprehension of the murderers. This was not enough to catch McGuire's attention, so the attorney general agreed to pay a two hundred dollar monthly salary and expenses. The famous detective signed on and went to work.

McGuire looked over the ground at Willow Creek, gathered a list of names of men who had left the country about the time of the murders, then went outside looking for them. He could not find the men first sought, but another suspect, Tony Tol, seemed a likely choice too. Tol was in the States somewhere and hard to find.

Almost a year passed and McGuire's supervisors grew restless. Some suspected that the detective preferred hanging around Seattle to slogging for clues along Alaska's trails. The attorney general ordered the new Bureau of Investigation office in Seattle to investigate McGuire. Agent W. B. Byron reported that McGuire roomed at the Berkshire Hotel on Third Avenue, a well-known house of prostitution, "in which I do not care to operate unless accompanied by a Special Agent." McGuire busied himself "attending theatres and functions, also going to meals nightly with a woman who formerly lived in the same hotel." McGuire did not report directly to the Seattle office or even leave his address there, but in informal meetings with Justice staff he let it slip that his girlfriend was really an English spy ferreting out German spies who were sending messages by wire to Berlin. McGuire had other resources as well; he had uncovered several men and women connected with German operations. Byron remained skeptical: "Either the women are fooling him or he the public."[7]

Obviously the Bureau of Investigation did not approve of freelancers like McGuire, particularly a phony who had been discovered passing information about Alaska fugitives gleaned from bureau staff to Valdez as his own investigative results. Alaska did have a legitimate outside officer based in Seattle: Joe Warren, extradition officer for the second division. Since the other three Alaska court divisions operated without a marshal's deputy assigned full time to transporting and tracing fugitives, they often asked for Warren's help. Warren always cooperated, but it confused the Seattle office when "no provision is made for reimbursement." Byron advised that if "the Department prefers Alaskan work done by the Bureau, additional force should be assigned to this headquarters."[8]

At any rate it looked like McGuire had lost a step or two, as sports announcers say, from his heroic days helping the Mounties get their man. He was summarily fired. The Willow Creek murders remained unsolved.

In all such cases the Department of Justice record was poor. It was one thing to apprehend an identified suspect who left Alaska for his former home and lived openly, in which case the Seattle bureau office or another nearer the suspect's domicile or Joe Warren could be dispatched to make the arrest. Deputies from the Alaska district involved would travel to the point of arrest and bring the suspect back. If evidence sustained a conviction, the case was closed satisfactorily, but solving a murder or other serious crime in which neither witnesses, physical evidence, nor circumstantial evidence pointed decisively at an individual virtually defied solution. Murders in remote districts, undetected for some time, were especially perplexing. It was always safe and reasonable to assume that the slayer had fled to the outside, but many Alaskans followed a seasonal cycle of wintering outside. Deputies could only try to identify men who had been in the section, had left in suspicious circumstances, and had had the opportunity of commiting the crime. Many fruitless searches were the usual result. If each division had retained a skilled detective for just such difficult cases, it probably would have helped, but the Justice Department did not expect deputies to have special skills in detection and was not prepared to carry the expense of full-time investigators.

The Bureau of Investigation was established in 1905 as part of the Department of Justice at President Teddy Roosevelt's direction and against the strongly expressed opposition of Congress. Roosevelt and his attorney general, Charles J. Bonaparte, investigating swindles involving federal land, borrowed investigators from the Post Office Department and the Secret Service and hired Pinkerton detectives. When Congress specifically prohibited Justice's use of borrowed or hired investigators, Bonaparte created his own force.

The bureau grew slowly under its first chief, A. Bruce Bielaski, and occupied itself with land and bank cases. By 1914 it had a Seattle office, which nominally could assist Alaska's officers, but its personnel were accountants who lacked skills in criminal investigation.

In 1915 when the Juneau district attorney wanted detection help, there was no reason for him to think of the bureau; he asked approval for hiring a private detective. James Smiser wanted to retain F. T. Lischke for help in the notorious Krause murder case, which will be discussed later. Lischke had already been of considerable help to authorities after being hired, through the Pinkerton agency, by fraternal organizations in Juneau. After paying the Pinkerton bill for some months the Juneau people thought the government should finish the investigation. Lischke was hired indirectly as a special deputy, but when Washington realized that he was a Pinkerton man, his appointment was withdrawn. The prohibitory federal law of 1905 was still in effect. Smiser kept trying, and the attorney general ordered the bureau to send him some help. The Seattle bureau office did not have anyone who was qualified and recommended the hiring of Charles Tennant, Seattle's chief of detectives, but Tennant declined. Finally a compromise was worked out: Lischke resigned from the Pinkertons and became a special deputy once again. [9]

Under both private employment and as a deputy, Lischke performed what was the most intensive criminal investigation in Alaska's history until more recent times. The successful conviction of Krause convinced Smiser that the detective was a key to his future well-being, and he was able to convince the attorney general as well. Several months passed before the attorney general approved of the detective's permanent employment, probably because he saw a use for a keen homicide investigator in solving recent murders in the interior, while Smiser seemed more worried about prostitution and liquor selling. By December 1916, Lischke had left Alaska, but he returned when Smiser finally gained permission to hire him.

The addition of a skilled detective to the first division's law forces might have had momentous effects if other divisions had clamored for and received the same privilege from Washington. Unfortunately, Smiser, seemingly a puritanical fellow who worried excessively about vice in a community traditionally much more tolerant at its prevalence, soon demanded Lischke's dismissal. The deputy's first assignment concerned white-slavery charges against E. B. and Esther Brown of San Francisco, who brought several prostitutes to Ketchikan, then moved on to Anchorage. Lischke went to Anchorage, arrested the Browns, and took them back to Ketchikan, ignoring Smiser's instructions to keep them separated en route. The Browns not only shared accommodations aboard ship and in hotels, they also shared their disdain for the vice-busting district attorney with the deputy, who must have agreed. Anyway the deputy compounded his neglect by lodging the Browns at a Ketchikan hotel rather than the jail, until the furious prosecutor learned of it, and even tried to convince Smiser that the Browns' law violation was only a "technical" one. Smiser resented Lischke's suggestion that charges be dismissed and secured E. B. Brown's conviction and a two-year sentence. Fearing the jurors would not convict Esther, he did not prosecute her. His court victory did not mitigate his contempt for his onetime favorite detective, whom he accused of reaching "some understanding" with Brown. Smiser also refused to approve Lischke's travel expenses to Alaska, but the attorney general overruled him. [10]

Smiser's disappointment set back the practice of hiring outside experts for a time, but the precedent had been set and district attorneys found occasion to revive the practice later on when they felt that the successful prosecution of certain cases required it. And the bureau did assign an agent to Juneau in 1917. Meanwhile there were other hard cases of the kind Alaska's geography dictated, most notably that of the Mad Trapper, which will be discussed later, and, of course, the liquor cases that regularly burdened the courts. Thanks to the Woman's Christian Temperance Union, Governor Strong, Delegate Wickersham, and a majority of Alaskans who succumbed to the argument that all political, social, and economic evils flowed from drinking, Alaskans voted dry in 1916 and a federal law established territory-wide prohibition in 1917. The governor's office was responsible for enforcement so the various marshals should have been spared pain, yet in the "Frozen Foot" Johnson case, as in so many later national prohibition efforts, the enforcers became corrupted and dragged other officers into the mire of scandal.

Dead men tell plenty of tales to careful detectives, but a missing person tells very little. If there is no body and uncertain evidence of foul play, who could say for sure that the missing person simply had left for the States? Given the maze of islands and waters in southeastern and the concentration of small boats in various ports, it is no surprise that a number of robbery and murder victims were boat skippers whose bodies were disposed of at sea. The most celebrated of these cases were those of Ed Krause, "the Monster of Juneau," and Burt McDonald, the slayer of Ketchikan fish buyer George Marshall.

Alaska's communities in earlier days were not populous, yet most of them had a large transitory segment. In mining towns, such as Fairbanks, Nome, Ruby, and Iditarod, there was a seasonal rhythm, an ebb and flow of residential traffic each spring and fall. In southeastern and south central the duration of the fishing and canning season set a similar work-residency pattern. Even Alaskans who were permanent residents were very mobile and likely to spend a winter or summer outside. But for all the restless and seasonal movement, people did wonder when someone disappeared without giving any explanation to acquaintances.

Folks in Juneau worked hard at fishing or in the gold mines, enjoying the town's beautiful setting of sea-ringed mountains and a sense of security peculiar to the sparsely populated forest region. All their security was suddenly dispelled when a number of men disappeared mysteriously between 1913 and 1915. Missing were Olaf Ekram, Kato Yamamoto, O. E. Moe, J. O. Plunkett, and William Christie. Could it be a mere coincidence that five men left the area without telling anyone, or, as seemed more likely, was some deadly monster preying on victims like a wolf falling on a flock of sheep? People became alarmed. Where was their protection against a wanton murderer? Their very helplessness enraged them; they turned on the federal authorities and demanded a solution: find the killer or we will do it ourselves. The fraternal societies of Juneau showed their resolve by raising fifteen hundred dollars and hiring a private detective.

The marshal and the U.S. attorney got the message. Their own well-being and job security was under attack. If mob violence erupted in the sylvan wilderness of southeastern, their superiors in Washington might replace them with more-effective lawmen. Thus aroused, they wired D.C. for authorization to spend more money, and the attorney general, sensing their predicament, promised the necessary help.

One of the missing men was Captain James O. Plunkett, fifty-five-year-old owner of the *Lue.* He had a cabin in Juneau but usually lived on the *Lue,* which he chartered to people who needed transportation. On October 24, 1915, a man who wanted to go to Snettisham talked to Plunkett in Tom McCall's cigar store on Front Street, but Plunkett was engaged and indicated that another man had retained him for a secret charter. Several people observed the *Lue* leaving the Juneau dock that Sunday with the captain and his passenger, the last time Plunkett was seen. Four days later the U.S. customs officer at Juneau received a letter, presumably from Plunkett, reporting the loss of the *Lue* by fire and enclosing the boat license.

In January 1913 a Japanese, Kato Yamamoto, had disappeared without a trace. Someone who identified himself as George Hartman corresponded with bankers in Vancouver, British Columbia, where Yamamoto owned real estate. Hamilton offered a mortgage on the property signed over to him in August 1913, and demanded foreclosure since Yamamoto apparently had drowned. The missing Yamamoto, a foreman at the Olympic mines near Petersburg, was an educated man with an excellent reputation. When he left the mine, he expected to return. The company owed him seven hundred dollars in wages.

The situation was the same with the other missing men. There seemed to be no reason why they would voluntarily vanish from the region. In the case of William Christie, the last man to disappear, the pattern of mystery broke down somewhat. There were rumors and facts that cast some light on his disappearance. The rumor was that Ed Krause had been in love with Christie's wife of two weeks, a German girl called Cecile, who had dated Krause before his marriage. Ed had not been happy with her decision, yet he had greeted her pleasantly on the street in Juneau and even took her and some of her relatives to dinner. But only insane jealousy or incredible contempt for the law and the community's anxiety about the missing men could explain Krause's open abduction of Christie. On October 29, 1915, he went over to Douglas Island, called at the Treadwell mine, posed as a deputy marshal, and took Christie right off his job. He had to take Christie to Juneau to see the marshal, he told the foreman, but would bring him back in the afternoon. That was the last anyone ever saw of William Christie.

The next day, Krause was seen near the Christie home, where a note, purporting to be from Christie to his wife and explaining his absence, was left. Krause then took his boat to Ketchikan, where he caught the passenger ship *Jefferson* for Seattle on November 8, traveling under the name of O. E. Moe. By this time Juneau lawmen were looking for Krause, and he was arrested when the *Jefferson* docked in Seattle.

Detective William Kent of the Seattle police interrogated the suspect, who initially denied that he was Krause. When police wondered that he used the name of another missing man, Krause admitted his identity, hired lawyers, and resisted extradition as long as he could.

Krause did not have a very good reputation in Juneau. Calvin H. Barkdull, a Sukoi Islets fox farmer, knew him as a fur poacher and the probable murderer of a neighboring fox farmer named Callahan, whose spread Krause and his gang took over when Callahan vanished. After one of Krause's gang warned Barkdull that they planned to take his pelts after the harvest, the fur man hired extra help and maintained an armed patrol around his island. Once some-one shot at him as he rowed along on his patrol. By pretending to be hit and letting his boat drift away, he escaped with his life. When Barkdull had his pelts ready for market, Krause landed on his is-land, hoping to steal them. The barking of his foxes alerted Bark-dull, who watched Krause land, armed with club and rifle. Krause watched the house for an hour; then, seeing that he was under ob-servation, he left.

Barkdull challenged Krause on a crowded Juneau street, calling him a "cold-blooded, low down sneak thief and a murdering skunk" and promising to kill Krause if Krause ever set foot on his island, unless the law got him first and hanged him." Krause walked away without saying anything, but he did not bother Barkdull again.

When Krause was brought back to Juneau, he was tried suc-cessively for larceny, kidnapping, fraud, and murder from April 1916. He was easily convicted of the Christie kidnapping and of several frauds involving the property of the missing men, but the prosecutor knew that a murder conviction would be difficult to get. Dragging likely places in search of the bodies of Christie, Plunkett, or the others had not achieved results. It seemed best to try Krause for the murder of Plunkett first because the circumstances of robbery and the identification of Krause with Plunkett on his last day in Juneau provided much circumstantial evidence.

The trial was a classic example of establishing the victim's death and the link with the accused in the absence of mortal remains. Con-victions in similar circumstances had been achieved often enough in American courts, but the prosecutor always had to hold his breath when the defense demanded dismissal on the ground that corpus delicti—that is, the death and the cause of it by the accused—had not been established.

The prosecutor stressed the ease with which a body could be disposed of in the water-rimmed world of southeastern. "Plunkett lies in many fathoms of cold water near the Taku Glacier."[12] And he put heavy emphasis on the unlikeliness of Plunkett's absence for any reason but for his murder. A large number of government wit-nesses, forty-six in all, testified that Plunkett was a sober man of good character who had no relatives outside to visit and had no reason not to tell his friends if he had planned to be away. This repetitious testimony to establish the probability of a forcible removal made sense because it was difficult to prove all the other elements of the crime.

It helped very much that on his arrest Krause had some of Plunkett's property in his possession. It appeared that Krause had planned to use the dead man's documents to acquire control of property, as with Yamamoto and others. It also helped to be able to show with expert testimony that Krause wrote the note to U.S. Customs on his own typewriter and signed Plunkett's name. But the prosecutor was still worried as he made his final argument to the jury and courted reversible error by commenting on Krause's failure to testify: "Krause has maintained a cat-like silence ever since he appeared in court . . . not even the rope dangling about his neck can induce him to talk. . . . He fears the consequences of cross-examination." For good measure the prosecutor called the accused a "sneaking wolf and a monster." To the general satisfaction of the people of Juneau, the jurors found Krause guilty of murder one; and they did not recommend mercy. In February 1917 the judge sentenced Krause to hang.

Krause's life did not end with his execution. Nor was his sentence commuted, as was often the case in Alaska death sentences. Krause thwarted the hangman with a spectacular escape on April 12, 1917.

Everyone in Juneau seemed to be on the streets as news of Krause's escape from the federal jail spread through town. Krause acted soon after his circuit-court appeal was rejected. Somehow he sawed through bars of the big tank used for the prisoners' day room, climbed through into the office section, and walked through the main door. His absence was discovered within moments. Guard James Bates ran out the same door and fired two shots in the air to raise the alarm.

Guards, law officers, and Governor J. F. A. Strong met in the U.S. attorney's office to plan a search. Armed parties were dispatched in all directions: ten men left in automobiles for Salmon Creek Road. Launches provided by the Treadwell mine and others chugged off to Petersburg, Sitka, Point Retreat, and the end of

Douglas Island. Volunteers were armed with guns stored in the jail to patrol the town, its environs, the docks, and the surrounding hills. Deputy marshals throughout the first division were notified, and firebells tolled in all the communities of Gastineau Channel.

Although Juneau is a mainland community, it is crammed close to the sea by mountains; its few roads and trails did not lead any considerable distance, hence it seemed probable that Krause, an experienced sailor, would steal a boat and hide out among the islands of the Alexander Archipelago until the pursuit cooled off.

The daring escape excited all southeastern because of Krause's notoriety. He was suspected of killing five men, although he was convicted only of the Plunkett murder, and it was assumed that if he had weapons he would readily kill anyone who interfered with his flight. Prosecution witnesses at his trial feared his vengeance; the Juneau Fire Department guarded the home of one of them, Mrs. William Christie, wife of one of Krause's victims.

On the day after the escape it was learned that Krause stole a rowboat at Norway Point, just two miles from city's center. As the search concentrated on the channel, there were several incidents. Men fired on a small boat manned by an attorney when he ignored their calls to come to shore. Police interrogated men known to be friendly with Krause; when one jeered, "You'll never get him. He's off with a pack and a boat," he was arrested.[13] This dampened the wise guy's mood; he complained that his intent was only to provide information.

Back at the jail Marshal Harry Bishop reviewed the escape evidence. Whether someone had smuggled in the knife Krause used as a saw could not be determined, but the guards' negligence in other respects was established. Krause had prevented the locking of his sleeping cell by inserting a wooden plug, leaving him free to open the door and file away at the day-room bars once the guards had left the area. Guards Peter Early, James Ester, and James Mahoney were fired.

Marshal Bishop resigned as well. His health was poor and he did not feel up to the stress of the search, which "promises more excitement and cares than his physical condition could endure."[14] The immediate replacement of Bishop with Josiah M. Tanner was announced. Tanner, a sixty-seven-year-old plumber from Skagway who had been a sheriff in Iowa and Pierce County, Washington, in the 1880s and 1890s, might have seemed a poor successor but for his fame in rounding up the Soapy Smith gang while he was a temporary marshal in 1898. Bishop, by contrast, had been a businessman, miner, water-company manager, and mayor before accepting his first law-enforcement job as U.S. marshal in 1914.

A Juneau newspaper editorial reflected on the escape: "Alaska for the greater part is a trackless desert but in many respects it is an easier country to catch a runaway in than anywhere because of the population scarcity and difficulty of getting provisions." Most man hunts had been successful, but "very few men would tackle Krause alone. He is a desperate man to handle."

Krause's liberty lasted from April 12 until the fifteenth, when his flight was halted at Doty's Cove on Admiralty Island fifteen miles from Juneau. Arvid Franzen, a Juneau shopkeeper, had been in town when Krause escaped. He knew Krause and hurried back to his home at Doty's Cove to alert residents and protect his family. On Sunday afternoon, the fifteenth, he saw a man landing a rowboat near his property and wondered whether it was the fugitive. Some time later he saw a man approaching the house and sent his wife out on the porch to sweep and distract the stranger while he scrambled for his rifle. After Mrs. Franzen and Krause exchanged greetings, Franzen showed himself with leveled rifle and called on Krause to halt where he stood, some thirty to forty feet from the house.

"Are you Krause?" challenged Franzen.

"Yes," said the fugitive, who was perhaps too exhausted for subterfuge.[15]

Krause kept coming defiantly. Franzen did not take any chances and fired twice. Bullets pierced Krause's heart and head.

After Krause fell dead, Franzen searched him. Krause's only weapon was the knife he had used as a file. Aside from that, his only possessions were a whiskey bottle and a jail blanket. It appeared that he had been in the boat most of the time since his escape.

Franzen sent a message to Juneau with an Indian: "I shot and killed Ed Krause at 2:30 this afternoon. My family is prostrated. Come and get body at once." By then Marshal Tanner was on the job, having arrived from Skagway the night before. Tanner and his deputies collected the body. An inquest the next day exonerated Franzen, and he was given the reward posted by the territory: one thousand dollars, dead or alive, had been offered. Krause's reputation as a gang leader worried Franzen. He feared revenge and carried his rifle into town; then, the next day, he asked for a pistol permit.

The enterprising editor of the *Alaska Daily Dispatch* called on Krause's attorney, Kazis Krauczunas, to clear up some of the Krause mysteries, since Krause was no more: Is Plunkett dead? Is Christie dead? What was Krause's motive in killing them? Where are their bodies? Have you instructions for disposal of Krause's body after his execution? Have you information on Krause's family or personal history? Krauczunas declined to answer: "Krause is dead. My advice is to forget him. Should I give out a statement now, it may be misconstrued." When the excitement dies down, 'maybe' I'll tell what I know."

During World War I radical and antiwar sentiment was no more welcome in Alaska than anywhere else in the nation, and law-enforcement officers responded swiftly to threats of disruption of the war effort. While some more centrally located Americans may have wondered how anyone could hurt the nation's mobilization on the distant, sparsely populated northern frontier, Alaska's officers seemed never to doubt that terrible things might occur but for their vigilance. In those days Alaskans were very proud of the Alaska Railroad, then under construction, and believed that long-sought boon to economic development might be a conspicuous target for the enemies of war. Officials in Alaska did not accept the cries of critics who had opposed the project as a gigantic boon-doggle, a railroad from nowhere to nowhere.

When Marshal L. T. Erwin and District Attorney Rhinehart Roth heard that the dreaded Wobblies (Industrial Workers of the World) were trying to strike railroad construction at Nenana, they rushed there with fire in their eyes. While they were not sure what specific laws had been breached by strike organizers, the lawmen were convinced "that the strike was not a *bona fide* strike but an IWW attempt to close work altogether."[16] Workers were upset because construction wages had fallen below Alaska's high living costs. Thomas Riggs, the railroad commissioner, insisted that the government had prohibited wage increases and refused to negotiate. Neither he nor Roth wanted the workers to petition the government as the strike leaders planned.

Robert Smith and other strike leaders believed that Roth's only concern was that a petition might motivate the government to halt construction during the war and cause "a great injustice . . . to the business people of the community." When Smith got a chance to complain of Roth's conduct to the attorney general, he claimed that Roth had conceded the justice of the workers' demands but explained that railroad construction "is only a joke . . . a gift from our Alaskan friends in congress and if we should now kick they are liable to close her down altogether."[17]

Perhaps Smith's whimsy colored his report on Roth's conversation, but regardless of what Roth said, he treated the strikers harshly. One man was convicted on what Smith labeled "a purely trumped-up charge" of disrespect for the flag, convicted, sentenced to a year in jail and fined one thousand dollars without having the opportunity to see a lawyer. Smith was held in the Fairbanks jail "incommunicado" for four months, then interred in the States as an enemy alien, although he had taken out his first papers for citizenship.

Roth and Erwin had kept the attorney general fully informed. Erwin described Smith as "a socialist, IWW, anarchist, and undesirable citizen" and recommended his deportation to Germany as an undesirable alien. The marshal appreciated that wartime ship movements prohibited Smith's immediate deportation, "but I want to take time by the forelock and have a reply so I can take steps when the war is over." Washington could not give Erwin the approval he sought, "as there is no suggestion in your letter that Smith is an enemy alien, or indeed an alien at all, it is not evident what action you think can be taken against him for deportation."[18] Roth followed up with a recommendation for permanent detention during the war. "Smith, et al., are not fit for parole, I consider them dangerous."[19]

From the Fairbanks jail Smith wrote the first of several letters to Washington over a two-year period protesting Roth's actions. Later

Tug-of-war in Fairbanks on the Fourth of July, 1913. University of Alaska Archives, Lulu Fairbanks Collection

he wrote long, amusing sketches of his life and attitudes, but in September he merely reported being "kidnapped three months ago in Nenana" when he was the officer of a "temporary organization formed to tell Washington, D.C. about the high cost of living."[20]

There was no sympathy for Smith in Washington. One assistant attorney general favored an indictment for treason. Another assured Roth that he might proceed against Smith under the penal code rather than worrying about treason charges. It is hard to see how any court might be expected to find Smith guilty of treason, and, in time, he was sent to Fort Douglas, Utah, for confinement.

Washington did ask Roth to answer charges Smith made in his letter from jail, and the routine request seemed to infuriate the district attorney. His reply suggests that he may have been unhinged by his radical-busting work: "It is humiliating, indeed, to be required to reply to the innuendo of an IWW alien enemy, that I am a representative of the White Pass Co." As for "my profit motive from big business, the accusation is just what one would expect from a man hoping and praying our government will be over run by the Imperial government of Germany." There was no ring of officialdom in Roth's division. "Smith lied to you" in saying that Roth bragged to him of scattering two hundred to three hundred men to the wind. "A few vicious characters did get frightened. All the rest went quietly back to work. Now the labor union at Nenana is affiliated with the A.F. of L. Smith, for years an IWW agitator, is the most dangerous character in every way and always advocated revolution in the United States."[21]

Obviously Roth had nothing to fear from Smith's charges against him, and it is strange that he reacted so stridently to his supervisor's request for information. Even radicals like Smith could complain, and the system required that answers be made. As time passed the department ignored Smith. His letter of March 1918 was not answered because of an "oversight." He tried again in May 1919 in a letter witty enough to catch the attorney general's interest and eventually gained his release from detention.[22]

Nome's prosecutor and district judge also exhibited patriotic vigilance against the Wobblies, but jurors there resisted what they considered the government's antilabor posture. The target for prosecution in Nome was Martin Kennelly, an Irishman who edited the *Daily Nome Industrial Worker,* an IWW paper sharply critical of America's participation in the war. Kennelly figured that the United States had no business bailing out an oppressive nation like England. Let the Kaiser and Johnny Bull fight their own battles, he argued. The same view was being expressed by radicals all over the States. Socialists and Wobblies viewed the war as a diversion to class warfare and a means of exploiting workers.

A Nome grand jury indicted the IWW editor for sedition in spring 1918. Many clippings from the newspaper in evidence showed that he favored stories on American grafters and war profiteers and on the battlefield victories of German forces. At trial Kennelly defended himself effectively. From Nome a newsman had little opportunity for investigating either government corruption or military campaigns, so he relied upon the syndicated news wires. Nine jurors concluded that Kennelly had not been guilty of sedition, and, most reluctantly, Judge William A. Holzheimer, discharged the jury.

The prosecutor, deciding his case was not strong enough for a conviction, asked the court to dismiss charges. This was routine procedure after a hung jury, and judges, who did not care to waste time, usually granted the district attorney's request without question. In this case the district attorney supported his petition with the assertion that the newspaper had ceased publication of articles said to be seditious. The paper's "conduct was now perfectly lawful and free from disloyalty or pro-Germanism"; Kennelly was no longer the editor. Judge Holzheimer was not pleased. "This is sedition," he scolded, "a character of case that the Department of Justice desires prosecuted vigorously, especially at this time, and the charge in the indictment is a meritorious one. The case should be tried."[23] The prosecutor was forced to do battle against sedition once more, but it appeared that his assessment of public opinion in Nome had been correct. Jurors acquitted Kennelly.

Judge Holzheimer felt better when Bruce Rogers, a staffer for the IWW newspaper, was tried. This time the newspaper language attributed to the accused went beyond a mere reporting of German victories. Rogers had written: "We must make the world safe for democracy, no matter if we have to bean the Goddess of Liberty to do it." He also wrote: "Recipe for being an American patriot: Be willing to die in the defense of the trade supremacy of the British Empire and her subjugation of India and Ireland." This time the jury came through with a conviction.[24]

Ed ("Frozen Foot") Johnson, an old-timer in Nome, took exception to repeated gambling indictments, which hindered fun and profit at his Arctic Saloon. The courts harassed him from 1915 to 1917 as if he were some kind of wicked character. After one fine of $500 and costs he got mad and appealed to the circuit court, eventually gaining a reversal and new trial. But the feds would not give up: they convicted him again. The fine was $250, and his lawyer's bill was staggering.

Too bad for Nome, then, sputtered Frozen Foot, who sold the Arctic Saloon and moved to Juneau, vowing to find a line of work less subject to persecution. His best course of action seemed a remote location, and he found a pleasant spot near Funter Bay. Since he lacked neighbors a gambling saloon was out of the question, so he built an efficient still and transported booze to thirsty residents of Juneau. From 1917 to January 1922, Frozen Foot did all right. The police did not bother him. Then for some reason the federal government decided Alaska needed a special agency devoted to prohibition enforcement, and Johnson's operation was placed under surveillance.

John B. Marshall, director of the new enforcement agency, sent J. W. Kirkland and W. C. Mayburn to investigate Johnson. The agents found the two-story cabin at Funter Bay, admired the stocks of moonshine-making material, and reported their findings. Then they were sent after Johnson with an arrest warrant. What happened subsequently provoked a storm of controversy and embarrassment for federal officials while elevating to heights of hysterical delight those who resented prohibition enforcers.

Agent Kirkland reported that the cabin was deserted; Johnson could not be found. Agent Mayburn told three different stories, one to the U.S. commissioner and two to the grand jury; each version conflicted sharply with Kirkland's. According to the most plausible version, the agents arrested Frozen Foot and started back to Juneau. Along the way Johnson bribed the agents and disappeared. Agents who followed up the first team's expedition took vengeance by raiding the still, seizing mash, sugar, and moonshine, and burning the cabin to the ground.

Puzzled and disgusted by the conflicting testimony, the grand jury indicted Johnson but censured Marshall for the unnecessary burning of the cabin and complained of the apparent lack of coordination among the various law officials. It seemed clear that trust and accord did not exist between the U.S. marshal's office and the prohibition office.

In the hope of salvaging some respect for the government, the U.S. attorney retained former Judge and Delegate James Wickersham as special prosecutor. Wickersham got Mayburn to confess his part in the bribe and release of Johnson by granting immunity from prosecution. The arrest of Johnson was set in motion, then stalled. U.S. Marshal Arthur Shoup claimed the prohibition director held up the warrant, telling him Johnson was leaving Alaska anyway and his arrest would disclose Mayburn's confession and endanger his life. The director denied making such a request. Everyone agreed that Johnson did get away.

The next round of the circus was the prosecution of Kirkland for perjury to the grand jury. Wickersham explained away the confusion of Mayburn's several narrations of events: the agent was now telling the truth, and jurors should convict Kirkland. The jury disagreed because the star witness's credibility was questionable; Kirkland was acquitted. Since Johnson had vanished and Mayburn had immunity, the federal prosecutor had batted zero for three in what should have been a cut-and-dried case. The score probably would have been zero for four if Johnson had been prosecuted. What jury would convict on the tangled testimony of two corrupted federal agents? [25]

"George Ming gave me cookies that made my stomach sick. I thought I was poisoned and took the pistol from my room to kill him as I thought I would be killed too."[26] Vicente Sanz's explanation of a triple killing was bizarre and unsatisfactory, yet it seemed to be the truth. Foreman George Ming of the Alaska Consolidated cannery on Rose Inlet (Dall Island, Alexander Archipelago) customarily gave crackers to men working overtime. On August 11, 1926, he ran out of crackers so he dispensed cookies. Sanz thought the foreman favored him until he suffered a violent attack of diarrhea; then he panicked and grabbed his roommate's gun to seek revenge.

Sanz came up behind Ming in the mess hall, shot him in the back, and rushed out through the kitchen, killing Louie Fon with another shot as he dashed for the door. Outside he ran into Gun Loon at the corner of the building and shot him dead, then fired a grazing shot at R. B. Palermo, a Filipino foreman. After this explosive destruction of three lives, Sanz went to his room, replaced the gun, then surrendered.

When the deputy marshal came over from Ketchikan to arrest Sanz and investigate the crimes, he did not learn very much. Sanz, a man of unduly suspicious disposition, had erupted spontaneously. At trial Sanz was convicted and sentenced to life. His lawyer offered an insanity defense, citing Sanz's treatment at a Tacoma hospital in 1923. But a check of the hospital records by the prosecutor revealed that Sanz's health problem then had been appendicitis.

Little was known about Sanz. He was one of the thousands of

cannery workers hired through contracting agencies in Seattle to put up the annual salmon pack in southeastern, south central, and Bristol Bay. These men, in large majority Filipinos, Chinese, Japanese, and Mexicans, rendered valuable service but had minimal contact with Alaska communities. Only a small number settled in Alaska's coastal towns; most were seasonal transients, birds of passage, who lived rather lonely lives away from their families and sometimes failed to cope with their monotonous regime. The incidence of assaults and killings was remarkably high; typically the homicides resembled the Sanz pattern. Men brooded over a real or fancied grievance and lacked opportunities to distract themselves from aggravating circumstances.

In June 1912, Demicio Flores attacked and killed Gararro Bararro with a knife at the Alaska Packers Association cannery near Coffee Creek, Nushagak. Flores' attorney argued that the men had quarreled; Flores got drunk and acted in a fit of insanity caused by intoxication. A month later there was another killing at a Nushagak cannery near Lackamak. The men involved were Italians. Frank Tragomene shot Francisco Cardinale while the latter rested on his bunk. No one knew of any trouble between the two workers; drink was not involved. In fact, the murder seemed inexplicable without reference to some sinister agency, and a juror was heard saying confidentially: "Tragomene was an agent of the Mafia, sent up here to kill this man."[27] When defense attorney O. H. Tucker heard about this statement, he tried unsuccessfully to use it to upset the conviction and life sentence given his client. Of course, the suspicion of the Black Hand, or Mafia, organizations was aroused anywhere in the nation during that era if one Italian killed another, and yet actual killing by the group was rare.

Conflicts between foremen and workers were the most common sources of trouble. There was no one to check a foreman who wished to make a packer's life miserable unless the victim took violent action. Dalmacio Bundoc was one man who resented the bullying of his foreman, so he shot him dead at Naknek in July 1947. Over the years there were many other cases of workers' killing or assaulting others in crazed desperation.[28] Jurors did not invariably find workers accused of murder in the wrong. In the Bundoc trial the evidence showed that the foreman had been carrying a gun and

had threatened Bundoc with it. The jury acquitted Bundoc on the ground of self-defense.

Of all the cannery slayings, the most grotesque was at Dundas Bay in 1913. O. Itow and E. Fushima expressed some grievance against fellow laborer Frank Dunn in the spirit of samurai warriors. Itow ran his cherished and ancient sword which had a twenty-three-inch blade, into Dunn's shoulder and through his body. Juneau jurors were appalled at the assassins; Itow was sentenced to hang and Fushima got twenty years for manslaughter.

In this case Itow was the foreman and Dunn was a dissatisfied worker who tired of "working for $50 a month alongside of the Japs" and planned to steal away from the cannery wharf to nearby Hoonah.[29] Itow got wind of Dunn's attempt to quit and confronted him on the wharf. Itow stabbed Dunn in the neck and in the back. As Dunn fell, other cannery workers ran up to disarm Itow, who threw down his sword, pulled a pistol and shot Thomas Costello, a Mexican, in the lung.

A small ethnic war threatened. The cannery superintendent mustered a group of men, armed them with rifles taken from the cannery store, and marched on the Japanese workers, who had gathered defensively around Itow. "The murderer would have been taken into custody at once," U.S. Deputy Marshal Goodell told newsmen, "but it was feared that a race war would have broken out that night and what might have happened in that event is a matter of conjecture." Itow remained at large until emotions cooled enough to bring him in. The situation was somewhat complicated by the remoteness of the cannery. Deputies were not alerted to the slaying until Costello was brought in for medical treatment. The marshal used the army's cable to charter the steamer *Georgia,* which was then at Sitka on its regular coastal voyage. Itow appealed without success to the U.S. Circuit Court, but President Woodrow Wilson's commutation order reduced Itow's sentence to life imprisonment in 1916.

The Itow case caused more comment than the ordinary cannery homicide. U.S. Attorney John Rustgard reflected darkly on the probability of undiscovered murders. He professed to believe that Asians traditionally punished with death the attempt of fellow workers to break their employment contracts.

Upset by the Itow murder and by a 1912 murder at the Weiss cannery near Shakan, where eight Japanese workers were charged with the murder of a Korean, "an Oriental of unusual intelligence who spoke four languages but was repelled by the unsalted rice diet," Rustgard wanted Alaskans to know that terrible things were going on. The Korean victim had tried to escape his duties and failed: "His skull was crushed in with a rock, a pistol bullet was fired through his neck, a stone was tied to his body, and he was thrown into the bay."[30] But for the body's surfacing two months later, the crime would not have been discovered. Cannery officials told Rustgard that they knew nothing of the murder or even that the victim had disappeared. As Rustgard and the marshal investigated the homicide, they were approached by a Japanese worker who offered to plead guilty if charges against the other suspects were dropped. Rustgard accepted the deal for lack of enough evidence to convict, then, to his embarrassment, learned that the confessor had been chosen by lot.

In the Itow case, Rustgard suspected that the cannery's Japanese bookkeeper had shot at Dunn the week before his slaying because Dunn claimed to be sick and refused to work. Under some pressure the bookkeeper confessed that he had scolded Dunn because the cannery needed his services, then shot at him to frighten him a bit!

The *Alaska Daily Dispatch* called for an investigation of cannery recruitment: "For a long time, refugees from canneries coming to Juneau have claimed not only that they were held as slaves, but that they were virtually shanghaied at San Francisco and Seattle." Most of the unfortunates are Orientals, Mexicans, and Spaniards, but "other American boys, like Frank Dunn, finding themselves impoverished in a strange city, have become victims of the system. And as these would find it more difficult than the others to endure the fare, it is probable that many of the victims buried beneath the waters of the sounds and straits of the inside passage were born on American soil."

The views of Rustgard and the *Dispatch* must be considered with their sensation-evoking intent in mind. The Department of Justice and territorial officials did not accept the notion of countless undiscovered murders in Alaska's canneries. Workers might complain about the food and working conditions, but the number of reported crimes of violence suggests that most malicious cannery occurrences commanded the attention of authorities.

The *Dispatch* did not exaggerate the pernicious exploitation of cannery workers, a condition that resulted from the traditional contractor system of hiring. Canneries negotiated directly with labor contractors in Seattle, Portland, and San Francisco for the seasonal work force, stipulating the number of workers needed and the price they would pay for each case packed. The contractor fixed the wage scale and provided food. Workers were in no position to bargain. Wages were low and the food poor.

Contractors fed workers on a budget of three or four dollars per month per man. Rice was the staple of their diet, with an occasional piece of fish, pork, or chicken. The salmon the workers packed was considered too valuable for their table; they got some rock cod and halibut caught locally instead. A worker who tired of this diet could buy fruits, vegetables, cheese, candy, and crackers from the contractor's agent at exorbitant prices. Nonfood items were available as well. Most sales were made on credit and charged against the worker's seasonal wages.

Compulsory gambling was another means of getting money from the workers. Labor contractors made it clear that anyone who expected to be hired for the next season must gamble at the contractor's tables. Professional gamblers saw to it that the house maintained an ascendant edge on the odds.

Unskilled cannery workers earned $100 to $250 in stipulated

wages for a season's work; wages were higher during the labor shortage of World War I but declined during the Great Depression. Actual wages differed from stipulated wages, as workers discovered when they returned to their hiring point. Deductions for bedding, eating utensils, disinfecting the ship, sick days, gambling debts, and store purchases reduced the pay packet. A net of $75 was average during the Depression.[31]

Cannery conditions were not the concern of the Department of Justice and its officers, however. In time, conditions improved radically as the Department of Labor put pressure on the contractors and workers organized a union.

As perhaps in all criminal cases, there is another side to the Itow case that is not revealed in archival records. Hjalmar Rutzebeck, author of *Alaska Man's Luck,* was Itow's cellmate in the Juneau jail and was very much impressed by him. "He is a remarkably nice little fellow," Rutzebeck wrote, "so pleasant, so little and dainty. He is like a little yellow pansy growing among tall weeds. It seems impossible that he would have killed anybody, and still more impossible that he is to be hanged."[32] Itow seemed a devoted, serene Christian, submissive to fate with an easy conscience and ever radiant face.

The story Itow told other prisoners about the killing stressed the difficulties posed by the contract-labor system. He admitted that he sometimes locked workers in the bunkhouse at night, but only when someone was suspected of wanting to run away. "I had to, then, to protection [*sic*] myself." Itow stood to lose fifty dollars' pay every time a worker got away, hence his nervous vigilance. Dunn's case was particularly aggravating because the Seattle contractor had advanced him forty dollars and made Itow the loser if Dunn reneged on either the advance or a sixty-dollar company-store bill. When Dunn threatened to leave, Itow faced a one hundred dollar loss he could ill afford. A watch was maintained on Dunn in the hope of holding him until he earned enough for his debt.

Dunn refused to work, demanded whiskey, and otherwise kept Itow in a state of anxiety. The killing was not the ceremonial samurai affair suggested by the press. One of Itow's assistants brandished a sheathed cane sword to quell a fight between Dunn and another worker. Dunn knocked both of Itow's helpers off the bunkhouse porch. Itow grabbed the cane and waved it at Dunn, who knocked him from the porch while grasping the cane. During the scuffle Dunn inadvertently unsheathed the sword and in falling from the porch impaled himself on it.

Whether Itow's version was true or not, the jurors did not believe it, perhaps because Itow immediately climbed back onto the porch, after pulling the sword from Dunn's body, to attack Mexican laborers who were throwing cans and bottles at him. He had a pistol too, that "went off without his knowing it," wounding a Japanese man who had been watching the fight.

Itow waited patiently for three days before a deputy marshal reached the cannery to arrest him. He could have escaped easily, "but he did not feel that he had committed any wrong but had merely carried out his duty according to the contract he was under."

Perhaps Itow was just another victim of the pernicious labor-contract system. Unfortunately the court lacked license to inquire into the strange ways canneries operated, and lawmen could not sympathize with a foreman who locked men up and resorted to the use of deadly weapons with fatal results. Besides, Mexican witnesses testified that Itow's two helpers were holding Dunn by the arms when Itow stabbed him. Itow and Rutzebeck figured jurors would have recognized the Mexicans' bias against Asians had they not shared it. Yet in retrospect it does not appear that the jury lacked reasonable support for its judgment.

15. Heroines and Experts

Alaska has, perhaps, its full quota of irresponsible blatherskites. —Governor J. F. A. Strong

IF Alaska had a ballad-singing tradition, there would have been many "Black Bear" songs, for her adventures were the natural stuff of literature. Black Bear was a bold, colorful, opportunistic figure of the demimonde, a lady of the night who gave solace to the lonely, loving men of the north. And she executed a daring robbery of the sacrosanct United States Mail with all the panache of a Jesse James, then defied the relentless pursuit of federal officers. Imagine a minstrel tuning up his fiddle for other roadhouse travelers along an Alaska trail, answering their spirited demand for a Black Bear ballad. "Yes," he would say, "join me if you like. The tune is that of 'Jeannie with the Light Brown Hair.'" Then he would start:

> *I'll sing of Nellie of the long black hair,*
> *Her we call our loving Black Bear.*
> *She is big and of great, stout heart,*
> *And the feds did find her far too smart.*[1]

By the time the minstrel got through all the verses, assuming that his voice was superior to his versification, the house would be rocking with enjoyment. Strangers to Alaska might wonder at the popularity of a thieving prostitute, but then they would recall the legends of Robin Hood and other bad actors celebrated by the people despite or because of their sins and would join the singing. Who could resist admiring a lone woman who outfoxed the ponderous government?

The facts of the great mail robbery are simple enough. Seattle's Dexter Horton Bank mailed thirty thousand dollars in cash to Thomas P. Atkins of McGrath on October 10, 1922. The currency disappeared the night of December 30, 1922, after traveling steadily by steamship to Seward, railroad to Nenana, and dog sled to Iditarod. The currency had reached Nenana on October 21. It was held there for two weeks until the 250-mile trail to McGrath was suitable for sled travel. Once snow packed the trails and the streams froze, the first of the relay teams of mail carriers dashed off behind yelping dogs with the precious burden. The second carrier in the relay, an inexperienced man, lost the trail and floundered around for days. He cached the unprotected mail in the woods until he finally got his bearings, reloaded the mail, and mushed off twenty days behind schedule.

Eventually the carrier reached McGrath. Owing to some bureaucratic mix-up the postmaster did not have the special key needed to open the currency pouch. It was not entirely clear that the pouch held McGrath mail, so he left it with carrier Bill Duffy, charging him with leaving it wherever the postmaster had the right key. Duffy reached the end of his line at the little mining town of Flat. There, Ralph Rivers, later to be the new state's first congressman, was helping his mother, the postmistress. He was able to open the bag to discover that it was addressed to McGrath. Duffy was told to drop it off on his return route.

Duffy visited the Flat prostitutes while resting up for his return. Nellie Bates and Nadine Saum wanted to travel with him. Nellie, widely known as Black Bear because of her statuesque figure and hirsute charms, hankered for the brighter lights of Seattle. Nadine only wanted to travel down the trail a short piece to Iditarod.

Nellie Bates, or Nellie Beattie, a reasonably attractive forty-year-old, was a businesswoman of some substance who had plied her trade at several mining centers in Alaska since 1901. Smart prostitutes in Alaska invested their earnings in mining ventures and lent money to miners at good interest rates. But in 1922–23, Nellie had lost $17,000 in an unprofitable mine on Chicken Creek, so she was a little sour on legitimate commerce when an unexpected opportunity came her way with Duffy.

The travelers pushed on to Iditarod. Nellie rode the runners behind the sled, Nadine bundled into the sled, and Duffy took the gee pole to direct the sled. At Iditarod, Duffy cached the currency pouch at the bank before joining the girls for a drink. The next day, Duffy and Nellie mushed only sixteen miles to reach Schermeyer's roadhouse, where Nellie had planned a going-away party with friends who would convene there. By this time Nellie had made other plans as well. Mail carriers did not worry much about the security when they were among friends. Duffy left the money bag on the sled, taking more care to secure his dogs than the mail. Dogs would devour anything edible left on a sled within their reach, but highway robbers on Alaska's winter trails were as rare as palm trees.

As the party roared on within the warm, joyous roadhouse, Nellie summoned proprietor William Schermeyer, a man in his late sixties who should have known better, and made him a proposition. Since she knew that word of the sled's valuable cargo probably had run in advance of their arrival, she had only to say, "Bill, are you game to make some money tonight?" "Nellie," he replied with macho instinct, "I'm always game."[2]

Bill Schermeyer was no more a crook than Nellie. He came to Alaska in 1900 as a prospector, joined the rush to Fairbanks in 1904, mined at Kantishna later on, then moved to Iditarod in 1912. While he had never struck it rich, he got by all right with his greenhouse business in the summer and his winter operation of the roadhouse. Naturally he sold a little moonshine to his guests, but bootlegging was a minor activity, one essential to his trade.

While the other guests drank and played cards, Nellie got Schermeyer aside once more. She had removed the mail pouch and stashed it in his fish cache outside. His job was to hide it. Schermeyer buried the sack in the snow. The next day he threw away the canvas bag and locks, stuffed the money into a gunnysack, and buried it some distance from the roadhouse. Then he ran his dog team and sled around the area to obliterate all signs of his work.

In May 1923, Schermeyer recovered the money and reburied it

near his greenhouse in Iditarod. Rumors were flying about investigations by the Post Office, so he changed the money's location
several times. By summer 1924 the heat had died down. It seemed
safe to divide the loot. Nellie ironed the bills that were damp, and
the two buried their shares in private places. Nellie used glass jars;
Schermeyer used flashlights with hollowed batteries. In September, Schermeyer felt secure enough to pass a couple of bills.
Nothing bad happened, so he dug up his treasure for the last time
and started for the outside. He was not getting any younger, he
had worked hard all his life, and it was time to have some fun.

Having fun is not all that easy. Schermeyer got sick in Eugene,
Oregon, and hired a private nurse who later decamped with one
thousand dollars worth of diamonds he had bought as an investment. He brought criminal and civil charges, but the nurse lied her
way out of trouble and kept her gains. In San Diego, Schermeyer
hooked up with a prostitute and another woman. They spent a lot
of time across the border in Mexico, attending the horse races
every day. Postal inspectors interrupted his idyll on a trip to Los
Angeles. His Oregon diamond affair had been given some newspaper publicity, and postal inspectors were still hotly interested in
the missing Iditarod money.

This was in spring 1925, when Schermeyer was seventy years
old, disenchanted with sunshine, fancy living, avaricious women,
and his uneasy conscience. Yes, he said, I'll go back to Alaska and
tell the whole story in court. Los Angeles newspapers were de-

lighted with what they heard of the affair, particularly the delicious irony of an aged lothario whose ill-gotten gains were fleeced by wicked young women in Oregon and California until he was down to his last thirteen cents (an exaggeration but necessary to the high moral tone newspapers aimed at). The postal inspectors were equally enchanted. And U.S. Marshal Lynn Smith of Fairbanks, who relished trips outside at government expense, got a trip to Los Angeles to convey the government's star witness back to Alaska.

Lynn Smith, an easygoing fellow, had been a deputy marshal at Flat when the theft was discovered in January 1923. He knew Schermeyer, liked him, and knew what was best for him. Smith planned to put him in charge of the hospital gardens in Fairbanks until the prosecutor could prepare his case against Nellie Bates. In Smith's eyes, Schermeyer had been victimized by Nellie, who stashed the mail sack at his place before he knew what was in it, then said, "It's up to you to get rid of the sack." He complied. "By the next morning there wasn't enough money in the world to get him to do it."[3] But there was no turning back.

Black Bear was tried at Fairbanks in February 1926. She denied involvement in the robbery, and her attorney, Tom Marquam, derided the inconsistencies in Schermeyer's testimony. Marquam also harped on the injustice of convicting an accused on the sole testimony of an accomplice, although the prosecutor tried to make much of evidence, gathered by an Internal Revenue examiner, bearing on Nellie's spending beyond her means.

Actually Schermeyer's testimony seemed both convincing and appealing in revealing a good man overthrown by a stronger woman. He told of paying a dollar for a pickle bucket that he filled with money and buried in his greenhouse. Nellie became worried when news came that a postal inspector was coming and hurried to call on her confederate: "Mr. Pinkham is on the road. What do you think about the cache?" Schermeyer thought it should be moved: "If he suspects me at all, he will dig all over God's creation to get it." His new cache in his garden remained secure until September, when freeze-up approached: "We didn't want to leave it in the ground to freeze up in case we wanted to do anything at all with it during the winter time," he told the jury, "so we decided to take it up from there and bury it in the root house." The uncomplaining money rested under two or three tons of carrots until June when the thieves felt inclined to uncover it once again. "I dug several days trying to locate it. I couldn't, seemingly, locate it so I got a crowbar and commenced working with that."[4] With the crowbar he found the loot, but its point damaged a few bills and all of them were damp. For several days Schermeyer locked up the house and stood guard while Nellie ironed the bills carefully. Then they put the money in canning jars and buried them in the field once more. With the thaw in June, Schermeyer dug up the jars and buried them in a hole under the barn.

All this activity and attendant anxiety took its toll on the old man. In September 1924 he decided to go outside for medical treatment: "I had lost thirty pounds in twenty-eight days." Nellie allowed him to take his share of the money. Just before he left Iditarod, Nellie arrived at his place in a state of panic. Bill Duffy, the mail carrier, had taken a lot of heat during the early months of the robbery investigation, although he had been guilty only of carelessness. Now he figured that the lawmen had given up, and after long reflection he also thought he knew who the thieves were. He told Nellie his suspicions. If they didn't share with him, Nellie told Schermeyer, "he is going to telegraph Pinkham to have every damn one of us searched." Schermeyer, longing for peace and not essentially a greedy man, urged Nellie to share with Duffy and immediately turned over four thousand dollars of his own portion of the loot. The old man professed no resentment at this shakedown: "He (Duffy) has stood the blame. I am only too glad to give him a share."[5]

Later, when Schermeyer, trying to enjoy the delights of the outside, had fallen into the hands of the scheming women of Oregon and California—"I had been robbed, cut and carved"—he remember his old friend and confederate, Nellie. He was broke and desperate, so he telegraphed a request for a five-hundred-dollar loan. Nellis replied with excuses: "Her place had been burned up and she had no money and she couldn't possibly let me have any money."[6] The old man tried two more pleading telegrams, to which Nellie replied in the same terms, although her responses grew more terse. It was this unfeeling treatment by Nellie that eventually triggered Schermeyer's confession to postal authorities.

The government was handicapped by the three-year limitation on prosecutions for larceny. Nellie could be tried for sharing in the division of the long-buried money, but not for its theft. With such constraints the government's case was not impressive, hence a hung jury. In February 1927 the government tried again. This time the jury acquitted Black Bear. Postal inspectors were disgruntled at the verdict. They believed Alaska juries were soft on all nonviolent criminals.

Ralph Rivers, then a law student at the University of Washington, was a witness at both trials. He marveled at the strategy of Tom Marquam in calling the jury's attention to the awesome resources of the government, displayed in the three Justice Department attorneys, a battery of postal inspectors, Internal Revenue accountants, and a pampered confessed felon who was the chief witness. Against this array of might and reams of documents compiled by a score of anonymous detectives and clerks, poor Nellie, dressed demurely in black, and her single defense attorney, looked like sacrificial lambs. Nellie did pay a price even if she was not convicted. Rivers could see the effect of two years of pressure in her appearance at the second trial. She was frayed, nervous, and had developed a tic in her right eye. And she was considerably out of pocket for the fees of her lawyer.

The Bureau of Investigation was called in to look into possible tampering with the case. Since the trial jurors would be unlikely to admit any influences upon their decision, the agent examined the grand jurors, who had voted thirteen to nine for indictment. The prosecutor believed the vote was suspiciously close, considering the overwhelming weight of evidence he submitted. Only one of the grand jurors admitted to anything like an approach by outside parties, and it was an amicable one without threats or bribes. Burly Dan Callahan, a leading figure in the Fairbanks demimonde, merely told the juror of his regard for Nellie, which was shared by many of his friends.

Authorities could not pursue the issue any further, but they learned something about Alaskans' loyalty. Nellie's "reputation has never been good; however, she has quite a following among the old time Alaskans." When Nellie and Bill Duffy received their subpoenas at Flat, they hurried to Fairbanks, arriving several days before the grand jury met. By this time Nellie and Duffy were living together, but only the most censorious found their liaison suspicious. "They surrounded themselves with the bootlegging and gambling element . . . and began to spread propaganda favorable to Nellie Beattie, recalling the early days of Alaska when Nellie Beattie assisted the 'down and out' miners and 'grub staked' several of them. This, of course, appealed to the old time Alaskans."[7]

Lynn Smith was relieved that his four years' involvement was over. Schermeyer was sentenced to a year in jail after the Bates trial and probably would not live too long, he thought: "He is a prince and his conscience is clear and he is contented and ready to go any time."[8] Schermeyer did indeed die within a year of his release. As befitted a legend, Nellie bounded back from her misfortune. She married Bill Duffy, the mail carrier. Some eyebrows were raised at this news. Had Duffy been involved in the robbery plan all along? "No," said Fairbanks cynics, he simply had to pay the marital price to share in her fortune. The big losers were the taxpayers. Ralph Rivers estimated that the tenacious prosecutions in defense of the sanctity of the United States Mail cost the government several times the amount of the thirty-thousand-dollar loss.

For once U.S. Attorney Howard D. Stabler of Juneau did not grumble about the omnipresent rain when the frugal Justice Department agreed to hire Luke May. The Burt McDonald murder case was one he wanted desperately to win; May's services as physical-evidence investigator and expert trial witness did not guarantee victory, but it improved his chances immeasurably. Stabler felt like the manager of a baseball team fighting for a playoff berth might feel if the owner secured the talents of a top-notch pitcher. Sunshine flooded Stabler's heart, and he left his umbrella in the office.

Luke May, Seattle criminologist, was a Northwest legend by 1931. He was a pioneer in scientific crime detection before the Federal Bureau of Investigation and larger city police departments established their own laboratories for physical-evidence investigation, handwriting analysis, ballistics, and other matters relating to crime solving. As a private investigator, he opened his agency in Seattle in 1919 after operating for several years in Pocatello, Idaho, and Salt Lake City. In most of the major murder cases of the northwestern and mountain states, particularly those in rural counties, Luke May's courtroom appearance was guaranteed to heighten public interest and improve the odds for the prosecuting attorney. County sheriffs and prosecutors appreciated their limitations when a sensatioinal murder aroused the community; usually they could pry May's fee from the budget dictators on the plausible grounds that May's expertise would make all the officials look better and help ensure protection for peaceful citizens.

The McDonald case in Ketchikan, much like the earlier Krause case in Juneau, had aroused all the southeastern district. Citizens demanded a conviction, and federal officers were anxious to comply.

Small boats like the *Phoenix IV,* used for fishing and transport, were as familiar to southeastern Alankans as riding horses are in range country, and the men who manned such boats included a good number of the industrious folks in coastal communities. So the discovery of George Marshall's body lying in a pool of his own blood on the drifting *Phoenix IV* in a cove near Point Higgins, ten miles northwest of Ketchikan, struck the nerve center of the community. Who was the brutal "sumbitch" who would use good old George so harshly? Who lashed his arms and ankles with manila rope and scattered gear and stores around the wheelhouse as if a gale had swept through?

George Marshall was a fish buyer. He was a former miner of Fairbanks and the Yukon who operated a fifty-foot gas boat to save local fishermen the time and trouble of going into dock with their catches by his regular appearance in Grindall Passage, where his two usual buying stations lay north and south of the entry to Kasan Bay. Of course, to buy fish he needed cash, as anyone who understood the rudiments of Ketchikan economics would appreciate. When the Coast Guard sailors boarded the ominously quiet *Phoenix IV* to view the gruesome carnage, they noted that George's safe and skiff were gone. Robbery seemed the clear motive; George usually sailed out of Ketchikan with eleven hundred dollars in cash and a store of canned goods to replenish the galley pantries

Luke May, Seattle criminologist, "America's Sherlock Holmes." University of Washington Archives

of fishermen. Someone had shot George in the foot with a .38 revolver. Subsequently, or before the shooting, the murderer had bashed the old man's skull in with a blunt instrument. The head wound took the victim's life.

Whoever would do such a thing must have had access in a good boat. Boat owners were solid citizens for the most part, always excepting, of course, those who earned their way smuggling booze or pirating fish traps; but smugglers and thieves did not stoop to vicious homicide. There were no reports of stolen boats, so the murderer must have had his own or the legitimate use of another's if he had intercepted Marshall. Later police abandoned the interception theory for the assumption that the murderer left Ketchikan with Marshall.

Weeks passed after the murder, which probably occurred on October 20, 1930, as U.S. Marshal Albert White and his deputies pulled their hair and rousted anyone in Ketchikan likely to have killed Marshall. Among Ketchikan's few thousand people, suspicious characters with the necessary boating skills, opportunity, and motive were few. The culprit could have been someone who drifted in and out of town without being noticed. The sea lanes were always open, and the seasonal flow of cannery workers, steamer passengers, and fishermen through town was as constant as the tide.

In January, Marshal White, who, like his colleagues in the other Alaska districts, did not boast of the detective capacity of his office, got a break. A deputy arrested Lloyd Close as he carried some blasting powder out of a warehouse. Close was a thief, bootlegger, ex-con, skilled boatman, a gimpy-legged, blond, nervous man—in short, a bad fellow who might well rob a fish buyer. Close also carried a .38 revolver, the same kind of gun that had been fired on the *Phoenix IV.*

With good reason the interrogation by the marshal and U.S. attorney terrified Close: "Sure, I stole the powder, but I ain't no killer."[9] As the questioning wore on, Close sensed the urgency of the prosecutor and his vulnerability. Why risk hanging, Close reasoned, when he could give the name of the guy who probably did the deed? The dictum "honor among thieves" must give way in emergencies. So it was that the authorities heard about Burton G. McDonald.

McDonald and Close were pals who had come to Ketchikan together after renewing a friendship that had flowered within the grim walls of the Washington state penitentiary. McDonald had been convicted twice for burglary and once for escaping from prison. Since he had since left Ketchikan for parts unknown, the officers were not as jubilant at Close's tattletelling as he had hoped. Tell us more, they cautioned; make it good or we'll have to go with you.

Close tried. My God, he tried, and he was reasonably convincing. He even recalled that Burt McDonald, after praising Close's skills as a safecracker and touting Alaska as "good country for a 'pete' man," told him about a well-stuffed safe on the *Phoenix IV.* McDonald suggested a charter of the boat for a supposed hunting trip to the Unuk River on which they could "stick up the old bird." This suggestion had been made in early October, two weeks before the crime. Close had not liked the robbery idea, although he did enjoy hanging around with Burt and the several excursions they made searching for a cache of contraband booze someone had hidden near Ward's Cove. Close had lent his .38 to McDonald a few days before the robbery, and the revolver was returned to him after October 20. McDonald lived aboard the *Comrade,* a boat owned by Cap Fowler, who was in the Ketchikan hospital during October. McDonald used the boat whenever he wished.

Another suspect was Kenneth Govro, also a friend of McDonald. Govro, an ex-con and drifter who left Ketchikan on October 30, was sought, and was arrested in Wyoming. Govro's claim of innocence survived his scrutiny by witnesses who had observed Marshall's meeting with an unidentified man on his last day in Ketchikan. Govro believed that McDonald probably committed the crime and told some pretty good stories about McDonald's sudden prosperity and suspicious conduct after October 20. McDonald bragged of his intent to buy a new Ford in Detroit and of a plan to buy the *Comrade* from Fowler for the purpose of converting it into a troller. Besides that, McDonald told him on October 20, "If, you are asked, you say that I was aboard this boat [docked at Ketchikan] all day today." Then Govro saw his pal throw a gunnysack filled with something into the bay. And when the newspaper reported a day or so later that a dark haired man had been seen helping Marshall load the *Phoenix IV* on the twentieth, McDonald quit making excursions to town from the dock until after nightfall.

U.S. Marshal White got a warrant for McDonald's arrest and the Seattle Bureau of Investigation ran the suspect down in Portland, Oregon. Eventually officers brought McDonald back to Ketchikan, where a grand jury delivered an indictment for murder one.

The Seattle Bureau originally hired Luke May to determine whether a bullet embedded in the deck of the *Phoenix IV* matched Close's .38 revolver and to compare Close's and McDonald's handwriting with the printing on the note notifying the Coast Guard that the *Phoenix IV* was adrift. May determined that the bullet fired into the boat had come from Close's gun. He could not say that McDonald printed the note but was sure that Close did not. Ballistic and handwriting investigatioins were routine work for May, who had extended his range of physical-evidence identification to hair, cloth fibers, fingernails, and knife shavings. At a very slow and deliberate pace that frustrated May, the Northwest courts had been admitting such findings when they established a link in the chain of evidence. Federal officers found black human hairs in George Marshall's hand; perhaps in grappling with his assailant the victim had torn the hair from the assailant's body. May urged the police to try to get some of McDonald's hair for comparison. If the two samples matched and if the court allowed the evidence, chances for a conviction would be improved.

McDonald's trial began April 13, 1931, in Ketchikan. Spectators competed for the limited courtroom seating, anxious to take part in one of the town's most notorious crimes. The local press whetted appetites for sensation even more with news stories on the celebrated criminologist Luke May, usually billed as "America's Sherlock Holmes."

Assistant District Attorney George Folta presented the government's case, which depended heavily on the jury's acceptance of the Close-Govro testimony. Other witnesses testified that Marshall was seen with a dark-haired man on October 20, that the man may have left Ketchikan on the *Phoenix IV,* and that Marshall's boat had performed erratically some miles out of Ketchikan.

Defense attorney George Grigsby, a tough character with thirty years' experience in Alaska's courts, did his best to shake the prosecution's witnesses. Close and Govro were not very creditable fellows, he argued. In fact, they were jailbirds who lied for the government to save their own necks. Grigsby and his associate, Harry G. McCain, treated Luke May cautiously but glowed with pleasure when the expert could not say with certainty that McDonald penned the note to the Coast Guard. Better yet for their hopes, May did not even mention his investigation of McDonald's hair. On cross-examination, Grigsby showed an intense interest in hair and probed the obvious reasons for May's reticence. May was forced to admit that he could not say that the hair in Marshall's hand matched the sample that McDonald had freely given his jailers. A battle royal raged among the lawyers as Grigsby fought to destroy the government's whole case on the hair issue. Even the judge gave way to shouting at times in ordering Grigsby to "sit down" and desist in his exposition of the hair matter.[10]

Fortunately for the prosecution, its case did not depend upon either hair or handwriting evidence. Other circumstantial evidence was more important, especially the hacksaw blades and acetylene torch found in McDonald's possession, equipment that might have been used to open Marshall's safe. Also of importance was McDonald's possession of the same kind of canned goods that Marshall usually carried on his voyages, although Grigsby's sarcasm hit heavily on the prosecution's efforts to build on the coincidental presence of standard store goods. But, as it seemed, star witnesses Close and Govro really made the prosecution's case. Despite their unsavory backgrounds, the jury believed their stories and found McDonald guilty. The judge sentenced him to life at McNeil Island, and folks in Ketchikan rejoiced.

In Seattle, where May's following was strong, the newspapers headlined his role thus: LUKE MAY CONVICTS SHIP KILLER. SEATTLE MAN GETS LIFE IN ALASKA TRIAL. While the papers exaggerated May's importance somewhat, they did recognize the importance of what the government had hoped to achieve "in one of the most unusual murder cases on record" in which "super scientific methods" and a "nationwide investigation" broke a case "rivalling anything to be found in detective fiction."[11] Clearly, the result was an outstanding victory for the marshal and the U.S. attorney in Ketchikan. If McDonald had been smart enough to throw Close's revolver into the sea instead of returning it, he might have escaped the consequences of his crime.

A certain rivalry existed among U.S. attorneys of the Alaska judicial districts. If, as in the conviction of Burt McDonald at Ketchikan in 1931, a prosecutor scored brilliantly, his colleagues in other places noted the triumph and learned from it. The first division's solution of a perplexing crime where the victim's body was never found was credited to Luke May. Maybe Luke could help the third division too in the difficult "Cap" Goodlataw case, reasoned Clyde Ellis, and Ellis got the Justice Department's approval of the necessary expenses.[12]

Superficially the Goodlataw murder near Chitina looked easier to

solve than the McDonald case. The chief suspect had not left the
area, and, as with the McDonald case, a good deal of circumstantial
evidence tied the suspect to the crime. H. L. Read lived on a tract
two miles from Chitina. Within this pleasant valley, through which
passed the Edgerton Cutoff from Richardson Highway, there was a
scattering of residents who lived and worked in the shadow of the
towering Chugach and Wrangell mountain ranges. Read had a one-
room cabin with adjoining storage buildings and barn. Across the
road from the cabin he had cleared enough ground to provide space
for small turnip and strawberry patches. His garden and the sale of
wood cut nearby gave Read some cash, and his carefully hidden
whiskey still yielded some income.

On occasion, the friendly Copper Indians would drop by Read's
tiny cabin for convivial drinks. The arrangement worked well until
several Indians became unruly while drinking at Read's place in
September 1931. The sixty-year-old proprietor, who was five-foot
seven and weighed 145 pounds, lacked the physical ability to keep
order, so he drew a pistol on the spirited drinkers. Cap Goodlataw
took exception to the gunplay. He was half Read's age, tall, burly,
and angry. His punishment cost Read a broken jaw and eighteen
days in the hospital. After Read returned home, the Indians, including Goodlataw, continued to frequent the grog shop. Goodlataw
thought Read bore him no grudge, although he may have misjudged
the other man's capacity for forgiveness.

Goodlataw disappeared on the morning of May 23, 1932, during
a walk down the highway to visit relatives eight miles away. Three
cabins lay along his route, one of them Read's. No one saw the Indian after he left Chitina, but the residents of the cabin just beyond
Read's, relatives of Goodlataw, were certain that the young man
would not have passed without visiting.

The Indians suspected Read of revenge. They searched for signs
of the missing man near Read's place and watched for a chance to
examine his property in his absence. After a few days they observed, from a distance, Read shoveling in his turnip patch in a
suspicious manner, then hurried off to see the deputy marshal and
U.S. commissioner. The marshal got a search warrant, ostensibly
to look for booze. Forty Indians arrived to help search as the
marshal served the warrant. Soon they found twenty gallons of

moonshine and a bed of ashes near the turnip patch. In the ashes were buttons, garter clips, and shoe nails; they found Goodlataw's belt and red woollen socks buried under a stump. Now they dug up the turnip patch to discover their friend's body. An autopsy revealed three gun wounds. The medical examiner guessed that the first two shots hit Goodlataw while he was running, the third after he fell.

Read denied any connection with the shooting. His revolver was taken as evidence, but none of the bullets that had hit Goodlataw was found.

Prosecutor Ellis hoped that Luke May's investigation of Goodlataw's and Read's clothing, a stained sack found in Read's cabin, stained gloves, a rifle and revolver, and other articles would reveal convincing evidence. In his Seattle lab May could not find any bloodstains on Read's clothing that could be identified as Goodlataw's, nor were any of Read's fingerprints on the Indian's possessions. May warned the prosecutor that the defense could readily explain away the blood found on the collar of Read's shirt as a shaving cut or some such thing.

With such inconclusive results Ellis did not bother bringing May up to Valdez for the murder trial. The prosecutor did his best with what he had, including the testimony of Goodlataw's brother bearing on the quarrel of the two men and the possible motive of revenge, but the evidence was not strong enough to remove all reasonable doubt of guilt. The jurors acquitted Read. The trial result was not an occasion of jubilation in Chitina, where suspicion of Read remained general. Officially, however, the Goodlataw slaying had to be considered an unsolved crime.

It would be unfair to leave the impression that the legendary Nellie "Black Bear" Bates is representative of the women who have been involved with crimes in Alaska. In fact, most of the women, whether perpetrators, victims, or incidental parties, seem to have resembled women elsewhere. They were not notably strong, with perhaps the exception of Hannah Nelson, one of the executioners in "Jack London's lynching," to be discussed later, or invariably steadfast in their loyalties, and like Josephine DeGroot they could cause confusion by changing their minds.

Harry DeGroot was a Juneau barber who got into serious trouble because his wife, Josephine, had what amounted to a fatal appeal to Abe Hansen. The trouble started in summer 1932 because Harry's wife, Josephine, left him to look for a job on Chichagof Island, a remote place thirty miles from Juneau. The family, which included four children, needed money, yet it was odd that she traveled so far. Perhaps Josephine left for other reasons, but she did get a job as housekeeper and companion to Abe Hansen, a moonshine purveyor. DeGroot wrote Josephine asking her to come home, telling her the children needed her and he needed her. After a long silence she wrote back, and DeGroot, thus encouraged, set forth to recover his erring spouse in March 1933.

The journey was not easy for a forty-six-year-old man inflicted with a rupture. Crossing Lynn Canal and Chatham Strait on the launch *Wa Wa* posed no difficulties, but Hansen lived outside the village of Chichagof. Deep snow lay on the ground, and DeGroot spent five hours wandering around before darkness caught him. He passed the night miserably next to a smoky fire that injured his eyes. In the morning some kindly men treated his eyes with boric acid and directed him to Hansen's place. By noon he arrived, hardly able to see. Josephine put Harry in the cabin's only bed and applied rags soaked in canned milk to his eyes. Then Hansen came home, saw his rival in his bed, and exploded wrathfully, telling Josephine: "Why don't you get that son of a bitch out of there so I can make some money? He will never take you away from me." [13]

Even without his eye afflication DeGroot was hardly the man to carry Josephine away against Hansen's resistance. He was a little fellow of five-seven and 145 pounds; Hansen, by contrast, towered at six-two and weighed 225 pounds—and was eleven years younger. Clearly, this confrontation resembled that between David and Goliath, although DeGroot could not even claim the advantage of youth.

Hours of Hansen's cursing and threats turned the cabin air blue. Hansen not only sold moonshine, he customarily drank plenty of it himself. The booze did not lighten his mood. DeGroot must go; Josephine must stay; and if they didn't watch out, he would kill them both. Hansen hammered home his meaning with repetitions of that awful phrase, the language described later by Circuit Judge Denman as assertions "of DeGroot's immediate female canine ances-

View of Juneau, Alaska Historical Library; Winters and Pond, photographers

try, and the suggestive silibants of the frontier phrase spoken in heated rage of the moonshiner, must have intensified the apprehension of the helpless husband."

Finally, at 4 A.M. the next day, a friend of Hansen persuaded him to retire to his boat while Doc McIver treated DeGroot. That afternoon Doc came by again to take DeGroot by motorboat to Juneau, then decided his patient was too ill for the long water passage. DeGroot could not keep food down and was forced to listen to Hansen's drunken tirades. "He will never live to sleep another night in my bed," said Hansen, glancing down smugly at the Colt revolver on his belt. Later he said: "You know too much about me and my business and I think I'll bump the both of you off."

Many uneasy, abusive hours later, Hansen took the DeGroots on his gasboat to Doc's boat at Chichagof. Hansen continued his

City Hall, Juneau, Alaska

Juneau city hall and jail. Alaska Historical Library, Alaska Postcard Collection

threats en route, even drawing his gun on DeGroot at one point. But for Josephine's heroics, that might have been his end. "Abe, you will have to kill me before you kill him. The man is sick and is going away. Let him go." Hansen put his boat alongside Doc's, and some hours of drinking followed. The booze did not soothe the burly bully, who eventually decided to shoot his rival. DeGroot, with the advantage of fear and sobriety, grabbed Doc's rifle and shot Hansen dead.

A clear case of self-defense? Evidently the prosecutor did not think so. DeGroot was indicted for murder. Although Josephine confirmed everything he told about the awful two days, there were no other witnesses to Hansen's bullying and assaults. It was the DeGroots' word against the prosecutor's showing that Hansen was shot as he tried to leave his boat. Josephine intended to stay with Hansen after helping DeGroot reach McIver's boat, and her husband shot Hansen to get her back. The jury, impressed because evidence showed that Hansen had been shot in the back, accepted the prosecutor's view. DeGroot was convicted of second-degree murder and sentenced to twenty years at McNeil Island in November 1933.

On appeal the circuit court discovered serious errors by the trial judge. The judge had instructed jurors that the defendant knew Hansen did not have a pistol, so he was not justified in shooting him. But the judge should have allowed jurors to consider from all the circumstances, including DeGroot's state of terror, whether he reasonably believed that Hansen was likely to kill him. The circuit court also found reversible error in the judge's remark during Josephine's testimony that she "has followed a steady course during the examination of trying to build herself up." When the defense objected, the judge realized that he had put his foot in his mouth and tried to correct his obvious bias by explaining that "my impugning of her purpose in building herself up is based upon my private opinion. My private opinion has nothing to do with the case." The circuit court pointed out the obvious: the judge's "private opinion . . . necessarily must have great weight" with the jury.

Harry DeGroot was returned to Juneau from McNeil Island for a new trial in January 1936. Betting men in town figured he had a good chance to go free, but the odds shifted overwhelmingly when Josephine changed sides. Poor Harry. Josephine had divorced him and remarried while he was languishing at McNeil Island. Now, as she reflected on Harry's dilemma, she lacked incentive to lie again about the fatal episode at Chichagof. U.S. Attorney George Folta cast her in a starring role as the government's chief witness.

Defense attorney H. L. Faulkner derided Josephine as an admitted perjurer. Yes, she said, she did lie at the first trial, and now she was telling the truth because she "learned what kind of a man he was." Attorneys did not probe her inscrutable logic, but there was little the defense could do to counter her testimony that DeGroot shot Hansen in the back because she refused to return to Juneau. DeGroot's silly attempt to intimidate her before the trial backfired. Josephine was approached by a friend of DeGroot who threatened to hurt her if she recanted her original testimony. The prosecutor swiftly filed charges against DeGroot's friend. The jurors made it clear that they considered DeGroot worthy of vile names. This time they found him guilty of murder one, and he got a mandatory life sentence.

16. Jack London's Lynching

Just what crooks, liquor dealers, and squaw men most desire.—Anonymous critic of Alaska's courts

CRIME can inspire literature, and social historians should review the bright and dark sides of efforts in creative and factual reporting. Jack London knew a great story when he read one, and the article in the Sunday section of the *San Francisco Examiner* of October 14, 1900, was as good as any he had ever heard in Alaska. It was headed: "WOMAN HANGS A MAN AND THE LAW UPHOLDS HER."[1] Illustrated with dramatic sketches, including a picture of a fashionably dressed woman holding a hangman's noose, the newspaper story described a murder and lynching that had occurred the year before in an isolated part of Alaska. The killings took place in Lituya Bay off the Gulf of Alaska in what is now Glacier Bay National Monument.

Six years after he read about the tragedy in the *Examiner,* the murder and lynching became the basis for one of London's most famous Alaska short stories. When his fictionalized version of the story, "The Unexpected," appeared in *McClure's Magazine* in August 1906 with a footnote that said it was based on a real incident, some readers claimed that the whole episode was a figment of the author's imagination. But the murder and lynching in 1899 actually occurred much as the novelist described them. Although there are many conflicting stories about the deaths, the true-to-life story of

Jack London's lynching tale ranks with the most astounding chapters in the history of frontier justice in Alaska.

Like those at Nome, the sands at Lituya were gold bearing, and the Lituya Bay Gold Placer Company worked through the summer of 1899 taking gold out of the beach. At the end of the summer a small crew was left to work the site during the winter. The winter crew included at least four men and one woman: the manager of the outfit, Hans Nelson; his wife, Hannah; Sam Christianson; Fragnalia Stefano; and Martin Severts. Until Severts tried to murder all of his companions on the night of October 6, 1899, everything seemed peaceful.

As usual Hannah had cooked the evening meal (though some sources say the shooting affair started at breakfast). After the meal everyone remained sitting at the table talking and laughing except Severts, who left the cabin and went outside. "In a short time he returned," survivor Sam Christianson said later, "and opening the door, leveled a .45 Colt's revolver at Stefano and shot him dead."[2] Severts then took aim at Christianson, fired, and missed, but the bullet ricocheted off a stone jar and hit Christianson in the back of the neck. "I was so stunned that I fell to the floor," he said. He watched as Severts then aimed at Hannah, but before he could fire, Hans Nelson jumped the killer and knocked him to the ground. During the struggle the gun went off, with "the ball tearing an ugly wound in Severts' leg." Hannah Nelson threw a dish towel around Severts' neck and choked him until Hans was able to tie him up.

After recovering from the shock, the Nelsons treated Christianson's wound. The bullet had only grazed his neck and was not so serious as Severts' leg wound. The Nelsons dragged the body of the murdered man outside and buried him the next day in a shallow grave. The survivors bandaged Severts, but they resolved at once to keep him tied up at all times and to keep close watch until they could deliver him to the authorities.

The mining camp was cut off from regular contact with the outside world. Hans Nelson tried to signal passing steamers, but none would stop. Mounting a guard day and night was hard on their nerves. Hannah was quoted as saying: "I would sit by the hour with a rifle across my lap opposite the bunk where he was tied and sew or knit, jumping at every move he made." The Nelsons hired Indians to hold Severts at a small cabin four miles away, but after a few days the Indians refused to watch him any longer.

The prospect of spending the entire winter with a madman seemed intolerable. The Nelsons finally gave up all hope of help from the outside and considered other options. Letting the slayer go was one, yet they would have no guarantee that he would leave the area; he might well try to kill them again. The only other option was to execute him. Only this drastic solution could assure their safety.

One thing that bothered the survivors about Severts was that he refused to explain why he had wished to kill them. When asked if it was for the money, his reply was "may be." Finally, speaking to Hannah alone, he said that he had planned to take all their gold and go back to Skagway with a story of an Indian killing.

The Nelsons hanged Severts early on the morning of October 26, 1899, according to one account, about three weeks after the shooting. "The execution was a very serious matter," Hannah said, "and was carried out as though it were under the order of a court by a deputized officer." She read the sentence, "You shall be hanged by the neck until you are dead," and placed the noose over his head. Severts stood on a barrel with the rope around his neck while Hannah read the story of the prodigal son from the Bible. When she had finished, Hans kicked the barrel out from under Severts' feet. A group of Indians witnesses watched the execution in silence, and they marveled at the workings of the white man's law, as Jack London put it, "that compelled a man to dance upon the air."[3]

When London's story "The Unexpected" was published, the *Seattle Post-Intelligencer* quoted a number of "prominent Alaskans" who denied that the bizarre incidents had ever taken place. One man who said he was the deputy marshal at Skagway in 1899 insisted that the story was "utterly ridiculous," while the paper claimed that "not a single Alaskan can be found who knows that the incidents happened."[4] The *Seattle Times,* archrival of the *P-I,* and some Alaska newspapers came to London's rescue. The *Times* interviewed a number of Alaskans who had heard of the lynching. "So true has been the story-teller," the *Times* said, "that a hundred men now in Seattle at once identified the real persons who figure as characters in the story."[5]

Although the *P-I* admitted the next day that London's story was based on fact, London himself felt it necessary to answer the original charges. In a letter to the editor he cited the *Examiner's* story of 1900. "Now, if no hanging occurred at Latuya Bay in the winter of 1899, then the whole story as published in the *Examiner,* with many of the thumb marks of verity, is all a newspaper lie written by newspapermen. In which case, it's up to you, not to lambaste me, as you have done, but to turn loose and lambaste your fellow newspapermen who are responsible for this."[6]

London did follow the story almost exactly, although to flesh out the brief article he invented a number of details. His recourse to a favorite theme—the ability of Hannah, a woman of superior Nordic stock, to adapt to unexpected circumstances and control the beastliness of savage men—conformed closely enough to the truth and was lifted directly from the news article. The three survivors of the tragedy were still living in the north in 1906 when the story appeared. Christianson said that although there were some errors in it and some names were changed, the story was right on the mark.

Jack London won the small battle for his literary reputation, but "The Unexpected" has displeased some of his modern critics, including Franklin Walker, who wrote a masterful account of London's actual and literary experiences in the north. The story proved to Walker that truth is stranger and less plausible than fiction. "The actual event remains quite incredible, even if it really took place, and the story based on it suffers in consequence."[7] In fact and fiction the final result was mostly a happy one. The authorities investigated the Nelson's story in 1900 and decided that the hanging of Serverts was a "judicial execution." The case was closed.

Informal executions or lynchings, aside from the Nelson case, have not been documented in Alaska's history. This may seem strange, given the region's remoteness and the propensity Americans have shown for deadly mob action elsewhere, and certainly we can be grateful that northern folks have been civilized. Alaska's jurors have also shown restraint in taking lives. They ordered the death sentence on only a handful of occasions, and sometimes their rulings were overturned.

Hot-tempered Homer Bird was one of the more unfortunate men who stampeded to the Yukon in 1898. His party, which included J. H. Hurlin, Charles Scheffler, R. S. Patterson, and Bird's girl friend, Naomi Strong, was organized in San Francisco. Each man contributed five hundred dollars for the purchase of a steam launch and provisions (although Bird paid Scheffler's share when the latter defaulted). With high hopes they disembarked at St. Michael on July 4, launched their thirty-two-foot boat, and headed upriver. By late September they had voyaged six hundred miles but were still far from their goal when they decided to establish winter quarters at Slaughter House Gulch eighty-five miles above Anvik. On September 26 they finished building their cabin. The next morning they ate breakfast on the launch and relaxed until their little world was suddenly shattered by violence.

The prospectors were talking about setting traps for grouse when Bird loaded his shotgun and fired point blank at Hurlin. Scheffler looked on as Hurlin fell to the floor of the boat, threw up his hands, and shouted, "For God's sake, don't shoot me!" Miss Strong and Patterson jumped up and ran ashore. She made it to the beach, but Patterson, who jumped into the water, could not avoid Bird, who waded after him, waving two guns and shouting, "Bob, you dirty son of a bitch, you're the cause of this!" On the beach Patterson begged Bird, "For God's sake, think of my poor family." "Bob," said Bird, "I have thought of our families."[8] And Bird shot him.

The trouble had begun before the stampeders stopped for winter quarters. As usual with inexperienced river men, they had run aground frequently on sandbars and Bird had villified Hurlin, the steersman. "The Dutch sons of bitches don't know where to run it," he would say without smiling. Hurlin also called Patterson a 'son of a bitch' on occasion and threatened to "hammer the devil out of him." With such ill feeling the five had agreed to divide their provisions and go their separate ways when navigation reopened in the spring. But how do you divide a boat? Quarrels continued until Bird ended discussions by killing Hurlin and wounding Patterson.

After Patterson was taken to Anvik for medical treatment, Miss Strong, Scheffler, and Bird returned to their camp. The winter passed slowly. Bird's temper was uncertain until he was finally arrested in April 1899. He was tried, convicted, and sentenced to hang in Juneau. He claimed self-defense as his excuse, but it was not convincing against the testimony of Miss Strong and Scheffler. The U.S. Supreme Court reviewed the conviction and ordered a new trial because the trial judge had admitted testimony on Bird's behavior after the shooting.

U.S. Attorney Robert Friedrich resented the quibbling of the Supreme Court, but, as he assured Governor Brady, "we will convict Bird again and shall try to hang him in accordance with the ideas of the Supreme Court as to how a gentleman should have his taking off in that behalf."[9] And the prospector gained the favor of jurors, who agreed again that Bird deserved to hang. The circuit court affirmed the trial court, then the Supreme Court reviewed the record; this time it found no errors. Bird was hanged March 6, 1903, at Sitka.

The slaying of Con Sullivan and others by Fred Hardy in 1901 was as brutal as any in Alaska's history. Con Sullivan was well known for his association with Idaho's Bunker Hill and Sullivan mine, a solid mountain of galena that produced silver from 1885 to 1982, discovered when Noah Kellogg's burro refused to move from the area. Sullivan was lucky enough to get in on the original staking and sold his share to Simeon G. Reed for seventy-five thousand dollars. The

Bunker Hill discovery made the Coeur d'Alene district one of the great silver-producing regions of the United States and contributed substantially to the growth of Spokane. Years later Sullivan was still prospecting while regretting that he sold out for a mere seventy-five thousand dollars. His luck ran out entirely when he ventured into the north, ignoring the regions of the Yukon interior and Seward Peninsula, where the important gold discoveries were made from 1897 to 1902, to investigate Unimak Island in the Aleutian chain. Failing to find gold was not the Sullivan party's biggest misfortune: what really devastated it was encountering Fred Hardy.

Tennessee drifter Fred Hardy was enrolled in the U.S. Army for the Spanish-American War, then ran afoul of authorities in the Philippines and was sentenced to a term at Alcatraz. He was one of the thousands who sought their fortunes in Alaska during the gold rush. A fair proportion of the adventurers lacked scruples, yet few were as depraved as Hardy, whose voracious reading of dime novels at the military prison earned him the sobriquet "Diamond Dick." Hardy had deserted the fishing schooner *Arago* on Unimak Island and now watched the well-equipped Sullivan party, which included Con and his brother Florence of Butte; P. J. Rooney of Seattle; and Owen Jackson of Wallace, Idaho. Of the four prospectors, only Jackson lived to tell the tale of Hardy's viciousness.

Sullivan and his group were occupied on June 6 and 7, 1901, in relocating their camp near Cape Lapin. Jackson and Rooney, returning with the party's dory and the last load of supplies to the new camp, heard four rifle shots as they approached the tent. Florence fell and the other men raced for the dory, hoping to escape by sea. The rifle fire continued, and Rooney was shot as the men boarded the dory. At this, Con and Jackson ran for the shelter of a nearby bluff. Before he got twenty feet Con fell with a bullet in his back. After trying to help the dying Rooney, Jackson kicked off his cumbersome rubber boots and ran like hell back to the original camp. He hid that night and set out the next morning for False Pass, resting en route at an abandoned trapper's cabin. Along the way he saw men he thought were natives, and since he assumed his assailants were natives, he changed directions for Unimak Pass on the west side of the island, keeping well up in the hills to avoid the massacre area.

On June 24, Jackson reached Scotch Cap in Unimak Pass. Save

for a little flour, water, and beans, he had eaten nothing since the attack. He crawled under a dory on the beach and passed out. Jackson was lucky enough to be found by a prospecting party before he died. He was near starvation and exhausted; he had no coat, blanket, or shoes, though he was wearing a worn-out pair of rubber-boot soles that he had tied to his feet. After two weeks' rest he was able to move. The party hailed the mail steamer *Newport* as it moved thorugh the narrow pass and reached Dutch Harbor on July 17. Nome's U.S. Marshal Frank Richards took Jackson's statement at Dutch Harbor, and soon a party consisting of the marshal, U.S. Commissioner R. E. Whipple, and a coroner's jury set off for Unimak Island.

Governor Brady, who called at Dutch Harbor on a tour of inspection, feared that the killer or killers would never be found. Richards wanted to post a reward, but Brady could not offer anything without sanction from the Interior Department or the attorney general. What the governor longed for was the police capacity of the Canadian Mounties in the Klondike. During the past winter three men traveling from Dawson to Skagway had been robbed, murdered, and dropped through the Yukon river ice. The Mounties performed magnificently in tracking down the killer, who was convicted and sentenced to hang. In Alaska, Brady believed that many prospectors had been murdered but not one had ever been hanged.[10]

As things turned out, Fred Hardy was not smart enough—or was perhaps too arrogant—to leave Unimak Island. He was found with the Sullivans' property and a large sum of money in his possession. He offered an array of alibis: he was still on the *Arago* on June 7; he had found Con Sullivan's rifle and other possessions; his cash was his army mustering-out pay. An Unalaska grand jury indicted Hardy and the second-division court convened to try his and other cases. John L. McGinn prosecuted, while Nome attorneys C. P. Sullivan and John W. Carson defended Hardy. The jury and Judge Wickersham listened as witnesses rebutted Hardy's cover-up stories and his effort to blame the murders on George Aston, who was arrested in Hardy's company. On September 7, three months after the murders, Wickersham sentenced Hardy to hang.

Hardy was taken to Nome after his sentence, where his fate created a sensation for residents of the Bering Sea gold town. From the jail Hardy provided good copy for eager newsmen speculating on "whether the authorities will use a silken rope when he is 'worked off.'" And when Hardy asked for pen and paper, Nome Nugget editor J. F. A. Strong, sometime composer of lyrical doggrel, commented: "Hardy, it is claimed by his jailers, gives evidence of insanity as he has taken to writing poetry."[11]

In June 1902 the circuit court rejected Hardy's appeal for a new trail. Meanwhile Hardy had hatched an escape plot with John Priess, another prisoner, which involved killing the guards and fleeing to Dutch Harbor, where Hardy knew of a man with thirty thousand dollars and a schooner. The fugitives would rob and kill the Dutch Harbor man and sail to South America to trade whiskey with the natives and enjoy the good life. When guards discovered Hardy's letters in Priess's possession, they clapped Hardy in irons and his fantasies diminished.

The appeal process moved Hardy's hanging date from December 1901 to September 1902. The prisoner's only diversion lay in visits from the Catholic priests and nuns and counting the words in the Bible. He reported a total of 407,283 words in the Old and New Testaments. By August the long confinement had taken its toll on the condemned man, though he managed some bravado for newsmen: "When I go up on that gallows you'll find me just as cool as I am now."[12] Hardy, 28, died on schedule September 19, protesting his innocence to the last.

In his book *Old Yukon*, Judge Wickersham described a dramatic courtroom confrontation as the prosecutor tried to fix an important date in the sequence of murder events. The important testimony of a man Hardy had met on Unimak Island could be substantiated through confirmation by an island Eskimo with "the general facial expression of a decrepit idiot," dressed in smelly, ragged skin garments. Defense lawyers smiled knowingly as the Eskimo testified that he was certain of the crucial date because "me lote [wrote] it me log."[13] On cross-examination the defense offered the witness a pen and the opportunity of demonstrating his literacy in log keeping. To Wickersham's delight, the Eskimo wrote his name in a clear, legible Russian script.

Jacob Jaconi followed gold prospectors to Dawson and later to the new town of Fairbanks in 1904, but he stuck to his trade as a fisherman. In both towns the quiet Greek was a familiar sight vending his daily catch of fresh fish in season and dried salmon after freeze-up. Four miles from Fairbanks he lived alone in a self-built log cabin with a tent roof along the bank of the Chena River and collected the yield from his fish wheel each summer's day.[14] Jaconi made his last visit to Fairbanks on October 28, 1904. He deposited some money in the bank, then drove his dog team back home. On the following day a neighbor heard two gunshots. Later he heard Jaconi's dogs barking; it sounded as if they wanted feeding. About noon a friend stopped by, saw Jaconi's cabin burning and recovered the remains of a man: a leg bone, a charred trunk, and the back part of a head. Someone had shot the fisherman in the head, then used his olive oil to fuel the cabin's firing.

A Fairbanks man told police that two weeks ealrier Vuko Perovich, once Jaconi's partner, suggested robbing an unidentified man who lived outside town, a man with five hundred dollars in cash, a valuable gold ring, a gold watch and chain, and a good rifle. Deputies started looking for Perovich and found him a week later in a camp about twenty miles away. Perovich not only had Jaconi's rifle, watch, and ring, he was wearing the fisherman's clothes. His efforts to explain the possession of this property did not make much sense.

Perovich was charged with murder and tried at Fairbanks in summer 1905. The prosecutor was a little worried about establishing his case because positive identification of the body had been difficult and because the link between the accused and the killing depended entirely upon his possession of what appeared to be Jaconi's property. It helped that a couple of witnesses had heard Perovich threaten Jaconi's life and that Perovich confessed when he was arrested, although he later repudiated the confession.

At trial Perovich denied that he had told any of the prosecuting witnesses about a plan to rob or murder Jaconi. He claimed that a miner's threats, not fear of arrest, had induced him to leave Fairbanks and that two strange men had given him Jaconi's clothing. Defense attorney Leroy Tozier insisted that jurors could not find Perovich guilty beyond a reasonable doubt. The condition of the charred body found in the ruins of Jaconi's cabin made positive identification impossible, and the evidence linking Perovich to a homicide was too thin for conviction.

The jury thought the evidence against the accused was persuasive enough. Because jurors found Perovich guilty of first-degree murder without deserving mercy, Judge Wickersham had no choice but to sentence him to hang. The judge was pleased with the result and pronounced the death sentence on October 15, 1905, giving Perovich the dubious distinction of being the first person in the interior to receive the death penalty. The jury's decision also was well received by the public in Fairbanks, except among the Montenegrins, who decided the conviction was unjust and a slur on their community of hard-working Slavic miners.

Perovich missed his December 8 date with the hangman while his appeals to the circuit court and the Supreme Court were pending. By March 1907 all his appeals had failed and the hanging was scheduled for August 14. Tozier then petitioned for a presidential commutation, and Alaska's governor, Wilford B. Hoggatt, granted a stay of execution until February 1, 1908. Perovich's new lawyer, John F. Dillon, applied for a writ of habeas corpus, arguing that Hoggatt had exceeded his authority in fixing a new execution date. The district court's refusal to grant a writ was appealed to the circuit court, and the president granted a reprieve until March 6, 1908. When the circuit court refused to overrule the district court, President W. H. Taft, in June 1909, commutated Perovich's sentence to life in prison.

While all this was going on, Perovich indulged in other means of pressure from his Fairbanks cell. After visiting the condemned man, the Reverend S. Hall Young rather excitedly called on James Wickersham, who had resigned his judgeship, and warned him the Perovich's "Black Hand" comrades had marked Wickersham for revenge. Wickersham was not impressed. "I've been killed a dozen times before by jaw smiths and I guess I can stand it again," he said. He was disturbed, however, when the same story was told to him by the marshal and defense attorney Dillon: "I'm surprised a U.S. Marshal, minister, and lawyer will repeat such talk and encourage it by repeating it seriously."[15]

Wickersham believed that Perovich should hang in order to encourage seemly conduct in the interior. The hanging of Fred Hardy several years earlier had, he felt, deterred crime in the Aleutians. Yet after meeting with Peter Vidovich, "the most sensible and enlightened of the Slavonians here," he suggested the habeas corpus tactic to Dillon.[16] The presidential reprieve may well have prevented violence in Fairbanks because Vidovich warned Wickersham that 120 Montenegrins planned to storm the jail and rescue Perovich.

After almost twenty years at McNeil Island and Leavenworth prisons, Perovich filed another habeas corpus writ, arguing that President Taft had lacked authority to change his sentence without his acceptance. A federal judge agreed in 1925 and Perovich was released. The U.S. attorney for Kansas petitioned to rescind the commutation and return Perovich to Alaska for a hanging. When the U.S. Supreme Court ruled that the president did indeed have authority to commute a death sentence to life imprisonment, Perovich won his permanent freedom with a pardon from President Calvin Coolidge in 1927. Thus ended the long legal battle. Meanwhile, Perovich, assisted by a church charity, had moved to Rochester, New York, where he operated the Golden Rule Barber Shop. There he married, had children, and worked hard and honestly until his death in 1976.[17]

Mailo Saguro will always be remembered for his profession of amazement that officers would want to arrest him for shooting another person. "Why are you going to put me in jail, I pay my bills?" he asked U.S. Deputy Marshal Guy Gehrity.[18] Gehrity just shook his head at the question while Charles Cadwallader and other Otter Creek miners guffawed uneasily. After a brief quarter-mile chase, the miners had caught Saguro after hearing two shots and seeing the woodcutter running away. At their command, Saguro stopped and told them where he had thrown his gun; it was found near the corpse of J. E. Riley.

Murder was a bad business anywhere, but when the victim was the biggest independent operator in the Iditarod region, a popular, influential man who indirectly supported a goodly number of residents, the excitement was intense. Some fellows muttered about a lynching's being the only fit way to handle a Bohunk's cold-blooded shooting of old Riley in the back. There did not seem to be any reason for the killing.

There was a reason, of course. Saguro's fury exploded as he made his last appeal to Riley for money owed him. For two years

Saguro had supplied split wood for the mine, yet the wealthy miner denied owing the eight hundred dollars Saguro claimed. Again and again Saguro had presented his bill. Now he was leaving the district and needed the money desperately. Once more Riley refused to pay, and Saguro, who was not a brave man, shot Riley in the back on May 5, 1918.

Defense attorney Leroy Tozier tried to have the trial shifted from Flat, alleging that witnesses who were aliens would be afraid to testify honestly for the defense. But a venue change was denied and Flat jurors convicted Saguro of murder one and did not recommend mercy. Judge Charles Bunnell set Saguro's hanging for October 4, 1918. The execution was delayed by an unsuccessful appeal to the circuit court and stays by the governor—which were probably illegal—to allow petitions for presidential clemency. Fairbanks attorney John A. Clark won the governor's stay of execution by arguing that Saguro shot in self-defense, although there was no convincing evidence of this. Clark also professed to believe that Riley was not really shot in the back; he had twisted his body somewhat while facing Saguro and reaching for his gun, causing Saguro's bullet to enter his back.

When the president refused to act, the execution was rescheduled for April 15, 1921, at Fairbanks. A rather unique scaffold was constructed by building a passageway between a second-floor window of the courthouse to a vacant building adjacent to it. Officials cut a trap door through the planks and set a two-by-ten frame over it for the rope. Frank Young and other deputies had to strap Saguro to a plank because he refused to stand; then they raised the plank into position for the hanging.

Margaret ("French Marguerite") Lavor plied her ancient trade in bustling Anchorage after construction of the Alaska Railroad got under way. C. W. Mossman, the U.S. deputy marshal, knew the buxom young blonde as a prostitute and made routine inquiries after the first reports on her disappearance were received on August 27, 1919. None of the local pimps, saloonkeepers, or prostitutes knew where she was. Her friends suspected foul play, so Mossman hired three men to comb the area for clues. Four days later the searchers discovered some startling evidence: a blood-

stained man's vest and shirt, half burned, stuffed in a toilet behind a
house on B Street between Sixth and Seventh avenues. A day later
the searchers looked closely at an abandoned well near Crazy John's
house at Ninth Avenue and East C Street after their dog started
jumping around it excitedly. From the surface the men could see
nothing but the usual debris, so one of the men lowered himself to
the bottom and dug around. Soon he found a woman's shoe. "Toss it
up," said his companion from above. W. H. Weaver tried to obey. "I
took hold of it," he told a jury, "but I didn't send it up. It was solid. I
found this shoe down in there with a foot in it . . . the woman was
in there."[19] The woman was Margaret Lavor, and the cause of her
death seemed obvious: "The back of her head was all caved in like
something had hit her from behind; her brains were all oozing; and
her clothes were bloody."

Several people told police that Miss Lavor had been seen with
young William Dempsey the night of August 25. A fellow who lived
with Margaret had watched her dress to go out for a meeting with
Dempsey. Later someone knocked on the door but did not wait
around upon hearing Margaret's friend come to answer. Whoever
knocked must have hoped to find the house empty. Mittie Hall, a
prostitute friend of Margaret, told officers that Dempsey came to
her house the same night and asked her to walk up to his cabin.
She refused. "Then he went up towards town, towards Margaret's
place." A couple of Dempsey's cronies admitted that he told them of
a scheme to rob the whores' houses while a partner took the
women for a walk. An acquaintance identified the bloody clothes
found in the toilet on B Street as those Dempsey was wearing the
night of the twenty-fifth.

Unfortunately for the marshals, Dempsey also was missing. Presumably he had left town to work at one of the railroad construction
camps between Anchorage and Seward. He had not been seen
since the day after Margaret's disappearance. Marshal F. R. Bren-
neman sent word to Deputy Marshal Isaac Evans in Seward to
watch for the murder suspect. Whether Dempsey was working on
construction or planned to catch a ship for passage outside, he
would probably surface in Seward. Sure enough, on September 3,
Dempsey strolled into the railroad's Seward office to cash a pay
check he had received for three days' work with a crew at Mile 40.

The clerk, who had been alerted by Evans, telephoned the marshal. Evans confronted the young man, who insisted that his name was Cummings. "I'll have to hold you on suspicion until we find out whether your name is Dempsey or Cummings," said Evans. "All right," said the suspect, who submitted to a superficial search for weapons, then walked across the street to the jail with Evans.

Evans, a railroad claims agent in Tacoma before becoming a deputy, paid severely for his careless search of the fugitive. Just as the men reached the jail, Dempsey dropped his blanket roll, bent, and pulled a revolver from the bundle. Evans ignored the lad's order to "put 'em up" and charged. Dempsey fired twice, then sprinted down the street for the railroad yard. Witnesses, including Dr. J. A. Romig, rushed to help Evans while others pursued Dempsey until they saw him speeding down the track on a handcar. Evans died the next morning as the aroused men of Seward formed posses to scour the country for the killer. Apparently Dempsey's taste for outdoor living was not highly developed; he came back to Seward the next day and turned himself in, explaining, "I didn't mean to kill him, I just wanted to get away."

Soon after the police lodged Dempsey in jail, news of the discovery of Margaret Lavor's body reached Seward. Dempsey told officers that he had smashed her head with a monkey wrench; he had no accomplice. Once Dempsey got to Valdez to await trial, he told another story and denied killing Margaret. His explanation for shooting Evans then became somewhat implausible; he had simply felt the urge to flee from the deputy's attention.

Judge Charles E. Bunnell appointed Anthony Dimond to defend the accused man. Dimond learned that the Ohio boy had suffered a serious skull fracture years earlier and had experienced periods of irrational behavior since then. On several occasions he had threatened his sister with a knife; he had complained of sleeplessness and acted in bizarre ways so frequently that family friends had advised the boy's father to commit him. All this background information was presented to jurors by Dimond as part of an insanity defense in the form of affidavits because family members could not afford the expense of traveling to Alaska and the court refused to pay their expenses as witnesses.

In jail Dempsey acted a bit crazy at times, although the stern authorities believed he was faking. During the trial he performed on one occasion with a flair that haunted the memories of the officials. The lights in the courtroom went out suddenly because of a power outage, and startled spectators heard the accused cry out: "The day of judgment has come, the day of judgment has come." The *Seward Gateway* reporter observed that "the darkness and the low tone sent the marrow creeping in the bones of those in the court room."[20] Dempsey followed up his macabre act the next day with a flash of wit that made everyone feel better. A clumsy court official was trying to remove bullets from the revolver that had been taken from Dempsey and offered as an exhibit. "Let me take the gun," Dempsey said with a willing smile, "I will take the bullets out and show you how to, as I know."

The trial for the murder of Evans was held in November; charges for the Lavor killing were heard in December. Each jury decided that Dempsey was guilty of first-degree murder and rejected the qualification of mercy they were entitled to make. By Alaska law the judge was required to order the hanging of anyone convicted of murder one who did not receive the jury's "without capital punishment" recommendation. In effect, Dempsey's life had been forfeited twice, and on December 12, Judge Bunnell repeated the dreadful words twice: "You shall be hanged by the neck until dead on February 20, 1920."[21]

Alaskans were generally happy over the trial results. Bunnell and others offset potential sympathy for the murderer by insisting that his claim to be only nineteen years old was a lie; he looked to be twenty-four or more, they argued. In fact, Dempsey was twenty when he stood trial.

Defense attorney Dimond did his duty in filing an appeal on grounds of procedural errors and even on the technical grounds of his incompetence as a criminal defense lawyer, alleging that most of his practice had been in civil cases. Dimond, who was born in New York in 1881, taught school in rural New York before moving to Alaska in 1905 as a prospector and freighter in the Copper River Valley. Only after an injury from an accidental gunshot wound did Dimond take up law, starting practice in 1913. Whatever his experience as a criminal lawyer in 1919, he gained plenty in later years and crowned an equally successful political career by serving as the congressional delegate for Alaska from 1932 to 1945, then as U.S. district judge for the Third Judicial District from 1945 until his death in 1953.

Dempsey's appeal record was not perfected in time for the U.S. Circuit Court of Appeals to consider his petition and was dismissed without a hearing. Judge Bunnell had not approved a government expenditure for the trial transcript and other appeal expenses, although Judge Fred Brown did extend Dempsey's time for filing. The failure of the appeal would have ended Dempsey's life but for the intervention of President Woodrow Wilson, through Attorney General Mitchell Palmer, with a commutation of the sentence to life imprisonment.

Bunnell and other law officers were highly vexed at Wilson and the attorney general and attempted to find out who had influenced the commutation. The attorney general had acted on a petition submitted by a Cleveland lawyer who had been retained by Dempsey's family, and since executive commutations were fairly common during Wilson's administration, the result should not have shocked Bunnell, but it did. There was something about Dempsey that worried the judge; he would have been relieved to see him hanged.

Dempsey was sent to McNeil Island until March 1921, when he was transferred to Leavenworth. As time passed, he tried to educate himself in the mysteries of law, finance, real estate, and English grammar, and in 1923 he campaigned for his freedom with letters to Governor Scott Bone, a former Seattle newspaperman, who was not familiar with the case. Bone consulted U.S. Attorney Sherman Duggan, who recalled the events: "No other Alaska case aroused such indignation and no crime committed since the foundation of the territory was so wanton and depraved," Duggan advised Bone: "People here think he should have paid with his life." [22]

Dempsey again wrote to Bone, hoping to set him right on the murder cases. By some logic peculiar to himself, he argued that his shooting of Evans, which could hardly be denied, was not done in "circumstances as to define it as first degree murder." It is hard to imagine what Dempsey thought first-degree murder was if the cold-blooded shooting of an arresting officer did not meet the test. His explanation of Lavor's death was easier since it had not been done in front of witnesses in downtown Seward: "I always had and always will deny having been responsible or even indirectly connected with it in any manner or form." He had been convicted of the crime because his lawyers lacked skill and he lacked the money to retain competent help. Now he was suffering in health because of his imprisonment, and his grieving and impecunious parents longed to have him free: "My parents need me and if I regain my liberty I shall return to their hearth and never, never leave it again," he told the governor. [23]

After an exchange of letters with Judge Bunnell in 1921, Dempsey was quiet for a while, then reopened the campaign in 1926. Bunnell, now president of Alaska Agricultural College and School of Mines, advised him to help authorities find out who actually did the killing if, as Dempsey claimed, he was innocent of the murder of Margaret Lavor. Later Bunnell wrote that there was no good reason for his intervention: "It seems to me that in view of all the circumstances society is best protected by keeping you where you are. . . . Men do not have to be at large to be good men. You were not a benefit to society or to yourself when you were at large." Be grateful that you escaped a death sentence, Bunnell wrote. [24]

With his first 1926 letter Dempsey enclosed a copy of the prison magazine *The New Era*. While Bunnell did not comment upon the coincidence, the lead article had been written by editor Dr. Frederick Cook, another man well known in Alaskan history. Cook was serving time at Leavenworth for mail fraud in his promotion of Texas oil fields. In Alaska he was known best for his fraudulent claim that he climbed Mount McKinley in 1906 and, of course, for his equally implausible claim to the first exploration of the North Pole in 1908.

Dempsey's arguments for his innocence were not too convincing, but it is noteworthy that he always claimed that he could have escaped en route to McNeil Island. Presumably he had amazed his guards by removing his Oregon boot (a thirty-pound leg shackle) and throwing it into Puget Sound as the prison launch conveyed him from the mainland to the island. While in jail at Valdez he had passed up other easy opportunities of escaping that had been given him by friends. In Dempsey's mind these refusals to take advantage of escape opportunities were grand, convincing testimonials to his good will toward men. "The only or main reason I did not escape," he wrote, "is that I feared I would probably of necessity have to also resort to violence of a fatal nature before completing my escape." [25]

Whether Dempsey's story was true or not, Bunnell did not like hearing anything about escape. He had taken the trouble to talk to Justice Department officials in Washington after Dempsey's death sentence was commuted to determine why the decision had been made. It was his understanding that President Wilson's wife opposed capital punishment and had acted in several cases during her husband's illness. Increasing Bunnell's uneasiness about Dempsey were such comments from him as this one: "I would like to regain my freedom and get a start in life anew, before I become a physical and mental wreck, feeling hatred against this world and those who caused my life's ruination." He had forgiven everyone involved, but he was afraid that he might "become calloused to human sentiments and become a menace to not only myself but all the gentle, organized society. This future, good or bad, lies in the hollow of your hand. . . . You undoubtably are a Christian, if so, prove your worthiness of its term or name."

This is rather forthright language for one in Dempsey's position. Men of good will and truly repentant slayers probably should not address judges in this fashion. Bunnell also had been particularly offended by a Christmas card that offered joy to the judge "despite the misery you have caused my family." Such communications were counterproductive in evoking a forgiving mood in Bunnell. In fact he became increasingly nervous about Dempsey and overreacted to those who spoke on his behalf. On a couple of occasions Dempsey, who apparently was not entirely without charm and guile, conned women into accepting his lies about his background. When they wrote to the judge asking for mercy, they received a sharp response and close questioning on their motivation, background, and details on what they heard from Dempsey.

In 1934, after a break in their correspondence, Dempsey asked Bunnell to write to the U.S. pardon attorney on his behalf. "I am now a totally different person, from what I was in 1919—mentally. So why do you insist on continuing to torture me, for what a mentally totally different person had committed." [26] Neither this nor any other communication moved Bunnell, who never discarded his belief that Dempsey should have been hanged.

Dempsey was returned to McNeil Island in 1939 and must have decided that he had little chance of getting out of prison unless he took matters into his own hands. So it was that on a foggy day, January 30, 1940, he escaped. As usual when escapes from the prison were discovered, guards beat the bushes on the island, figuring the fugitive would lie low until he saw a chance, or got the nerve, to swim the two miles to the mainland. Swimmers had made it in the past, most notably the Robin Hoodish mail bandit Roy Gardner, who enlivened a Labor Day baseball game in 1921 by cutting a fence and disappearing among a herd of dairy cows. The guards did not find Dempsey on the island. He may have survived the swim and made it to safety. There was a report of a suspicious-looking man asking charity of a minister in a community near the prison island.

Bunnell heard the escape news that he had long feared with much alarm. He was convinced that Dempsey blamed him for his twenty years of confinement and would take revenge. The former judge wired the FBI in Juneau, then followed up with a letter to FBI chief J. Edgar Hoover: "Dempsey may head for Alaska. . . . He is a desperate killer. . . . His letters during the last five years have been abusive. It challenges my attention to know that murderers are permitted to send out the kind of stuff they do." [27] Hoover wrote a soothing letter of reply, but Bunnell worried about Dempsey until his own death in 1956.

If he survived his escape, Dempsey presumably did not go back to Alaska. He was never recaptured, although the usual efforts were made. Readers of true-crime stories learned about his career in several articles published in 1940 and between 1953 and 1956. Whether Dempsey was the nastiest of Alaska's killers is a moot question, but there is no doubt that he caused more anxiety to others after his conviction than any other.

Aside from the consequences, the circumstances of the 1946 killing of Jim Ellen in Juneau were not remarkable. Ellen, who kept a grocery and liquor store on Willoughby Avenue, was robbed for two thousand dollars and stabbed fatally in his store the night of December 22. His murder seemed a senseless act of violence. It did not appear that he had resisted the robber.

Men who hung around Juneau's saloons without visible means of support were hauled in by U.S. Marshal Walter Hellan and FBI agent Jack Hayes. One of these was Austin Nelson, who could not give a coherent account of his sudden splurging at Juneau's bars or of his activities on December 22. Witnesses had seen him and another man near Ellen's store that night. Nelson was indicted for murder one. At trial another Juneau drifter, Eugene La Moore, offered an alibi for Nelson. He and his wife had been with Nelson on the evening in question, drinking in several bars. Jurors found no truth in Nelson's defense. He was convicted without a recommendation for mercy, and his hanging was scheduled for July 1, 1947.

La Moore's testimony struck a false note. The police decided that he was a blatant liar and charged him with perjury. It seemed likely that La Moore testified less for altruistic reasons than to protect an accomplice. La Moore was jailed and interrogated intensively. The day before Nelson's execution, officials brought Nelson and La Moore together. Nelson begged for help and perhaps threatened to expose La Moore. La Moore confessed his part in the robbery.

According to La Moore the two men resolved on a holdup while sitting in Blackie's Bar wondering where their next drink was coming from. They set off for Ellen's place. Nelson had a gun, but it was not loaded. La Moore urged him not to kill Ellen. At the store Nelson showed his gun and pushed Ellen from the grocery store to the back room while La Moore looted the cash register. La Moore heard a scuffle, then the sound of running water. The thieves left the store, hurried to the Alaska Hotel and divided their takings. Blood on Nelson's clothes frightened La Moore. "Good God, man. What happened? What did you do?" "I had to do it. I had to do it," Nelson answered. [28] After Nelson left, La Moore burned his hat and rubbers and threw his coat in Gold Creek. He hid his money in a woodshed, where it was discovered and taken by another thief.

With La Moore's confession, which he later claimed had been tampered with, Nelson got a reprieve, but only for possible testimony at La Moore's trial. Nelson was hanged on March 1, 1948, at Juneau, still proclaiming his innocence. La Moore denied his confession at trial. He also denied that he had ever been convicted of a crime, then changed his testimony after the prosecutor introduced evidence that he had been convicted of robbery in California. Under the name Austin Rollan, La Moore had been sentenced to five years at San Quentin in 1927. In the only instance in Alaska of a double hanging for the same murder, La Moore was hanged in Juneau on April 14, 1950.

17. Busting Out

The official class . . . is so dastardly cowardly and corrupt. —James
Wickersham

By digging, chipping, sawing, forcing bars, or getting the drop on
guards with sly tricks, prisoners sometimes escaped from Alaska's
early jails, which were no more secure than beautiful. A legend that
in early times the Circle jailer allowed prisoners to roam during the
day but warned against a tardy return, punished by being locked
out for the night, suggests a certain laxity. But in truth the deputy
marshal in charge of the jail was vigilant. He often earned a helpful
income from fees allowed for prisoners' subsistence because they
exceeded the cost of food; but, more significantly, he stood a good
chance of losing his job if his negligence contributed to an escape.

With each escape the marshal reported immediately to the attorney general and to the Federal Bureau of Prisons. The attorney
general's office responded faster to such messages than it did to a
request for funds. Officials wanted to know why there had been an
escape and who was to blame. A telegram of dismissal was a common response.

For towering audacity, the escape of William T. ("Slim") Birch
from the Juneau jail in 1897 is without parallel in Alaska crime annals, and its aftermath is equally incredible. Several armed masked
men barged into the jailer's office, forced him to open Birch's cell, and

fled town without difficulty. Birch had been charged with mayhem, but many people in Juneau felt he was comparatively innocent.

After the authorities recovered from their initial shock and heard from informants that the jailbreakers were holed up on Admiralty Island, they devised a plan of pursuit. Five deputies boarded the tugboat *Lucy* for a voyage to Bear Creek on Admiralty Island. When they saw a canoe on the beach and a faint trail in the snow, they knew their information was accurate. Three miles inland, they reached an inhabited log cabin. The deputies saw Birch and three or four men inside and made the fatal mistake of calling for the fugitives' surrender rather than rushing the cabin without notice. All they got in exchange for their demand was a volley of gunfire that drove them to cover behind a tree ten yards from the cabin. As the gun battle raged the posse got the worst of it. Two deputies were wounded and another, William Watts, broke his leg. After the cabin defenders threw a burning bundle of rags at the deputies' position to smoke them out, the latter retreated to the beach in confusion. An Indian deputy performed heroically in covering the retreat but had to leave William Watts because of Watts's broken leg. Later Watts was fatally wounded by gunfire from the cabin. The survivors steamed back to Juneau on the *Lucy* to report their failure. Juneau men rallied to form another posse, and help from the U.S. Navy gunboat *Pinta* was requested.

Alaskans seethed. "All men talk about death in a whisper," said Sitka's newspaper. "It is fearful in itself and horrible to think of. . . . It is greatly to be deplored that Alaska's choice young men should be murdered at the hands of such a miserable wretch as this fiend Birch has proved to be."[1] The Admiralty Island killings also served as a stick to beat those "who have openly sympathized with Birch and thus emboldened him to defy the law and stain his hands in blood." It is time, said the *Alaskan*, "for the people to stand by law and order and cease sympathizing with criminals when an attempt is made to punish them. We believe now is the time for us as true citizens to crush out this evil element so fast coming in among us."

When the large posse voyaged to Admiralty Island, it stumbled onto Birch and Hiram Schell sleeping in the woods and captured them without difficulty. Both men claimed that Schell had not been involved in Birch's escape from the Juneau jail. Birch and those who had helped him escape had forced Schell to leave Juneau with them. The *Alaskan* ridiculed this alibi: "The idea of an escaping criminal capturing a man, taking him 25 miles by water and three miles up the mountain, then keeping him for days and weeks cannot be believed a moment." Birch would not have saddled himself with a hostile captive, and why did Schell not try to escape when the first posse cornered the fugitives? Schell insisted that he had not been involved in shooting at the arresting officers, and Birch supported his story. Birch's explanation of his own conduct was simple. He had been outside the cabin when the posse started shooting without warning. He had no idea that the men were law officers and fired back through chinks in the cabin walls in self-defense.

Birch and Schell were charged with the murder of William Watts and tried at Sitka in December 1898. The jury found them not guilty. Despite this result, the *Alaskan* praised the efforts of the prosecutor and the judge, even publishing the judge's routine instructions to the jury in full—"one of the best charges to the jury . . . that has ever issued from the court of this district."[2]

The defense had maintained that Birch had been compelled to leave the Juneau jail against his will by the gang that sprang him. He stuck to his story that he had fired a few random shots in self-defense at the Admiralty Island shootout but had not shot Watts. Schell repeated the story he told when he was arrested. Prosecutor Burton Bennett had no witnesses who could refute the defendants' stories. None of the men who had freed Birch and occupied the cabin on Admiralty Island could be found. It appeared that jurors took seriously the judge's charge that the evidence must show "beyond a reasonable doubt" that the accused knew the men outside were law officers and shot at them. Through no fault of his own, the prosecutor's evidence was simply not good enough, according to the *Alaskan*.

The newspaper's benign view of the culmination of such dastardly crimes perhaps reflected other undisclosed policies. The editor, who had reflected earlier on the need of Alaskans to support law-and-order efforts, saw fit to praise the "conscientious jurors" and court officers rather than abuse them for failing to convict. Heavy praise of the prosecutor in a losing cause is somewhat suspect.

Whether the editor's moderation expressed the court's view or was designed to encourage Alaskans to an appreciation of their court, despite the acquittal, cannot be determined. Superficially it would appear that the prosecutor had a good-enough case for manslaughter at least. And one interested observer of the trial, Governor John Brady, put his horrified opinion of the jury's decision on record. Writing to the secretary of the interior, Brady lumped the Sitka trial with the outrageous domination of Skagway by Soapy Smith's gang in pleading for law-enforcement help. Police were at the mercy of "ruffians . . . one of this class . . . was acquitted by a jury in the face of positive evidence. In fact these influences seem joined hand and hand and will go unpunished unless the government takes immediate action and provides the necessary force at Skagway and Dyea."[3] Brady was obviously very angry at the Sitka jurors and saw no reason to distinguish events in the comparatively orderly capital from affairs in Skagway.

Ice fog settled over Fairbanks in late January 1906 as daily temperatures ranged from thirty to fifty degrees below. This climatic condition, created by the release of warmer air into the frigid surroundings to form a dense fog, is one aspect of the interior's winters that no one praises. It complicates life in the communities by obscuring visibility, and it tends to grate on people's nerves. For Fairbanks jailbirds Charles Hendrickson and Thomas Thornton, however, the ice fog promised opportunity. Their guards' senses might be dulled enough to give them an edge in breaking jail; and pursuers would be baffled in the fog. Both prisoners had escaped the Fairbanks jail before. The jail was a poorly constructed log house, thirty by twenty-four feet, divided into three cells. It had been built in 1903, as prospectors flocked to Fairbanks and adjacent creeks in the latest northern stampede, by carpenters anxious to get on with other building jobs, and they were sparing of scarce, expensive building materials.

Hendrickson, known as the "Blue Parka bandit" after a notorious series of trail holdups, a most uncommon crime in Alaska, first broke out August 8, 1905. He and a cellmate fashioned a saw out of an iron hoop and sawed their way through the cabin's fourteen-inch-thick log foundation. Judge Wickersham heard of Hendrickson's escape on the same day a jury angered him by acquitting Harry Owens of murder. Why did Hendrickson bother? the judge sneered in his diary. He could have trusted the jury to free him.

Thornton had served a year in the Fairbanks jail for breaking into a Fourth Avenue cabin. He was released in June 1905, and in July he was charged with stealing two horses at Cleary City. Like road holdups, horse thefts were unfamiliar crimes in Alaska. It was as if Hendrickson and Thornton wished to enhance the interior's culture by introducing felonies traditional in other climes. A month passed before Thornton was captured with the help of soldiers at Fort Gibbon and returned to his old quarters in the Fairbanks jail. This time he cut his way out, headed for the Canadian border, and was apprehended at Eagle in November.

Since the guards watched scrupulously for any signs of tampering with the logs, Hendrickson and Thornton hatched a bolder scheme. They struck as a guard served them breakfast on the morning of January 29. Thornton threw pepper in the server's eyes and, as the men grappled, stabbed him three times with a knife. Meanwhile, Hendrickson dashed at the other guard and laid him out with desperate punches. Somehow he had managed to get his leg shackles off before attacking the guard and was free to barge out the door to freedom. Thornton, still in leg irons, hobbled after him.

Hendrickson may have expected help once he got out of the jail, but if he had arranged to get a parka and other winter clothing, his expectations were not met. His movements after escape verged on the suicidal. He started down the Valdez Trail at fifty degrees below zero wearing only a light shirt and trousers. After twelve miles he found an empty cabin and stopped, but the cabin had no stove or blankets, so the exhausted fugitive folded up in a corner and shivered until deputies ran him down a few hours later. The drinking men in Fairbanks were unhappy about the stabbing of a guard and did not distinguish Hendrickson from Thornton, the actual culprit. But for the extreme cold and the determined stand of Deputy Marshal George Dreibelis, they would have lynched Hendrickson. The guard did recover, but at the time his death was expected.

A month passed before Thornton was captured. He had rendezvoused with friends in Fairbanks, who removed his leg irons

and got him refuge in a woodcutter's tent fifteen miles below Chena. An informant tipped his location to deputies, who converged on Thornton's tent, after calling for his surrender, to find him bleeding from four self-inflicted throat slashes. It was a near thing, but after three weeks in the Fairbanks hospital, Thornton was back in jail.

Hendrickson and Thornton had other adventures in May 1906 when a fire raged through the town, leaving most buildings in shambles. Before the jail ignited, the prisoners were marched to a vacant lot at Third Avenue and Wickersham Street and guarded there until a new jail was constructed.

Their trials were delayed by the absence of Judge Wickersham, who had been called to Washington, D.C., to defend his appointment against his influential detractors and did not return until late summer. Finally, on August 17, they stood trial. Officers took no chances with the escape artists, who had been wearing riveted leg irons day and night since their capture. For court appearances the irons were removed in favor of Oregon boots: circular iron disks weighing thirty pounds each, clamped around the ankles by means of an inside hinge and held by a bolt sunk in a small socket. A key screwed the bolt tight. Iron bars with upturned ends screwed to the prisoner's shoes held the Oregon boots above the ankles so that it was possible to hobble from jail to courthouse. Once back in jail the prisoners' iron-bound shoes were removed and the Oregon boots fell to their usual ankle position, making walking virtually impossible.

In court both men looked older than their thirty-odd years because of their long, close confinement. Thornton, an unpleasant-looking, ignorant, nasty-mannered type and would-be killer, was the object of much hostility from the courtroom crowd. Hendrickson, however, was a young man of flair and education, good looking and dapper in dress. Because he had established himself as a non-violent Robin Hood stereotype, he was an object of fascination for Fairbanks folks, particularly the women.

District Attorney Nathan Harlan allowed both men to amend their pleas in open court. In exchange for their pleading guilty to all crimes charged, Harlan would recommend leniency. Thornton hurt his chances by complaining of jail conditions and the alleged brutality of one of the guards—unfortunately, not the one he had assaulted. "I am not a vicious man," cried Thornton. "Since coming North it seems that everything has gone wrong. Judge Wickersham, I have a wife and family. I would like to see them again." [4] The judge was not touched and rejected the argument that bad jail conditions were mitigating circumstances. Thornton got fifteen years.

Hendrickson, who had not committed a severe assault, may have expected a lighter sentence, but he refused to beg for mercy. It is unlikely that he would have been favored anyway because Wickersham was fed up with a character who had mocked the law repeatedly with daring robberies and dramatic escapes. Wickersham had been distressed in 1905 when a "soft headed, soft hearted" jury acquitted Hendrickson of three holdup charges. [5] Judges and prosecutors do not generally succumb to romance concerning felons, even Robin Hoods. Hendrickson got fifteen years and the court spectators murmured in surprise. Actually, as Hendrickson's biographer has pointed out, both defendants gained from defense lawyer Leroy Tozier's deal with Harlan. All charges except the escape assaults were dropped, and, of course, the government saved the trouble and expense of long trials.

Deputy George Dreibelis exercised devoted vigilance until he could ship the prisoners out on the *Lavelle Young*. At odd hours he appeared at the jail to check the alertness of the guards and the security of the prisoners' manacles. Town wits commented that the court officers had permitted the plea bargaining only out of anxiety to rid themselves sooner of the embarrassment of another escape. Other gossips argued that the accused men pleaded guilty only as a means of getting out of the new "escape-proof" jail to less-restrained conditions.

As long as Hendrickson and Thornton remained in town, the officials could expect some heat. U.S. Marshal George Perry took an editorial blast from the *Fairbanks Times* when he named the four guards for the voyage to McNeil Island. Jack Sowerby and Charles Webb were experienced men, but James Darlington and Jack Noon were known to be friends of Perry. "They are not men of experience in handling prisoners. The fact that they were employed as guards was not due to such experience, or because of any ability in that line, but solely because they wanted to get outside without paying their way and had sufficient pull with the marshal's office to accomplish it."[6]

The *Lavelle Young* left Fairbanks on September 24. Deputy Marshal Frank Wiseman and four guards had four prisoners in the steamboat's centrally situated double stateroom. Robert ("Bobby") Miller, the gold-heist bandit, and a forger named Kunz completed the prisoner party. Stern precautions were taken: Hendrickson and Thornton wore Oregon boots. Before boarding the prisoners, Wiseman examined the stateroom carefully and removed a wooden rod supporting a thin brass tube used for a window curtain. Wiseman wanted iron bars placed outside the only window, but the captain objected. Sowerby and Webb were daytime guards; Darlington and Noon stood night watches. Wiseman was always present at feeding times and inspected at odd hours during the night and day.

The passengers, many of them returning outside with well-filled gold pokes, were not affected by the presence of prisoners. They were pleased with themselves and comfortable in the warm sunshine enjoyed each day on the Tanana and middle-Yukon rivers. Nights were cool. Winter was coming, but they would not be around to feel its icy grip this time. Some of their serenity vanished at Rampart, where a lively mob of prospectors boarded to fill every corner of the vessel. They were not going far, only to Fort Yukon, where they would stampede north of the Arctic Circle to the hot new gold discovery in the Chandalar River region. However, the extra burden may have caused the engine breakdown that occurred fifty miles below Fort Yukon. As repairs were made, a crewman dropped a bearing overboard; that concluded hopes of further progress until repairs or a tow could be arranged. The breakdown occurred on September 28. Slush ice floated in the river, and food was running low. On October 1 another steamer, the *Ida May*, fully loaded, came by but could only tow the *Lavelle Young* downriver to a better moorage place and promise to send help. Relief came with the arrival of the steamer *Seattle No. 3*. It was empty and had been dispatched for winter moorage at Dawson before anyone heard about the *Lavelle Young*'s plight. All the passengers were delirious with joy as the *Seattle No. 3* took the stranded steamer in tow.

Meanwhile, the indomitable Hendrickson and Thornton laid plans for an escape. Hendrickson had secured a tiny jeweler's tool in his pipe, and while the others kept watch he fashioned a key for the Oregon boots and a saw from the brass curtain rod. Bobbie Miller, who bragged about his short term for the gold heist from the *Tanana* and his plan to enjoy the gold he did not surrender when he was arrested, was a tremendous help. Unlike the surly, tempestuous Thornton, Miller exuded charm and enjoyed enlivening the night watch (Darlington and Noon) with conversation while Hendrickson and Thornton cut an escape hatch in the stateroom ceiling. In his many inspections, Wiseman observed no sign of the men's work.

The break was planned for a scheduled wood stop at Nation City. Hendrickson and Thornton crawled through the hatch. Their escape was detected when the slow-witted Darlington bumped into Thornton outside the stateroom, pondered a few moments, checked the stateroom, and then, instead of firing his rifle as a warning, as he had been instructed to do, ran for Wiseman. The latter launched a search involving most of the male passengers on the steamer, but the captain demanded their return by midnight; he would wait no longer before sailing. The fugitives were not found, and Wiseman paced the deck until the steamer moved slowly along the forty-six-mile stretch to Eagle and the telegraph.

Before leaving Nation City, Wiseman posed a $250 reward and

deputized two men, ordering them to spread the word to a nearby Indian village and a mining camp on Fourth of July Creek. This was a decisive impediment to Hendrickson's plan. He had chosen Nation City for his escape because he knew the area and could get clothes and provisions from the miners. Once before he had learned the futility of an unprepared flight, and had the miners not been alerted by Wiseman, he would have plundered them for his needs. The fugitives quickly discovered that the miners were on the watch and eager to win the reward. With overwhelming dread they faced the alternative: living off the land without proper clothing, arms, or food. Nighttime temperatures fell to near zero, and all the chilled land offered in the way of food was frozen berries.

In a desperate bid for survival, the fugitives took over a roadhouse at Montauk, charging in with clubs and looking wild enough to stun the four men gathered there. With the roadhouse keeper's reluctant help, the jailbirds secured a winter outfit and packed food. Then they headed across difficult country for the Canadian border before detouring for the established trail to Seventymile. Neither man was strong enough, after their many months of close confinement, for the exertion of rugged travel. Thornton gave himself up at a roadhouse; Hendrickson pushed on. He did not get far before a man whose boat he commandeered for a river crossing got the drop on him. Deputy Wiseman came along to collect the fugitives.

Charles Sheldon, the big-game hunter, was aboard the *Jefferson,* preparing to leave Skagway for Seattle, when Hendrickson and Thornton were marched aboard. Sheldon and other Skagway passengers had been the prisoners' shipmates on the *Lavelle Young,* and their reunion signified that for all of Hendrickson's brilliance and audacity, he had not been able to miss the ship the government had booked him on. This time Wiseman removed the prisoners' stateroom door, and extremely sharp eyes kept them under scrutiny all the way down the picturesque Inside Passage. At Dawson, Wiseman had hired a pair of retiring Mounties for guards to replace Darlington and Noon, who had been summarily fired, and the voyage passed without further alarm.

The prisoners were well known by the time they reached McNeil Island, and it must be presumed that the warden was wary of them. Nevertheless, Hendrickson broke away from confinement two months after his arrival. He escaped the prison but was captured before he got off the island. As was customary, federal prison authorities transferred him to the maximum-security prison at Leavenworth. Thornton died in prison, but the exceedingly wily Hendrickson escaped twice, for very brief periods, before his release in 1920; had it not been for his escape attempts, he might have been released in 1916. It is not known what Hendrickson did after his release. He apparently did not return to Alaska, where his exploits had made him a legend.

Lawmen who arrested Lee H. Johnston in September 1908 stood by in embarrassment as his wife, Cora, crying furiously, clung to him and begged for an explanation. Cora Tosh, who had married Johnston at Omaha, Nebraska, in 1903, was bitterly shocked to learn of his bigamy. To special agent Joe Warren and Seattle detectives, bigamy was the least of Johnston's offenses; they wondered when the hysterical woman might recover enough to count her blessings. Cora's world had been dashed but she was alive, while Johnston's other wife was dead. And it was the apparent slaying of Belle Gilchrist in Nome that led Warren to Johnston in Seattle. Johnston and Belle apparently met on the *Ohio* en route to Nome in 1905. Cora remained in Seattle while Johnston sought his fortune in Alaska, and she knew nothing of his shipboard romance and marriage in Nome.

In Nome, Johnston sent Cora money each month and persuaded Belle to give him power of attorney over her property in Alaska. When the *Ohio* made its last voyage to Seattle in October 1905, Belle was aboard or at least that's what Johnston told those who asked. A Nome friend of Belle doubted that Belle would leave without saying anything and wrote to her friends in Butte, Montana, and Seattle. No one had heard from Belle, and the affair seemed suspicious. Marshal T. C. Powell was alerted. He made some inquiries, then dug up the area around the Johnston cabin without finding anything of interest. Meanwhile, Johnston worked at odd jobs in Nome until the fall of 1906, when he returned to Cora in Seattle.

Marshal Powell assigned Joe Warren the case in spring 1907. Warren learned that Johnston had appeared in Butte, demanding

$4,800 that Belle had left in a lawyer's control, displaying Belle's power of attorney. The lawyer smelled a forgery and refused to turn over the money. Subsequently the lawyer received several letters purporting to be from Belle. The writer of these letters explained that she could sign only crudely because her rheumatism was so bad. The attorney, still wondering, sent only $1,100 of the money demanded.

Warren's attention was stimulated when he saw letters Johnston wrote to other people from Seattle, claiming that Belle remained in Nome, and discovered the bigamous marriage. Finally Warren confronted Johnston in Seattle and listened to an implausible story of Belle's suicide. Where is her body? asked Warren. Well, said Johnston, he buried it under the cabin to avoid embarrassment, then dug it up, dismembered it, and burned it. These had been Belle's instructions on her suicide note, which Johnston had misplaced. Oh, and the note also directed him to take possession of her money in Butte. Warren figured a Nome grand jury might well indict Johnston for murder, particularly after the search he ordered in Nome turned up portions of Belle's body. It was also learned that Johnston had purchased cyanide at a Nome drugstore sometime before Belle's disappearance.

Deputies W. O. Robb and E. B. Bowen were assigned to take Johnston back to Nome on the *Victoria,* sailing September 5, 1908, but lost their sense of vigilance during the long voyage. As the *Victoria* passed through the narrow Aleutian Islands gap at Unimak Pass, Johnston climbed over his sleeping guard and vanished. The embarrassed deputies had no idea whether their prisoner jumped overboard and struck out for shore or hid on board. At Nome a careful watch was maintained over the ship and its disembarking passengers; there was no sign of the fugitive. When the ship returned to Seattle, a fuming Joe Warren supervised a thorough examination of the *Victoria's* six hundred passengers, then moved into the ship with a squad of officers. The search revealed nothing so Warren arranged a fumigation of the old *Victoria,* hoping to smoke out Johnston in the unlikely event that he had remained aboard.[7] Johnston was never heard of again. If he drowned swimming from the ship, his body apparently did not wash ashore. Whether he gained the shore in safety, then evaded discovery, remains a mystery. It is probable that he drowned, unless, as some evidence indicated, he found on the ship's deck a canoe that later was said to be missing and paddled off to secure obscurity.

Another man who got away from the law was Tom Johnson, better known as "Blueberry Kid." The Kid was suspected of murder, although the circumstances of the case might have made conviction difficult even if he had been found. The pursuit of the Blueberry Kid was long drawn out and instructive on the peculiar character of law enforcement in Alaska. Distances and remoteness were factors, as was a certain lack of vigor not peculiar to Alaska.

Bob Marshall's *Arctic Village,* a classic volume of Alaskana focusing on Wiseman and published in 1933, describes the three Koyukuk murders the author had heard about. Marshall knew nothing of the region's greatest mystery, a crime as brutal as any in territorial history. The incident's omission in Koyukuk folklore is understandable. The victims and their assailant were equally illusive, yet the facts point conclusively to the deliberate robbery and slaying of three people: John Holmberg, Marie Schmidt, and Frank Adams.

John Holmberg, alias "Fiddler John," a prosperous Koyukuk miner, leased his mines in September 1912 and prepared to retire in the States. He arranged transportation on Tom Johnson's launch, the *Seal Pup,* from Wiseman down the Koyukuk to meet a Yukon steamboat. Voyaging with him were Marie Schmidt, a Fairbanks prostitute known as "Dutch Marie" who may have been married to Holmberg, and Frank Adams. Carrying passengers was convenient for Johnson because he had finished his seasonal work operating the *Seal Pup* on the upper Koyukuk, collecting wages of nine hundred dollars due him and paying two hundred dollars in debts. He too planned to winter outside, to enjoy the good life as long as his money lasted.

At some point Johnson must have reflected on the disparity between his savings and the eight thousand dollars Holmberg carried. In Seattle and San Francisco he could revel for months with Holmberg's money if the voyage downriver provided an opportunity for redistributing wealth. Apparently it did. According to an investigation conducted by special agent Joe Warren, the Blueberry Kid hit Seattle's watering resorts with an impressive splash after selling

$8,000 in gold dust to the U.S. Mint. Johnson lodged at the Hotel Victoria on Second Avenue and caroused with another Alaskan named Masura, who helped the Kid spend his money and lifted $400 in nuggets from him. After exhausting himself with the city's pleasures the Kid reportedly took off for San Francisco, then moved on to Wisconsin or Michigan for recuperation. Warren followed without success. Back in Fairbanks, U.S. Marshal L. T. Erwin disputed Warren's need to comb the Midwest or otherwise found fault with the special agent's work and may have managed to get him fired, although government economy was cited as the reason for eliminating the Seattle-based special agent's position.

While Warren had searched for the Kid in the States, lawmen in Alaska turned up some startling events in the Kid's earlier career that, if true, should have prevented his Koyukuk adventures. Johnson left his job as engineer at a Wrangell cannery in 1910 after bartering for a young Indian girl. The girl's stepfather wanted $250 bride money; Johnson paid $50 of the agreed fee, then reneged. There ensued a conflict, which Johnson may have resolved by killing the stepfather, mother, and his bride. The stepfather was said to have $220 in his possession, while the mother owned a necklace of nice gold nuggets. Since the deputy marshal could not find any conclusive evidence of foul play except some burned clothes of one of the women and their canoe hidden in brush, Johnson was not pursued. By this time he had left Wrangell in his launch.

The investigation of the 1912 Koyukuk voyage did not get under way until 1914, and even that effort was later described by officials as desultory. E. P. Heppenstall, deputy marshal at Wiseman, apologized to Marshal Erwin for not following through on a planned search of the Koyukuk in the summer of 1914 because Erwin's firm orders did not reach him in time to catch the launch *Reliance,* which carried commercial traffic on the river. Captain Green of the *Reliance* found the *Seal Pup* scuttled in the shallow water of a slough 120 miles below Bettles. "I sure would have liked to have been there at the launch raising and made a body search," said Heppenstall. "My opinion is that the bodies were not tied to the launch and would be found buried within 20 miles above the launch. The water is too clear for him to put them in."[8]

In September a deputy marshal from Ruby ran a launch up and

down the Koyukuk, its tributaries, and backwaters for two weeks without finding any sign of the missing passengers. Despite the paucity of evidence, the U.S. attorney got a Ruby grand jury to indict Johnson and issued a warrant for his arrest in August 1915. The government's expenditure in Alaska and the States in 1914 seemed to discourage more searching for the bodies or the Blueberry Kid, although the appointment of four special agents for the investigation of this and other murders was proposed in 1914. Marshal Erwin apparently opposed the use of special agents, and the plan was not pursued. Some action followed in 1918 when an anonymous source advised the Fairbanks U.S. attorney's office that information on Johnson's whereabouts would be exchanged for a suitable record. A $50 reward was publicized, but no information was received.

Four years later the Fairbanks U.S. attorney admitted that it was "disconcerting that such affairs could go so long without definite results." Evidence could be gained only ten years after the event through "systematic, secret, and determined investigation." If Johnson were alive, he might feel overconfident enough to make exposures. U.S. Attorney G. B. Erwin recommended that the "matter be sifted to the last for the good of the service and assurance of security to persons and property in Alaska."

William J. Burns, the legendary detective who in 1924 headed the government's Bureau of Investigation, precursor of the FBI, asked Erwin whether he wanted to continue the investigation. Erwin's enthusiasm for more work had faded: "This office, the Seattle office, and others since the resumption of the investigation, have used every effort. I am inclined to endorse Warren's view." Warren's view, expressed back in 1914–15, had cooled the search for Johnson at that time. Warren figured that the Kid sallied into the fleshpots of San Francisco's notorious Barbary Coast flashing money. Thugs took his money and bumped him off. Erwin told the Department of Justice that his office had closed its Johnson file in March 1923. The matter seemed dead until April 1927, when a rumor of Johnson's presence in Alaska motivated U.S. Marshal Lynn Smith to ask for a bench warrant. Nothing came of Smith's hopes to solve the ancient mystery.

The federal bureaucracy moves slowly at times. In January 1938 the U.S. attorney petitioned the district court for dismissal of the murder indictment against Tom Johnson on the ground that evidence was insufficient for prosecution. Twenty-five years had passed; the Blueberry Kid, if alive, need no longer fear the law.

Alaska was not too good to Hjalmar Rutzebeck, a young Danish immigrant who voyaged there in 1914. He had traveled to Seattle the hard way, riding the rods across the country, battling with train crews, detectives and policemen who tried to bar his way, then boarded the SS *Mariposa* for Juneau. After years as a sailor and soldier he had met Marian, the girl of his dreams; now he wished to marry and settle down, but first he required a stake. Since he had once been stationed at Fort Seward near Haines, he knew where to go. As a soldier, he had heard many stories of men making fortunes in Alaska.

In Haines the young man felt the moving sensation of homecoming. "I thought I knew how much I loved this beautiful land but I didn't until I came back among its protecting mountains."[9] From Haines, Rutzebeck mushed up the icebound Chilkat River to Porcupine, where he got a job right away. But the job did not last long. Rutzebeck soon ran through his small savings. By August he was joining other unemployed hustlers trying to get work as longshoremen in Skagway and missing most of his meals; if he could get to Haines, his friends would help him. For want of passage money he tried to stow away on a steamer. He was detected and put ashore before the ship left the dock. In his desperation the young man gave way to impulse. Bacon, canned meats, biscuits, and candy lay tantalizingly near: just behind a grocery store's window. "My mouth watered at the sight. . . . I would eat. I would not starve or beg like a low down dog! I would eat and live and take the consequences."

He did eat and live but swiftly regretted the consequences of his decision. Perhaps if he had responded to his immediate impulse, smashed the window, grabbed food, and fled, he might have suffered less. Instead, he returned at night and broke open the store's back door. After filling a gunnysack with food, he could not resist checking the cash register and took the $13.25 it held. Then he stole a rowboat for a voyage to Haines, a passage that ended abruptly at a deserted cove after hours of terror induced by wind and raging sea.

For a few days the fugitive made his way toward Haines on foot, wondering how he would get across the channel to the town. He was arrested and brought back to Skagway before he resolved the problem. "They shoved me into the cage. Then came the heavy thud of the door, the rattle and clang of the lock and bar, and I was in jail. My head was thumping. . . . I was at the bottom of the pit. I crawled into a bunk in one of the cells and faded away." The U.S. commissioner bound Rutzebeck over for the grand jury session in Juneau. Cheerful guards assured him of a five-year term. Such a prospect frightened the young Dane, who quickly exposed the security of Skagway's jail by dashing out the door when the guard roused him in the morning. Soon he was in the woods, moving along the old White Pass Trail, then climbing higher to cross a glacier.

While the fugitive's woodcraft lacked elements of skill, his sense of direction brought him to the dwelling of a friend who equipped him with a rifle and grub for further flight into the interior. He made it to Whitehorse, where watchful Mounties clapped him in jail. Before a Skagway marshal could arrive, Rutzebeck took to his heels once more, knocking over a guard and running for the woods. The following day, a Mountie ran him down and brought him back to Whitehorse. A five-day ration of bread and water diminished his escape energies, then a bracing plate of pork and beans strengthened him enough to protest his extradition—to no avail. On the train to Skagway he tried to run away once more, manacled though he was, but the deputy subdued him.

In Skagway the Dane enjoyed temporary celebrity status because of his daring. His jailer, a replacement for the man fired when he first escaped, kept him in leg irons. Soon he was moved to Juneau, where jail security standards were higher. It was some comfort to receive three letters from his girl friend, yet thoughts of her intensified his longing for freedom. "I walk and walk around the cage, staring at the infernal bars that are barriers between me and life. Yes, it is life out there! I can hear the blasts of the mines up in

the hills and the rattle of the ore trains. I can hear the steamboat whistles echo from mountain range to mountain range."

After a week in jail Rutzebeck determined to escape once more, even if rushing the guards imperiled his life. To put the wary guards at ease, since they refused to enter his cell until he backed into a far corner, the prisoner confessed his crime to the prosecutor and asked for immediate sentencing. The guards relaxed after this exhibition of candor and submission. Before long they regretted their lack of vigilance. The nimble Dane sped out the open cell door past three guards as a trusty was gathering supper dishes. The prisoner's only diversion consisted of grabbing the dishpan full of dishes and throwing it to the ceiling. Before the guards could gather their scattered powers of concentration, the fugitive gained the street and was gone. Outside town Rutzebeck got help from an acquaintance he encountered. As in every other escape, the elusive Dane admitted breaking out of jail to those he asked to help him. His story invariably aroused sympathy and enthusiastic offers of support. Either he was very persuasive or the general citizenry did not venerate the law-enforcement people.

As usual the fugitive's post-escape plans were no more imaginative than the headlong dashes that sprang him. This time he would steal a boat and row the one hundred miles or so to Skagway. Once

McNeil Island prison near Tacoma, Washington, with Mount Rainier in the background. University of Washington Library

there he would borrow money from soldiers he knew and take passage on a Canadian steamer. Near Haines, Rutzebeck left his boat and hid out in the woods. Several days of rowing on scant food had exhausted him. He made two sorties to Fort Seward looking for a friend who might give him some money. Returning fruitlessly from the second attempt to find his friend, he ran into one of his jail guards, well equipped with a revolver and leg irons.

The next morning the prisoner was taken aboard the SS *Admiral Evans* for the short voyage back to the Juneau jail. This time he settled down until he was taken to Ketchikan for a grand-jury hearing. There, as in Juneau, the courthouse stood on a hill, as if to dominate the town. In Europe, he recalled, churches were placed in such prominent positions. "Could it be that this courthouse stands in the position of the church and that I am really a wolf about to be tried by the good shepherd?"

After the incident Rutzebeck pleaded guilty and waived a trial. He told the judge how hunger had caused his grief and how jail depressions induced his various flights. The judge took his honorable discharge from the U.S. Army into consideration in sentencing him to fifteen months in the Juneau jail. But for the escapes, the judge would have given him a suspended sentence, or so he said.

Rutzebeck served good time, busying himself with school texts lent by the Juneau high school and writing a memoir of jail life, which eventually became the book *Alaska Man's Luck.* Still, time dragged by until the last, long day of his sentence passed in November 1915. "I longed for the woods and the mountains, so I put on my new boots, as soon as I established myself in a room, and hiked out of town on the Salmon Creek road." It was a great day. Now he was free—and certainly not disillusioned with Alaska. He got a job at the Perseverance mine and started saving money. Later

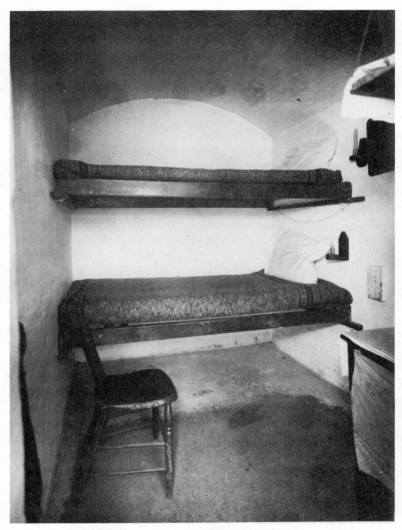

A cell at McNeil Island prison. University of Washington Library

he went into commercial fishing and subsequently built a cabin outside Haines, close to the forest lair he occupied when he was hiding
from the law. His long dream of bringing his fiancée to Alaska was
achieved, and then he launched his writing career.

Rutzebeck's book is unique in describing a criminal episode in
Alaska with style and verisimilitude. Its publication was quite an
achievement for a man who left school and his native land at age
twelve. As the years rushed by, he did not have many opportunities
to fulfill his boyish ambition to become an author. Life taught him
much, but earning a living required all his powers. How could he
hope to write a book in the English language he was still struggling
with? Yet, by the strange circumstances attending his second trip
to Alaska, he did convert a remarkable disruptive event into literature. In 1920 publisher Horace Liveright was particularly interested in obtaining proletarian literature, and Rutzebeck's story held
the direct, simple, earthy qualities that were in demand.

Meanwhile, Marshal Harry Bishop had had a heavy time in explaining the Juneau jail escape to Washington. The attorney general
was perplexed: "The Department doesn't understand why the prisoner was allowed so much liberty and we desire a statement."[10]
Bishop acknowledged that Juneau prisoners no longer carried their
own dishes but stressed his charge's physical capabilities. "Rutzebeck is an exceptionally rugged mountaineer" whose first escape
featured an eighty-six-mile trek through mountain wilderness,
while his Juneau dash involved a leap over a thirty-foot embank-
ment to gain the street below. "We didn't expect anyone to do
that." In his memoirs, Rutzebeck took no credit for this daring
leap: he had fallen in the dark while seeking the path.[11]

Frugal policies of the Department of Justice dictated that any expenses incurred in recapturing an escaped prisoner be paid by the
deputy in charge if he showed negligence. Marshal L. T. Erwin
strenuously resisted this rule in 1915 when it was applied to the
escape of an insane man in custody for the long voyage to Oregon's
Morningside Sanitarium. The patient ran off the Yukon steamboat
at a wood stop while the deputy attended to a little girl who had
fallen down. Immediate pursuit into the woods produced no results, but the next day the fugitive recovered his senses and hailed
another steamboat from the shore.

Erwin explained the circumstances to Washington while putting forward a little lesson in Alaska geography. Conditions were singular in interior Alaska; a trip of three thousand miles could take a month:

No marshal in the states has any such trips as this to make; he could traverse the country from New York to San Francisco six times in less time that it requires me to land a bunch of prisoners from Fairbanks to the Morningside Hospital in Portland, Oregon. We have more than 1500 miles upstream traveling where the boats make slow progress and are compelled to tie up at the banks several hours each day and night to take on wood.
It is not possible to exercise a vigilance night and day over the number of prisoners on these long trips that would be so effective . . . unless there were two guards for each prisoner or each prisoner was ironed all the time. . . . It would be cruel and inhuman to keep insane prisoners manacled on these long, tedious journeys.[12]

Erwin prevailed in this instance and again a couple of years later when a prisoner who escaped at Fairbanks complained to the governor and attorney general and asked that Erwin be forced to return fifty dollars confiscated from him after his recapture. During his period of freedom the prisoner moved down the Yukon to Marshall and earned his fifty dollars working in a placer mine. Erwin applied the fifty dollars to the cost of pursuit. "His time belonged to the government," Erwin argued, and so did any money he earned during his unsanctioned leave.[13]

In July 1915, Robert Dupee, sentenced to seven years for assault, left Juneau in irons with two guards for a voyage to Seattle on the *Mariposa*. South of Wrangell the ship struck a rock, took in water, and listed precariously. After temporary repairs, the ship voyaged on, but the guards, who had freed Dupee from his leg irons during the emergency, decided not to shackle him again. After all, the ship might founder at any time. As the crippled ship approached the Seattle dock the guards relaxed. Dupee, locked in a stateroom, unscrewed a porthole, jumped to the wharf, found a taxi, and disappeared as the *Mariposa* tied up.

In Washington federal officials ordered the firing of the deputy in charge. Intercession by the marshal and Governor Strong, who stressed the near-shipwreck conditions and the deputy's record as

A prison gate at McNeil Island. University of Washington Library

a "good Democrat and officer," saved his job. The Justice Department settled for a fifteen-day suspension.[14]

McNeil Island may have been a home away from home for many
Alaskans, but incarceration there was no pleasure to offenders who

were sentenced in the north. A description of it by Robert Franklin Stroud makes this clear. Stroud, the only convicted felon from Alaska to increase his notoriety in captivity as the much publicized "Birdman of Alcatraz," was a nineteen-year-old pimp in Juneau when he got into trouble. He shot and killed a bartender who battered Stroud's girl friend, was convicted of manslaughter, and was sentenced to twelve years at McNeil; then, after viciously killing a guard, he was moved on to Leavenworth and Alcatraz.

When he reached McNeil, Stroud was struck by the stench: "a dead stench, as from the grave . . . the stench was that of dead, cold air, the old odor of unwashed bodies, unsanitary night buckets, the accumulated filth of years." He felt cold from the time he arrived in spite of his heavy woollen striped uniform and the warm sun outside. Everything he saw was filthy, and the floors were worn from the hobnailed shoes of the thousands of prisoners who had been marched through the passages. "The gloom, the chill, the filth, the rutted floors, the stench of the night buckets, the silence, almost like that of the grave, fell upon my spirit." The cells appeared to be "black, evil-smelling caverns . . . symbolic of all the misery of the ages—of man's inhumanity to man."[15]

Many other prisoners must have felt as Stroud did and marveled that in some deliberate or perhaps impetuous act they had caused themselves to be imprisoned. In justice to the old prison on Puget Sound, finally abandoned by the federal government in the late 1970s but reopened by the state of Washington for its overflow of convicts, Stroud was sad to leave the place for Leavenworth, where discipline was tougher. McNeil was never considered a resort, but its record, spanning many decades, has not been marred by commonplace instances of bruality and sadism.[16]

18. Native Legends

It seems well-nigh impossible ever to be sure that we have got a decent man in Alaska. —Theodore Roosevelt

IT is no revelation to note that liquor has been a scourge to Alaska's natives from its introduction until the present. The vast majority of criminal prosecutions involving natives were for liquor violations or for crimes they committed while intoxicated. This significant social problem is outside the scope of this book, just as the administration of natives was outside the responsibilities of the Department of Justice and its agents. Federal policy making on native matters lay with the Department of the Interior and other agencies.

There were law-enforcement problems involving natives that were of direct concern to the Justice Department. Missionaries complained often that white juries would not convict whites charged of committing crimes against natives. While this may have been true on occasion in early territorial days, when natives did not sit on juries, nothing could be done about the dominant community's bias. However, it does appear that most of the complaints arose in the prosecution of liquor cases, and liquor prosecutions were not too popular; yet in spite of this there were countless convictions of whites who sold liquor to natives. The lawmen also showed zeal in prosecuting whites for cohabitation with natives. The Edwards case is interesting for public discussion showing bias toward natives and missionaries, but neither this case nor others demonstrates that the rights of natives were treated lightly in Alaska's courts.

C. H. Edwards, a young missionary and government teacher at Douglas, showed vigor in rooting out vice in 1891, touring Douglas dance halls so he could testify in court to the corruption of native girls. He was also alert to liquor selling and responded to the report of a sloop lying off Kake Island, waiting to land its pernicious cargo, by organizing a party of Indians to intercept the sloop. The sloop's crew, Malcomb Campbell and another man, were actually on a hunting expedition, or so they claimed later. They were anchored off Kake after dark, they said, when a canoe swooped down on them and Indians swarmed aboard the sloop. Campbell was thrown onto his back. Someone knelt on his chest and gripped his head while others tried to tie his feet. Campbell grabbed his pistol and put three shots into the man who was wrestling with him. Edwards fell back, mortally wounded.

Missionaries cried that Edwards had been slain by liquor smugglers. The district attorney and marshal were not entirely sure that Campbell's version of events was wholly accurate, but the case for prosecuting Campbell for homicide seemed rather weak. Sheldon Jackson, now commissioner of education and based in Washington, demanded a prosecution. He and others complained to the secretary of the interior and the attorney general. The attorney general asked his Juneau subordinate to explain the "extreme leniency with which the Edwards' murder was treated." Juneau's U.S. attorney replied that "public sentiment was with Campbell." He thought Campbell was guilty of manslaughter, "but [I] have little hope of a conviction."[1]

The Juneau press saw no ambiguity. The shooting was "a most unfortunate affair . . . a tragedy," but no crime. "It may serve as a warning to people who are disposed to be too zealous in matters in which they have no authority to act." The coroner's jury ruled that Campbell had a right to protect his life and property. Edwards, "a very exemplary young man" with "many friends . . . a thorough Christian . . . stepped beyond the bounds of propriety to impress the world with his sincerity in the cause of christianity." His faith in the "noble siwash . . . and his zeal caused his death."[2]

A native village policeman. Alaska Historical Library; Vince Soboleff, photographer

To interpret the Edwards affair, as did a Chicago critic who wrote to the secretary of the interior, as proof that "the administration of law in Alaska is, in many instances, a mere travesty of justice," was unfair. It is also unjust to use the case, as has been done, as an illustration of Alaskans' approval of the liquor traffic, because the coroner's jury finding seems reasonable enough. The affair does illuminate the public's antipathy to missionaries and to natives. This bias was well spelled out in the Juneau press. According to one writer, missionaries had abused the white pioneers to Indians and the "outside world." Authorities, influenced by "the maudlin sympathy of Indian sympathizers," had been too lenient with Indians who had shown hostility to whites. The "irresponsible savages employed by Edwards" should be dealt with severely.[3]

There are more singular incidents involving natives than the dreary liquor cases. One concerns the prosecution of Indians who tried to maintain an ancient tradition founded in superstition, and two others depict natives as legendary outlaws.

Authorities often complained about the practice of witchcraft and the undue influence of shamans or medicine men in some native villages. Unlike the keeping of slaves, which could be attended to quickly once a complaint was made, the eradication of superstition had to be left to processes of social change and education—unless a clear crime was the result. An incident among the Tlingits in 1902 did indeed involve a terrible crime.

The residents of the little village of Hoonah on Baranof Island, twenty-five miles west of Juneau, worshiped at the Russian Orthodox and Presbyterian churches, fished for canneries and their own needs, and hunted game for additional subsistence. Most natives had anglicized their names, although some used the old form as well. The principals in a curious homicide-by-starvation case were Moses (Kes-tee-ish), George Smalley (Ked-Kitch-ish), Benjamin (Keh-suk-dahe), Jeremiah King (Kui-da-qua), Aron Sharp, and just plain Archie. It was Archie who told Aron Sharp that George Smalley was a warlock. It embarrased Aron to have his old friend indicate a belief in witchcraft despite the teachings of the churches. He understood Archie's lapse, however. Archie was dying of consumption and still grieving over the loss of his wife, who had died of the same disease a short time before.

As Archie told it, the revelation that George Smalley was a warlock came to him in a dream; in fact, the revelation came to Archie from George Smalley himself. George tried to take advantage of Archie's wavering mind to extort money from him in return for driving away other evil spirits that had caused his illness. Obviously George did not believe such things himself. He was a bit of a hustler who had scandalized other Indians by joining the Russian Orthodox church, then converting to Presbyterianism, and then converting to the Salvation Army, possibly to gain benefits that were of this world.

Aron Sharp and Archie talked the witchcraft matter over with Jeremiah King, an old man recognized as a chief. In the course of discussion an idea was born. Why not try a remedy used in former times against evil spirits? Our fathers used to tie up witches for eight days without food, and the fast deprived them of their awful powers. Earlier, Aron Sharp had warned George against doing evil things, such as speaking of witches and joining so many churches, but it had not helped. George must be purged!

The older men ordered three young men, Moses, Benjamin, and John Smith, to carry George away to some lonely place. In obedience to their elders, the youngsters bundled George into their canoe, paddled off to a remote forested cove, set up a tent, and maintained a vigil over George. After three days of fasting the boys untied their prisoner but did not relax their guard or feed him until the mandatory eight-day cleansing period had elapsed. On the ninth day, George did not seem interested in food or anything else. His captors were taking him back to Hoonah when he died.

U.S. Deputy Marshal John B. Heyburn arrested all six Indians involved when George's death was reported. A Juneau grand jury indicted them for murder, but in separate trials for Moses, Benjamin and John Smith, jurors delivered convictions for manslaughter. In December 1902 each was sentenced to serve four years at McNeil Island prison. U.S. Attorney John Boyce dallied over the other prosecutions until Archie died in April 1903. Boyce decided that Archie had the chief responsibility for appealing to old Indian traditions. Since Archie could not answer for his crime, Boyce asked for a dismissal of charges against the others.[4]

"Alaskan Indians paddling in their baidarkas or clustered at camp-fires in their cedar forests are telling with awe the strange tale of Kebeth the Aleut. Eskimos meeting on the ice pack pass along the amazing story and recount its tragic details as they huddle around their stone lamps of sputtering whale oil in their underground ig-loos beyond the Arctic Circle."[5] This lead to a 1901 article in pres-tigious *McClure's Magazine* whets one's appetite for the adven-tures of Kebeth. Good heavens! If even the Eskimos meeting on the ice pack paused to broadcast the story, it must be a good one. And if the legend Kebeth inspired could make heroes of his com-rades, "who roamed over frozen mountains with this mighty hunter or sailed with him on any of his annual returns in his pelt-laden umiak . . . to Kotzebue Sound or Bristol Bay," he must have been a colossus. Since the *McClure's* article bore the title "The True Story of Kebeth, the Aleut," readers knew they were getting the straight goods on a man whose death sentence was commuted by President William McKinley. Alaskans who read the story may have been amazed at the range of Kebeth's hunting from south-eastern to Barrow and including the upper Yukon, the Kuskok-wim, the St. Elias mountain range, and the Aleutians, but as the author pointed out, "Kebeth was a prodigious rover."

How, then, did this heroic figure run afoul of the law? Demon rum caused the trouble. At the end of each wide-ranging hunting season Kebeth and his comrades retired to Juneau, Sitka, or Skag-way, "their goat-skins filled with gold, their puksaks of wolverine fur bulging with tobacco and their canteens of sealskin brimming with the unholy brews and distillations," for their saturnalia. Their revels went unchecked because "these rude hunters were greatly feared, their leader particularly, and even white men noted for their scorn of sudden death, treated him with discreet civilty." Yet until 1899, Kebeth and his followers sobered up each fall to commence another hunting season. In 1899, Kebeth was having so much fun in Skagway that he hated to leave. His chief counselor, Artikoor the Silent, spoke up loudly, noted the movements of the walrus, ptar-migan, and gray plover, and urged Kebeth to "leave the kasheem, the house of dancing, to white men and their women." For once Kebeth ignored Artikoor's advice, so the counselor paddled off in a kayak with his wife and child. A week later Kebeth sobered up, missed Artikoor, and started looking for his valued friend. But all the searchers found were broken bits of his kayak and pieces of clothing scattered along a Lynn Canal beach. Kebeth jumped to the conclusion that white men had murdered Artikoor and his family. He swore mighty oaths of vengeance, and he also swore off booze until the holy task of retribution had been completed.

Finding the murderers perplexed Kebeth until he consulted a shaman, who advised him to camp near the spot where Artikoor's belongings were found and wait there until an amulet the shaman provided brought the slayer to him. Kebeth and his men followed instructions in October 1899. Within a couple of days they were gratified at the beach landing of Burt and Florence Horton. The Hortons, a young couple from Skagway, planned to hunt, fish, and prospect in the area, little realizing the perils of their visit. With swift, ugly purpose the natives fell upon the Hortons. They shot Burt and disemboweled him, slashed Florence's throat, buried the two bodies in the woods, and returned to Skagway. The shaman advised Kebeth to postpone his hunting expedition until spring. Kebeth complied and continued the ban on booze for himself and his people. Skagway's whites were intrigued at the abstinence of these notable revelers.

Kebeth surprised people even more by harkening to the eloquent call of a Salvation Army preacher to embrace Christianity. His name was Barabbas, he told the joyful proselyters; he had taken the new name after hearing a sermon promising God's mercy to even such bloodstained sinners as the thief who died with Jesus. "Glory be to God, who saveth even to the uttermost," cried the preacher. "Amen. Hallelujah," responded Barabbas.

Now Kebeth-Barabbas, to the disgust of his old hunting comrades, made a tambourine and took to the streets of Skagway with the Salvation Army forces. Great delight swept the "Salleys" as Kebeth's lusty thumping and hallelujahs shocked the ears of drunks and sinners. Soon Kebeth discovered a new form of intoxication in the presence of marveling crowds. Enraptured with his born-again joy and keen to emulate the oratorial triumphs of his companions, he told the best story he knew of God's mercy by confessing the Hortons' murders.

Kebeth's narrative fascinated his listeners. Others had testified of their sins, but Kebeth excelled all the confessors, just as he had excelled all the hunters. With experience gained in public exhortation, Kebeth's story magnified in power. "I, Kebeth, called the Brown Bear," he would begin with thundering tone, "an Indian known to you, a man of sin, have seen that Light and heard the Voice." That Light and Voice, of course, were the same encountered by St. Paul on the road to Damascus.

Listeners did not doubt Kebeth's sincerity. Wags commented that the Salvation Army "had struck pay dirt" in its conversion of Kebeth. "With that wild Aleut convert," a miner argued, "Skagway may be represented in Heaven yet." Another man expected to hear "that Soapy Smith is twanging a harp somewhere near those regions now." Hearing about Kebeth's performance, the marshal invited him to repeat his compelling narrative, then clapped him in jail. According to *McClure's,* Kebeth sweetly offered to take all the blame and die for his sins, yet he took the precaution of explaining that his followers, who had deserted him after his conversion, had agreed to place the entire guilt for the murders on anyone who confessed.

Despite Kebeth's willingness to take all the blame and die well, federal officers insisted upon trying his former associates, who "were gathered from the four corners of the Arctic." These rogues tried desperately to shift full responsibility to Kebeth but were undone by his testimony and the savage cross-examination of their own. Six natives were sentenced to prison terms ranging from twenty-three to fifty years, thanks to Kebeth's cooperation with authorities. Kebeth got the death sentence after urging Judge Melville C. Brown: "My brother, I have done my duty, now do yours." Everyone in the courtroom, including natives from all over the territory, felt compassion for Kebeth. "Seamed and grizzled miners," said *McClure's,* "who had held unflinching roles in barroom fights, where pistol shots punctuated profanity, hurried away to hide feelings they would not willingly betray, and at nearby saloons sought to reassure themselves that their sympathy for their Indian brother had not resulted in any unmanly incapacity for drink."

Judge Brown, clergymen, and hoards of Skagway's better element joined in the petition for clemency sent to President McKinley: "This Indian," said the judge, "has done much for the cause of justice in Alaska. To hang him would in my opinion be unwise." And the Great White Father in Washington showed his mercy with a commutation order. Kebeth would remain imprisoned at McNeil Island, but, said *McClure's,* he became "canonized in the imagination" of Alaska's natives and figured largely in artists' carvings of stone, ivory, and totem poles.

In checking this exciting *McClure's* story against the court records, a few discrepancies emerge. Kebeth, or Jim Hanson, was indeed tried at Sitka in June 1900, sentenced to hang, and saved by the president's commutation in November. Defense attorneys W. E. Crews and R. W. Jennings made all the usual moves in pretrial skirmishes and at trial argued that Hanson had killed in compliance with tribal custom, an excuse the court had encountered in every previous homicide case involving natives. Judge Brown instructed jurors that no one could excuse the law's violation for religious reasons. Religious beliefs made the crimes "a more emphatic wrong, because of the determination to commit crime in cold blood," and men professing such beliefs were more dangerous than those who kill for gain or personal hatred.[6] While it was not the judge's obligation to ask jurors to be merciful, he did note that "if anything in this case commends this man to mercy or favor," it was his truthful statements. The jury ignored Brown's hint. They were free to convict the accused of murder one without the death penalty, but they chose to call for a hanging.

Records of the trial of Hanson's associates show that he may not have been the heroic leader *McClure's* depicted. The other natives were keen to show his bad reputation and note that "he has implicated others in this court and escaped punishment." But for his willingness to testify against others, Hanson would have been tried and convicted of offenses committed before the Horton murders, they alleged.

The commutation probably did not prolong Hanson's life too long. Most natives did not last long in jail. Jim Williams, whose fifty-year sentence was the most severe, except for Hanson's, died in a Tacoma hospital in May 1902. When Hanson died is not disclosed by the court records, but certainly he did not become a cultural hero among southeastern natives as *McClure's* had predicted. Natives of Alaska were not inclined to honor killers just because they joined the Salvation Army and excited a New York journalist. And anyone, native or white, in Alaska who read the magazine would have laughed at some of the picturesque details of Kebeth's travels and natives' lifestyle.

The article is worth savoring, however, even if its exaggerations bordered on farce. Seen in the best light, it represents a conscious attempt to present a cultural clash in sympathetic terms. Whites did feel bad sometimes about applying their laws to natives. They could do little about the harshness of the situation, although it would seem that many other incidents were more likely to command sympathy than the horrible slaying of the Hortons. Literature and legend making, such as "The True Story of Kebeth, the Aleut," gave the dominant culture some solace. And, of course, the story itself lives on as a monument to Kebeth, or at least as an appreciation of Alaska's earlier native culture.

Everyone agreed that the development of mining should be Alaska's first priority. By 1930 the industry had been in decline for years. A shortage of risk capital and the government's neglect in providing surveys and roads were usually singled out as the chief detriments to development, although a certain area's lawlessness cropped up as an issue in the late 1920s and early 1930s. The lower Kuskokwim region was having a little mining activity until reports of a "notorious Indian outlaw" threatened to frighten investors away. B. D. Stewart of the U.S. Geological Survey wrote to Governor George Parks in some alarm. "Klutak is a real menace to development work. It slows the country down if a criminal is left at large who can intimidate those wishing to mine so they fear to send their men into the country."[7] Stewart was not the only one who was upset with the elusive outlaw. In 1929 the territorial legislators in Juneau had reviewed the Justice Department's handling of the case without finding grounds for criticism, but they were not happy.

Lawmen had been watching for Klutak for a long time. The government did not post many five hundred dollar rewards, but U.S. Marshal H. P. Sullivan of Valdez did so in 1927. Klutak, described as an Indian thirty-six to thirty-eight years old, five-foot-four, 140 pounds, who wore an old parka patched with odd skins, was wanted for killing Andrew Kallenvik near Dillingham.

Concern over Klutak dated back to May 1927. Trappers Charles Anderson and Arvid Sackarson had been expected to return to Dillingham in March after their season's trapping but did not appear. In May a search was made. Sackarson's body was found caught in a pile of driftwood on a river sandbar. Searchers also found the trappers' canoe. They did not find Anderson, but there was no evidence of anything but accidental death. As usual when white men disappeared in the wilderness, rumors of foul play by natives were circulated. Someone claimed that Klutak, an Eskimo trapper who openly resented white men's trapping near the place where he ran his own lines, had killed Sackarson and Anderson.

Nothing was done to bother Klutak until he wandered into the camp of R. A. Smith, F. F. Peterson, and Andrew Kallenvik on Harris Creek, a tributary that flows into the Nushagak River seventy-five miles northeast of Dillingham. The three men were bound for the Nushagak with provisions for the coming winter. Smith, who had heard the rumors about Klutak, left Kallenvik to watch him while he and Peterson packed provisions over to the Nushagak. When they returned to camp they found Kallenvik lying face down in a pool of blood, his head gashed with an ax and a bullet wound in his arm. Klutak was gone. A quick reconnaissance of his trail ended at a slough where further movements could not be traced.

In Dillingham the body was examined and a coroner's jury prepared to visit the murder site. A storm held up departure for a week. Klutak had eight days' start before Deputy Frank Wiseman was prepared to look for him. The season was too advanced for serious searching; Wiseman would wait for freeze-up, then mush up the Nushagak to Klutak's cabin.

Bad news reached Dillingham in December. Someone had stolen fish and food at Togiak, shot at an Eskimo girl, and wounded a boy. Klutak and his black dog had been seen in the area. Other reports placed Klutak at the Hoholitna headwaters, so Wiseman sent the arrest warrant to his colleague at Bethel. In January Wiseman trekked fifty miles of hard-going trail to Togiak to learn that Klutak had not actually been seen there. It seems that a hunter had mistaken a boy for a fox in 1924 and wounded him. A similar accident in 1926 explained the report of a shot fired at a girl.

By June 1928, Wiseman's superiors ardently desired news of Klutak's arrest. Wiseman had no news except that no boats were available for a search until the Bristol Bay fishing season was over; then, when boats were available, the weather turned bad. Wiseman finally started on August 3, chugging up the Nushagak River with six men in two boats. They voyaged 155 miles upriver, "beating the country for news along the way."[8] At Kiliganek, Wiseman sent one boat up the Tikchik River, then moved upriver another 120 miles to investigate Klutak's cabin. It did not appear that anyone had been there for months. The deputies searched the country within a radius of 15 miles, then started downriver, checking the cabins of Charlie Nielsen and Jackako, a native missing since spring and possibly one of Klutak's victims. With a skin boat he had towed along, Wiseman ascended the Chichitnok River 30 miles above its mouth on the Nushagak. No trace of Klutak. He checked Jack Hale's cabin. No luck.

Wiseman's search was not only fruitless, it was damn hard work. The men wore rubber boots and tramped for miles through swamps and high grass. "It is an impossible country to travel in once you leave the river; there are not even animal trails to follow." Back at Kiliganek, Wiseman's other boat party met him. It had gone all the way up to Tikchik Lake without finding anyone.

After seventeen days and an expenditure of $1,455, Wiseman got back to Dillingham, feeling that he had done his best. His superiors seemed reasonably content, but whenever fresh rumors concerning the "mad trapper" surfaced, federal officials had to review the frustrating Klutak file once more.

Illustrating the region's lack of appeal to anyone save a few trappers during the winter is the fact that Wiseman encountered only one native family on his trip. Its members had not seen Klutak for two years. If they were truthful, it meant that the fugitive was living off the country. But Wiseman did not think anyone could live in such a barren region without access to ammunition and other provisions.

Wiseman was at Bethel in March 1929 when new reports on Klutak stirred him to search south of the Kukokwim. Guides re-

fused to take him out because the winter trails were breaking up. Later, when there had been no confirmation of Klutak's movements, he saw no reason to travel. Thus in 1930 when B. D. Stewart started worrying about the outlaw, lawmen groaned but did not reach for their rubber boots. The mad trapper was a phantom. He might be dead or thumbing his nose at occasional travelers in the vast, empty land between Cook Inlet and the Kuskokwim River, but there was little point in random searching.

What happened between Klutak and Andrew Kallenvik remained a mystery. The dead man had a reputation for being quarrelsome when he was drinking, and he had been drinking when Klutak came into the camp. In January 1927, Kallenvik broke into a home, beat up the man and woman living there, and was sentenced to three months in jail. Maybe Kallenvik abused Klutak and let slip Smith's plan of taking him to Dillingham. But it was hard to figure out how Klutak got the drop on a big, tough guy who had reason to be wary.

A story published in 1984 may be considered an explanation of Klutak's end. The author, Fred Hatfield, trapped in the Dillingham region during the 1930s. He had heard about the various slayings attributed to Klutak and later found the body of trapper Jake Savolly on the Nuyukuk River. It looked like Klutak had shot Savolly and cleared out his cabin. Hatfield figured that he could be the next victim unless he became aggressive and killed the murderer himself. After burying the dead trapper he investigated the area until the found Klutak's mink traps, all of which he set off to make them useless. Then he retreated to his own cabin, knowing that Klutak could pick up his trail but believing that the killer would not dare pursue for fear of falling into an ambush. After the winter passed Hatfield gathered his furs and made a rendezvous with the charter plane from Dillingham he had arranged for transportation. As he flew off he could imagine Klutak watching the plane and plotting revenge.

In the fall Hatfield flew back to the interior for another season of trapping. As he anticipated that Klutak would be waiting at his usual landing place, Hatfield directed his pilot to Rat Lake, where he could use the empty cabin of another trapper. Klutak would be disappointed once again and would be reluctant to approach Hatfield's base, knowing that he would have to be patient to catch his foe by surprise. But Hatfield did not intend to play a cat-mouse game indefinitely. This time he had brought along something that could lure Klutak to destruction.

In the spring, Hatfield, who had seen no sign of Klutak over the winter, was picked up by charter plane as usual. When he departed, he left his unused provisions in the cabin, expecting Klutak to arrive soon to take any supplies and set a trap for Hatfield's arrival in the fall. Among the items the trapper left was the familiar sugar jar commonly used in the bush, but Hatfield had substituted strychnine for the sugar. He was so confident of his plan that he did not hesitate to have his pilot fly him directly to the Rat Lake cabin in the fall, although he did ask the pilot to stand by for possible assistance. It took only an hour or two of searching before Hatfield found Klutak's disorderly camp about two miles from the cabin. The camp had been unattended for some time, and bears had marauded to make a mess of Klutak's gear. Quite near the camp he found Klutak's body, or what was left of it; the mad trapper had been dead for a long time. Hatfield covered the bones and rejoiced. Now the country was free of the phantom killer, and "my two years of feeling hunted were over."[9]

19. "What's Going on in Alaska?"

It is undoubtably true that any slander or lying statement can be confirmed by affidavits and reports from Alaska.—Governor J. F. A. Strong

"NOT infrequently as many as 1,500 complaints reach the Department of Justice in a single day," said Attorney General Thomas Gregory during the busy days of World War I.[1] He did not say how many of them came from Alaska, but the northern territory never lacked for critics, and Washington officials experienced difficulty in weighing their merits.

Many complaints about the courts and law officers could be attributed to the public's suspicion of lawyers and imperfect understanding of court proceedings, coupled with an ardent belief in the existence of a "courthouse ring" that was unfairly dominating small-town affairs. It goes without saying that Democrats noticed the ring when Republican appointees took over and vice versa.

Although the governors of Alaska had nothing to do with the Department of Justice or the courts, they were nevertheless the recipients of all manner of accusations against Justice officers. "The trouble with the court," wrote a critic of the fourth division to Governor George Parks in 1925, "is a ring of lawyers who haul you in on any excuse that will make a case." It was all a put-up job. "The judge manhandles you and allows what evidence they desire to make a verdict that gives the most money to the ring." The U.S. attorney was crooked and took money from prostitutes, "who call the law a bunch of dirty crooks." The only solution was to "get us a judge from the outside to break the ring."[2]

The demand for a judge from the outside was evidence of the writer's desperation and did not reflect the prevalent view of Alaskans that the appointment of outsiders showed the harshness and indifference of the federal government. It was the heartfelt popular view that only Alaskans understood Alaska well enough to administer justice, particularly Alaskans who were friends of the petitioners. While it is true that even today most Alaskans have gone there recently from some other place and that there never has been a substantial class of "old Alaskans," as such an element would be understood elsewhere, in the 1920s this was not reflected in Alaskans' views of themselves.

Just as it was not easy to please Alaskans with federal appointees, it was hard for Washington to figure out the political currents among Alaskans. While an appreciation of a distant community's political structure and biases was not legally required of Washington bureaucrats, such knowledge did help them evaluate complaints and recommendations for office. All Justice Department staff might have done well to have Governor Scott Bone's advice to the attorney general posted at their desks. Bone, defending alleged malfeasance of first-division U.S. Attorney Arthur G. Shoup in 1922, pointed out that bitter politics lay behind most defamation of Alaska officeholders. This much was not news to Washington men, but Bone elucidated the Alaska situation by further defining politics: "Politics in Alaska is personal and factional, and party politics (like party discipline) is a thing unknown."[3]

Officeholders had to answer nasty tales carried to their supervisors by disgruntled citizens and endure backbiting from colleagues. "The vain-glorious conceit of Crossley . . . leads him to believe that he alone is honorable or disposed to do his duty," U.S. Marshal Henry K. Love reported to the attorney general in 1913.[4] Love's anger at the district attorney may or may not have been well founded, but Washington clearly considered it better form for law-enforcement officers to cooperate amicably against the common foe who transgressed the law.

Love had a good reputation. He fought in Cuba in 1898–99 with

The aftermath of a 1902 holdup of Skagway's Canadian Bank of Commerce. The robber threatened tellers with a bomb which accidentally exploded. The bomber's head was a popular town exhibit for many years.
Alaska Historical Library; Paul Sincic, photographer

Teddy Roosevelt's Rough Riders and joined the civil government of Guam and the Philippines (1899–1903). After Love's stints with the U.S. Land Office in Oregon (1903–1904) and as special timber agent for Alaska (1904–1908), new President William Howard Taft gave him the Fairbanks marshal job in 1909. It was a big year in Alaska's judicial history because the government had finally responded to the many pleas for a new court. It had been apparent for some years, particularly since the rapid growth of the canned-salmon industry had brought thousands of workers to coastal Alaska, that Fairbanks was not well placed for administration of the developing region. The solution was to redesignate Fairbanks as

the new fourth division and make Valdez on the coast a court center for the third division. In effect the creation of a new court divided the original third division into northern and southern parts.

District Attorney James Crossley was appointed in 1908. He was
from Iowa, studied law at Iowa State, took advanced work at Yale,
and served nine years in the Iowa state senate before moving to
Alaska. Love made a serious charge against Crossley, claiming that
he had advised a deputy marshal to "have in his pocket a list of business men from which to select jurors." Even the hint of jury fixing
created concern, as it was rightfully regarded as the unforgiveable
sin. Other charges were more trivial. Crossley had "denounced"
Love in the presence of some lawyers, had been drunk at a party,
"and urged the mothers and the ladies of the town there present,
and who should be examples of propriety in a community, to excessive drinking, with incessant 'Bottoms up, ladies.'" Then he invited
a married woman to sit on his lap and capped this risqué performance by doing a drunken clog dance in the middle of the room.

The attorney general saw little evil in Love's tattle but reacted
more strongly in a serious scandal in spring 1912 when Crossley's
assistant attorney, Cecil Clegg, engaged in local politics and saloon
rowdiness. Clegg and others opposed the dominant Republican
clique with a slate of their own for the election of delegates to the
Alaska Republican party convention. In an exuberant spirit of party
factionalism, Clegg uttered uncomplimentary remarks about Judge
Peter Overfield—"the vilest names in the language," reported
Marshal Love. Clegg paid a heavy price for whatever he said. Republican Thomas Marquam, a fan of Overfield who resented Clegg's
attempt to oust his faction from control of the party, knocked Clegg
down, to the delight of other saloon patrons.

Clegg insisted that he had taken only a few drinks in the saloon
and then had been drugged. In a helpless condition he was "brutally
and wantonly attacked" by Marquam, the Republican leader and a
criminal lawyer who was a "bitter professional rival" in many trials.
"His purpose was to deprive me of office and strengthen enemies
of the D.A.'s office and embarrass Crossley through me."[5] Whether
Clegg was drugged or drunk, he certainly succeeded in embarrassing Crossley, who tried without success to defend his assistant
to the Justice Department. Clegg lost his job in 1913, yet was in

good graces in 1921 when he was elevated to the fourth division's judgeship.

Love had resigned in March 1913 before writing his long complaint about four years' unpleasant service with Crossley. Even if Washington officials had taken his charges against Crossley seriously it would not have mattered too much. The Democrats won the presidential election in 1913. Judge Overfield left office that year, and Crossley left in 1914.

Love's successor was a Democrat, Lewis T. Erwin, a Georgian who had been city magistrate and clerk in Fairbanks for some years. He must have been Love's friend because Republican Love advised the attorney general that Erwin would make "the most efficient occupant" the marshal's office ever had.[6] Erwin did do a fine job, but he did not get along any better with Crossley than his predecessor. The officials clashed over the best means of investigating a number of unsolved murders. Crossley wanted the marshal to have special deputies assigned, while Erwin believed that too much was being made of the unsolved cases. He and his deputies had apprehended the murders in two of the three slayings committed during the first two years; the others were ancient affairs that would defy solution regardless of the number of investigators.

Crossley haunted Erwin even after leaving the service. Complaints were made against Erwin for employing his wife as a matron to accompany an insane woman outside. Her daughter, a Fairbanks prostitute, had wanted the job herself. Erwin answered these charges with relative ease. He employed his wife because there was no other suitable woman available. The daughter "was not fit to be a matron" and practiced her trade on the voyage outside. Since the patient went to work for the Crossley household in Portland when she had been discharged from Morningside Sanitarium, it seemed obvious to Erwin that Crossley had helped draw up the papers accusing him of misconduct.[7]

All Alaska towns were small enough so that a sensational case could cause conflict when someone charged with a crime was a popular or influential individual. This was the case in Fairbanks in 1916–17 when Dan Callahan and others were charged with rape. Callahan had been acquitted on similar charges of trifling with

young Indian girls at Circle in 1900 and always had been a conspicuous member of the rowdy class. Yet because he had influence in
town it was easy for his friends to whip up word-of-mouth and
newspaper support for his insistence that the district attorney was
out to get him.

In answering these complaints, District Attorney R. F. Roth,
smarting from the circuit court's reversal of the district court's conviction of Callahan, passed along his impressions of Alaskans' attitudes to the attorney general. He did not mention it, but the reversal probably irked him even more because James Crossley, his
predecessor in office and opponent in an acrimonious campaign of
slander, had been a member of the victorious defendants' team.
Crossley had tried to hold his office against Roth's determination to
get it after President Wilson's election, but as a Republican hold-
over he wasted his time.

Now Roth had to try Callahan again and he had to explain that
personal spite was not an issue, although it was true that he did not
admire old Dan, then fifty-one years old and married for the last
sixteen years to an Indian woman. "He is an immense man, six
foot, two inches, 275 pounds, strong as a horse, and always known
as a fighting man . . . generally a bully and people are afraid of
him." Yet Callahan possessed a "keen intellect . . . a brilliant mind,"
even if he lacked other virtues. "There is not a single moral con-
ception in his entire make-up and he is about the most bare faced
liar that ever lived." He was a "criminal by instinct, a notorious
character among the women of the underworld and he has the
pimps under his thumb." In fact he reigned as the "boss of the restricted district."[8] As the people's choice for city council, he had no
peers, having been elected to that body every term save one since
the town's founding in 1905 through various tricks, support of the
saloon crowd, and control of half the region's criminals. Dan did not
campaign on a law-and-order platform; in fact, he showed his contempt for lawmen openly and at all times and had written a number
of affidavits for others bringing nasty charges against Roth and
Marshal Erwin.

Roth believed in protecting young girls from men like Callahan
and the other defendants because he had young daughters himself.
For the benefit of the attorney general he described himself as a

man who had been married "for over twenty-five years, who has taken no drink in this division of Alaska since 1908," and, by implication, was something of an expert on interior Alaskans, among whom a remarkable climate of opinion existed. "No one who has not lived here for a considerable time can understand it at all." Most of the residents left their homes outside because they were constrained. "When they got here they felt a certain freedom in certain respects and this freedom, not freedom at all, but license, they have come to regard as a certain right." On the whole, the community was law abiding, but not when it came to sex: "Any attempt to bear down on sex crimes meets violent opposition."[9]

Some delicacy was required of the attorney general in dealing with the judges. Unlike the marshals and district attorneys, the judges, despite owing their appointments to the president, represented a separate branch of government. The Constitution prohibited executive-branch interference with judicial decisions. Incompetence or corruption were matters subject to the attorney general's supervision, but the line marking proper areas for investigation had to be—and was—carefully observed. By law the attorney general did have more power over territorial courts, such as Alaska's, than over federal courts in the States. For Alaska the attorney general prescribed special court terms and the places of hearing and was entitled to approve all fees for judicial officers. It was permissible for the Justice Department to investigate a judge and recommend that the president dismiss him, as was done on several occasions, but removal before a term's end was rare. It was much easier and less embarrassing to wait until the end of term and thus avoid charges of exceeding powers placed with the attorney general.

Charges of abuse of power were brought against Judge Melville Brown in 1904 by District Attorney John Boyce. William Day, first assistant to the attorney general, looked into matters on the trip he took to investigate Judge Wickersham and Judge Noyes. Day, noting the general disapproval of Brown among the Juneau public and the perverse influence of Brown's clerk, recommended his dismissal. After the president communicated his acceptance of Day's recommendation, Brown protested to the attorney general. "I have had no hearing." Day read the charges to me; all "were refuted by court records; those not refuted are too silly to consider." Like Judge Wickersham, Brown objected to Day's public hearings: "an invitation to slander" attracting "a few disgruntled Democrats and litigants." What particularly infuriated the judge were Day's conclusions that Brown's personal integrity remained unimpeached: "In the name of all that is holy, upon what were charges based unless it was slander and spume of a class of people before him in what is commonly called his dark-lantern procedure." And how could Day say that Brown had a hearing? "Anyone who says I neglected my duty is a liar. . . . I'm proud of my record. . . . The time will come when the president and those acting under him will be convinced of this error and, I hope, repent this action."[10] In spite of his protest, however, Brown did resign.

While the eight-year career of James Wickersham as district judge was important because of his pioneer role in the interior and his cleanup work in Nome, another aspect of his tenure highlights some complexities in Alaska's criminal administration. If the attorney general and president agreed that the incumbent of the four-year office had done a good job and if the same president or a successor of the same party held appointment powers, reappointment to another four-year term could be expected. But there was another potential obstacle to appointments in that they had to be confirmed by the U.S. Senate. A senator holding power on the Judiciary Committee could resist the president's desires, and he need not publicize his real reasons for withholding approval.

Wickersham's first term ran until June 1904. He was aware, as he wrote many years later, that his decisions in civil cases, particularly those dealing with mining claims, had earned him many vindictive foes. "Lust for gold when frustrated by adverse decisions not infrequently turns to malice toward the judge. Then no slander is too vile, no means of revenge is too base to satisfy the thirst for vengeance." Any disappointed litigant was free to make confidential charges to Washington, and the accused judge had no right to a hearing on such charges. "There was never a closed season for protection of district judges in Alaska as there was for brown bear and other varmints." Wickersham knew judicial history and could name many judges who "were removed from office upon secret charges without notice," and he knew that all of them "were maliciously assailed and more or less intimidated in the performance of their judicial duty."[11]

In a letter of February 1904 to the attorney general reviewing his case for reappointment, Wickersham boasted of his docket clearing in the interior, in Valdez, and in Nome, where he was assigned because of Judge Noyes's corruption and incompetence without the support of his own loyal court officials, yet he prevailed, after eleven months of labor, in clearing the docket of four hundred cases.[12]

The judge expected the strongest opposition to his reappointment to come from friends of Nome's marshal, Frank Richards, and the losers of mining cases in the interior and Valdez. Richards had dealt the judge a low blow by resurrecting scandalous charges of seduction that had resulted in criminal prosecution of Wickersham at Tacoma, Washington, in 1889. At the time, Wickersham was county probate judge, a handsome, virile, married man with lots of political enemies. His was a sensational trial, heavily publicized in the Northwest press. Women of the WCTU, who were then flexing their political muscle, thronged the courtroom in support of complaining witness Sadie Brantner.[13] Wickersham lost his campaign for reelection between the time of Sadie's accusations and his trial. And in spite of the forensic splendor of Washington's greatest attorney, James Hamilton Lewis, later a prominent U.S. senator for Indiana, Wickersham was found guilty. But the wily judge did not give up. He had never denied that he had had sexual relations with Sadie, but he did insist that he was not responsible for her pregnancy, that she was anything but the virtuous young woman entitled by law to accuse a man of seduction, and that the whole sordid business had been concocted by a political rival. Five months after Wickersham was convicted, the prosecutor had admissions from Sadie that she had misrepresented herself as an unsullied victim. The judge ordered a new trial, and the prosecutor asked for the dismissal of the case. Wickersham enclosed a record of the old scandal with his letter, hoping to head off further embarrassment.

In July 1904, William A. Day, first assistant to the attorney general, voyaged to Alaska to investigate both Wickersham and the first-division judge, Melville C. Brown (1900–1904). Day reported directly to President Teddy Roosevelt on Alaska's scandals. He had been shocked to find that O. P. Hubbard, one of the movers in the spoilers conspiracy at Nome, was holding office as deputy district attorney in Valdez, "although charges against him had been filed with the Department of Justice eight months since."[14]

Day's proceedings in Fairbanks seemed a bit unusual to Wickersham. After giving public notice of his purpose, Day invited anyone in town with something to say about the court to meet him at the town hall. Wickersham was not invited, but later Day gave him a summary of charges and heard his explanations. Many of Day's questions concerned the Richards jury-fixing case at Nome. When Day left Fairbanks for Nome to continue his investigation, the public interest died down, although, as the judge noted "it continued to afford the sporting element a subject of much talk and some betting on the result in the cigar stores, pool halls and saloons."[15]

For all of Wickersham's foreboding, Day recommended reappointment in glowing terms: "He is an able, honest, and upright judge . . . and possesses the confidence of the people of his division."[16] Day found Judge Brown of Juneau too weak for his responsibilities and recommended against Judge Alfred Moore (1902–1910) of Nome too, but the president kept Moore on "because he had been surrounded by the worst kind of officials" and did not have a fair chance.[17] It was on this same tour of investigation that Day recommended that Marshal Richards of Nome be removed.

President Roosevelt reappointed Wickersham and sent his name to the Senate, but the Judiciary Committee blocked his immediate confirmation and directed a subcommittee to investigate charges against him. The two North Dakota senators, Henry Hansbrough and Porter McCumber, creatures of Alexander McKenzie, had lobbied the president against Wickersham's reappointment but were not members of the Judiciary Committee. Its chairman, Knute Nelson of Minnesota, was a relentless enemy, probably because friends with Alaska interests has been disappointed in civil litigation or because of McKenzie's very strong influence in Minnesota political circles. Despite the opposition of Nelson and others, however, the subcommittee and the Judiciary Committee voted in favor of Wickersham. Confirmation by the full Senate was expected until a journalistic bombshell infuriated the North Dakota senators. Rex Beach's series "The Looting of Alaska" appeared in a magazine, and newspapers picked up the exposure of the spoilers and their backers in Washington. Hansbrough told his Senate colleagues that Wickersham had been seen hurrying a copy of the Beach article to the *Washington Times*.

Wickersham telegraphed Beach in New York, urging him to come to Washington for the latest episode of the Nome scandals: "I wanted him to see for himself how the Dakota Boss is yet able to 'pack a jury' in the United States Senate, and when he loses in that way, to filibuster and defy the Senate through his power and influence on North Dakotan and Minnesotan politicians." [18]

Hansbrough, Nelson, and others filibustered to good effect, and Congress adjourned without voting on confirmation. President Roosevelt was empowered to grant a one-year appointment in such a case. Similar stalemates with similar results followed for several years until Wickersham, eager to be congressional delegate, sent Roosevelt his letter of resignation in September 1907. "I am a poor man and now have a reasonable and proper opportunity to reenter the law practice [and] it seems hopeless to expect those senators who have opposed my confirmation to ever cease to do so," he wrote. [19]

Washington had to listen and wonder whenever their local officers in Alaska were slandered. Since most of the charges were ill founded, the attorney general may have been pleased on the rare occasion a judge talked back to a detractor with eloquent force. In 1921 attorney John Rustgard, a former U.S. attorney, filed an affidavit in a civil suit that scorched Judge Robert W. Jennings of Juneau. Neither the facts in litigation nor the implications of Rustgard's insults are worth reviewing, but Jennings' anger was expressed in some fine, vituperative language. Once the judge had delivered his opinion of Rustgard, he felt more judicial and dismissed the contempt charges he had brought against the attorney for his offensive affidavit. This is what Jennings said:

This affidavit is so puerile, it is so asinine, it is so far fetched, that really it fails of its purpose. To say that the Judge of a court, because he is a friend of the Governor of the Territory, because he belongs to the same political party that the Governor belongs to, cannot fairly decide a case which does not mean one cent to that Governor—a suit, too, brought against a person who will not have to pay personally one cent if the case is decided against him—is, to my mind, so ridiculous, so absurd, so much the mark of those whose mental horizon is limited and whose moral bankruptcy is imminent,—and the testimony adduced here in explanation thereof is so plainly the mark of a paranoiac, filled to overflowing with his self-satisfied sufficiency, and of a brain of mush and a heart of a crook, a disordered fancy and a twisted tongue, that it merits very little consideration. That this affidavit was intended as an insult to the Judge of this court I have not the slightest doubt in the world;—but speaking of insults, the question as to whether an insult is conveyed depends as much upon the character and standing of the would-be insulter as it does upon the language employed. John Randolph of Roanoke said, "A gentleman will not insult me, and no other can." It is perfectly obvious that a knave cannot really insult an honest man,—he may irritate him and annoy him, but he cannot insult any one. A weakling and an idiot with no moral backbone and with only a thimbleful of brains cannot insult any one,—the only person such characters can insult are their inferiors, and as there are no inferiors there are none for them to insult. They themselves are at the bottom of the pit, and they cannot look below,—self-satisfied paranoiacs, liars from the pure love of a lie, canting hypocrites, attempting to cleanse their hands with invisible soap, defamers of men, slanderers of women, assassins of character, sneaking, cowardly curs,—what do they do among decent men? Why such objects on the fair face of the earth? Their place is not on the earth but in the earth—in the privies of the earth. The station in life, in human affairs, of such men as that corresponds to the position which "the foul bird of Patagonia" occupies in bird life. "The foul bird of Patagonia" is not the buzzard that feeds on the carrion—it is a smaller bird that perches on the back of the buzzard and by continually pecking causes the buzzard to vomit forth the carrion that it has fed upon and then hops down to the ground to eat the vomit which the buzzard has spewed from its foul belly.[20]

Because their areas of jurisdiction were well defined, conflicts between the attorney general and the secretary of the interior or between Justice Department officials and the governors of Alaska were few. The governor's advice on Justice officials was sometimes solicited and his recommendations on office seekers were often heard, whether solicited or not, but each executive officer protected his prerogatives.

The attorney general did become disturbed when governors acted on a 1919 revision of the U.S. Civil Code to pardon criminals convicted of misdemeanors. Since territorial governors served under the president, whose executive-pardon privilege was administered by the pardon attorney in the Department of Justice, the attorney general had opposed this legislation. In 1924, Governor Scott Bone pardoned a couple of gamblers and drew a sharp rebuke from the attorney general: "The 1919 Act which empowers pardons for misdemeanors is, in our opinion, unconstitutional."[21] In time the attorney general prevailed and the grounds of conflict between the two departments were removed.

When the governor received complaints about Justice Department officers, he usually passed them on to the secretary of the interior or to the attorney general. Governors recognized that many citizens could not figure out the governmental lines of authority and assumed that the governors supervised court officers.

Individual deputy marshals often were accused of abusing their authority. Alaskans had little occasion to show bias against an entire race, except natives, or another community, but one critic displayed both biases. "A Norwegian can't do wrong in Petersburg," said Commissioner A. P. Williams to Governor Strong. Williams' chief complaint was against Deputy Marshal Martin Kildall, "a big Norwegian who is not a citizen."[22] Possibly Williams did not like Norwegians, who made up about three-quarters of Petersburg's seven hundred souls, or perhaps he disdained the picturesque island fishing community for other reasons. He had lived there only six months and had discovered "a different class of people from any I've met in Alaska before." Significantly, no Norwegian had yet appeared before his court, although some of them openly sold booze to natives. Williams urged the appointment of a "good, clean American for us" to end the lamentable condition of having "one law for Americans and another for Norwegians." As an instance of this he cited the prosecution of prostitutes at the June court term in Ketchikan. Kildall handled the fine levied against a Norwegian madame, "who never had to leave her business," but two Americans had to close up in Petersburg to appear in court at Ketchikan. If Williams' was right, it appears that the marshal had contributed to unfair commercial competition.

In the same vein Williams wrote to U.S. Marshal H. A. Bishop in Juneau. Whenever Williams wanted swift action from the marshal, he seemed to be out shrimping; he even allowed individuals who deserved prosecution to leave town. "I don't think it is my business to produce evidence in criminal cases and try them too," he said. [23] The Petersburg jailer was worthless too, a common drunk who had to be pulled out of the saloon when he was needed. "The jail and marshal's office here are more like kindergarten than a place to keep criminals. I visited the jail six times last week and never found either the marshal or the jailer there." Apparently the marshal had seized a fishing boat in some sort of legal action and wanted to harvest while he could. Were conditions in Petersburg as terrible as Williams claimed? Verily, the record is hazy, but it is instructive to note that Petersburg got a new commissioner in 1916, while Deputy Marshal Kildall remained on the job.

"I don't know what it is about the atmosphere of Alaska that seems to be so destructive of good morals," said Attorney General George W. Wickersham (a distant relation to James Wickersham, judge and congressional delegate). [24] The attorney general was upset about the small corruptions of Marshal Harvey P. Sullivan of Valdez, and his despairing remarks were similar to others that echoed through the Justice Department building over the years. Alaskans believed that their ordinary citizens, if not their officials, were more virtuous than those elsewhere because the distinct lifestyle promoted all man's best qualities. Without attempting to settle the vexing question of relative morality, let's look at Sullivan, a reasonably typical Alaskan but one who had been tempted by the curious system with which jails were financed. Sullivan, a Minnesotan, stampeded to Dawson in 1898, then mined at Circle and Nome. Sponsors for his appointment as third-division marshal in 1909 included the powerful western railroad man James J. Hill.

There were several accusations against Sullivan. A trusty told of carrying supplies from the jail to the Sullivan family home and cooking meals for the Sullivans there. Fresh-baked bread from the jail kitchen, as well as government coal, sustained the Sullivans. Cornelius L. Vawter, then a deputy marshal at Iditarod, claimed that he was fired from his deputy job in Dillingham in 1909 because he refused to share money allotted for prisoners' upkeep with the marshal. Vawter, whose service as a deputy continuously from 1898 to 1922 except for a short, turbulent stretch as marshal at

Nome (1900–1901), was a testament to his good repute, had corroborating witnesses. As corruption went, Sullivan's misdeeds were not so alarming, but, as in all such cases, the handling of them by Washington involved some complexities. Special examiner Plato Mountjoy voyaged to south-central Alaska to investigate and confront Sullivan. The marshal admitted "borrowing" blankets and coal because of the coal shortage in the winter of 1909–1910, and he also admitted having enjoyed jail food on occasion. He did return some of the coal when his own supply reached town: seven sacks against the two tons he used.

Mountjoy's investigation in January–February 1911 left the attorney general undecided about a course of action. Should Sullivan merely be reprimanded or should he be removed? Should he be prosecuted? Prosecutions of federal officers were embarrassing, and even removals raised controversy. James J. Hill was concerned enough to write President Taft in May questioning the investigation, so the attorney general had to be wary. Special assistant T. J. Butler, sent to report on September, thought "there is no chance of a prosecution but evidence of irregularities sufficient to demand removal." Still the attorney general hesitated. B. J. Townsend, another special assistant, looked into the affair in November. No need for prosecution, he said, "and I don't want to advise on firing." It may be a good idea, but perhaps "a reprimand is enough." [25] This advice seemed to be what the attorney general had been waiting for. Sullivan kept his job until the Democrats took over in 1913, got it back in 1922, and served until 1933 in spite of repeated outcries against his drinking habits.

When questions were raised about judges, marshals, or district attorneys, the investigative process worked slowly because of the distances involved. Lesser functionaries—court clerks, deputies, and assistant attorneys—might be quickly fired by telegram, but the principal officeholders, selected after much agony over their qualifications (and much more over the relative political weight of their patrons) got more consideration. Field examiners on their tours, usually during the summer, to audit office bookkeeping and review management could be asked to investigate, or an attorney general's assistant could be dispatched from Washington. Even for the marshal's office, which was actually an arm of the court, there was no direct supervision by the district judge. Giving the judge such authority might have helped in some instances, but it could also cause feuds and disruptions. There was nothing to prevent the solicitation of a judge's opinion, but it was seldom done.

One instance in which a judge's views were solicited occurred in 1915. Attorney General Thomas Gregory, an Austin lawyer who proved himself an effective, fair-minded administrator and declined the ultimate reward of a Supreme Court appointment, asked Judge Charles F. Bunnell about Marshal L. T. Erwin. This was the period during which Fairbanks was Alaska Territory's largest town and site of the court for a huge outlying section, so affairs in the fourth division were often the concern of Washington. Gregory had been hearing serious charges from Fort Yukon missionary Dr. Grafton Burke about Erwin and his deputy, Thomas E. Winecoff. Burke's unhappiness could have been related to his removal as U.S. commissioner, yet the Justice Department in Washington did not ignore his charges. According to Burke, the marshal's office is "just what crooks, liquor dealers, and squaw-men most desire." Erwin routinely cooperated with saloonkeepers and his deputies were corrupt, charged Burke. One deputy, Winecoff, "is not a fit person for a deputy; is a deposed clergyman, and his removal from Fort Yukon would be a victory for righteousness."[26] Gregory conceded that similar charges had "been coming into this office for a long time, and have in each case been investigated."[27] Obviously the investigations had reflected favorably on Erwin, but it was exasperating to hear them again and again, and Gregory wanted the matter laid to rest.

Judge Bunnell reported on the "character, integrity, reliability, personally and officially," of Erwin and on what he knew of the Fort Yukon situation from court records and Burke's reputation as a troublemaker. Bunnell, an Episcopalian himself, took an interest in the church's mission at Fort Yukon. Because he had been an Alaskan since 1900, he knew Archdeacon Hudson Stuck and Bishop P. T. Rowe and was not hesitant about talking to them. Stuck did not want a commissioner. Bunnell wanted one but had not been able to find anyone willing to take the job except another missionary.[28] Playing the peacemaker was not a foreign role for district judges, and advising the attorney general about the peculiar condition of Alaska was a favorite occupation of field officers whenever they were given the opportunity. Bunnell appreciated that Gregory heard accusations against everyone holding public office, "especially in Alaska," but counseled against paying any attention to anonymous letters.

Judge Bunnell was able to help Erwin get reappointed in 1917 and enlighten the attorney general somewhat more on the perils encountered by Alaska's officers. "Many enemies" thrust at men of positive opinions and positive qualities, he said. "Ever since I have been in Fairbanks I have seen at his heels, snarling and snapping, the most motley pack of hounds and curs it has ever been my experience to meet," Bunnell wrote. "Their yelping is not because of any alleged incompetency on his part . . . but simply because they don't like him. They disliked him because they could not handle him—and disliked the district attorney and the judge for the same reason. Generally speaking they are trouble makers of the most virulent type, singers of sacred music on Sundays, and on all other days character witnesses for defendants on trial and makers of scurrilous affidavits." Bunnell singled out J. Harmon Caskey, publisher of a "libelous newspaper" called the *Alaska Daily Citizen,* a candidate for every appointment from "jail guard to governor," who endeavored to compel federal officers to "comply with his wishes. He and his crowd have at all times and under all circumstances both day and night sought to misrepresent, malign and discredit any and every one honestly engaged in the administration of justice."[29] The judge grew warm on his theme. The Caskey crowd would love to stir up strife among the court officials. To this end they were pushing for the appointment as marshal a "moral leper," a man whose notorious behavior "I shrink from detailing. . . . To this element the innocence of childhood, the purity of womanhood, and even the sacredness of the home are mere pawns in the game of life."

One of the facts of life in Alaska for federal officials was the uncertainty of whether the next attack on them would come locally or from the outside, on behalf of a local individual who had been aggrieved or in support of some entrenched commercial interest. Foes of officers had perfected the boldness of big-lie techniques, particularly slanders calculated to show that the target official pos-

Judge Charles Bunnell. Alaska Historical Library, Alaska Transportation Museum Collection

sessed extraordinary cupidity. Alaska newspapers could even joke about this, as with the story that "a Washington, D.C. lobbyist wired his Seattle friend that Mr. . . . had been appointed to a federal job in Alaska." The recipient, knowing just what to do, would wire immediately to his lobbyist: "Who the hell is Mr. . . . ? File charges against him at once."[30]

Bunnell's own travails with regard to reappointment show a certain ironic continuity in the appointment system. He had done a good job from 1915 to 1918 and was renominated by the president. Then, as with his pioneer predecessor, Judge James Wickersham, the U.S. Senate balked at his confirmation. And who was behind Bunnell's anguish and embarrassment? Why, his old political foe, James Wickersham, then Alaska's delegate to Congress.

Wickersham's lockhold on the delegate's job from 1909 to 1921 had not been threatened too seriously by Bunnell's campaign against him in 1914. Rumors were that Bunnell agreed to sacrifice himself by running for the Democrats against Wickersham in return for the promise of a judgeship. Bunnell campaigned hard against the popular incumbent and strenuously denied other rumors that he disdained the drinking of hard liquor and was a secret prohibitionist. He also hoped to convince voters that a Democratic delegate would work better with the new national Democratic administration. But of 10,806 votes cast, Bunnell got only 3,416, compared to Wickersham's 6,283. The total number of voters should be noted. Not many Alaskans were active in the political wars, but these few created as much discord as more numerous individuals in other regions.

Wickersham, rather pleased to run against Bunnell instead of a stronger candidate, became vengeful only when Judge Bunnell and District Attorney Roth campaigned against him in 1916. Wickersham lost this election until his showing of irregularities at the polls resulted in the unseating of the winner, Charles Sulzer, but not until the delegate's two-year term had nearly elapsed. The same thing happened with the 1918 election of George Grigsby. Again, long after the election, the House of Representatives declared that Wickersham would have won but for poll fraud. Of the 1916 campaign Wickersham believed, or professed to believe, that Bunnell and Roth had advised soldiers at Fort Gibbon and Fort Liscum to vote, although they were not eligible to do so.

In Congress, Wickersham enlisted the aid of Senator Wesley L. Jones, a Washington Republican, against Bunnell's reappointment. Again, as in Wickersham's situation earlier, the president kept Bunnell in office with recess appointments. Visiting Washington in November 1920 after the president once more had asked the Senate for confirmation, Bunnell thought he had convinced Jones and other senators that Wickersham had not "fully advised" them on the controversy. Yet confirmation was withheld, and in 1921 a Republican president replaced Bunnell. [31]

Judge Bunnell's tenure ended about the time Alaska's bush-pilot era commenced. Since the early 1920s, commercial flying had been proving its worth in Alaska and making inroads on the traditional modes of travel. The possibilities of flight did not affect the court

very much because there were no more boom towns to cry for immediate attention during the quiet years of declining population between the world wars. It was excitement about the Black Bear
case in Fairbanks, however, that saved the town's first commercial
air service from bankruptcy when bush dwellers flocked in by air to
attend the trial. [32]

20. How Justice Fared

It appears in some instances that the temptation has proved too strong.
—Governor John Brady

WORLD WAR II's effects on Alaska compared with those of the gold rushes in economic and political significance. After the Japanese attack on Pearl Harbor, the government launched military construction projects all over the territory. More than a billion dollars was spent in Alaska during the war, and the consequent growth of population did not abate after the war ended.

During the war Alaska's law officers had a busy time policing construction workers and military men who swelled the population in Kodiak, Anchorage, Fairbanks, and other places. Although the marshals and deputies carried on as before, they had help in criminal investigations and arrests related to more serious crimes after the FBI posted resident agents to Alaska. But the work of the officers and the courts was no longer very singular in nature. The spread of commercial air transportation had greatly reduced the territory's distances and isolation. Law enforcement in the field and its administration from Washington lost much of their peculiar—and often colorful—flavor. Few of the wartime or postwar criminal matters stand out. More than ever, crime was concentrated in urban settings and appeared as banal as that committed outside, even with those few instances that excited communities and, as with killers Nelson and La Moore, resulted in executions.

Alaskans were more excited by political developments in the postwar years than in criminal affairs. With perhaps some of the same energy and intensity that formerly had been reserved for local politics and the backbiting of officials, a considerable body of Alaskans began agitating for statehood. That joyous goal was achieved when Alaska joined the Union as the forty-ninth state in 1959. The result long had been anticipated by the Department of Justice and other federal agencies. Congressional legislation in 1953 provided for the merger of Alaska's four court districts into a single one, but the reduction in force was withheld until after 1959.

Advocates of statehood realized that it would be the responsibility of the new state to establish its own police forces, prosecutors, civil and criminal courts, and jails. They made light of the expense of this and other services in their briefs to other residents and the federal government, and lawyers pointed out the difficulties federal courts had in recent years keeping up with increased case loads.

Some harsh assessments have been made of the early period of Alaska's criminal justice system and its administration. Thomas O. Murton, studying the system as it existed from 1867 to 1902, concluded that political pressures, corruption, carpetbagger administrations, and inadequate financing created a travesty of justice. He found that conditions were chaotic before 1885 and scarcely improved as the new court system faced the effects of the gold rushes. "None of the officials sent to govern Alaska, civil or military, had the benefit of any instructions," Murton wrote. "The only exception to that was the inauguration of the court at Nome. In this instance the Attorney General sent a man to advise the officers of the court in the performance of their duties. But, he resigned and joined with the corrupt court of officials to use his advisory talents in the subversion of justice."[1]

Murton's dim view is understandable considering the time frame of his focus. Here we have not been concerned with the early period (1867–84) of gross neglect and sometimes military ineptness, and we have gone on after the turmoil of the gold rushes to follow consider more settled conditions. The administration of justice certainly did improve after thousands of stampeders abandoned their hopes of wringing fortunes from the ground and returned to their

homes. Their exodus left Alaska with four functioning court districts, a fluctuating economy based on the declining mining industry and the fisheries, and a dependence on the federal government for most services and even the prospects of further development. There were a few other booms and busts up to the 1940s, but the conditions that led to the deplorable conditions of early Skagway and Nome never had to be faced again. In such frenzy as then occurred it is a little hard to fix blame for the breakdown of criminal administration solely in the Department of Justice. The rot of national politics and the corruption that characterized the McKinley era emanated from the highest executive offices and from Congress. The justice system established in 1885 and 1900 for Alaska was well short of perfection, but it might have worked well enough except for the corruption of a handful of officers in Alaska and their backers in Washington.

All was not sweetness and light after the gold rushes. There were scandals, corrupt deals, incompetent officials, irregular proceedings, mindless administrative dictates, and nasty partisanship to enliven and impede the work of dealing with criminals, themselves enough of a disruptive force, but the target the government agents were supposed to give their full attention. It is not possible to measure the efficiency of the officers in the struggle to provide order and bring criminals to justice except perhaps by some comparative statistical analysis that is beyond my powers and interest. But some reflection on the work of the Department of Justice and its officers convinces me that a high standard of performance was usually demanded by Washington and that those charged with duties in the field usually either met the standards or got out of office. What clearly distinguished the administration of justice in Alaska were the particular difficulties of communication and transportation in the vast and distant land where the winter climate, in every section except southeastern, can be severely taxing.

The work of historians of other parts of the West provides some insights to Alaska's history. Glenn Shirley's study of criminals and federal officers in Oklahoma Territory from 1889 to 1907 is close in time to the first years of Alaska's court, and Oklahoma's land rushes were settings comparable to northern gold rushes. Shirley records incidents of official corruption and public discord, as well as the determined efforts of federal and local peace officers to bring the last frontier bandit gang to justice. Yet it really is difficult to compare conditions in Oklahoma and Alaska. The northern territory seems to have been more law abiding. It had fewer people; it had fewer outlaws; it did not suffer from outlaw bands, with the exception of the Soapy Smith gang in Skagway. Oklahoma was a refuge for hard characters from Texas and elsewhere, a place where they could avoid pursuit by their home officers yet continue their larcenous ways in a more lightly policed environment. Few rogues ever thought of Alaska as a refuge, and it was only for a brief time at Nome that the region attracted large numbers of what used to be called the sporting crowd. Differences in political organization, population, economy, and geographic proximity between the two territories were even more significant than other factors that have been noted, and taking all the differences together forces the conclusion that grounds for comparison are interesting but strictly limited.[2]

The same conclusion can be made for Arizona and New Mexico territories, the marshals of which were studied by Larry D. Ball. As in Oklahoma, federal officers played a large role in keeping the peace and were not always appreciated by political factions. Unlike Shirley, Ball passes judgment on the federal administration, criticizing "a complacent Congress, armed with the ideal of limited law enforcement, [that] failed miserably to comprehend the unique problems of the federal officers. . . . The national lawmakers provided weak and inefficient courts. The marshals, whom Congress regarded as mere ministerial officers, grappled with criminal activities that only a strong detective with resources for pursuit could have overcome. The Department of Justice encumbered these lawmen with 'utterly impractical' bureaucratic restrictions and then left them 'to keep the peace as best they could.' One scholar has rightly concluded that the territorial judiciary was one of the 'weakest parts' of that jerry-rigged government.'"[3]

Again, it is difficult to compare Arizona–New Mexico with Alaska, yet Ball's more general conclusions can be examined for their applicability. Obviously all Ball says of his territories' "unique problems" (particularly geographic conditions) and Washington's failure to understand them tempts one to say amen for Alaska. Alaskans and Alaska historians must be wary of referring to their "unique problems." It is not that Alaska was not as unusual as residents considered it, but in Washington federal officials also had to listen to claims of uniqueness from Arizona, New Mexico, Oklahoma, and other places, and every acceptance of uniqueness, every expression of particularly sympathetic understanding, had its price. If Alaska got more, Arizona might get less. After all, the funds available were limited and the denial of requests for assistance did not necessarily mean that the Washington bureaucrats lacked understanding.

I think Alaska's experience supports Ball's judgment that certain geographic realities and the needs of criminal investigation exposed the shortcomings of the marshals. Another kind of police agency was needed in the Far North and in the Southwest, but authority for it would have to come from Congress and neither Congress nor the public ever smiled on proposals for other kinds of national police; they even resisted the Secret Service's investigations for the Justice Department and, until the Bureau of Investigation became popular in the 1920s, its evolution into the huge agency that the F.B.I. became. The U.S. Marshal Service was traditional and acceptable. It made more political sense to make it work in the territories than to create some other organization.

Ball's judgment that the judiciary was the weakest part of the law-enforcement machinery in Arizona–New Mexico is not one that parallels the Alaska experience. Judges in Alaska held more powers than their counterparts elsewhere, but even in the exercise of criminal trial functions the Alaska judges seemed superior in strength, honesty, and efficiency to the handicapped U.S. Marshal Service or the district attorneys, who were tempted by politics and moved by their ambition to replace sitting judges.

Despite these different views, I could accept Ball's ultimate praise for the marshals and extend it to Alaska's other court officers as well: "For more than six decades the marshals . . . guided the destiny of federal law enforcement through numerous crises. . . . They ran the gauntlet of political partisanship, sometimes succumbing to selfish party influences, but at other times transcending political dogmas. All these activities, when viewed collectively, reveal considerable achievement on the part of federal lawmen. In spite of a rather doctrinaire attitude on the part of their superiors in Washington, the marshals demonstrated some ability to adapt to the peculiar problems of the frontier."[4]

In *The Western Peace Officer,* Frank R. Prassel includes U.S. marshals in his review of officers. He pays particular attention to Oklahoma Territory because of the lawlessness there near the end of the nineteenth century and rates the marshals highly, but he does not mention Alaska.[5]

Judging by the historical literature, lawlessness in Alaska cannot be compared in volume and intensity with other regions of the frontier. There are no legendary Alaska outlaws (except for Soapy Smith, the subject of a drama produced in New York in 1984), no Billy the Kid, Butch Cassidy, Jesse James, or John Hardin, to name only a few of the many richly celebrated bad men. Frank Canton and Wyatt Earp were quiet and good in Alaska. And Alaska lacked that great tie to larceny and related crimes, the great cattle herds and corrals filled with tempting horses, and thus was deprived of the impetus for the dozens of bloody feuds that enlivened Texas history or for the large-scale conflicts, such as New Mexico's Lincoln County War and Wyoming's Johnson County Invasion. Alaska did not get by without some vigilante incidents, but none of them has achieved the celebrity of such affairs in California, Montana, and elsewhere. Alaska's two major contributions to that strange fusion of fact and fiction that is the outlaw tradition were Soapy Smith and the Nome spoilers. The spoilers did not hold the popular imagination, despite the work of Rex Beach, and this is unfortunate because their story is a most meaningful moral tale in a democracy where so much depends upon the rectitude of judges.

A statistical analysis of Alaska felonies from 1935 to 1965 sheds light on earlier times as well. Kermit Kynell shows that Alaska's homicide rate has been below the national average and its homicides have not been related to geographic location so much as they have been factors of environmental conditions: heavy drinking, isolation, lack of social services.[6]

In summary, it appears that the major deficiencies in the Justice Department's organization for Alaska can be attributed to concern for high costs. As has been said, neither Congress nor the department was allured by repeated calls for some kind of territorial police force possessing the mobility and investigative talents of Canada's Mounties. Nor did appeals for special transport gain much response, although the first division did acquire a patrol boat in the late 1920s, a rum runner seized by the court. Whether the marshal's efficiency soared to new heights through the acquisition is not clear, but there was a complaint that Marshal Albert White used his vessel to spread good will among fellow Republicans.[7]

The floating court was Alaska's only significant innovation, although the tradition of a circuit court was a venerable one. Even this measure to bring speedier justice to outlying areas lasted only a few years. Judge James Wickersham inaugurated the practice in 1903 with a thirty-seven-day, three-thousand-mile voyage on the Revenue Cutter Service's *Rush* to coastal ports between Yakutat and Bristol Bay, including Unalaska in the Aleutians and Kodiak Island. Other judges held similar sessions through 1913 to handle the huge seasonal influx of cannery workers and fishermen. In 1913 the U.S. attorney in Valdez recommended that a new position be authorized for a traveling prosecutor. The attorney could travel in advance of the court party to prepare his cases and thus improve efficiency. Washington not only refused this request but abolished floating-court sessions in 1915. It cost less to let the commissioners deal with petty crimes within their jurisdictions and dispatch accused felons to Valdez for the regular court session.

Another call never answered in Washington was that for a prison in Alaska to house long-termers. Governor Brady suggested the need in 1902, recommending one of the picturesque islands in Sitka Harbor as a likely site. But the government always found the transport of prisoners to McNeil Island, although expensive and disruptive to the ordinary routine of deputies, a better alternative.

Alaskans did not mind exporting its felons to McNeil Island off Tacoma, Washington. They were rather pleased to annex effectively a little Puget Sound country for people who behaved unsocially. And the name McNeil Island, constantly misstated as McNeil's Island, fluttered from the tongues of Alaskans with alarming frequency. In countless saloon disputes, fellows threatened one another with exile to McNeil to win arguments. Many newcomers to the territory must have believed that McNeil was just down the trail since the resort figured so largely in conversations of residents. Today all but a few Alaskan convicts are lodged in the state's own prison.

Notes

ABBREVIATIONS USED IN THE NOTES

ASL: Alaska State Library, Juneau
DJ: Department of Justice
FRC: Federal Records Center, Seattle
GP: Correspondence of the Governors of Alaska. Record Group 348. Microfilm at Federal Records Center, Seattle
IP: Interior Department, Alaska Territorial Papers. Record Group 48. Microfilm at Federal Records Center, Seattle
NA: National Archives, Washington, D.C.
RG: Record Group of the National Archives
TT: Texas Tech University
UA: University of Alaska Archives, Fairbanks, Rasmuson Library
UO: University of Oklahoma Archives
UW: University of Washington Archives, Suzzallo Library

CHAPTER 1. PETROFF'S ALASKA

1. Hinckley, *Americanization of Alaska,* p. 31.
2. Sherwood, *Exploration of Alaska,* p. 62.
3. Carlson, "Alaska's First Census: 1880," pp. 48–53. See Swineford's newspaper, *The Alaskan,* May 8, 1886, for complaints that Petroff did not even visit Sitka.
4. Sherwood, *Exploration of Alaska,* p. 68.
5. Bancroft, *History of Alaska,* pp. 368–74. The Juvenal story also can be found in Sherwood, *Cook Inlet Collection,* pp. 61–66, and Chevigny, *Lord of Alaska,* pp. 152–56.
6. Trevor-Roper, *Hermit of Peking,* passim.

7. W. G. Morris to Secretary of Treasury, November 7, 1881, quoted in Hinckley, *Americanization of Alaska,* p. 159.

8. Elliott, *Condition of Affairs in Alaska,* p. 25.

9. Morris, *Report on the Resources of Alaska,* pp. 61–62.

10. Ibid., p. 62.

11. *Alaska Census 1870,* pp. 19, 21, 23.

12. Teichmann, *A Journey to Alaska in the Year 1868,* pp. 187–91.

CHAPTER 2. UNEASY BEGINNINGS

1. Samuel Ward McAllister was the full name of father and son, but both preferred to use Ward McAllister.

2. Malone, *Dictionary of American Biography,* pp. 945–47.

3. Hillyer to Attorney General, December 5, 1884, April 13, 1885, NA, RG 60, Letters Received.

4. Haskett to Attorney General, July 1, 1885, NA, RG 60, Letters Received.

5. Hillyer to Attorney General, January 8, 1885, NA, RG 60, Letters Received.

6. Hinckley, *Americanization of Alaska,* p. 113.

7. Hinckley, *Alaskan John G. Brady,* p. 58.

8. Haskett's successor also had to deal with the bad feeling engendered by the uncertainty of the land laws. See Ball to Attorney General, October 7, 1885, NA, RG 60, Letters Received.

9. Hinckley, *Alaskan John G. Brady,* pp. 90–96.

10. Jackson to Rev. William M. Cleveland, May 5, 1885, DJ Correspondence, copy at ASL. ASL copies were made from NA, RG 60, Letters Received.

11. Jackson to Rev. William M. Cleveland, May 5, 1885, DJ Correspondence, copy at ASL.

12. Kinkead to President Cleveland, January 5, 1886, DJ Correspondence, copy at ASL.

13. Henry Clews to President Cleveland, September 9, 1885, DJ Correspondence, copy at ASL; Malone, *Dictionary of American Biography,* pp. 945–47; McAllister v. The United States, 1 *Alaska Federal Reports,* 189, 114 *US* 174 (1891), deciding that, as a territorial judge, McAllister could be removed.

14. *The Alaskan,* November 21, 1885, March 6, 27, 1886.

15. The ASL has a copy of the Dawne petition; Jackson to Rev. William M. Cleveland, May 5, 1885, DJ Correspondence, copy at ASL.

16. Samuel Ramp to President Cleveland, August 11, 1885; R. W. Thompson to President Cleveland, August 28, 1885, DJ Correspondence, copies at ASL.

17. Samuel Ramp to President Cleveland, August 11, 1885; anonymous letter from Salem, Oregon, to President Cleveland, October 28, 1885, DJ Correspondence, copies at ASL.

18. *The Alaskan,* November 7, 21, 28, 1885, February 6, 1886.

19. Ibid., February 13, 1885.

20. Jackson to Attorney General, March 27, 1889, DJ Correspondence, copy at ASL.

21. Nightingale's report, November 23, 1888, NA, RG 60, Letters Received.

22. Hinckley, *Americanization of Alaska,* p. 166; *The Alaskan,* November 21, 1885.

23. Nightingale's report, November 23, 1888, NA, RG 60, Letters Received.

24. Ibid.

25. Atkins to Attorney General, April 21, 1886, NA, RG 60, Letters Received.

26. Atkins to Attorney General, January 10, 1889.

27. Nightingale to Attorney General, February 17, 1890, NA, RG 60, Letters Received.

28. Haydon, *Cases Reported . . . by Lafayette Dawson,* p. 155. Other quotes that follow are from pp. 113, 115–16, 119, and 120–21.

29. McCafferty to Solicitor General, February 16, 1887, DJ Correspondence, copy at ASL.

30. U.S. v. John McCafferty, court record, cases 119B, 344, FRC.

31. U.S. v. John McCafferty, court record, cases 119B, 344, FRC.

32. McCafferty to Judge Dawson, January 26, 1887, DJ Correspondence, copy at ASL.

33. McCafferty to Solicitor General, February 16, 1887, DJ Correspondence, copy at ASL.

34. DeLorme, "Liquor Smuggling in Alaska," p. 150.

35. Ibid., p. 146.

36. For this and following quotes, Murray to C. A. Hamlin, June 1, 1895, NA, RG 60, Letters Received.

37. Murray to C. A. Hamlin, June 1, 1895, NA, RG 60, Letters Received.

38. Moore to Murray, May 31, 1895; Rogers to Murray, May 31, 1895. These letters and the substance of Sheakley's letter to the president were included with Murray to Hamlin, June 1, 1895, NA, RG 60, Letters Received.

39. DeLorme, "Liquor Smuggling in Alaska," p. 151.

40. Governor Brady to Secretary of Interior, October 5, 1897, GP.

41. Bennett to Attorney General, June 17, July 3, 1898, NA, RG 60, Letters Received.

42. U.S. v. W. E. Crews, Thomas Marquam, et al., court record, case 999, FRC.

43. DeLorme, "Liquor Smuggling in Alaska," p. 152.

CHAPTER 3. DREADFUL MURDERS

1. U.S. v. Charles Kie, court record, case 1, FRC.

2. Ibid.

3. Ibid.

4. Ibid.

5. Ibid.

6. Kie v. United States, 1 *Alaska Federal Reports* 125; 27 *F* 351 (1886).

7. In re Sah Quah, 1 *Alaska Federal Reports,* 140.

8. In re Sah Quah, 1 *Alaska Federal Reports,* 142.

9. Steckler, "Charles John Seghers," p. 434. Other quotes that follow are from pp. 435, 494, 501, 521, 522–23, 535, and 538. For the trial documents, see U.S. v. Frank Fuller, court record, case 160, FRC.

CHAPTER 4. JUSTICE QUESTIONED

1. Berton, *Klondike,* has the best general account of events preceding the great gold rush. See also Hunt, *North of 53°,* passim.

2. U.S. v. Jack Dalton, court record, case 383, FRC.

3. *Juneau Mining Record,* March 9, 1893.

4. U.S. v. Jack Dalton, court record, case 383, FRC.

5. U.S. v. Jack Dalton, court record, case 383, FRC.

6. *Alaskan,* July 1, 1893.

7. Ibid.

8. Ibid., November 18, 1893.

9. Heid to Attorney General, August 9, 1893, Maloney Collection, ASL.

10. U.S. v. Maloney, case 99, Maloney Collection, ASL.

11. The *Star* story was quoted in the *Fairbanks Daily News-Miner* on May 15, 1915, with the snide comment that the "sensational" *Star* "tells a good story in the *Star* fashion."

12. *Alaska Mining Record,* April 15, 1895.

13. Ibid., April 22, 1895, for this and following quotes.

14. Ibid., April 29, 1895, for this and following quotes.

15. Ibid., May 6, 1895.

16. *Alaska News,* April 18, 1895; April 25, 1895.

CHAPTER 5. VIGILANTES

1. Steele, *Forty Years in Canada,* p. 297; pp. 295–96.

2. Brady to Secretary of Interior, March 2, 1898; September 14, 1900, IP, FRC.

3. Smith to McBride, September 25, 1897, IP, FRC.

4. Report on John U. Smith, November 18, 1897, IP, FRC.

5. Brady to Secretary of the Interior, March 2, 1898, IP, FRC.

6. Ibid.

7. Brady to Secretary of the Interior, December 21, 1897; July 7, 1898, IP, FRC.

8. Brady to Secretary of the Interior, July 7, 1898, IP, FRC.

9. All three public notices relating to the vigilantes are from the *Dyea Trail*, March 11, 1898.

10. *Seattle Times,* June 3, 1898.

11. Ibid.

12. Levy to S. A. Perkins, June 6, 1898, NA, RG 60, Letters Received.

13. Levy to Attorney General, June 9, 1898, NA, RG 60, Letters Received.

14. Bennett to Attorney General, July 3, 1898, NA, RG 60, Letters Received.

15. *Skagway News,* July 8, 1898, for this and following quote.

16. Shoup to Attorney General, July 3, 1898, NA, RG 60, Letters Received.

17. *Alaskan,* July 23, 1898.

18. Shoup to Attorney General, July 22, 1898, NA, RG 60, Letters Received, for this and following quote.

19. Capt. R. T. Yeatman to Adjutant General, July 8, 1898, NA, RG 60, Letters Received.

20. U.S. v. Turner Jackson, court record, case 1014, FRC.

21. U.S. v. Sylvester Taylor, court record, case 1028, FRC.

22. U.S. v. John Fitzpatrick, court record, case 819, FRC.

23. Brady to Secretary of Interior, July 11, 1898, IP, FRC, for this and following quote.

24. Undated clipping from the *Alaskan, Third Annual Edition,* c. 1901. Author's file.

CHAPTER 6. POLICING THE INTERIOR

1. James Shoup to Attorney General, January 28, 1898; Rutledge to Shoup, September 28, 1897; Shoup to Rutledge, January 28, 1898, NA, RG 60, Letters Received.

2. Weare to George Shoup, January 17, 1894; May 20, 1897, UO.

3. Beach, *Personal Exposures,* p. 46.

4. Canton's letter of November 26, 1897, as published in the *Buffalo* (Wyo.) *Bulletin,* March 3, 1898, UO.

5. *Compilation of Explorations in Alaska,* p. 527.

6. Ibid.

7. Ibid., p. 531.

8. Ibid., pp. 553–54.

9. Canton, *Frontier Trails,* p. 203.

10. Ibid., p. 205.

11. Ibid., pp. 206, 207.

12. Canton to J. M. Shoup, December 31, 1898, UO.

13. Canton to J. M. Shoup, December 31, 1898, UO.

14. Canton to J. M. Shoup, January 2, 1899, UO.

15. *Ex parte Horner,* July 17, 1894, Governors' Pardon Papers, Texas State Archives.

16. Canton to J. M. Shoup, March 28, 1899, UO.

17. Canton to J. M. Shoup, May 24, 1899. The 1893 and 1896 correspondence files of the Department of Justice for Oklahoma in the National Archives include the files relevant to Canton's record. These are summarized in National Archives to G. C. Boyer, September 30, 1966, UO.

18. Canton, *Frontier Trails,* pp. xvii, 221.

CHAPTER 7. NO PLACE LIKE NOME

1. Harrison, *Nome and the Seward Peninsula,* p. 57.

2. Cole, *Nome,* p. 73. If Chief Eddy is the same man as William M. Eddy (as seems likely), who was fired as a U.S. deputy marshal at Nome in 1905, he had an interesting criminal record himself in Colorado as a robbery suspect, possible burglar, and disturber of the peace, and in other suspicious activities before that in Utah. Attorney General to T. C. Powell, September 12, 1905, NA, RG 60, Letters Received.

3. *Nome News,* March 18, 1900.

4. Cole, *Nome,* p. 74.

5. *Nome Chronicle,* October 6, 1900.

6. *Nome News,* December 8, 1900.

CHAPTER 8. THE NEW COURT

1. Wickersham, *Old Yukon,* p. 4. In his published memoirs, Wickersham professed a preference for the Alaskan assignment over the consul's job, but his diary indicates otherwise. See Wickersham Diary, May 4, 1900, UA.

2. Shirley, *West of Hell's Fringe,* pp. 405–406.

3. Wickersham, *Old Yukon,* pp. 38–39.

4. Wickersham Diary, September 4, 1900, UA.

5. U.S. v. Charles Hubbard, court record, case 4, FRC.

6. Minutes of the Fort Yukon Miners' Meeting, May 20, 1900 (with U.S. v. Charles Hubbard, court record, case 4, FRC). Few written records of miners' meetings exist. This one was made because the men expected a formal court to be established soon.

7. Wickersham Diary, February 16, 1906, UA. In his struggle for reappointment, Wickersham wanted to accommodate a senator from Washington state who was urging Hubbard's release.

8. Wickersham Diary, December 11, 1900, UA. See J. L. Waller to wife, October 24, 1898, for Waller's claim to have prepared the first case presented to a miners' meeting at Eagle. His letter to his wife of November 28, 1898, is interesting for recording a shift of sentiment against miners' meetings after the men decreed some unspecified physical punishment: "Sentiment . . . is changing. The beast's thirst for gore is satisfied and many are beginning to

think that perhaps Hall was punished more than he deserved." Waller Collection, UA.

9. Wickersham, *Old Yukon,* pp. 60–61.

CHAPTER 9. ALEXANDER THE GREAT

1. Cole, "History of the Nome Gold Rush," p. 168.
2. Ibid., p. 171.
3. Ibid., pp. 171–73.
4. Ibid., p. 174.
5. Ibid., p. 175.
6. Ibid., p. 179.
7. U.S. Ninth Circuit Court of Appeals, "In the Matter of Arthur H. Noyes, et al.," *Transcript of Proceedings and Testimony,* Statement of W. T. Hume, 2:394, 2:391.
8. Cole, "History of the Nome Gold Rush," p. 198.
9. Ibid., p. 201.
10. In re Noyes, 121 *F* 209 (1902); see also Wickersham, *Old Yukon,* p. 360.
11. Beach, "Looting of Alaska," p. 41.
12. Vawter to Attorney General, August 7, 1900, NA, RG 60, Letters Received.
13. Frost to Attorney General, August 16, 1900, NA, RG 60, Letters Received.
14. Noyes to Attorney General, August 20, 1900, NA, RG 60, Letters Received.
15. Vawter to Attorney General, September 13, 1901, NA, RG 60, Letters Received.
16. Vawter to Attorney General, September 13, 1901; Vawter's affidavit, August 31, 1901; Leekley's affidavit, August 10, 1901, NA, RG 60, Letters Received.
17. Cole, "History of the Nome Gold Rush," p. 204.
18. *Nome Chronicle,* September 14, 1900.
19. Noyes to Attorney General, October 12, 1900, NA, RG 60, Letters Received.
20. Sutherland, Memoirs, p. 9, Sutherland Collection, UA.
21. Frost to Major Frank Strong, General Agent, Department of Justice, October 27, 1900, NA, RG 60, Letters Received.
22. Leland to Stewart, February 27, 1901; H. G. Orton to President McKinley, January 18, 1901, NA, RG 60, Letters Received.
23. Tornanses v. Melsing, 106 *F* 775 (1901).
24. *Nome Chronicle,* December 15, 1900.
25. Noyes to Griggs, March 30, 1901; James W. Bell to Noyes, June 1, 1901 (with Noyes to Attorney General cover letter, July 18, 1901), NA, RG 60, Letters Received.

26. Wood to Attorney General, June 21, 1901, NA, RG 60, Letters Received.

27. Noyes to Attorney General, July 19, 1901; the following quote is from Noyes to Attorney General, August 23, 1901, NA, RG 60, Letters Received.

28. *Nome Nugget,* July 12, 1901.

29. Reed to Attorney General, August 13, 1901, NA, RG 60, Letters Received.

30. W. T. Hune et al. to President McKinley, August 15, 1901, NA, RG 60, Letters Received.

31. Wiley to President Roosevelt, October 23, 1901, NA, RG 60, Letters Received.

32. In re Noyes, 212 *F* 209 (1902).

33. Pillsbury to Knox, February 6, 1902, NA, RG 60, Letters Received.

34. Oral Argument on Motion to Dismiss Judge Noyes, February 8, 1902, NA, RG 60, Appointments File.

35. Oral Argument on Motion to Dismiss Judge Noyes, February 8, 1902, NA, RG 60, Appointments File.

36. Dunham to Knox, February 4, 1902. For examples of Dunham's poetry, see Hunt, *North of 53°,* pp. 106, 132, or *Nome Nugget,* August 2, 1901. Sam Dunham had originally been sent to Alaska by the Department of Labor to report on conditions.

37. Coy to President Roosevelt, February 10, 1902, NA, RG 60, Letters Received.

38. Unsigned memo with cover letter, Presidential Secretary to Knox, February 6, 1902, NA, RG 60, Letters Received.

39. Dr. J. Rosenstirn to Knox, February 14, 1902; Auditor to Attorney General, July 29, 1902, NA, RG 60, Letters Received.

40. *Nome Nugget,* February 19, 1902.

41. Ibid.

42. Wickersham Diary, October 30, 1902, UA.

43. Beach, "Looting of Alaska," p. 2. There was actually a short Senate debate in 1902 when Senator Ben Tillman read into the record an article from the *Washington Post* describing the affair. Hansbrough responded "that the record in this transaction will fully vindicate Mr. McKenzie and acquit him of the miserable charges against his character and integrity." See Lillo, *Alaska Gold Mining Company,* pp. 296–98.

CHAPTER 10. TEDDY WANTS ANSWERS

1. Wickersham to Attorney General, February 17, 1904, NA, RG 60, Appointments File.

2. Wickersham, *Old Yukon,* p. 366.

3. Ibid., p. 362.

4. Ibid., p. 372.

5. Ibid., p. 373.

6. Ibid., p. 375.

7. U.S. v. Joseph Wright, court record, case 107, FRC; U.S. v. Frank Richards and Joseph D. Jourden, court record, case 176, FRC.

8. Fink to Attorney General, June 9, 1902, NA, RG 60, Letters Received.

9. Wickersham to Attorney General, February 17, 1904, NA, RG 60, Appointments File.

10. "Report of Finch and McNish," November 14, 1903, NA, RG 60, Letters Received.

11. Brady to Secretary of Interior, May 18, 1903, IP, FRC, RG 48.

12. Wickersham to Attorney General, February 17, 1904, NA, RG 60, Appointments File.

13. Day to Henry M. Hoyt, October 24, 1904, NA, RG 60, Appointments File.

14. "Report to the Attorney General," November 1904, NA, RG 60, Appointments File.

15. Richards to Attorney General, November 25, 1904, NA, RG 60, Letters Received.

16. Attorney general to Melvin Grigsby, July 11, 1903; Melvin Grigsby to Attorney General, August 8, 10, 1903, NA, RG 60, Letters Received.

17. Clum to George B. Cortelyou, February 9, 1903, for this and following quotes, NA, RG 60, Letters Received.

18. Whitehead to President Roosevelt, January 14, 1903, NA, RG 60, Letters Received.

19. Presidential Secretary to Attorney General, January 30, 1903, NA, RG 60, Letters Received. In 1904, William H. Moody replaced Knox as attorney general.

20. Melvin Grigsby to President Roosevelt, March 10, 1904, NA, RG 60, Letters Received.

CHAPTER 11. NOME SETTLES DOWN?

1. *Nome News,* September 12, 1902.

2. *Nome Nugget,* February 7, 1903.

3. Ibid., August 13, 1903.

4. Ibid., February 7, 1903. George Grigsby to Melvin Grigsby, June 15, 1903, DJ Correspondence, copy at ASL.

5. *Nome Nugget,* February 18, 1903.

6. *Nome News,* December 15, 1903.

7. Ibid.

8. Ibid.

9. U.S. v. John J. Jolley, court record, case 216, FRC.

10. U.S. v. John J. Jolley, court record, case 216, FRC, for this and the quotes that follow.

11. Cravez, *Seizing the Frontier,* p. 25; George Grigsby to Melvin Grigsby, June 15, 1903, DJ Correspondence, copy at ASL.

12. Borchsenius to Day, August 22, 1904, NA, RG 60, Letters Received.

13. *Nome Nugget,* May 4, 1904.

14. Ibid., October 26, 1904.

15. Borchsenius to Day, August 22, 1904, NA, RG 60, Letters Received.

16. *Nome Nugget,* October 22, 1904.

17. Ibid., July 19, 1905.

18. Hunt, *North of 53°,* pp. 198–201.

19. *Nome Gold Digger,* July 22, 1903.

20. *Nome News,* July 24, 1903.

21. U.S. v. Allen, court record, case 49, FRC.

22. *Nome Chronicle,* February 15, 1901.

23. U.S. v. Allen, 115 *Federal Reporter,* 3, 12.

24. Ibid.

25. Ibid.

26. Allen to Attorney General, September 4, 1902, John P. Allen Collection, UW.

27. Ibid.

28. U.S. v. Allen, court record, case 49, FRC.

29. Wood to Attorney General, June 21, 1901, NA, RG 60, Letters Received.

30. *Klondike Nugget,* July 30, 1898.

31. Ibid., September 13, 1899.

32. Crane, *Smiles and Tears from the Klondyke,* p. 8; Countess Morajeski to President Roosevelt, July 1, 1904, GP, FRC.

33. Countess Morajeski to President Roosevelt, July 1, 1904, GP, FRC.

34. Countess Morajeski to President Roosevelt, July 1, 1904, GP, FRC.

35. Countess Morajeski to President Roosevelt, July 1, 1904, GP, FRC.

36. *Nome Nugget,* January 12, 1905.

37. U.S. v. Victor Morajeski, court record, case 282, Ogilvie to Galpin, July 12, 1903, FRC.

38. Ogilvie to Galpin, July 12, 1903, FRC.

39. U.S. v. Victor and Alice Morajeski, court record, case 284, FRC.

40. U.S. v. Victor and Alice Morajeski, court record, case 284, FRC.

41. U.S. v. Victor Morajeski, court record, case 282, FRC.

CHAPTER 12. TOUGH CHARACTERS

1. Wickersham to Balliet, November 6, 1900, Wickersham Correspondence, UA.

2. *Klondike Nugget,* August 17, 1902.

3. Wickersham to Balliet, November 6, 1900, Wickersham Correspondence, UA.

4. U.S. v. Carolan, court record, case 17, FRC.

5. U.S. v. Harry Owens, court record, case 40, FRC.

6. U.S. v. Harry Owens, 2 *Alaska Federal Reports* 279, 282.

7. Owens to Attorney General, November 19, 1904, for this and other Owens quotes, NA, RG 60, Letters Received.

8. Harlan to Attorney General, February 22, 1905, NA, RG 60, Letters Received.

9. Wickersham Diary, July 13, 1905, UA.

10. U.S. v. Harry Owens, court record, case 40, FRC.

11. *Fairbanks Times*, July 23, 1906.

12. Ibid., July 28, August 18, 1906.

13. *Seattle Times*, October 20, 1908, for these and following quote.

14. U.S. v. Frederick Wright and R. P. Quinn, court record, case 275, FRC.

15. Pilcher Diary, July 9, January 25–26, 1898, February 1, 1908, for this and following quotes, UA.

16. U.S. v. Pilcher, court record, case 583, FRC, for this and following quotes.

17. Morison, *Maritime History of Massachusetts*, p. 324.

18. Bodfish, *Chasing the Bowhead*, pp. 232–33, 237.

19. Ibid., p. 234.

20. Ibid., p. 241.

21. Ibid., pp. 244–45.

22. Stefansson, *Discovery*, p. 73.

23. Bruce to Root, March 4, 1907, NA, RG 60, Letters Received.

24. Robert T. Devlin to Attorney General, November 6, 1907, NA, RG 60, Letters Received.

25. Undated newspaper clip with Robert T. Devlin to Attorney General, November 6, 1907, NA, RG 60, Letters Received.

26. Undated newspaper clipping with Robert T. Devlin to Attorney General, November 6, 1907, NA, RG 60, Letters Received.

27. Landers to Attorney General, December 9, 1907, NA, RG 60, Letters Received.

28. Wickersham to President Warren Harding, January 6, 1921, NA, RG 60, Letters Received.

29. See Melody Webb Grauman, "Kennecott: Alaska Origins of a Copper Empire, 1900–1938," *Western Historical Quarterly* 5, no. 2 (April 1978): 197–211; Robert A. Stearns, "The Morgan-Guggenheim Syndicate and the Development of Alaska, 1906–1915, Ph.D. diss., University of California, Santa Barbara, 1967, passim.

30. Hazelet to Hasey, September 2, 1907, Keystone Canyon Collection, UA, microfilm 140.

31. McAdams to Chief Wilkie, March 18, 1908, Keystone Canyon Collection, UA, microfilm 140.

32. Hoggatt to Secretary of Interior, October 26, 1907, Keystone Canyon Collection, UA, microfilm 140; Wickersham diary, March 27, March 28, April 1, 1908, UA. Wickersham attributed Harlan's behavior to grief caused by his son's death.

33. Roosevelt to attorney general, December 27, 1907, February 10, 1908, Library of Congress, Bonaparte Papers.

34. McAdams to Chief Wilkie, March 20, 1908, Keystone Canyon Collection, UA, microfilm 140.

35. Ostrander to Tom Donohoe, March 28, 1908, UA, Donohoe-Ostrander Collection.

36. Ostrander to Tom Donohoe, April 12, 1908, UA, Ostrander-Donohoe Collection. The district court record is U.S. v. Hasey, case 545 B, FRC.

37. Wickersham diary, April 30, 1910, UA.

38. Carson to Jarvis, May 6, 1908, Keystone Canyon Collection, UA, microfilm 140.

39. John Boyce file, appointments file, NA, RG 60, passim.

40. McNamara to attorney general, February 11, 1911, Keystone Canyon Collection, UA, microfilm 140; Elmer Todd to attorney general, April 14, 1911, Keystone Canyon Collection, UA, microfilm 140.

41. Janson, *Copper Spike,* p. 64; Wickersham diary, June 24, 1911, with clipping of *New York Times* story of the same date, UA.

CHAPTER 13. LONG TRAILS

1. U.S. v. Boucher, court record, case 418, FRC.

2. U.S. v. Boucher, court record, case 418, FRC.

3. Edingtons' *Tundra,* p. 166.

4. Ibid., p. 214. Other quotes that follow are from p. 215, p. 226, pp. 242–43, p. 300, p. 299, p. 307, p. 311, p. 328, and p. 213.

5. Nicholson to Attorney General, September 20, 1911, NA, RG 60, Letters Received, for this and following quote.

6. Nicholson's Affidavit, August 30, 1912, NA, RG 60, Letters Received.

7. Nicholson to Attorney General, September 20, 1911, NA, RG 60, Letters Received.

8. Stuck, *Voyages on the Yukon,* pp. 255–56. Contrary to Stuck's understanding, it was not true that the marshal needed an arrest warrant charging a specific person before a deputy could search for a body. A John Doe warrant or, as in this case, authorization from Washington was enough.

9. Erwin to Attorney General, April 11, 1914, NA, RG 60, Letters Received, for this and following quotes.

10. Carroll, *First Ten Years,* p. 60.

11. Erwin to Attorney General, April 11, 1914, NA, RG 60, Letters Received, for this and following quote.

12. Delmas C. Stutler, Examiner, December 17, 1914, NA, RG 60, Letters Received.

CHAPTER 14. HARD TO CONVICT

1. U.S. v. Joseph MacDonald, court record, case 865B, FRC, for this and following quotes.

2. U.S. v. Joseph MacDonald, court record, case 468B, FRC, for this and following quote. The U.S. Attorney's Office in Juneau wanted an indict-

ment badly: "We all feel at this time that there is an opportunity to end Mac-Donald's tyranny," wrote prosecutor Thomas Lyons to Thomas Donohoe, June 19, 1904, UA, Donohoe-Ostrander Collection.

3. U.S. v. Joseph MacDonald, court record, case 865B, FRC.

4. Masterson to Attorney General, January 18, 1911, NA, RG 60, Letters Received.

5. Attorney General to Rustgard, March 7, 1911, NA, RG 60, Letters Sent.

6. Attorney General to Rustgard, April 14, 1911, NA, RG 60, Letters Sent.

7. Byron to Bielaski, December 5, 1914, NA, RG 60, Letters Received.

8. Byron to Bielaski, December 5, 1914, NA, RG 60, Letters Received.

9. Bishop to Attorney General, April 17, 1916; Smiser to Attorney General, October 7, 1917, NA, RG 60, Letters Received.

10. Smiser to Attorney General, May 29, 1917, NA, RG 60, Letters Received.

11. Barkdull, "The Murder Gang," p. 28.

12. U.S. v. Ed Krause, court record, case 1149, FRC, for this and following quotes. Other material on the Krause case can be found at the ASL in the collection gathered by Gerald Williams and in Williams' unpublished history of the case.

13. *Alaska Daily Dispatch,* April 14, 1917.

14. Ibid., April 15, 1917, for this and following quote.

15. Ibid., April 17, 1917, for this and following quotes.

16. Roth to Attorney General, December 3, 1917, NA, RG 60, Letters Received.

17. Smith to T. W. Gregory, March 6, 1918, NA, RG 60, Letters Received, for this and following quotes.

18. Erwin to Attorney General, September 13, 1917; Attorney General to Erwin, October 18, 1917, NA, RG 60, Letters Received.

19. Roth to Attorney General, November 3, 1917, NA, RG 60, Letters Received.

20. Smith to Attorney General, September 26, 1917, NA, RG 60, Letters Received.

21. Roth to Attorney General, December 3, 1917, NA, RG 60, Letters Received.

22. Smith to Attorney General, March 6, 1918, May 28, August 6, 1919, NA, RG 60, Letters Received.

23. U.S. v. Martin Kennelly, court record, case 1073, FRC.

24. U.S. v. Bruce Rogers, court record, case 1083, FRC.

25. U.S. v. Ed Johnson, court record, cases 1035 and 1054, FRC, for the Nome gambling trials. Details of the Juneau scandal can be found in GP (1922), FRC.

26. U.S. v. Vicente Sanz, court record, case 1865, FRC.

27. U.S. v. Frank Tragomene, court record, case 344, FRC.

28. U.S. v. Dalmacio Bundoc, court record, case 2053, FRC.

29. *Alaska Daily Dispatch,* July 16, 1912, for this and following quote.

30. Undated *Alaska Daily Dispatch* clipping in U.S. v. O. Itow and E. Fushima, court record, case 863B, FRC.

31. Masson and Guimary, "Asian Labor Contractors in the Alaskan Canned Salmon Industry," p. 392.

32. Rutzebeck, *Alaska Man's Luck,* pp. 163, 189, and 190, for this and following quotes.

CHAPTER 15. HEROINES AND EXPERTS

1. The author takes the blame for this wretched verse.

2. *Fairbanks Daily News-Miner,* February 18, 1927.

3. Smith to Mary Smith, March 1, 1927, Lynn Smith Collection, UA.

4. U.S. v. Nellie Bates, trial transcripts in Bureau of Investigation Files 48–7, NA, RG 60.

5. U.S. v. Nellie Bates, trial transcripts in Bureau of Investigation Files 48–7, NA, RG 60.

6. U.S. v. Nellie Bates, trial transcripts in Bureau of Investigation Files 48–7, NA, RG 60.

7. Affidavit of J. G. Buzby; Report of agent H. J. Wade, Bureau of Investigation Files 48–7, NA, RG 60.

8. Smith to Mary Smith, March 1, 1927, Lynn Smith Collection, UA.

9. U.S. v. Burton McDonald, court record, case 790, FRC, for this and following quotes.

10. *Ketchikan Tribune,* April 16, 1931.

11. *Seattle Post-Intelligencer,* April 20, 1931.

12. U.S. v. H. L. Read, court record, case 1293, FRC; Luke May Collection, case 891, UW.

13. DeGroot v. U.S., 5 *Alaska Federal Reports* 790, and following quotes from pp. 791, 792, 796, 797.

CHAPTER 16. JACK LONDON'S LYNCHING

1. *San Francisco Examiner,* October 14, 1900.

2. *Sitka Alaskan,* October 13, 1906, for this and other quotes on the event. The original brief mention of "the elevation" was made in the edition of May 12, 1900.

3. London, *Love of Life,* p. 165.

4. *Seattle Post-Intelligencer,* July 28, 1906.

5. *Seattle Times,* July 28, 1906.

6. *Seattle Post-Intelligencer,* August 12, 1906.

7. Walker, *Jack London and the Klondike,* p. 245.

8. U.S. v. Homer Bird, 1 *Alaska Federal Reports,* 673, for this and following quote.

9. Friedrich to Brady, August 30, 1901, GP.

10. Brady to Secretary of Interior, August 1, 1901, GP; U.S. v. Fred Hardy, court record, case 109, FRC.

11. *Nome Nugget,* September 14, 1901.

12. *Ibid.,* August 23, 1902.

13. Wickersham, *Old Yukon,* p. 334.

14. Cole, "Dead Man on Deadman's Slough," and U.S. v. Perovich, court record, case 104, FRC; the U.S. Supreme Court decision is in 2 *Alaska Federal Reports* 750.

15. Wickersham Diary, January 13–14, 1908, UA.

16. Wickersham Diary, January 30, 1908, UA.

17. *Fairbanks Daily News-Miner,* October 20, 1985.

18. Cadwallader Reminiscenses, pages unnumbered, UA; U.S. v. Mailo Saguro, court record, case 792, FRC. The hanging is described in Cashen, *Farthest North College President,* p. 73.

19. U.S. v. William Stewart a.k.a. Dempsey, court record, case 766, FRC, for this and following quotes.

20. *Seward Gateway,* December 4, 1919.

21. U.S. v. William Stewart a.k.a. Dempsey, court record, case 766, FRC.

22. Sherman Duggan to Governor Bone, May 10, 1923, GP.

23. Dempsey to Governor Bone, June 15, 1923, GP.

24. Bunnell to Dempsey, June 11, 1926, Bunnell Collection, UA.

25. Dempsey to Bunnell, May 7, 1926, Bunnell Collection, UA.

26. Dempsey to Bunnell, February 7, 1934, Bunnell Collection, UA.

27. Bunnell to Hoover, February 1, 1940, Bunnell Collection, UA.

28. U.S. v. LaMoore, court record, case 2471B, FRC.

CHAPTER 17. BUSTING OUT

1. *Alaskan,* December 30, 1897, for this and following quote. Prisoners fared reasonably well, as the 1901 menu for Sitka's jail indicates: breakfast was mush and molasses (or beans), bread, potatoes, and coffee; dinner was stew, bread, potatoes, and coffee; supper was fish, bread, potatoes, and coffee. A Justice Department examiner calculated the cost per day at twenty cents, giving the marshal a profit of sixty cents per day. The examiner considered the profit outrageous and called for an end to a system so lucrative to the lawman (Stanley W. Finch to Attorney General, October 28, 1901, NA, RG 60, Letters Received).

2. Ibid., January 1, 1898.

3. Brady to Secretary of Interior, February 3, 1898, GP.

4. Landru, *Blue Parka Man,* p. 148.

5. Wickersham Diary, July 13, 1905, UA.

6. Quoted in Landru, *Blue Parka Man,* p. 151.

7. U.S. v. Lee Johnston, court record, case 768, FRC.

8. U.S. v. Tom Johnson, court record, case 813, FRC; Tom Johnson case file, Bureau of Investigation Files, NA, RG 60, Letters Received.

9. Rutzeback, *Alaska Man's Luck,* p. 23, and following quotes from pp. 64, 75, 144, 166, and 199.

10. Attorney General to Bishop, November 19, 1914, NA, RG 60, Letters Received.

11. Bishop to Attorney General, October 26, 1914, NA, RG 60, Letters Received.

12. Erwin to Comptroller, March 8, 1916, NA, RG 60, Letters Received.

13. Erwin to Governor Riggs, April 4, 1919, GP.

14. Erwin to Attorney General, July 15, 1915, NA, RG 60, Letters Received.

15. Keve, *The McNeil Century,* pp. 222–23; Gaddis, *Birdman of Alcatraz,* passim.

16. McNeil Island records are part of RG 129, Bureau of Prisons, at FRC.

CHAPTER 18. NATIVE LEGENDS

1. W. R. Maury to Secretary of Interior, April 16, May 28, 1892, GP.

2. *Juneau Mining Record,* January 28, 1892.

3. Louis K. Gillson to Secretary of Interior, February 25, 1892, GP; *Juneau Mining Record,* February 4, 1892.

4. U.S. v. Kes-Tee-ish et al., court record, case 344, FRC.

5. "The True Story of Kebeth," typescript, pages unnumbered, a copy of the *McClure's* article of June 1901, located with U.S. v. Jim Hanson, court record, case 1467, FRC.

6. U.S. v. Jim Hanson, court record, case 1467, FRC.

7. Stewart to Governor Parks, January 20, 1930, GP.

8. Wiseman to Attorney General, June 21, 1928, GP.

9. Hatfield, "Of Traps and Treasures," p. 61.

CHAPTER 19. "WHAT'S GOING ON IN ALASKA?"

1. Address to the American Bar Association, 1917, Gregory Papers, TT.

2. McConnell to Parks, August 22, 1925, GP.

3. Bone to Attorney General, September 8, 1922, GP.

4. Love to Attorney General, March 9, 1913, for this and following quotes.

5. Clegg's Affidavit, March 23, 1912, NA, RG 60, Letters Received.

6. Love to Attorney General, August 11, 1912, NA, RG 60, Letters Received.

7. Erwin to Attorney General, September 25, 1915, NA, RG 60, Letters Received.

8. Roth to Attorney General, June 10, 1916, NA, RG 60, Letters Received.

9. Roth to Attorney General, June 10, 1916, NA, RG 60, Letters Received.

10. Brown to Attorney General, November 25, 1904, NA, RG 60, Letters Received.

11. Wickersham, *Old Yukon,* pp. 433–34.

12. Wickersham to Attorney General, February 17, 1904, NA, RG 60, Letters Received.

13. *Seattle Daily Press,* February 19, 1889, cited in Atwood, *Frontier Politics,* p. 406.

14. Investigation of Alaska: Wickersham Investigation, NA, RG 60, Appointments File.

15. Wickersham, *Old Yukon,* p. 437.

16. Day's Report to the Attorney General, November 1904, NA, RG 60, Appointments File.

17. Wickersham, *Old Yukon,* p. 440.

18. Atwood, *Frontier Politics,* p. 127.

19. Ibid., p. 161.

20. U.S. v. W. G. Smith and John Rustgard, Decision of Contempt Proceeding, July 21, 1921, Bunnell Collection, UA.

21. Attorney General to Bone, December 27, 1924, GP.

22. Williams to Strong, October 4, 1915, GP.

23. Williams to Bishop, September 16, 1915, GP, for this and following quote.

24. Attorney General to Clark, February 9, 1911, NA, RG 60, Letters Sent.

25. Masterson Report, January 27, 1911; Townsend Report, November 20, 1911; Butler Report, October 3, 1911, NA, RG 60, Letters Received.

26. Erwin to Attorney General, April 11, 1914, NA, RG 60, Letters Received.

27. Gregory to Bunnell, February 1, 1915, Bunnell Collection, UA.

28. Bunnell to Gregory, undated, Bunnell Collection, UA, for this and following quotes.

29. Bunnell to Attorney General, April 17, 1917, for this and following quote.

30. Nichols, *History of Alaska,* p. 237, citing the *Alaska Daily Dispatch,* August 26, 1904.

31. Bunnell to Senator P. C. Knox, February 7, 1921, Bunnell Collection, UA.

32. Potter, *The Flying North,* p. 71.

CHAPTER 20. HOW JUSTICE FARED

1. Murton, "Administration of Criminal Justice in Alaska," p. 192.

2. Shirley, *West of Hell's Fringe,* passim.

3. Ball, *The United States Marshals of New Mexico and Arizona Territories,* p. 192.

4. Ibid., p. 244.

5. Prassel, *The Western Peace Officer,* pp. 220–43.

6. Kynell, "A Different Frontier," passim.

7. William L. Paul to Attorney General, undated entry in Department of Justice Index Card File, probably 1929, DJ.

Bibliography

GOVERNMENT ARCHIVAL SOURCES

Alaska District Court Records. Record Group 21.
Bureau of Prisons. Record Group 129. McNeil Island Commitment Logs, 1891–1951.
Correspondence of the Governors of Alaska. Record Group 348.
Department of the Interior, Alaska Territorial Papers, 1869–1911. Record Group 48.
Department of Justice. Index Card File.
Federal Records Center, Seattle.
National Archives. Record Group 60. Department of Justice Records. Most note citations in the text are to this archival source.

OTHER ARCHIVES

Alaska State Library, Juneau.
Library of Congress. Charles J. Bonaparte Papers.
Texas State Archives. Governors' Pardon Papers.
Texas Tech University. Gregory Papers.
University of Alaska, Fairbanks. Rasmuson Library. Bunnell Collection. Cadwallader Collection. Donohoe-Ostrander Collection. Heller Collection. Keystone Canyon Collection. Pilcher Diary. Riggs Autobiography. Lynn Smith Collection. Sutherland Collection. Waller Collection. Wickersham Diary.
University of Oklahoma, Western History Collections. Frank Canton Papers.
University of Oregon. James Crossley Papers. Judge Joseph W. Kehoe Papers.
University of Washington, Suzzallo Library. John P. Allen Papers.
University of Wyoming, American Heritage Center. Melville C. Brown Collection.

NEWSPAPERS

There are gaps in the files of some early Alaskan newspapers, but those of Sitka, Juneau, Ketchikan, Rampart, Nome, Iditarod, and Fairbanks have been examined for relevant material. The newspapers of Seattle and the Klondike also have been useful.

GOVERNMENT PUBLICATIONS

Except where otherwise noted, these publications originated in the Government Printing Office, Washington, D.C.

Alaska Census. 1870. 1871.

Alaska Federal Reports.

Annual Report of the Governors of Alaska, 1885–1940.

Brooks, Alfred H. *Geography and Geology of Alaska.* 1906.

———. *A Reconnaissance in Cape Nome, 1900.* 1901.

Cantwell, J. C. *Report of the Operations of the U.S. Revenue Steamer* Nunivak *on the Yukon River Station, Alaska, 1899–1901.* 1902.

Compilation of Narratives of Explorations in Alaska. 1900.

Elliott, Henry W. *Condition of Affairs in Alaska.* 1875.

Morris, William G. *Report on the Resources of Alaska.* 1879.

Ninth U.S. Circuit Court of Appeals. "In the Matter of Arthur H. Noyes, et al.," *Transcript of Proceedings and Testimony.* San Francisco, Government Printing Office.

Petroff, Ivan. *Population, Industries, and Resources of Alaska, 1880.* Report for the Tenth Census of the United States. 1884.

Rosse, Irving C. *Cruise of the Revenue-Steamer* Corwin *in Alaska . . . 1881.* 1883.

Wickersham, James. *Alaska Reports.* St. Paul, Minn.: West Publishing Company, 1903–1906.

THESES, DISSERTATIONS, AND UNPUBLISHED WORK

Cole, Terrence. "History of the Nome Gold Rush." Ph.D. diss., University of Washington, 1983.

Kynell, Kermit. "A Different Frontier: Alaska Criminal Justice, 1935–65." Ph.D. diss., Carnegie-Mellon University, 1981.

Lain, Bobby. "North of 53." Ph.D. diss., University of Texas, Austin, 1974.

Lillo, Waldemar R. E. "The Alaska Gold Mining Company and the Cape Nome Conspiracy." Ph.D. diss., North Dakota State University, Fargo, 1933.

Murton, Thomas O. "Administration of Criminal Justice in Alaska, 1867–1902." M.A. thesis, University of California, Berkeley, 1967.

Stearns, Robert A. "The Morgan-Guggenheim Syndicate and the Development of Alaska, 1906–1915." Ph.D. diss., University of California, Santa Barbara, 1967.

Steckler, Gerald. "Charles John Seghers." Ph.D. diss., University of Washington, 1963.

Williams, Gerald. "Alaska Enigma: The Legend of Ed Krause." Unpublished manuscript.

ARTICLES AND BOOKS

Atwood, Evangeline. *Frontier Politics.* Portland, Ore.: Binford and Mort, 1979.

——— and Robert N. DeArmond. *Who's Who in Alaskan Politics.* Portland, Ore.: Binford and Mort for the Alaska Historical Commission, 1977.

Ball, Larry D. *The United States Marshals of New Mexico and Arizona Territories, 1846–1912.* Albuquerque: University of New Mexico Press, 1978.

Bancroft, Hubert H. *History of Alaska.* San Francisco: Hubert Howe Bancroft, 1886.

Barkdull, Calvin H. "The Murder Gang." *Alaska Sportsman,* January 1956, pp. 6–7, 9, 26–29.

Beach, Rex. *The Spoilers.* New York: Harper, 1906.

———. "The Looting of Alaska." *Appleton's Booklovers Magazine,* January 1906, pp. 3–12; February, pp. 131–40; March, pp. 294–301; April, pp. 540–47; May, pp. 606–613.

———. *The Barrier.* New York: Harper, 1908.

———. *Personal Exposures.* New York: Harper, 1940.

Berton, Pierre. *Klondike.* Toronto: McClelland and Steward, 1962.

Bodfish, Harston H. *Chasing the Bowhead.* Cambridge, Mass.: Harvard University Press, 1936.

Brooks, Alfred H. *Blazing Alaska's Trails.* College, Alaska: University of Alaska, 1953.

Canton, Frank. *Frontier Trails.* Norman: University of Oklahoma Press, 1966.

Carlson, L. H. *An Alaskan Gold Mine: The Story of Number 9 Above.* Evanston, Ill.: Northwestern University Press, 1951.

Carlson, Phyllis D. "Alaska's First Census: 1880." *Alaska Journal,* Winter 1971, pp. 48–53.

Carroll, James. *First Ten Years in Alaska.* New York: Exposition Press, 1957.

Cashen, William R. *Farthest North College President.* Fairbanks: University of Alaska, 1972.

Chevigny, Hector. *Lord of Alaska.* New York: Viking Press, 1942.

Clifton, Robert B. *Murder by Mail.* Ardmore, Pa.: Dorrance Publishing Company, 1979.

Cole, Terrence. "Dead Man on Deadman's Slough." *Alaska,* September 1978, pp. A9–A10.

———. *E. T. Barnette.* Edmonds, Wash.: Alaska Northwest Publishing Co.

———. *Nome.* Edmonds, Wash.: Alaska Geographic Society, 1984.

Crane, Alice Rollins. *Smiles and Tears from the Klondyke.* New York: Doxey's Press, 1901.

Cravez, Pamela. *Seizing the Frontier.* Alaska: Alaska Historical Commission, microfiche, 1983.

DeArmond, Robert N. *The Founding of Juneau.* Seattle, Wash.: Olney Press, 1967.

DeLorme, Roland. "Liquor Smuggling in Alaska." *Pacific Northwest Quarterly,* October 1975, pp. 145–52.

Douthwaite, Charles L. *Royal Canadian Mounted Police.* London: Blackie and Son, 1939.

Dufresne, Frank. *My Way Up North.* New York: Holt, Rinehart and Winston, 1966.

Edingtons, The. *Tundra.* New York: Century Publishing Company, 1930.

Fell, Sarah. *Threads of Alaskan Gold.* N.p., n.d.

French, L. H. *Seward's Land of Gold.* New York: Montross, Clarke and Emmons, 1905.

Fritz, Frances. *Lady Sourdough.* New York: Macmillan, 1941.

Gaddis, Thomas E. *Birdman of Alcatraz.* New York: New American Library, 1958.

Gard, Wayne. *Frontier Justice.* Norman: University of Oklahoma Press, 1949.

Godwin, John. *Alcatraz 1868–1963.* Garden City, N.Y.: Doubleday, 1963.

Grauman, Melody Webb. "Kennecott: Alaska Origins of a Copper Empire, 1900–1938." *Western Historical Quarterly* 9, no. 2 (April 1978): 197–211.

Gruening, Ernest. *State of Alaska.* New York: Random House, 1968.

Harrison, E. S. *Nome and the Seward Peninsula.* Seattle, Wash.: E. S. Harrison, 1905.

Hatfield, Fred. "Of Traps and Treasures." *Alaska,* September 1984, pp. 13–16, 61–62.

Haydon, Henry E. *Cases Reported . . . by Lafayette Dawson, Judge, 1886–88.* Maryville, Mo.: Republican Press, n.d.

Heller, Herbert L. *Sourdough Sagas.* Cleveland, Ohio: World, 1967.

Hinckley, Theodore C. *The Americanization of Alaska, 1867–1897.* Palo Alto, Calif.: Pacific Books, 1972.

———. *Alaskan John G. Brady.* Miami, Fla.: Miami University Press, 1982.

Hollon, W. Eugene. *Frontier Violence.* New York: Oxford University Press, 1974.

Hunt, William R. *Arctic Passage.* New York: Charles Scribner's Sons, 1975.

———. *North of 53 Degrees.* New York: Macmillan, 1974.

Janson, Lone E. *Copper Spike.* Anchorage: Alaska Northwest Publishing Company, 1975.

Jordan, Philip D. *Frontier Law and Order.* Lincoln: University of Nebraska Press, 1970.

Landru, H. C. *The Blue Parka Man.* New York: Dodd, Mead, 1980.

Langeluttig, Albert. *The Department of Justice of the United States.* Baltimore: Johns Hopkins University Press, 1927.

Lomen, Carl. *Fifty Years in Alaska*. New York: McKay, 1954.

London, Jack. *Love of Life and Other Stories*. New York: Macmillan, 1907.

Lowenthal, Max. *The Federal Bureau of Investigation*. New York: William Sloan, 1950.

MacInnes, Tom. *Klengenberg of the Arctic*. London: Jonathan Cape, 1932.

Malcomb, M. J. *Murder in the Yukon*. Saskatoon, Sask.: Prairie Books, 1982.

Malone, Dumas, ed. *Dictionary of American Biography*. New York: Charles Scribner's Sons, 1933.

Marshall, Robert. *Arctic Village*. New York: Literary Guild, 1933.

Masson, Jack, and Donald Guimary. "Asian Labor Contractors in the Alaskan Canned Salmon Industry." *Labor History* 22, no. 3 (Summer 1981).

Moore, J. Bernard. *Skagway in Days Primeval*. New York: Vantage Press, 1968.

Morison, Samuel E. *Maritime History of Massachusetts*. Boston: Houghton Mifflin Company, 1941.

Naske, Claus. "Vuko Perovich." *Fairbanks News-Miner*, October 20, 1985.

———— and Herman Slotnick. *Alaska*. Grand Rapids, Mich.: Eerdmans, 1979.

Nichols, Jeannette P. *Alaska: A History*. Cleveland, Ohio: Arthur H. Clark Company, 1924.

Pierce, Richard. "New Light on Ivan Petroff, Historian of Alaska." *Pacific Northwest Quarterly*, January 1968, pp. 1–10.

Potter, Jean. *The Flying North*. New York: Ballantine Books, 1973.

Prassel, Frank R. *The Western Peace Officer*. Norman: University of Oklahoma Press, 1972.

Ricks, Melvin. *Alaska Bibliography*. Edited by Stephen W. and Betty J. Haycox. Portland, Ore.: Binford and Mort for the Alaska Historical Commission, 1977.

Rivers, Ralph J. "The Black Bear Case." *Alaska Journal*, Autumn 1975, pp. 211–16.

Rudensky, Morris, and Don Riley. *The Gonif*. Blue Earth, Minn.: Piper Publishing Company, 1970.

Rutzebeck, Hjalmar. *Alaska Man's Luck*. New York: Boni and Liveright, 1920.

Sheldon, Charles. *Wilderness of Denali*. New York: Charles Scribner's Sons, 1960.

Sherwood, Morgan. *Exploration of Alaska 1865–1900*. New Haven, Conn.: Yale University Press, 1965.

————. *The Cook Inlet Collection*. Edmonds, Wash.: Alaska Northwest Publishing Co., 1974.

Shirley, Glenn. *West of Hell's Fringe*. Norman: University of Oklahoma Press, 1978.

Steele, Colonel S. B. *Forty Years in Canada*. London: Jenkins Press, 1915.

Stefansson, Vilhjalmur. *Discovery*. New York: McGraw-Hill, 1964.

Stuck, Hudson. *Voyages on the Yukon*. New York: Charles Scribner's Sons, 1917.

————. *A Winter Circuit of Our Arctic Coast*. New York: Charles Scribner's Sons, 1920.

Teichman, Emil. *A Journey to Alaska in the Year 1868.* New York: Argosy-Anti-
    quarian, Limited, 1963.
Trevor-Roper, Hugh. *Hermit of Peking.* New York: Alfred A. Knopf, 1977.
Walker, Franklin. *Jack London and the Klondike.* San Marino, Calif.: Hunt-
    ington Library, 1966.
Wickersham, James. *Old Yukon.* Washington, D.C.: Washington Law Book,
    1938.
Wilson, William. "To Make a Stake: Fred Kimball in Alaska, 1899–1909."
    Alaska Journal, Winter, 1983, pp. 108–14.

Index

Distant Justice,

designed by Bill Cason, was set in Century Old Style by G&S Type-
setters and printed offset on 60-pound Glatfelter's Smooth Antique
B-31 by Cushing-Malloy, Inc., with case binding by John H. Dekker
& Sons.